Reading by Numbe.

Anthem Scholarship in the Digital Age

Anthem Scholarship in the Digital Age investigates the global impact of technology and computing on knowledge and society. Tracing transformations in communication, learning and research, the ground-breaking titles in this series demonstrate the far-reaching effects of the digital revolution across disciplines, cultures and languages.

Series Editors

Paul Arthur – University of Western Sydney, Australia
Willard McCarty – King's College London, UK
Patrik Svensson – Umeå University, Sweden

Editorial Board

Edward Ayers – University of Richmond, USA
Katherine Hayles – Duke University, USA
Marsha Kinder – University of Southern California, USA
Mark Kornbluh – University of Kentucky, USA
Lewis Lancaster – University of California, Berkeley, USA
Tara McPherson – University of Southern California, USA
Janet Murray – Georgia Institute of Technology, USA
Peter Robinson – University of Saskatchewan, Canada
Geoffrey Rockwell – University of Alberta, Canada
Marie-Laure Ryan – University of Colorado, Boulder, USA
Paul Turnbull – University of Queensland, Australia

Reading by Numbers

Recalibrating the Literary Field

KATHERINE BODE

ANTHEM PRESS
LONDON · NEW YORK · DELHI

Anthem Press
An imprint of Wimbledon Publishing Company
www.anthempress.com

This edition first published in UK and USA 2014
by ANTHEM PRESS
75–76 Blackfriars Road, London SE1 8HA, UK
or PO Box 9779, London SW19 7ZG, UK
and
244 Madison Ave. #116, New York, NY 10016, USA

First published in hardback by Anthem Press in 2012

Copyright © Katherine Bode 2014

The author asserts the moral right to be identified as the author of this work.

Cover photograph 'Bookshelves' © Alexandre Duret-Lutz 2006
Licensed under a Creative Commons Attribution-ShareAlike 2.0 Generic License

All rights reserved. Without limiting the rights under copyright reserved above,
no part of this publication may be reproduced, stored or introduced into
a retrieval system, or transmitted, in any form or by any means
(electronic, mechanical, photocopying, recording or otherwise),
without the prior written permission of both the copyright
owner and the above publisher of this book.

British Library Cataloguing-in-Publication Data
A catalogue record for this book is available from the British Library.

Library of Congress Cataloging-in-Publication Data
The Library of Congress has catalogued the hardcover edition as follows:
Bode, Katherine.
Reading by numbers : recalibrating the literary field / Katherine Bode.
p. cm.
Includes bibliographical references and index.
ISBN 978-0-85728-454-9 (hardback : alk. paper)
1. Australian literature–History and criticism.
2. Publishers and publishing–Australia–History.
3. Booksellers and bookselling–Australia–History. I. Title.
PR9604.6.B63 2012
820.9'994–dc23
2012013680

ISBN-13: 978 1 78308 308 4 (Pbk)
ISBN-10: 1 78308 308 5 (Pbk)

This title is also available as an ebook.

CONTENTS

Acknowledgements		vii
List of Tables and Figures		ix
Introduction	**A New History of the Australian Novel**	1
Chapter 1	**Literary Studies in the Digital Age**	7
I	Quantitative Method and its Critics	8
II	Critical Quantification: Book History and the Digital Humanities	13
Chapter 2	**Beyond the Book: Publishing in the Nineteenth Century**	27
I	Book Publishing: 1830s to 1850s	30
II	Serial Publishing	34
III	The Cycle of Serial and Book Publishing	40
IV	Book Publishing: 1860s to 1880s	43
V	Book Publishing: 1890s	47
Chapter 3	**Nostalgia and the Novel: Looking Back, Looking Forward**	57
I	British Domination? 1940s to 1960s	62
II	The Golden Age? 1970s to 1980s	70
III	Multinational Domination? 1990s to 2000s	79
IV	The End of Local Publishing? 1990s to 2000s	88
Chapter 4	**Recovering Gender: Rethinking the Nineteenth Century**	105
I	Feminist Literary Criticism and the Nineteenth Century	107
II	Serial Publishing	113

III	Book Publishing: 1860s to 1880s	120
IV	Gender and the 1890s	124

Chapter 5 **The 'Rise' of the Woman Novelist: Popular and Literary Trends** — 131

I	Male Domination? 1940s to 1960s	135
II	Female Liberation? 1970s to 1980s	143
III	Beyond Gender? 1990s to 2000s	153

Conclusion **Literary Studies in the Digital Future** — 169

Notes — 175
Bibliography — 215
Index — 237

ACKNOWLEDGEMENTS

Some of the arguments and ideas present in this book were initially explored in journal articles published in *Australian Literary Studies*, *Australian Feminist Studies*, *Cultural Studies Review* and the *Journal of the Association for the Study of Australian Literature*, and in *Resourceful Reading*, a collection of essays I co-edited with Robert Dixon. However, in these cases, what appears here is greatly expanded and significantly altered. *Reading by Numbers* also includes a revised and extended version of an article published in *Book History*.

Much of this book was written with the support of an Australian Postdoctoral Fellowship from the Australian Research Council at the University of Sydney and the University of Tasmania. It was completed at the Digital Humanities Hub at the Australian National University.

There are many people who have advised and assisted me during this project. I am grateful to the colleagues who have read, and commented on, parts of this manuscript, or earlier versions of these arguments and ideas, including Mark Davis, Robert Dixon, Ken Gelder, Julieanne Lamond, Elizabeth Morrison, Nicola Parsons, Susan Sheridan, Ryan Walter and Elizabeth Webby. I am particularly grateful to Paul Eggert and Williard McCarty, who read, and incisively responded to, the entire manuscript, and to Leigh Dale, who has always offered me invaluable guidance and advice, including in the development and drafting of this book. For their friendship and encouragement during this project, my thanks goes to Miranda Harman, Rebecca Johinke, Kate Mitchell, Tara Murphy, Kaz Ross and Nicola Parsons. Tara also provided lots of very useful advice about collecting and processing the data in *AustLit*. I am also grateful to Anthem Press for helping me bring this book to press.

Not a word of *Reading by Numbers* could have been written without the dedication and careful attention to detail of hundreds of people, most of whom I do not know. I am referring to the dedicated bibliographers who have developed the *AustLit* database during its long history and in its many incarnations. My work has also greatly benefited from detailed discussion with, and advice from, those I do know at *AustLit*, especially Carol Hetherington and Roger Osborne. I write these acknowledgements at a time when the future of *AustLit* appears uncertain. It will be an enormous loss for Australian literary studies, and for current and future research in book history and digital humanities, if this database closes or is no longer maintained to its current level. I hope that, in demonstrating some of what is possible with *AustLit*, this book will contribute to the arguments for the ongoing funding of this resource and other digital archives. *Reading by Numbers* is dedicated to all who have worked at *AustLit*, and to the careful scholarship, and fascinating permutations of bibliography, that this resource demonstrates.

Finally, I am grateful, not only for support in the writing of this book but for all sorts of things, to my wonderful family, including my brother Michael (for answering many mathematical questions), my sisters Helen and Rachael (for always having time to talk and always encouraging me) and my parents (for everything – including proof reading). Very special thanks has to go to Ben Williams, for his patience during the long time it took to write this book, and especially for listening to me talk, at length, about quantitative methods and trends in literary history, while really wanting to talk about the latest books we'd both read.

LIST OF TABLES AND FIGURES

Tables

Table 1	Top ten book publishers of Australian novels, 1830 to 1859	30
Table 2	Top ten periodical publishers of Australian novels, 1860 to 1889	36
Table 3	Top ten book publishers of Australian novels, 1860 to 1889	44
Table 4	Top ten book publishers of Australian novels, 1890 to 1899	49
Table 5	Top ten publishers of Australian novels, 1945 to 1969	64
Table 6	Top ten publishers of Australian novels, 1970s and 1980s	74
Table 7	Top ten publishers of Australian novels, 1990s and 2000s	82

Figures

Figure 1	Place of first book publication of Australian novels, percentages, 1830 to 1899 (by decade)	29
Figure 2	Form of publication of Australian novels, percentages, 1830 to 1899 (by decade and date of first publication)	29
Figure 3	Number of serialised Australian novels, published in Australia and total, 1860 to 1899 (two-yearly totals)	38
Figure 4	Australian novels by category of publisher, percentages, 1945 to 2009 (five-yearly averages)	59
Figure 5	Number of Australian novels, overall and by Australian, British and multinational publishers, 1945 to 2009 (five-yearly totals)	60
Figure 6	Australian novels by category of publisher, percentages, 1930 to 1969 (five-yearly averages)	61
Figure 7	Number of Australian novels by category of publisher, 1930 to 1969 (five-yearly totals)	65
Figure 8	Australian novels by category of publisher, percentages, 1970 to 1989 (five-yearly averages)	73
Figure 9	Australian novels (excluding local pulp fiction) by category of publisher, percentages, 1970 to 1989 (five-yearly averages)	76

Figure 10	Australian novels by Australian and multinational publishers, percentages, 1950 to 1989 (five-yearly averages)	77
Figure 11	Australian genre/non-genre novels, percentages, 1970 to 2009 (two-yearly averages)	86
Figure 12	Australian genre/non-genre novels published in Australia (excluding Horwitz and Cleveland titles), percentages, 1970 to 2009 (two-yearly averages)	87
Figure 13	Australian genre novels by category of publisher, percentages, 1970 to 2009 (two-yearly averages)	88
Figure 14	Proportion of locally published Australian novels by companies categorised by the number of Australian novels published per decade, 1970 to 2009 (by decade)	90
Figure 15	Australian novels by gender of author, percentages, 1830 to 1939 (five-yearly averages)	108
Figure 16	Australian novels serialised, overall and by men and women, percentages, 1860 to 1899 (five-yearly averages)	114
Figure 17	Number of serialised Australian novels, by men and women, in Australian and British periodicals, 1860 to 1899 (five-yearly totals)	116
Figure 18	Australian novels published as books in Australia and Britain, overall and by men and women, percentages, 1880s and 1890s	126
Figure 19	Australian novels by gender of author, percentages, 1945 to 2009 (five-yearly averages)	132
Figure 20	Number of Australian novels by gender of author, 1945 to 2009 (yearly totals)	133
Figure 21	Australian novels (excluding pulp fiction) published in Australia by gender of author, percentages, 1945 to 2009 (five-yearly averages)	134
Figure 22	Men and women in the top twenty most critically discussed Australian authors, percentages, 1945 to 2006 (by decade)	134
Figure 23	Australian novels (excluding pulp fiction) by men and women, published by Australian and multinational companies (with and without Torstar), percentages, 1965 to 2009 (five-yearly averages)	149
Figure 24	Number of Australian novels (excluding pulp fiction) by men and women, published by Australian and multinational companies (with and without Torstar), 1965 to 2009 (five-yearly totals)	150

Introduction

A NEW HISTORY OF THE AUSTRALIAN NOVEL

> Often engaging and well-written, [literary histories] are also in general derivative and conservative... New histories cannot but rely to a considerable extent on previous ones... It remains to be seen whether the possibilities offered by the web, and by electronic communications in general, will allow for a 'flatter', more horizontal and extensive, even more 'democratic' form of history production in the future.[1]

In the popular imagination, archives remain dusty, hidden, forgotten places; in fact, they are increasingly likely to be digital and available online.[2] By changing the form that archives take, technology also transforms the ways in which they can be searched and the types of questions that can be asked of them. This shift affords opportunities for more extensive, data-rich and quantitative approaches to literary historical scholarship. But it does not negate – it actually increases – the potential for what we find in the archives to challenge and transform the way we understand the past. That, in a nutshell, is the premise and the aim of *Reading by Numbers*. By mining, modelling and analysing data in a digital archive – *AustLit*, a comprehensive, online bibliographical record of Australian literature[3] – I present a new history of the Australian novel: one that concentrates on the nineteenth century and the decades since the end of the Second World War, and aims precisely for the more 'extensive' and 'democratic' historiography encouraged by the epigraph.

As these words imply, this is not a history of the great authors of Australian novels, nor of the canonical texts in this tradition. It is a history of the 'routine configurations' of this literary form,[4] and of the 'patterns, conjunctions, connections, and absences'[5] in that history that only emerge in aggregate: when the Australian novel is approached as a field and a system rather than a collection of individual authors and texts. This approach is possible because Australia is leading the world in the scope and comprehensiveness of its digital bibliographical archive. Analysing the extensive data in *AustLit* has enabled me to ask questions about trends in the authorship of Australian novels as well as their form, place of publication, circulation and the reading communities they accessed. This exploration of trends both challenges established ideas about, and provides the basis for new understandings of, the history of the Australian novel.

Established arguments in Australian literary history that this book addresses and challenges include: that colonial authors were entirely – or even predominantly – reliant on British publishers; that men were the most successful authors of nineteenth-century Australian novels; that the 1970s and 1980s were a period of considerable growth in the Australian novel field; and that contemporary Australian literature and publishing are currently in crisis due to the dominance of multinational conglomerates. In other cases, the historical trends suggested by analysis of the bibliographical data indicate new features of the Australian novel's history. Among the many arguments in this book are new propositions regarding gender trends in the authorship of such titles; the circulation of Australian novels within Australia and beyond; and the readerships, in Australia and elsewhere, for this literary form.

Two main themes pervade this new literary history. The first is transnationalism. Despite the recent 'transnational turn' in humanities scholarship, most literary histories – and indeed, many book histories – still analyse literature in relation to a particular national space.[6] Although the data I use in *Reading by Numbers* come from a national bibliographical archive, I explore the production, dissemination and reception of the Australian novel within and beyond the nation's boundaries. For the nineteenth century I consider the relationship between the constructions of authorship, operations of publishing and formation of reading communities in Britain and the Australian colonies, as well as the movement of literature – in book and serial form – between these two places. In the contemporary period, I chart the history of the Australian novel in relation to a shift from a largely (though also generally unacknowledged) nation-based publishing industry to an explicitly globalised, or multinational, one. I demonstrate how the tension between nationalism and globalism shapes contemporary literary criticism, and explore the impact of transnational literary and political discourses on gender trends in the production and reception of Australian novels.

The second overarching theme in this book is the issue – and the question – of value. As I discuss in Chapter 1, quantitative analyses are frequently criticised for neglecting this aspect of the literary field. Because such analyses rarely, if ever, attend to what might be called the aesthetic features of particular literary works, they are seen as failing to appreciate – or, in stronger terms, as ignoring and desecrating – literary value. This book does not deny that such value exists; rather, my point – and my concern – is that these constructions of value are too determining of literary history. Not only do particular (but loosely defined) value judgements about literature stand for many literary scholars as the only legitimate way of understanding that field, when translated into literary history, these decisions about what works are worthy of attention come to comprise the entirety of what we understand that history to be. The literary field contains multiple – changing, and often competing – ideas about the value of particular literary forms, and of the uses and meanings of literature. This book considers how the history of the Australian novel changes when forms not traditionally valued by literary critics are incorporated. There are many of these, but the main ones that emerge in this study are serialised fiction in the nineteenth century, and in the twentieth, pulp fiction and popular genres more broadly. A history of the Australian novel that does not simply dismiss or deny the various regimes of value circulating in literary culture not only alters our understanding of that form and its development, but exposes and challenges assumptions – particularly regarding gender, class, geography and commerce – that lie beneath the value judgements made by Australian literary scholars and historians, and that shape large- as well as author-scale studies.

***

I have emphasised how *Reading by Numbers* differs from previous studies; but it also builds on the cultural materialist approach that has characterised most histories of Australian literature since at least the late 1980s. One of the most influential early books to demonstrate this approach was Ken Gelder and Paul Salzman's *The New Diversity: Australian Fiction 1970–1988*. Published in 1989, this study foregrounds the material contexts under which Australian literature was produced and consumed in that period.[7] More recently, in 2000, Elizabeth Webby's introduction to *The Cambridge Companion to Australian Literature* describes the commitment of that collection, and of Australian literary studies generally, to a 'culturally materialist perspective', which she defines as a view of

> literary works not as aesthetic objects produced by gifted intellectuals but as cultural artefacts inevitably influenced and constrained by the social, political and economic circumstances of their times, as well as by geographical and environmental factors.[8]

Alternatively, David Carter describes contemporary Australian literary studies in terms of 'a kind of new empiricism' – an approach developing 'precisely through engagement with theories of culture that point beyond literary autonomy'.[9]

While empirical approaches to Australian literature in bibliography and scholarly editing have always considered this context,[10] the emphasis on cultural materialism spread to the discipline more broadly through the influence of identity-based political and theoretical movements including Marxism, feminism and post-colonialism. These approaches motivated an interest in the position or construction of authors and texts, and to a lesser extent readers, in relation to historical and cultural discourses of class, gender, sexuality, race and geography. In the last decade or so, this focus on the contexts of production and consumption has taken a more specifically economic and material turn, with attention shifting to the ways in which literary works relate to and are incorporated within broader literary and commodity culture.[11] Although related to the impact of cultural studies on the discipline, this shift is increasingly attributable to the rise of the history of the book, an interdisciplinary field that emphasises 'print culture and the role of the book as material object within that culture'[12] (the book, here, is taken to mean 'script and print in any medium, including books, newspapers, periodicals, manuscripts and ephemera'[13]). Indeed, much contemporary research into the history of Australian literature – especially in respect to the nineteenth century, but increasingly in relation to the twentieth – occurs at the boundaries of literary and book history.

It is at these boundaries that quantitative methods are playing a growing and prominent role in Australian literary studies. Recent quantitative work in this field, some of which I discuss in detail in this book, explores Australian literature in relation to publishing, sales, reviewing and readerships.[14] Of course, simply because they are increasingly common does not mean such approaches are accepted by everyone. Susan Lever, for instance, associates the rise of book history, 'distant reading', and 'quantifying skills' with the decline of evaluative criticism, which she claims must remain 'the main game for a literary academic' and the focus of Australian literary studies.[15] However, I see this incorporation of quantitative approaches not as a dramatic departure from, but as a logical next step in, the cultural materialist approach.

A central feature of cultural materialist studies has been a move beyond the canonical perspective of earlier histories of Australian literature,[16] to a broader conception of the literary field. This widening perspective is foregrounded in the title of *The New Diversity*, which discusses a much greater range of authors and books than was the case in earlier histories. Eleven years later, Delys Bird's chapter on contemporary fiction in *The Cambridge Companion* referred to 107 authors.[17] Although not even approaching the more than 2,500 Australian authors who published novels in the years she surveys (from 1970 to 1999), this figure demonstrates the shift in Australian literary studies to trying to survey the range of what was written, published and read, rather than a selective canon of great works.[18] Quantitative research into Australian literature enables this ongoing attempt to perceive and represent literary culture in as broad and comprehensive a way as possible. Rather than detracting from evaluative criticism, my work on trends in the production and reception of Australian literature has the potential to alleviate some of the pressure for coverage by providing a context in which to discuss individual works, including those of the canon. It could, in other words, allow literary scholars to concentrate more effectively on providing detailed and nuanced readings of particular literary works, without having to abandon a sense of those works as 'cultural artefacts', embedded in a social, political, economic and material world.

At the same time, quantitative methods – and the computational strategies that enable them – should not be accepted uncritically. Their incorporation into literary studies raises a range of theoretical, methodological and epistemological issues that need to be considered if such approaches are to make a valuable and ongoing contribution to humanities scholarship. Considering these issues is the focus of my first chapter, 'Literary Studies in the Digital Age'. This chapter outlines the main criticisms that have been made of quantitative approaches to literary history: that they ignore the complexity of literary texts and privilege a simplistic understanding of literary culture; make false claims to absolute knowledge; and resonate, in problematic and complicit ways, with dominant institutional and political discourses. While acknowledging the importance of these criticisms, I show that these characteristics are not intrinsic to the quantitative method. Drawing on methodological discussions in book history and the digital humanities, I outline a critical approach to working with data and computers in literary history, and the humanities more broadly. This approach is one that maintains a view of the importance of empirical data and the historical understandings they can enable, while conceptualising the creation, presentation and interpretation of data as a form of representation and argument, rather than an expression of objective truth. Such an understanding enables a productive integration of – rather than a hostile stand off between – empirical analysis and humanities inquiry.

The remaining four chapters deploy the theoretical and methodological framework outlined in Chapter 1 to explore the history of the Australian novel. These chapters are divided in two ways: by period and focus. In respect to period, Chapters 2 and 4 consider the nineteenth century, and Chapters 3 and 5 investigate the decades since the end of the Second World War. One chapter for each of these periods focuses on trends in publishing (Chapters 2 and 3), the other on gender trends in authorship (Chapters 4 and 5). My concern throughout is to explore how trends in the authorship, publication, distribution and reception of Australian novels challenge received wisdom about, and add to our understanding of, the history of that form.

Recent histories of publishing and reading in Australia during the nineteenth century emphasise the dominance of British publishers and books for colonial authors and readers, in a framework that presents local publishers and authors as largely marginal to colonial literary culture. Chapter 2, 'Beyond the Book: Publishing in the Nineteenth Century', argues that Australian publishers – especially of periodicals – and local readers were of foundational importance to the history of the Australian novel. Although British book publishers played a major role in the colonial market, in the first half of the nineteenth century local publishers provided essentially the only avenues of publication for authors who remained in the colonies. In the second half of the century, until the 1890s, more Australian novels were first published in the colonies than were first published in Britain. The local readerships for Australian novels indicated by these publishing trends – and other data on circulation and pricing – suggest alternative modes of reading existed alongside the 'Anglocentric reading model' that currently dominates understandings of colonial literary culture.[19] These local readerships also provide a reason why, when seeking access to the lucrative colonial book market in the 1890s, British presses substantially increased their publication of Australian novels. The findings outlined in this chapter show that relationships between British publishers and colonial authors and readers were more interactive than the top-down exercise of power implied by histories emphasising the dominance of the imperial centre.

Chapter 3, 'Nostalgia and the Novel: Looking Back, Looking Forward', also analyses publication data, but for Australian novels since the end of the Second World War. I use this data to complicate the widespread conception of the 1970s and 1980s as a 'golden age' for Australian literature and publishing. While this understanding – and the cultural or literary nationalist paradigm that underpins it – organises contemporary Australian literary history, including recent book histories, the periodisation it institutes bears little resemblance to the production and circulation of Australian novels in these decades. In particular, this nostalgic nationalist framework conceals the importance of the local publishing industry to Australian authors and readers immediately following the war, and can only perceive recent trends in publishing negatively. I highlight the continuities in publishing trends before, during and after this purported 'golden age', while also exploring the growth and implications of self- and subsidy-funded publishing in the 1990s and 2000s. The periodisation, industry dynamics, and relationships between authorship, publishing and reading presented in this chapter are significantly more complex, but also more interesting and challenging, than existing histories of contemporary Australian literature and publishing allow.

Chapters 4 and 5 also focus, respectively, on the nineteenth century and the decades since the end of the Second World War. In exploring gender trends in the authorship of Australian novels they add another layer to the revised history already presented. Chapter 4, 'Recovering Gender: Rethinking the Nineteenth Century', shows that the three major forms in which colonial novels were published – local serialisation, and British and Australian book publication – manifested distinct gender trends in authorship. Women's novels were more likely to be serialised than men's, while men's novels were more likely to be published as books. At the same time, and despite the fact that men outnumbered women as authors of nineteenth-century Australian novels, more titles by women were published as books in Britain. Women authors, in other words, were overrepresented in the two areas of publication for colonial novels – as serials and as British books – that offered the greatest economic and/or cultural rewards. I argue that competing gendered constructions of the novel and authorship in Britain and the colonies profoundly shaped the transnational circulation of nineteenth-century Australian novels and that, in the cultural terms of the day, women novelists – although outnumbered by their male counterparts – were more successful. At least, this was the case until the 1890s, when book publication in Britain became common for colonial male novelists. As well as offering a new perspective on Australian literary culture in this decade, gender trends in the 1890s suggest another way in which British publishers responded to local practices and preferences to gain entry to the colonial book market.

Chapter 5, 'The "Rise" of the Woman Novelist: Popular and Literary Trends', explores gender trends in the publication of Australian novels since the end of the Second World War. The empirical data strongly support the claim by feminist critics that, around 1970, Australian literature shifted from a predominantly male-oriented field to one where women played an increasingly prominent and important role. However, I also show that this gendered shift, while occurring in the literary and critical spheres that are the predominant focus of feminist analyses, was most pronounced in genre fiction publishing. The parallels between gender trends in popular and literary spheres emphasise the importance of gender-alert analyses for understanding Australian literary history. But they challenge the meanings that feminist literary critics have attached to this shift, specifically, the interpretation of growth in Australian women's writing in the 1970s and 1980s as an indication of women's political and social emancipation. I argue that political changes were influential, but that this shift was also – and primarily – a commercial trend, driven by new awareness of a female market for fiction, popular and literary. Challenging the established association of women's writing and women's liberation is especially important for understanding gender trends in the 1990s and 2000s. Although it has not been acknowledged, women now dominate the Australian novel field. Far from being a sign of women's liberation, I argue that this gender trend in authorship has produced both a devaluing of this literary form, and a re-establishment of male novelists at the centre of critical discussion and acclaim. As I demonstrate through these case studies, quantitative analysis and computational methods have significant potential to offer new perspectives on existing debates in literary studies, as well as new ways of conceptualising the field, and new research questions and directions for literary scholarship in the future.

Chapter 1

LITERARY STUDIES IN THE DIGITAL AGE

[T]here is no method, however well adapted to a given science, that literary history can transplant and apply to its own researches. The illusion that this is possible is responsible for much poor and childish work: statistics and charts, evolution of species, and quantitative analysis are processes, methods, and hypotheses excellent in their place, but their place is not literary history.[1]

In the last decade, and especially in the last four or five years, the insistence in this epigraph – that quantitative methods have no place in literary history – has been repeated many times. The fact that this particular passage comes from a book first published in 1922, and intended as a guide for graduate students, should demonstrate that both the application of such methods, and the resistance to them, are of considerably longer standing in debates about literary history than is generally acknowledged. Nonetheless, discussion of quantitative methods has almost certainly never been as heated or as widespread – or as apparent to the majority of literary scholars – as it is today. While there are a number of quantitative approaches to literature,[2] the current debate focuses on Franco Moretti's work in literary history. As Priya Joshi says, literary scholars have for a long time 'regarded quantitative analysis with suspicion bordering on contempt'.[3] But in the response to the publication in 2000 of Moretti's 'Conjectures on World Literature', and in 2005 of his book *Graphs, Maps, Trees*,[4] this contempt has escalated – especially in the American humanities – to an intense stand-off.[5]

The controversy surrounding Moretti's work is, to a significant extent, specific to it. But this debate also presents important criticisms of quantitative methods that need to be engaged with if such studies are to make a productive contribution to literary history and humanities scholarship generally. This chapter considers three closely related criticisms that have been levelled at quantitative literary research (predominantly at Moretti's 'experiments' in literary history): first, that such approaches reduce the inherent complexity and multiplicity of literature and language to uniform data; second, that quantitative methods make false claims to authoritative and objective knowledge; and finally, that such studies resonate, in problematic and complicit ways, with contemporary institutional discourses, especially neoliberal or economic rationalist managerial practices.

I am not proposing that such criticisms are never applicable to quantitative approaches; like all research practices, these can be applied in varying ways. Nor is this chapter a defence of Moretti's scholarship. Although his centrality to the debate makes an engagement with his arguments and methods unavoidable – and while I find his work well worth the engagement – some aspects of Moretti's research justify some of the criticisms that have been made. However, I will argue that reductionism, absolutism and acquiescence to neoliberalism are not intrinsic to quantitative methods. In this chapter I discuss work in book history and the digital humanities that I have found useful in developing my approach to literary historical data. Specifically, I argue that an approach based on book history's methodological pragmatism regarding the nature and use of data, and the digital humanities' method of modelling, offers a productive way of integrating empirical data with the paradigm of humanities knowledge as a critical, analytic and speculative process of inquiry. This approach maintains what Donna Haraway calls 'a no-nonsense commitment to a faithful account of the "real" world',[6] while preserving, in George Levine's words, 'a tentativeness that keeps all aspirations to knowledge from becoming aspirations to power as well'.[7]

I Quantitative Method and its Critics

As the criticisms of quantitative approaches to literature are largely directed at Moretti's work, I will begin with a brief summary of his arguments: both against conventional approaches to literary history and for quantitative methods. For decades, Moretti has argued that a literary history based only on the texts that make up the canon offers no insight into the vast 'mass' of literature, and no basis for understanding the causes and processes of literary change. In 1983 he wrote that:

> [A]t present, our knowledge of literary history closely resembles the maps of Africa of a century and a half ago: the coastal strips are familiar but an entire continent is unknown. Dazzled by the great estuaries of mythical rivers, when it comes to pinpointing the source we still trust too often to bizarre hypotheses or even to legends.[8]

More recently, Moretti has refined this critique into a specific challenge to the reliance of literary history on detailed textual analysis or 'close reading' as the source of historical evidence. He identifies 'close reading' – where the 'representative individual' defines the 'whole', or the 'one per cent of the canon' signifies 'the lost 99 per cent of the archive' – as a form of 'topographical thinking'.[9] The main problem with this approach, and the source of what Moretti considers as irrationality, lies in the fact that the 'rare and... exceptional' works of the canon are by definition not representative.[10] In taking the canon as its object, literary history fails to consider the 'banal, everyday, normal' operations of the literary field and the wider context in which literary change occurs.[11]

For Moretti, the means of overcoming this unrepresentative focus cannot be more reading. The size of the archive renders this potential solution impossible to achieve: even 'a novel a day every day of the year would take a century or so' to cover nineteenth-century British fiction. As well as a matter of scale, close reading gives no insight into the workings of the literary system:

> [A] field this large cannot be understood by stitching together separate bits of knowledge about individual cases, because it *isn't* a sum of individual cases: it's a collective system, that should be grasped as such, as a whole.[12]

To this end, Moretti offers a paradigm of 'distant reading' that deliberately abstracts both the material and textual features of literary works to provide new accounts of literary history based on 'a specific form of knowledge: fewer elements, hence a sharper sense of their overall interconnection. Shapes, relations, structures. Forms. Models.'[13] Moretti's work provides an important statement of the contribution quantitative methods can make to literary history: namely, their potential to represent historical trends and, in so doing, enable a form of analysis that moves beyond the handful of exceptional texts and authors that are repeatedly discussed in literary history. However, and although he is often perceived as such,[14] Moretti is not the only scholar to make these arguments: both his challenge to established practices in literary history and his rationale for quantitative analyses align closely with ideas in book history.

Since the emergence of this interdisciplinary field in the 1980s,[15] book historians have – like Moretti – rejected a canonical approach to literary history and challenged that discipline's reliance on theory, insufficiently grounded in empirical, historical evidence (what Moretti calls literary history's basis in 'bizarre hypotheses' and 'legends'). Robert Darnton, for instance, describes the canonical approach to – or 'great-man, great-book variety' of – literary history as

> an artifice, pieced together over many generations, shortened here and lengthened there, worn thin in some places, patched over in others, and laced through everywhere with anachronism. It bears little relation to the actual experience of literature in the past.[16]

As a substitute for this canonical focus, Darnton recommends that literary scholars 'work through theoretical issues by incorporating them more thoroughly in more research of a concrete, empirical character'.[17] Darnton's focus on reception – the 'experience of literature in the past' – is characteristic of most work in book history.[18] This signals another connection between such scholarship and Moretti's analyses in *Graphs*, many of which treat the reading community as the catalyst for literary development.[19] Other connections include the identification of social history – especially the *Annales* school – as an important historical and intellectual antecedent,[20] and a focus on literature as a system (or, as book historians tend to call it, a 'communications circuit')[21] rather than a collection of individual texts. Finally, and most importantly for the purposes of this chapter, like Moretti, many book historians use quantitative methods to explore this system or circuit. This aspect of book history includes studies that focus on the operations of the publishing industry and the reception of literature in history,[22] as well as an emerging body of work that uses historical data – as this book does – to explore changes and developments in particular literary forms.[23]

In presenting these connections, I am not aiming to minimise the innovation and uniqueness of Moretti's work. His application of quantitative methods extends well beyond any other work in book history, especially in his use of what might be called textual as well as material or historical data. While the first chapter of *Graphs* is (as Moretti acknowledges) essentially an exercise in quantitative book history – drawing on historical data to explore trends in book publication, authorship and genre across a range of national fields – the other two chapters are based on datasets created from elements within particular literary texts, such as character, setting, plot and device. From this textual dataset, Moretti produces visual representations (in his words, 'abstract models') of what is occurring within the pages of books. In more recent work, Moretti employs quantitative methods to analyse language patterns in much larger groups of texts.[24] These other studies have their own antecedents: Literary Darwinists use textual data,[25] and Moretti's analyses of language patterns draw on methods developed in linguistics and digital humanities (or humanities computing).[26] But no one else incorporates this range of approaches, or combines them in ways as original and provocative as Moretti. My intention in establishing these connections between Moretti's work and other quantitative approaches to literature, particularly those of book history, is to signal the relevance of ongoing methodological discussions in these other fields to the current debate about Moretti's quantitative 'experiments' and, in particular, to the criticisms these experiments have received.

The most general of these criticisms is that, in reducing aspects of the literary field to data, quantitative approaches provide and privilege a simplistic view of literature, one that fails to understand – or more pointedly, dismisses and violates – such things as aesthetic value and literary complexity.[27] Discussing Moretti's analysis of British book titles,[28] Katie Trumpener describes

> [t]he designation of a novel as a novel, a poetry volume as poems…[as] alienating, reducing books to mere commodities – a box of salt with the generic label 'Salt', a bag of flour announcing itself 'Flour' – as if the book's content (and the irreducibility of authorial style) was virtually irrelevant.

According to Trumpener, such designations – and Moretti's 'statistically driven model of literary history' more broadly – 'violate the individuality of the text'.[29] Similarly, in a review of *Graphs*, Robert Tally argues that, in relying on data, the 'literary historian will overlook, or deliberately elide, the particulars that make the study of literature critical. The practice leads to, and even encourages, generalisations that critics would normally eschew.'[30] Referring specifically to analyses that use words as data, but also discussing Moretti's *Graphs* as a whole, Michael Rothberg asks whether 'quantitative cultural historians [can] prevent the massification of word-based data from performing a reduction of the inherent polysemy or aporetic nature of the signifier?… Can we quantify without losing the disruptive detail and splitting significations to which we have learned to attend?'[31]

This perception that quantitative analysis will replace complexity with simplistic explanation underpins another criticism of such methods, also made primarily in relation to Moretti's work: that quantitative approaches make a false claim to absolute knowledge and objective truth. In similar terms to Rothberg, Gayatri Spivak perceives in Moretti's quantitative experiments an attempt to control the inherent 'undecidability' of literary culture by creating 'authoritative totalizing patterns' that reduce the complexity of the literary field to simplistic models. However, she identifies the 'real problem' with distant reading as its 'claim to scopic vision'.[32] Such vision – described by Haraway as a 'god trick', claiming to see everything 'from everywhere and nowhere equally and fully'[33] – asserts a form of knowledge that is transcendent, central, total and true.[34] This charge of false objectivity is probably the most developed aspect of the critiques of Moretti's work, and I will return to it in detail later in this chapter.

The association of quantitative research with objective knowledge is seen as having major implications for power relations between literary scholars and within the institution of the university. Jonathan Arac describes Moretti's model of 'distant reading' as 'covert imperialism' due to the hierarchical difference it creates between 'readers' and the 'global synthesizer, who becomes the *maestro di color che sanno* ("master of those who know")'.[35] Similarly, though focusing on the different national locations and languages of these readers, Spivak criticises Moretti's use of 'native informants', predominantly from non-Anglophone literary cultures, to provide 'close reading[s] from the periphery' that are amassed at the Anglophone centre.[36] These critics are responding, specifically, to Moretti's proposal for world literary studies and the implicit hegemony of the English language (and for Spivak, of American nationalism) they perceive in his framing of this agenda. However, similar claims regarding the inequalities between readers and synthesisers could be made of all projects that use the scholarship of others – as I do with the bibliographical work in *AustLit* – to identify trends in literary history.

More broadly in terms of power inequalities, there is the view that quantitative analyses resonate, and are complicit, with other paradigms that foreground numerical measures, especially the neoliberal or economic rationalist ideology underpinning managerial practices in today's universities and in capitalist societies generally. Referring to the American academy, James English describes the ascendancy of a 'naïve or cynical quantitative paradigm that has become the doxa of higher-educational management'. This 'hegemony of numbers' favours the social and natural sciences – disciplines that also deploy statistics. Under these conditions, 'antagonism toward counting has begun to feel like an urgent struggle for survival' for literary studies.[37] Susan Lever makes a similar argument in relation to the Australian university system, arguing that literary criticism – a practice which requires 'time rather than money' – falls between the gaps in terms of gaining funding in an institutional context that values research based on a 'science model'. Projects that require 'research assistants, travel, even equipment', speak to this model in ways that marginalise traditional humanities research: '[t]hat's one reason', Lever proposes, 'why cultural history, media studies, "distant reading" are now the fashion' for literary studies in Australia.[38] The idea that quantitative methods support and institute power inequalities between disciplines relates to a wider argument regarding the oppressive consequences – for society generally – of forms of knowledge based on statistical evidence, numerical data and averages.[39]

There can be no doubt that numbers and statistics are imbued with significant power in modern society, and that much of this power comes from the rhetoric of objectivity and truth surrounding such measures or, as Sally Engle Merry puts it, 'the magic of numbers and the appearance of certainty and objectivity that they convey'.[40] I strongly agree with many of the scholars above that this rhetoric is employed in contemporary universities to channel and control research, and that this configuring of knowledge is having major negative consequences for the humanities. These institutional factors are perhaps one of the main reasons why Moretti's work has received so much attention and criticism:[41] he stands, in the American academy, as a symbol of broader changes that are only beginning to be articulated by humanities scholars. It is much easier to criticise an individual than the system as a whole, especially as this is a system that humanities scholars are ensconced within and reliant upon.[42]

With computers and computation embedded in the same rhetoric of objectivity and truth that surrounds quantitative approaches, there is also significant potential for the integration of digital methods in humanities scholarship to reinforce and compound institutional trends. In a review of *A Companion to Digital Literary Studies*, Scott Hermanson echoes many of the concerns above, but locates them specifically in relation to digital research. Hermanson worries that 'data-driven scholarship' will be 'misconstrued as more valuable or more legitimate because it relies on hard numbers'.[43] In a social and institutional context where the humanities 'have lately struggled…adequately [to] explain themselves to outside viewers', Hermanson is concerned that 'this type of data-driven research becomes elevated above others because it is easy to sell, quantifiable, and a product of exact numbers. The danger exists', he says, returning us to the issue of reductionism discussed above, 'in privileging the 1 and the 0 and obscuring the infinite gradations in between'.[44] The strategies for visualising data that modern technology make available arguably represent the epitome of this rhetoric of truth and objectivity. In particular, the slippage between seeing and knowing functions to accord graphs and charts – what are, in essence, arguments made using visual rhetoric – the status of self-evident fact or, precisely, 'scopic vision'.[45] As a result, and in an extension of the division that Spivak and Arac describe between close reading's 'native informants' and their quantitative masters, there is a clear possibility – with universities privileging paradigms of knowledge and funding that produce measurable outcomes and productivity – that a divide will open up between humanities scholars with the opportunities and technological abilities to frame their arguments in terms of quantitative evidence, and those without.

However, recognising the implication of quantitative and computational methods in complex and challenging power dynamics does not constitute an argument for excluding such approaches from literary historical research. If we avoided all methods implicated in difficult power relations, literary scholars would long ago have abandoned language. As poststructuralist theory emphasises, language is a form of knowledge and a means of representation that carries, in its structure, values that privilege some voices and attempt to silence others. Instead of abandoning language, literary scholars have sought to understand the ways it works and to challenge and critique the relations of power it perpetuates. We need to do the same with numbers: to recognise them as a form of representation and, as such, to explore how they operate and the ways in which numbers accrue authenticity and authority. Like language, numbers provide an imperfect and mediated way of accessing the world; but in the absence of any perfect or unmediated access, they are tools we can use in our attempts to understand and investigate the literary field.

While this sense of numbers as an imperfect and mediated representation might not be the exact way they are discussed in the sciences, no scientist approaches statistics as neutral, true and infallible. Awareness of the way scientists interrogate – rather than simply accept or promote – statistical measures is often lacking in current humanities' debate about quantitative approaches and their ideological resonances. As part of the contemporary, corporate university system, the sciences – like the humanities – are implicated in its managerial strategies and neoliberal or economic rationalist political ideology. This does not mean that scientists adopt the positivistic approach to quantification that prevails among 'the doxa of higher education management'.[46] Instead, significant effort is devoted in scientific studies to addressing the 'problems of categorisation, bias, rhetorical presentation and distortion'. (Pat Hudson provides this list, her point being that these precise problems afflict 'detailed description or narrative' as much as 'quantitative approaches'.)[47]

On one level, developing a more sophisticated and theorised understanding of numbers and statistical analysis is necessary for the humanities whether or not such approaches are employed directly. This is simply because of the status of quantification and, increasingly, computation as central regimes of knowledge and forms of power in contemporary society. In this context, understanding the way social relations are organised and institutions function requires a framework for engaging critically – rather than contemptuously or fearfully – with quantitative forms of representation. On another level, such engagement is worthwhile because – as I will discuss in more detail in what follows, and as the case studies in this book aim to demonstrate – quantitative methods allow us to explore aspects of the literary field, especially trends and patterns, broad developments and directions, that would otherwise remain unrepresented and unrepresentable.

For both purposes – and particularly because, rather than in spite, of the potential collusions between quantitative analyses and various forms of neoliberal ideology – literary scholars need to reconceptualise data and computation not as inevitably reductive and absolute regimes of power, but as products of theoretical processes and decisions, and as means of argumentation and theorisation. Although there has been little direct conversation between the two fields, the methodological underpinnings of both book history and the digital humanities signal important directions for developing a critical and theoretically aware approach to working with data – one that has significant potential for quantitative literary history, and for the humanities generally. Importantly, the methodological frameworks of both fields either anticipates and avoids, or answers, the criticism of quantitative approaches I have outlined above, while at the same time circumventing blind spots that emerge in the defence of close reading.

II Critical Quantification: Book History and the Digital Humanities

Many quantitative book histories begin with the deceptively simple statement that, like all cultural fields, the literary one includes features that 'cannot be "counted"', such as 'the reading experiences of an individual'[48] and the 'quality' of a literary work.[49] But it also contains elements that 'can be quantified…for example, the number of books printed; the number of books sold, the quantities of books exported'.[50] In such accounts, instead of qualitative and quantitative methods being inherently divided and opposed practices, they become, in Darnton's words, 'a matter of perspective', their use suited to the investigation of different aspects of the literary field. Close readings can reveal information that numbers cannot just as '[s]tatistics can reveal configurations and proportions that escape other kinds of observation'.⁵¹ As Joshi writes, 'rather than forcing a divide between quantitative method and literary study, between statistics and cultural understanding', quantitative book historians acknowledge the potential of each approach to 'enhance the other'.⁵²

These book historians do not deny that quantitative methods suppress the 'particularities' and 'singularities' of individual literary works, as critics of such methods contend. However, they do argue that the trends and patterns – the 'generalisations' – that emerge from this process justify the loss of detail. As Jonathan Zwicker says:

> [N]umbers flatten out the peculiarities and individuality of their object, but this is also part of their value, they 'simplify the better to come to grips with their subject' and so make accessible – through patterns and series – solutions to problems that are virtually inaccessible through the methods of traditional literary history.⁵³

In similar terms, while acknowledging the vital role of detailed case studies for publishing history, Simon Eliot insists that:

> Any number of individual studies would not be sufficient, because you could never be certain that you had assembled a reliable sample that did justice to the particular period or area you were studying. Also the individual studies need a context to confer on their details a proper significance.⁵⁴

Quantitative methods, in other words, do not tell us everything about the literary field; but they provide a way of exploring aspects of that field that could not be investigated by other means. From this perspective, identifying one approach as inherently better simply results in 'an impoverished understanding of a [complex] phenomenon'.⁵⁵

It may seem almost bizarre for book historians to devote so much energy to insisting on the presence of both quantitative and qualitative features of the literary field and, hence, the value of both qualitative and quantitative forms of understanding. Indeed, Literary Darwinist Jonathan Gottschall simply dismisses the dichotomisation of methodological debate:

> To argue for the superiority of quantitative over qualitative approaches (or vice versa) would be as vacuous as arguing that hammers are better than drills. As the carpenter requires a collection of widely varied and subtle tools for effectively confronting widely varied challenges, so too does the scholar.⁵⁶

Yet in the broader controversy about quantitative methods, it is often difficult to determine what value, if any, Moretti and his critics accord to the methodology other than the one they champion. For instance, in her critique of Moretti's work, Trumpener identifies book history as a potential 'middle ground' between statistical methods and close reading, and describes as 'brilliant' the 'statistical work of bibliographers and book historians like Peter Garside and James Raven'.⁵⁷ However, the type of book history she subsequently delineates and advocates is one that replicates the individualised focus of close reading. Thus, she valorises the book historian who endeavours 'to figure out, book for book, who determined' – in this case – 'each novel's title: author, publisher or publicist'. As Trumpener puts it, this approach involves 'real footwork – and…commitment to specific novels'.[58] Trumpener thus appears to endorse, or at least allow space for, quantitative approaches to literature (admittedly in a book history realm that she separates from literary history). However, the moral associations she draws between the study of particular texts – signifying commitment and hard work – and quantitative approaches – which 'violate' the integrity or 'individuality' of the object of study – denigrates any form of history not based on direct acquaintance with each literary object.[59]

Moretti's views on the appropriate fate of close reading are similarly opaque. Sometimes, like the book historians above, he appears to accord value to qualitative as well as quantitative approaches. In 'Conjectures on World Literature', he notes, '[r]eading "more" is always a good thing',[60] and describes 'distant reading' as 'a little pact with the devil'.[61] In the introduction to *Graphs*, he claims, 'for me, abstraction is not an end in itself, but a way to widen the domain of the literary historian, and enrich its internal problematic'.[62] 'Distant reading', from this perspective, is a way of addressing particular questions. Rachel Serlen, who has written a detailed critique of Moretti's oeuvre, notes that such instances – where Moretti 'appears to say that both methods can peacefully coexist' – are the ones '[h]is most sympathetic critics' seize upon.[63] Timothy Burke, for instance, contends: 'There is no requirement to purchase the entire methodological inventory [Moretti] makes available, or to throw overboard close reading'.[64]

But, Serlen continues, 'In more recent restatements of the problem…Moretti takes the more radical stance that the distant turn he advocates entails the rejection of interpretation'.[65] In one of his many responses to the commentary his work has evoked, Moretti asserts: 'Between interpretation (that tends to make a close reading of a single text) and explanation (that works with abstract models on a large groups [sic] of texts) I see an antithesis. Not just difference, but an either/or choice'. He makes this proclamation even while acknowledging that, '[i]t may be tactically silly for me to say so now, given that the general consensus is that what I do could be interesting, as long as it doesn't want to get rid of current procedures'.[66] As Moretti elsewhere describes 'close reading' as less 'rational' than distant reading,[67] this 'either/or choice' between interpretation and explanation – like Trumpener's association of close reading with commitment and hard work – raises methodology from *modus operandi* to moral imperative. Where Trumpener's moral/methodological framework suggests the Protestant work ethic, Moretti's invokes the Kantian view of rationality as the basis of morality. In light of this morally loaded bifurcation of debate about qualitative and quantitative methods, the careful and pragmatic insistence by book historians that different questions – and different features of the literary field – require different approaches appears, far from simple-minded or bizarre, astute and necessary.

As I have said, critics such as Spivak have attacked what they see as Moretti's false claim to objective truth and totalising knowledge. To my mind, this is the most pertinent criticism of Moretti's approach, and I want to spend some time detailing its elements, and adding my own criticism, before describing how book history's approach to data avoids this charge. While Spivak broadly criticises Moretti's assumption of scopic vision,[68] other commentators focus on two aspects of his work that they argue underpin this assertion of absolute knowledge: his definition and use of data. John Frow criticises Moretti's understanding of data, arguing that he takes 'genres or forms as given and then derive[s] structures from large data sets based on them in such a way that literary history can be conceived as an objective account of patterns and trends'. In this process, Moretti 'ignore[s] the crucial point that these morphological categories he takes as his base units are not pre-given but are constituted in an interpretive encounter by means of an interpretive decision'.[69] In other words, although Moretti's data – which include such abstract concepts as clues in detective fiction, free indirect style,[70] and formal compromise[71] – are the results of the subjective process of reading, his analysis disregards 'that moment of interpretive constitution of the categories of analysis' to produce a historical approach that is uncritically positivist.

Related to this, Serlen highlights Moretti's 'ad hoc' categorisations of data, and proposes that he 'runs the risk of identifying genres and devices whose totality is as artificial as that of the individual texts he is trying to displace'.[72] I would add that, even when Moretti uses data constructed by others, he is inclined to overplay its accuracy. For instance, in the first chapter of *Graphs* he claims that: '[q]uantitative data can tell us when Britain produced one new novel per month or week or day, or hour for that matter'.[73] Moretti may intend this claim to refer to average levels of production; or to the possibilities of future datasets, more complete than current records of eighteenth- and nineteenth-century British book publication. Yet in not making these distinctions, and instead asserting an impossible level of precision – it is certain that not even the titles of all British novels are recorded, let alone the hour of their production – Moretti accords to his results an accuracy and objectivity they cannot (and probably can never) possess.

This quote regarding the quantitative data on British book publishing (which continues, 'where the significant turning points lie along the continuum – and why – is something that must be decided on a different basis') is one that Serlen uses as an example of where Moretti acknowledges the subjective nature of his interpretations.[74] Quantitative research provides, he argues in this case, '*data*, not interpretation'.[75] However, she sees this example as exceptional, arguing that Moretti generally describes his method in ways that downplay or occlude the subjective and interpretive aspects of data analysis:

> While Moretti's own work shows interpretation to be as important to distant reading as the accumulation of data…interpretation is curiously elided in his descriptions of distant reading as a method…ma[de to] seem easy, natural – the inevitable result of the accumulated data.[76]

This minimisation of interpretation is another way Moretti presents his arguments as objective descriptions or – the word he prefers – explanations of the literary field.

Significantly, and resonating with Spivak's charge of 'scopic vision',[77] Moretti's elision of the subjective process of interpretation is particularly apparent in respect to the visualisation of data. Quantitative analysis and the visual models it enables are presented not as representations and arguments but as essentially transparent windows into the literary text or the field more broadly. At the beginning of *Graphs*, Moretti announces: 'graphs, maps, and trees place the literary field literally in front of our eyes – and show us how little we still know about it'.[78] Elsewhere he describes these 'three models' as 'three snapshots of the literary field', implying the capacity of a camera's lens to capture the view (with the speed with which these snapshots are taken further minimising the process of interpretation).[79] If these visualisations present the literary field itself, then seeing what is there – and explaining it – can be substituted for the subjective processes involved in collecting and constructing the data for these graphs, and in deciding how the data will be visualised and what it means. As Serlen remarks, '[h]ow the data get interpreted is replaced by how the data are seen, which minimizes the explanatory work involved in distant reading'.[80]

Another consequence of what Spivak calls Moretti's 'claim to scopic vision' is the transition this assumption supports from context-specific, socio-historical accounts of literary data to explanations that are 'global rather than local'. Michael Friedman describes a global focus as characteristic of 'scientific explanation': what is explained in such accounts is 'a general regularity or pattern of behavior – a law if you like – i.e. that water turns to steam when heated'.[81] Moretti aims in *Graphs* to reveal the 'hidden thread of literary history': its cycles.[82] As '[v]ariations in a conflict that remains constant',[83] these cycles operate separately from and beyond the social world and events in it. Moretti ties this focus on cycles to the *Annales* school of history – an approach, as I said earlier, that is also foundational to book history. However, where the *Annaliste* historians investigate the persistence of cultural ideas (or *mentalities*) over long stretches of time (as well as the effects of geographical and geological realities on the social world), Moretti aims to discover general regularities or patterns that, like global scientific 'laws', exist beneath or beyond social or historical context.

This understanding of cycles as literary 'laws' leads Moretti, in some cases, to neglect obvious differences in context when comparing literary fields in different places and times and, in other cases, to propose explanations that relate changes in the literary field solely to features internal to that field. In relation to this first tendency, Moretti attributes the 'pattern' that emerges in the first graph in *Graphs* (the much-discussed rise of the novel in five separate countries) to a general theory of

> the horizon of novel-reading… As long as only a handful of texts are published each year…the novel is an unreliable commodity: it disappears for long stretches of time, and cannot really command the loyalty of the reading public; it resembles a fashion, more than a literary genre. With a new text every week, however, the novel becomes that great modern oxymoron of the *regular novelty*: the unexpected that consumers expect so often and eagerly that they can no longer do without it.[84]

Leaving aside the issue of whether five instances constitutes a pattern – and disregarding the important fact that novels are published and read in many forms besides the book – this hypothesis might have relevance to understanding growth in the production of British novels in the early eighteenth century. However, in identifying the same 'horizon of novel-reading' in late nineteenth-century Nigeria, for instance, Moretti overlooks the vital contextual point that, while Britain may have had a relatively isolated book market, there were novels circulating in Nigeria before the 1960s and the emergence of the Nigerian novel. Thus, the same relationship between the publication of novels by Nigerian authors and the reading habits of those in that country – Moretti's 'horizon of novel-reading' – is not inevitable, and cannot be assumed.

Elsewhere, Moretti's search for literary cycles leads him to propose explanations that are, as Serlen puts it, 'purely internal to the formal structure of the literary object': what she calls 'depoliticized form'.[85] For instance, in Moretti's explanation of gender trends in authorship, the novel – and other, unspecified, literary forms – become not only active, but the only participants in this literary cycle. Noting the various rises and falls in the number of novels by British men and women in the eighteenth and nineteenth centuries, Moretti asserts:

> [I]f the conflict remains constant, then the point is not who prevails in this or that skirmish, but exactly the opposite: no victory is ever definitive, neither men nor women writers 'occupy' the British novel once and for all, and the form keeps oscillating back and forth between the two groups…allow[ing] the novel to use a double pool of talents and of forms, thereby boosting its productivity, and giving it an edge over its many competitors.[86]

I agree with Moretti that gender trends in authorship tend to oscillate. Certainly, the Australian data shows this same 'back and forth' movement between a predominance of novels by men and women. However, in abstracting this phenomenon from the social world, Moretti's explanation adds little to our understanding of the operations of gender in the literary field. While it seems clear that, throughout history, writing by men and women has been constructed and received differently, Moretti presents this gendered distinction and dichotomisation as itself a law: men and women have different 'talents' and produce contrasting 'forms' across space and time. The British novel is personified, and plays men and women off against each other to gain what Moretti proposes as an evolutionary advantage over other literary forms ('its many competitors'). Although Moretti defines '[f]orms…as the abstract of social relationships', such that 'formal analysis is in its own modest way an analysis of power',[87] in his explanations of gender trends Moretti substitutes a consideration of social power relations for a seemingly uncritical mixture of literary statistics and evolutionary and economic theory.

Such explanations, as Serlen argues, make it 'unclear what weight historical forces can have if their results cannot change';[88] or, we might add, if they change randomly. Moretti has responded to criticisms of his use of scientific paradigms to explain literature by asking: 'why on earth should I drop a perfectly plausible explanation? Because it sounds politically wrong?'[89] My problem with these particular explanations is not that they are politically incorrect, but that they miss important features of, or do not add to our understanding of, literary change. This step that Moretti takes in abstracting literature from its social and historical context occurs because, as critics like Frow and Serlen argue, Moretti imagines his data as being objective, in the sense of being separate from the social world. Admittedly, Moretti moves very quickly through a number of different historical and literary trends, and is, as he says, more interested in 'opening new conceptual possibilities...than justifying these in every detail'.[90] However, in some cases, the conceptual possibilities that are offered do not seem to me to attain the level of understanding and insight that should be the aim of humanities scholarship. In this book I offer an alternative approach to both of the issues I have just addressed in relation to Moretti's work: that is, a form of 'distant reading' that attends to the complex historical, social, geographical, political and economic factors involved in the rise of the novel and its relationship to reading communities, and in the shifts or oscillations in gender trends in authorship.

These criticisms of Moretti's 'claim to scopic vision' describe an association between a conception of data as a direct reflection of what is in the literary field, and a form of analysis that proposes to tell and, indeed, to show the truth of that field. Methodological discussions in quantitative book history work against both tendencies, acknowledging that literary statistics are mediated and limited, and that the understanding or knowledge gained from such studies is necessarily partial and qualified. Eliot provides an apt summary of the understanding of data in book history when he asserts:

> The past has left us some data, but they were not produced in laboratory conditions; they were not designed to answer our questions; they were not collected as a representative sample – and they rarely used a classification system that we might find at all helpful. However, they are all we have got and we must work with them.[91]

Such acknowledgements of the limitations of data are often 'pounce[d] upon', Joshi says, by 'quantitative history's detractors...as "further" evidence of the dubious value of statistical methods'.[92] However, in book history, this understanding simply demonstrates the need for a clear and detailed account of the origins, biases and limitations of literary historical data. This is a process that Eliot describes as providing the 'biography of the [data] source':

> If we are to use our sources well (that is, exploit them to the full without asking them to bear a weight of interpretation that they are not strong enough to carry) we need to know our sources well: who compiled them, why they were compiled, and how they were compiled.[93]

All archives are the outcome of what Frow terms 'interpretive encounter[s] by means of...interpretive decision[s]'.[94] The biography of an archive – data-based or otherwise; historical or modern – attempts to identify the ideas, values, definitions and meanings, the theories and biases, that underpin and produce the collection, so as to enable a more critical and astute reading of the information it contains.

As I said in the introduction, the new history of the Australian novel I present in this book draws predominantly on the *AustLit* database, a non-profit, electronic archive that, it announces on its website, 'aim[s] to be the definitive virtual research environment and information resource for Australian literary, print, and narrative culture scholars, students, and the public'.[95] Created in 2000, *AustLit* merged a number of existing specialist databases and bibliographies, and has subsequently involved well over a hundred individual researchers – from multiple Australian universities and the National Library of Australia – in an effort to 'correct unevenness and gaps in bibliographical coverage'[96] and continually update the collection. The database has received significant government and institutional funding and support, and includes bibliographical details on hundreds of thousands of works and authors.[97]

AustLit is well suited for quantitative analysis. The database has a high degree of comprehensiveness, due to the substantial and longstanding investment of money and scholarly energy in its creation, and because of the relatively recent origins of 'Australian literature'. Its construction according to established bibliographical standards and fields, which give the data a high degree of consistency across the collection, also facilitates quantitative and computational approaches. However, none of this implies that the data in *AustLit* is complete or perfect. I focus on novels predominantly for historiographical reasons: they are the fictional form most directly tied, in general as well as academic discussion, to the state and status of Australian literary culture.[98] But there is also an important pragmatic reason for this focus: novels are the most comprehensively recorded fictional form in *AustLit*. Even so, not every Australian novel is included. *AustLit* notes that its 'coverage of some popular fiction genres such as westerns and romances, and of self-published works, is representative rather than full'.[99] Likewise, although over a thousand different periodicals are indexed, this coverage is not comprehensive.[100]

My datasets are also not identical with *AustLit*'s.[101] This is partly because there are instances where I have chosen to exclude titles that *AustLit* includes, such as entries for 'Non-*AustLit* Novels',[102] and novels by overseas authors included because they were banned in Australia.[103] There is also a considerable amount of data in *AustLit* that my study does not explore. In particular, while many titles are reprinted multiple times, due to the complexity of this dataset and the certainty of substantial gaps in coverage, I only consider the first publication in book and/or serial form. Most significantly, as an online rather than a print bibliography,[104] *AustLit* is updated continually as Australian authors write more fiction and as historical authors and works are included or excluded. I updated my datasets approximately every six months during the four years of this project.[105] This process enhanced my awareness of the fluid nature of the dataset and, in particular, of the adjustments – including retrospective ones – that occur as *AustLit* modifies its parameters for inclusion or its interpretation of them. But it also confirmed for me the general stability of this collection, in that these adjustments did not change the overall trends.

Even leaving aside the authors and works not discovered by *AustLit*, and the differences between this dataset and my own, in a fundamental and important way, it is impossible for any bibliographical record of the Australian novel to be complete. As *AustLit* acknowledges, '[t]he definition of "Australian" and "Literature" moves according to current debates and changing reading, teaching and research patterns'.[106] *AustLit*, in other words, is engaged in an ongoing process of representing and constructing the category of Australian literature, including the Australian novel. The complexity of this process of construction comes to the fore in relation to the question of who or what is an Australian author. Drawing on a set of parameters for defining an Australian author – including such considerations as where they were born, where they spent their formative years, and the content of their fiction[107] – decisions about which texts and authors to incorporate are made on an individual basis. The effects of these decisions are particularly apparent for nineteenth-century records. In certain cases, some of an author's titles are included while others are not (as with novels by Fergus Hume and B. L. Farjeon, for example).[108] However, Australian literature's status as a constructed category is true for all periods: as Maryanne Dever says of the 1920s and 1930s, 'the concept of an "Australian Author"… was by no means a fixed and fully-constituted category'.[109] More broadly, the notion of Australian literature as it currently stands is a product – like the *AustLit* database itself – of a particular period and paradigm of cultural nationalist research into, and funding for, Australian literature. Indeed, a peculiar irony of this book is that, while I criticise aspects of this cultural nationalist ideology (especially in Chapter 3), this new history of the Australian novel is only possible because of the research and infrastructural outcomes of that paradigm.

In book historical accounts, awareness of the inevitably constructed or mediated and limited nature of any cultural data strongly tempers the type of knowledge or understanding scholars claim for their quantitative analyses. This point is often made through metaphors that relate the results of quantitative studies to other forms of partial representation. Darnton, for instance, compares the 'general picture of literary culture' provided by book historical data 'to the early maps of the New World, which showed the contours of continents, even though they did not correspond very well to the actual landscape'.[110] While acknowledging that Moretti's analogy of literary history with 'the maps of Africa of a century and a half ago'[111] – quoted at the start of this chapter – is from his earlier work, comparing it with Darnton's map provides a salutary demonstration of the different epistemological claims made for quantitative analysis by the two historians. Both refer to historical maps, but whereas for Darnton the 'general picture' offered by statistics is the point – because literary data is inevitably 'flawed or distorted'[112] – Moretti's analogy implies that quantitative analyses will provide literary scholars with the framework to fill in the map and 'pinpoint' the source of changes in the 'coastal' canon (in effect, regarding quantitative analyses as GPS technology).

Similar metaphors to Darnton's appear in many other descriptions of the potential and limitations of quantitative book history. Joshi builds on Darnton's analogy of statistics and maps of the new world, arguing:

> [Q]uantitative methods expand literary history and make all sorts of discoveries possible, much the way that early maps did in the dissemination of knowledge about 'new' worlds. Statistics, like maps, are indeed lies to some extent…but they are lies that tell a truth that would not otherwise be evident.[113]

Discussing '[l]iterary statistics from a poorly documented book culture' – such as the Nigerian novels she explores – Wendy Griswold argues that quantitative analyses are 'like a very rough sketch: some of the lines may be off, but a picture emerges anyway'.[114] These metaphors in book history serve to acknowledge the limitations of literary data and present the results of quantitative analyses as indications, rather than proof, of historical trends.[115] At the same time, in emphasising the wider perspective such studies enable, these metaphors maintain the importance of quantitative perspectives. The refusal of an objective standpoint does not, in other words, slide into a claim of equivalence between qualitative and quantitative studies. Any reading of statistics is, like any reading of a text, a subjective process of selection and decision-making; and in both cases, there are readings that are more accurate and enlightening than others. But for identifying literary trends over time, quantitative analyses enable a broad, historical and comparative perspective not achievable based on studies of particular texts or publishers' records.

These discussions in book history – regarding the mediated nature of data and the form of knowledge that quantitative analyses make possible – provide an important critical framework for data-rich literary history. But they have a significant blind-spot: although the majority (if not all) recent quantitative book histories use computers and computational techniques, especially in collating and visualising data, their methodological framework does not acknowledge the adoption of this technology, let alone reflect on its methodological and epistemological implications. Accordingly, while these book historical studies show, for instance, precisely why the archive is not an unmediated repository of information, computational processes are rendered entirely transparent. The nature of the metaphors employed to describe the visualisation of data makes this assumed lack of mediation apparent: both quill on parchment (to produce the historical maps) and pencil on paper (for Griswold's 'rough sketch') signify forms of representation where there is no apparent intermediary between input and output. As well as determinedly analogue, these metaphors present the visualisation of data as a final (and singular) end product, whereas computer visualisations – like the data on which they are based – can exist in temporary and transitionary, as well as multiple and transferable, forms.

A failure to acknowledge – let alone interrogate – the implications of working with computers is not unique to book history, but occurs throughout the humanities. While the established view is of humanities scholars and technology as 'virtual strangers',[116] the ready acceptance of the computer as simply a tool – a 'system to deliver results', entirely separate from analysis and no more worthy of mention than the use of a word processing program to prepare an article for publication[117] – suggests that 'we are all too comfortably at home in the digital'. As Rothberg continues, lacking the critical distance to question and 'defamiliarize powerful technological framings',[118] there is a significant risk that humanities scholars will not perceive computation for what it is: a new set of representational and epistemological practices and processes, whose adoption has profound consequences for humanities scholarship, and requires careful consideration.

This perception of computers, to use Willard McCarty's formulation, as 'knowledge jukeboxes' – that simply play whatever is loaded into them[119] – has two major implications. First, it reinforces the same rhetoric of objectivity and certainty for computational approaches that book historians have worked so hard to challenge in relation to quantitative analyses. Given that computational approaches always involve quantification, and that quantitative studies are increasingly carried out with the computer, this uncritical view of computational analyses has the potential to cancel out the important methodological insights of quantitative book history. This uncritical understanding of computers as providing objective and certain information – rather than a way of knowing (or 'prosthetic extensions…for critical reflection', as Jerome McGann puts it)[120] – also unconsciously replicates the understanding of knowledge production privileged in contemporary university management practices. As McCarty writes, the 'knowledge jukebox' view of computers 'harkens to the commodification of knowledge as something that can be packaged in units, stored somewhere else and delivered to a consumer or dispensed from a machine on demand'.[121] Second, in viewing computers as simply tools, humanities scholars risk not taking full advantage of the critical possibilities computers can enable, nor of playing an active part in developing such approaches 'in ways we wish to develop them'.[122]

Although the theorised nature of data does not receive the same focused attention in the digital humanities as it does in book history, both fields share a basic view of data as shaped by ideas and values circulating in the world. For instance, Cathy Davidson's description of 'data collection…[as] data selection', as well as her contention that '[d]ata transform theory; theory, stated or assumed, transforms data into interpretation',[123] clearly resonate with many of the claims I have discussed in relation to quantitative book history. In integrating what might be called the analogue conception of quantitative analysis in book history, with an understanding of how working with a computer informs and remediates my approach to data, I have found McCarty's notion of modelling particularly useful. Although McCarty develops this approach for use with language, his description of modelling – as an exploratory and experimental practice, aimed not at producing final and definitive answers but at enabling a process of investigation and speculation – can be adapted for quantitative analysis of literary historical data, and its visualisation in particular.

Like quantitative book historians, McCarty acknowledges that his method 'obfuscates difference': a 'model *of* something' is, of necessity, 'an abstraction or simple representation of a more complex real phenomenon'. And like book historians, he justifies this process of reduction because it facilitates the development of a form of understanding and knowledge that would not be possible by other means. Indeed, McCarty argues that models are necessary precisely because the object of study – such as, in my case, historical trends in the production and reception of Australian novels – is otherwise 'inaccessible or intractable'.[124] While this aspect of modelling resembles the approach to data and quantitative analysis in book history, what I find particularly enabling about McCarty's methodology is the emphasis it places on the analysis and representation of data as a process of knowledge production and experimentation, enabled by the computer.

McCarty emphasises the status of models as 'pragmatic instruments of investigation'.[125] Where Moretti's 'abstract models' present transparent windows into, or snapshots of, the literary field – and where book historical metaphors emphasise partial but completed indications of historical trends – McCarty describes models as 'experimental device[s]', and as constructs or stages in a 'process of coming to know'.[126] To ground this notion in an example from my own research, the publishing data for a particular period in the history of the Australian novel might lead me to suppose a particular influence on the field: for instance, that a particular government funding model, supporting a particular group of local publishers, enabled the rise of a particular Australian novel genre. The manipulability of a digital representation, and the fluid nature of the computing environment more broadly, encourages and enables modification of, or experimentation with, data – for instance, subtracting particular publishers or genres – as a way of testing such hypotheses. This process might fulfil my expectations – thus strengthening my original hypothesis – or challenge them, bringing that hypothesis into question and compelling me to seek an alternative account of the data.[127] Although the codex form does not allow me to display the literally hundreds of models I developed in exploring the history of the Australian novel, this practice of trying and testing a range of hypotheses underpins all the graphs, and informs all the arguments, that I present in the pages that follow. I have also made the datasets used for this book available, so that others can explore and experiment with them, and in doing so, check, extend or challenge my categorisations, visualisations and interpretations.[128]

Modelling as McCarty theorises it, then, is directed at 'making new knowledge' using quantitative information and a digital research environment. However, the emphasis on manipulation also transforms the meaning of these representations. Models are built to be modified, and this process of modification emphasises their status as fictions: 'not only by being a representation, and so not the thing itself, but also by selective omission and perhaps by distortion or inclusion as well'.[129] As a result, what is emphasised in modelling is not knowledge as an end product but the development of knowledge as an ongoing process. As McCarty elaborates:

> The drastically reduced investment in an obviously temporary product, plus the means at hand to alter it immediately, mean that one is much less likely to mistake this product for a true or final representation, indeed unlikely to think that any such product would ever reach perfection.

No matter how complete the graphs in this book might appear, as McCarty says of his models, they 'are better understood as *temporary states in a process of coming to know* rather than fixed structures of knowledge'.[130]

This description of modelling resonates productively with *AustLit*'s status as an online and, hence, fluid archive. While the established comprehensiveness of *AustLit* remains important in this context – as it means the data used for modelling will not change radically and render the process of hypothesis testing so abstract as to be redundant – McCarty provides a framework wherein potential shifts in the data do not disallow quantitative analysis. To put this another way, where the perception of a graph as a final product would prevent – or at least, significantly curtail – the critical potential of mining, modelling and visualising an online (and hence changeable) database, modelling enables a relationship between data and argumentation that is, explicitly, an ongoing and evolving one. Data is contingent: inherently due to its constructed nature and, as is increasingly the case, because of the online environment in which it is presented. Understanding data representation as a process of research rather than an end-product signifies a quantitative approach that resonates with the humanities process of interpretation: an approach that is explicitly contingent and speculative while remaining critical and committed to scholarly rigour.

***

As I have proposed in this chapter, there are some who view all quantitative approaches to literature as pointlessly reductive, falsely totalising in their knowledge claims, and inherently complicit with the neoliberal or economic rationalist managerial practices increasingly prominent in today's corporate university. But any claim to knowledge (including the defence of close reading) that does not admit its partiality – and thus, inherently, the value of other ways of knowing – is bound to transform the will to knowledge into the will to power, and to enable only an impoverished understanding of any complex phenomenon. Combined, the book history and digital humanities approaches I have discussed offer a critical way of working and thinking with literary and digital data that does not fall into this trap. Quantitative book histories provide a framework for acknowledging the limitations of data while upholding the importance of analyses based on empirical evidence. As Eliot says, such studies are not 'exercise[s] in justifying the use of any figures at any time in any context'. Rather, they propose that, 'interpreted cautiously and used intelligently', literary data indicates trends in the literary field that cannot be investigated otherwise.[131] The digital humanities – and McCarty's method of modelling in particular – extends the possibilities of quantitative analysis by outlining a speculative and experimental approach to computation and data visualisation. The new history of the Australian novel I offer in the pages that follow draws on both sets of approaches to provide an account that is, of necessity, partial. However, due to the perspective enabled by quantitative representation and analysis, it is also an account that enables insights into the literary field: insights that challenge established interpretations and offer new understandings of the history of the Australian novel.

Chapter 2

BEYOND THE BOOK: PUBLISHING IN THE NINETEENTH CENTURY

The history of the book in Australia may be characterised as the movement of durable cultural goods over very large distances. Raw material was dispatched to Britain in the form of stories and other texts to be converted into books at the industrial heart of Empire. These were then shipped back to the Antipodes along with numerous other books to satisfy the prodigious appetites of Australian readers. Local publishing was a sideline undertaken by enterprising printers and booksellers.[1]

Over the last decade, Australian literary studies has undergone a 'transnational turn',[2] with a number of the field's leading scholars urging a shift 'beyond the national paradigm'[3] to 'explore and elaborate the many ways in which the national literature has always been connected to the world'.[4] Book histories have been at the forefront of this process, with particularly profound consequences for conceptions of nineteenth-century literary culture. Where earlier literary histories sought in this century – especially the 1890s – the origins of a recognisably national literary tradition and canon,[5] histories of the book (and of publishing and reading) in Australia emphasise the fundamental importance of British publishers and books for colonial authors and readers. This recent scholarship highlights Australia's position as a major export market for British books, 'the largest…from at least 1889',[6] and according to Alexis Weedon, since 1878.[7] British publishers are described as not only the main source of books for colonial readers but, as Craig Munro and John Curtain state in the epigraph to this chapter, essentially the only avenue of publication for Australian authors.

Perhaps the major renovation of this transnational turn is the emphasis placed on colonial readers' lack of interest in local fiction. Martyn Lyons and Tim Dolin make this argument based on analyses of the records of different lending and reading institutions in the late nineteenth and early twentieth centuries, with Lyons noting the pre-eminence of an 'Anglocentric reading model',[8] and Dolin describing Australian readers' preference for popular British books or, as he puts it, 'bad literature from somewhere else'.[9] Likewise, drawing on the 'minutes of three Hobart reading groups established in the late nineteenth century', Elizabeth Webby proposes that Hobart's cultural elite, '[l]ike most Australian readers of the 1890s…were not especially interested in Australian literature'.[10] Taken together, these studies of publishing and reading argue, as Webby writes elsewhere, that 'for much of the nineteenth century and indeed afterwards, Australian readers were mainly interested in books by English authors, and Australian authors were largely dependent on the English publishing industry'.[11]

But were Australian authors and publishers really so marginal, if not largely irrelevant, to the development of literary culture in Australia and to colonial readers? Based on quantitative analysis of trends in the place and form of publication of nineteenth-century Australian novels, I argue that local publishing – especially, but not only, in colonial periodicals – was more important to the history of the Australian novel, and to colonial reading practices, than these accounts allow. Indeed, from the 1860s to the 1880s, most Australian novels were first published in Australia, and in the majority of cases, only ever read there. These results challenge the prevailing view that there was essentially no publishing in Australia in the nineteenth century. In turn, the local readerships indicated by this local publishing activity demonstrate an interest in, and market for, Australian fiction in the colonies. As well as providing a new perspective on the nineteenth-century Australian novel, and the conditions under which it emerged, these local readerships for Australian fiction help to explain why, when seeking increased access to the colonial market in the 1890s, British publishers substantially increased their production of Australian novels. Instead of colonial readers and authors completely dependent on British authors and publishers, I emphasise the importance of local practices in shaping colonial literary culture, including the activities of British publishers in that market. This chapter shows there is much about the history of colonial authorship, publishing and reading – both within and beyond Australia – to be learned from analysis of the publishing history of the Australian novel, and much about that history that has been overlooked in the recent focus on British publishers and authors, and the longstanding preoccupation of Australian literary scholars with the book as the vehicle of literary culture.

My argument builds on the results shown in the following two graphs. Figure 1 depicts the place of initial book publication for Australian novels from the 1830s to the 1890s.[12] This graph clearly supports, in relation to the Australian novel, the main argument about book publishing in this period: the dominance of British publishers. My analysis also confirms Munro and Curtain's description of local book publishing as a 'sideline'. At the same time, I argue that, during the first half of the nineteenth century, 'enterprising booksellers and publishers' were essentially the only avenue of publication for authors resident in the colonies. In the second half of that century, this 'sideline' expanded considerably, such that, in the 1870s and 1880s, one in every three book editions of Australian novels were first, and in most cases only, published in the colonies.

While the contribution of local book publishers to the history of the Australian novel is greater than previously acknowledged, it pales in comparison with that of local periodical publishers. Figure 2 indicates the form of publication of Australian novels from the 1830s to the 1890s: specifically, whether titles were published only in book form; as serials and – in most cases, subsequently – as books; or only as serials.[13] In addition to overall growth in serial publication of Australian novels from the 1830s to the 1880s, this graph demonstrates that, from the 1860s to the 1880s, approximately half of all titles were serialised, and an increasing proportion of these only appeared in serial form. The vast majority of Australian serialised novels were first published in colonial periodicals, especially the weekly companions to the major metropolitan daily newspapers; the large circulations of these publications indicate substantial local readerships for Australian fiction. Where serial fiction predominantly circulated within colonies, rather than between them, local serialisation also

Figure 1. Place of first book publication of Australian novels, percentages, 1830 to 1899 (by decade)

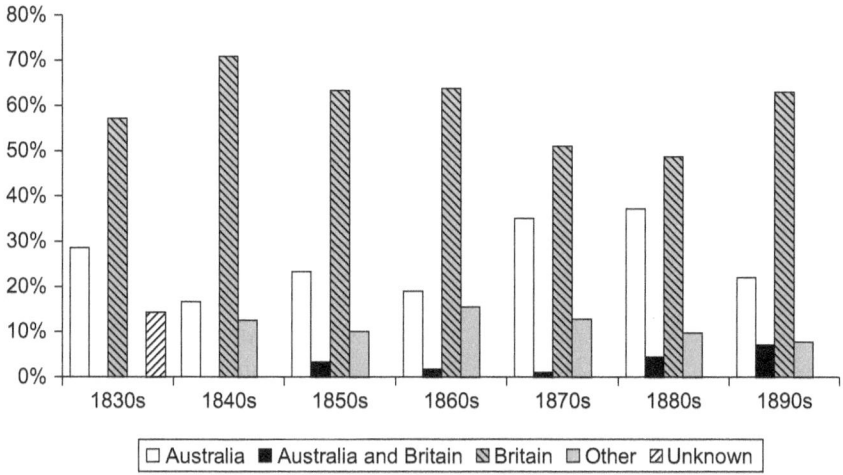

Figure 2. Form of publication of Australian novels, percentages, 1830 to 1899 (by decade and date of first publication)

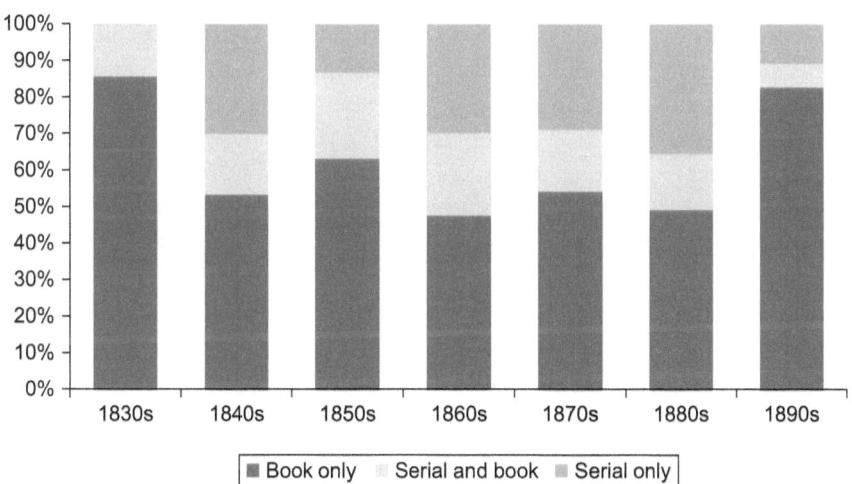

played a role in facilitating British publication of Australian authors. This capacity of serial publication has long been recognised as important in the careers of certain authors, but this chapter demonstrates the extent of this practice. It also locates the rise of serialised fiction in Australia in the early 1860s, more than a decade earlier than has been proposed.

My discussion in this chapter is divided in five parts: part one considers book publication of Australian novels from the 1830s to the 1850s; part two explores the serial publication of Australian novels throughout the nineteenth century; part three analyses the relationship between serial and book publication in the history of this form; part four returns to book publication, focusing on the decades from 1860 to 1889; and part five demonstrates and explores the profound shifts in colonial literary culture that occurred in the final decade of the nineteenth century.

I Book Publishing: 1830s to 1850s

Relatively few Australian novels were published in these early decades: seven in the 1830s, 30 in the 1840s and 38 in the 1850s. Nevertheless, trends in the form and place of publication of such titles indicate features of colonial and British book publishing relevant to the history of the Australian novel throughout the nineteenth century: specifically, the different approaches of these two groups of publishers and the contrasting rewards, for authors, of publication in Britain and the colonies. In this section I argue that, while Munro and Curtain's description of local publishing as 'a sideline undertaken by enterprising printers and booksellers'[14] nicely captures the range of activities in which these publishers engaged, and the financial precariousness of such ventures, it underplays local book publishers' unique contribution to the emergence and development of the Australian novel and colonial literary culture.

Although some Australian novels (nine in the 1840s and five in the 1850s) only appeared as serials,[15] the book was the main form in which such titles were published, as Figure 2 indicates. Figure 1 shows the extent to which British companies dominated in this area, publishing 66 per cent of book editions of Australian novels in these three decades, compared with 21 per cent by colonial book publishers (the second highest producers). The majority of publishers of Australian novels in this period were responsible for only one title, and in most cases, this was the only Australian novel that those companies ever published. However, one local publisher – J. R. Clarke – as well as one American and seven British presses published multiple titles (see Table 1). For two of these British publishers – Routledge and Ward, Lock – a connection with a particular (and particularly prolific) author, John Lang, was a major factor in their early engagement in the colonial novel field.[16]

The main difference between the British and colonial publishers of Australian novels in this early period – and throughout the nineteenth century – was their degree of specialisation.

Table 1. Top ten book publishers of Australian novels, 1830 to 1859

Publishers	Nation	# Titles	% Titles
1. Routledge	British	5	7
2. Smith, Elder	British	4	5
2. Ward, Lock	British	4	5
4. J. R. Clarke	Australian	3	4
4. Richard Bentley	British	3	4
4. Saunders and Otley	British	3	4
7. F. Gleason's Publishing Hall	American	2	3
7. Longman	British	2	3
7. Simmonds and Ward	British	2	3
7. The Author	Australian	2	3

In *A History of British Publishing*, John Feather describes the transformation, '[b]y the end of the second decade of the nineteenth century', of the 'British book trade' into a 'recognisably... modern publishing industry'. A series of changes from the 1770s – associated with the cessation of perpetual copyrights and the industrial revolution (which gave rise to new technologies for book production and new groups of book-buyers) – compelled a 'process of gradual separation of the several functions of the printer, the publisher and the bookseller'.[17] This transition took its 'toll on the old', with established companies either adapting to the newly specialised, competitive industry, or folding. But it also 'offered opportunities for the new'. Established houses like Rivington and Longman, which Feather argues survived because they 'disposed of their retail stock and concentrated entirely on publishing',[18] were among the British publishers of Australian novels at this time. But most were of the new breed, houses like Routledge, Saunders and Otley, Macmillan, Chapman and Hall, and Smith, Elder that arose and prospered in the industrial age by focusing on publishing, and by identifying and exploiting newly available technologies, means of distribution and markets.

Although they emerged at the same time as this new breed of British publishers, the colonial companies responsible for book editions of Australian novels were not specialised publishers. Instead, they performed a range of print-related (and in some cases, non-print-related) activities, particularly bookselling, general printing and periodical publishing. Despite publishing the most novels of any local publisher in this era,[19] Sydney-based J. R. Clarke specialised in music selling and publishing, and also printed artworks and photographs. Likewise based in Sydney and responsible for publishing one Australian novel in the 1840s,[20] James Tegg was typical of other local publishers in his involvement in printing and retail bookselling, but atypical in his role as a wholesaler of British books.[21] George Slater, who published one title in the 1850s,[22] ran a Melbourne bookstore, publisher, printer, stationer, newsagency and library that also dealt in homeopathic medicines;[23] James Turner Grocott (proprietor of J. T. Grocott, publisher of one Australian novel in the 1840s)[24] sold prints, music and stationery in George Street, Sydney, but was also, at various times, licensee of the Pier Hotel and charterer of a steamer that took sightseers to Manly and Watsons Bay.[25] Two local publishers of Australian novels also produced periodicals: Henry Melville, who published *Quintus Servinton*, the first Australian novel published in the colonies,[26] was a prominent Hobart newspaper proprietor and printer; Tegg published two short-lived magazines (both of which featured local writers): *Tegg's Monthly Magazine* and *The Literary News; A Review and Magazine of Fact and Fiction, The Arts, Sciences, & Belles Lettres*.[27]

An obvious reason for the differing degrees of specialisation of local and British publishers was the different markets the two groups served. Feather describes the concurrent emergence, and interdependence, of a mass audience for books in Britain and a 'recognisably...modern publishing industry'.[28] The colonial reading market was minute compared with Britain's: in 1841, the combined population of the colonies was only a tenth of London's.[29] As a nineteenth-century English commentator remarked of Australian periodicals, one consequence of this smaller market was that: '[t]here is not population enough to support the specialist as we know him at home'.[30] And local publishers did not have this population to themselves: this early period of the Australian novel coincides with the beginning of major growth in the export of British books to the colonies.[31] As part of a wider expansion of industrial output – sometimes called the 'great Victorian boom'[32] – British publishers greatly increased their export trade. According to Weedon, already by 1838 almost a quarter (24 per cent) of the 'declared value at customs of books manufactured in the UK' and exported to the British colonies came to Australia. Although India was clearly the leading market at this time, receiving more than half of such exports, by 1868, 'five times the weight of books were being shipped to Australia as to India'.[33]

Engagement in foreign markets led to an unprecedented expansion of the British publishing industry. In contrast, the relatively small colonial market, combined with the largely unidirectional flow of books between Britain and Australia (from the former to the latter, rarely vice versa),[34] made local publishing a financially risky venture. Bankruptcy was not uncommon even for British publishers at this time;[35] but even the most successful of local publishers barely made ends meet. In addition to his wholesale and retail bookselling business, and periodical ventures, James Tegg had an extremely active and varied publishing list, which included the *New South Wales Pocket Almanac*, appearing yearly from 1836 to 1844; protocol manuals like Lady Darling's *Simple Rules for the Guidance of Persons in Humble Life* (1837); and curiosities such as William Lee's *Brandy and Salt; Being an Effectual Remedy for Most of the Diseases Which Afflict Humanity* (1842).[36] Despite this varied list – and his family connection with one of Britain's largest publishers[37] – Tegg died in 1845 'leaving an estate valued at under £100'.[38] Although Jacob Richard Clarke (proprietor of J. R. Clarke) was 'an influential publisher with important connections in the social and political elite of the day',[39] his business went bankrupt and he died in poverty.[40]

A question that hangs over a consideration of publishing in this period – and throughout the nineteenth century – is the relative cultural and economic value of book publication in the colonies as opposed to Britain. British publication was almost certainly preferred by colonial novelists, as it reached a wider audience and had the benefit of potentially multiple reprintings (as three-deckers, in single volumes, and later in the century, as colonial editions).[41] More broadly, and probably more powerfully, the orientation of colonial culture to the trends and judgements of the mother country suggests that British books were accorded greater cultural value than the local product. The financial precariousness of the existence of local publishers – and their non-specialist nature (specifically, their involvement in a range of commissioned printing activities) – also raises the possibility that some (or even many) of these enterprises required authors to contribute to the costs of publication. Certainly, Elizabeth Morrison argues that this practice was widespread among colonial book publishers.[42] This was not an absolute point of distinction between local and British companies, with some of the latter also requiring copayment from authors.[43] However, as these British companies were operating in an industry where there were much greater opportunities for sales and expansion than in the colonies, the existence of this practice in Britain strongly reinforces the possibility of its wider occurrence in the colonies. At the same time, the presence – in these early decades and subsequently – of self-published titles (that is, books imprinted with the author's rather than the publisher's name)[44] implies some level of financial investment by local publishers in the majority of Australian novels published in the colonies.

To my mind, the strong possibility that colonial authors were more likely to have to contribute financially toward the costs of local than British book publication, combined with a view of publication in Britain as more culturally esteemed and financially rewarding, has played a role in the scholarly neglect of these local enterprises. Put bluntly, these factors – and the cultural cringe they bring to the fore – produced a view of colonial publication as the avenue of last resort for authors unable to gain publication in Britain. In Chapter 4, I interrogate this perception in light of gender trends in publication – specifically, the much greater tendency for men's novels to be published locally than women's – and argue that local publishing in the nineteenth century potentially signified an alternative regime of value, focused on the expression of colonial, and later national, identity.

For now though, I want to highlight another trend that complicates a dismissal of local publishing in these early decades as signifying lack of quality: the strong correlation that emerges between the place of publication and the author's location. The majority of authors whose novels were published overseas from 1830 to 1859 were themselves overseas, many having returned 'home', usually to England and usually for good, after stays of varying lengths (from months to decades) in the colonies. Only William Ross (in the 1830s), Thomas McCombie (in the 1840s) and Catherine Helen Spence (in the 1850s) have their novels published as first edition books in Britain without also being in that country. Initially, it appeared Lang was a similar exception, in that he spent much of his life in India but had multiple novels published as books in Britain. But even with his many literary connections in England and a reputation established through extensive serialisation, Lang only achieved British publication for his novels during his extended visits to that country. While there is a perception that British publication signifies the quality of colonial titles, this correlation between the author's location and place of publication indicates that a willingness or ability to travel was as (and arguably more) important than an author's talent in determining where a book was published.

For the colonial novels published as books in Britain from 1830 to 1859, the correspondence between author location and place of publication foregrounds the ambiguity of the definition of 'Australian author', and hence, 'Australian novel' in this period.[45] Given that the vast majority of novelists whose books were published in Britain were themselves in Britain – and *AustLit*'s focus, in such cases, on novels with Australian content – we can assume that such works would have been understood, in the British market, as 'emigrant literature'.[46] These titles would have been aimed, first and foremost, at British readers (those planning to emigrate to Australia as well as those seeking narratives of imperial adventure).

In respect to locally published books, this correlation between author location and place of publication highlights the fact that, with limited exceptions, local publishers provided the only means by which authors who remained in Australia could have their novels published as books. These locally published titles were also the only ones targeted primarily at colonial readers. From this perspective, such books represent the first examples, in novel form, of the correspondence of local publishing, authorship and reading typically conceptualised in terms of national literary culture. Although local book publishers were responsible for a very small number of Australian novels, in representing essentially the only avenue of publication for authors who remained in the colonies, they played a unique role in the emergence of the Australian novel. The extent to which these, and the titles published in Britain, circulated in the colonies (and in Britain) is another question, and one I will return to in part four of this chapter.

II Serial Publishing

There has been considerable, and important, bibliographical and editorial research on Australian periodicals highlighting their importance in publishing nineteenth-century Australian fiction.[47] Toni Johnson-Woods, for instance, describes 'colonial periodicals' as '*de facto* publishers [that] offered many colonial writers their only publishing outlet'.[48] It is because of this research that the data in *AustLit* – underpinning this chapter – is available. But in contrast to America and Britain, where major studies have foregrounded the importance of this form of publication,[49] the majority of Australian literary scholars either ignore serial publication,[50] or mention it only in passing, without any detailed consideration of its role for colonial authors and readers.[51] Certainly, the significance of the serial in the history of the Australian novel, especially from the 1860s to the 1880s, has not been fully appreciated. Analysis of this area of publishing history – including the nature of serialisation prior to the 1860s, the growth in this form of publication of Australian novels from the start of that decade (more than ten years earlier than has been appreciated), and the reading communities this growth indicates – demonstrates the importance of the Australian novel to the development of colonial literary culture.

Australian novels have always been serialised. Between 1830 and 1859, 39 per cent of titles were serialised (and 19 per cent appeared only in serial form). While this statistic might seem to indicate a major trend, the vital qualification is Lang's authorship of half of these titles, a circumstance that reinforces the relatively small size of the novel field in these early decades, as well as Lang's high productivity and predilection for serial publication. Lang was the author of eighteen novels in total, all but one of which was published in this early period (his final novel appeared in 1862). Of the seventeen novels by Lang that were published serially, all but three appeared in the *Mofussilite*, the Indian newspaper he owned and edited. The other titles were first published in prominent British periodicals.[52]

Although Lang epitomises the trend, serial publication of Australian novels in the 1830s and 1840s can largely be understood at the level of the individual author. Four of the five novels not by Lang were by two authors – Charles Rowcroft and David Burn – with the final title published anonymously. Rowcroft, who lived in Van Diemen's Land from 1821 to 1826, had two novels published serially in British periodicals a number of years after he left the colony.[53] Lang and Rowcroft's status as the only 'Australian' authors with novels published in non-Australian periodicals before the 1860s suggests that, as with book publication, overseas serialisation relied on the physical proximity of author and publisher (a phenomenon ironically underscored by Lang's editorship of the *Mofussilite*, and Rowcroft's editorship of two of the periodicals in which his novels appeared).[54] Of the three novels serialised in local periodicals, the two by Burn appeared in the *South Briton, or, Tasmanian Literary Journal*, but were not completed due to the short-lived nature of that publication. Until the 1850s, the only completed serialised novel by an Australian author in an Australian periodical was published anonymously. *Tom Bourke of 'Ours'* appeared in 24 instalments in 1844 in the (also short-lived) New South Wales based *Guardian*. This periodical's subtitle – *A Weekly Journal of Politics, Commerce, Literature, Science and Arts for the Middle and Working Classes of New South Wales* – aptly demonstrates the broad scope of local periodicals in this period (a scope that resonates with the non-specialist nature of local book publishers).

This rather scant field – constituted by a few individuals, a handful of overseas periodicals and two short-lived local journals – began to undergo a series of significant shifts in the 1850s. Webby has highlighted the importance of this decade in the history of local periodical publishing, noting the significant growth in the number of such publications at this time, as well as a shift in their focus from poetry and overseas authors to prose and the promotion – or at least, deliberate inclusion – of local writers.[55] Where serial publication in the 1840s was limited to a few individual contributors, in the 1850s, local serialisation involved as many authors as there were novel titles. And while overseas publication was the norm in the 1830s and 1840s, the eight titles not by Lang serialised in the 1850s all appeared in local periodicals, and, with the exception of Friedrich Gerstaecker's *The Two Convicts*,[56] all appeared first or only in serial form. Gerstaecker was also the only author published in a local periodical who was not, at the time, in the colonies. The general correlation between an author's residence in the colonies and local serialisation shows that local periodicals shared with local book publishers the distinction of being virtually the only avenue of publication for authors who remained in Australia. The type of local periodicals in which novels appeared also began to shift: from magazines and journals only in the 1840s, to include newspapers in the 1850s.

While the 1850s mark the beginning of serial publication, and local serialisation, as an important avenue of publication of Australian novels, it was from the 1860s to the 1880s that this trend was particularly prominent. As Figure 2 indicates, half of all Australian novels published in these decades were serialised (52 per cent in the 1860s, 46 per cent in the 1870s, 51 per cent in the 1880s), and an increasing majority of these appeared only in serial form (57 per cent in the 1860s, 63 per cent in the 1870s and 70 per cent in the 1880s). Most serialised Australian novels first appeared in local periodicals (84 per cent in the 1860s, 86 per cent in the 1870s and 93 per cent in the 1880s), with almost all of the remaining titles in British publications. Given the ephemeral nature of serial publication,[57] it is likely that these statistics underrepresent the importance of this type of publishing to the history of the Australian novel. Yet even on the basis of available records, for the period from 1860 to 1889, periodicals emerge as not only the major local publishers of Australian novels, but the major category of publishers of such titles overall (where British book publishers were responsible for 139 Australian novels in these three decades, 188 were published in local periodicals).

Table 2 lists the most prolific periodical publishers of Australian novels in these decades. With 35 titles, the *Australian Journal* – a magazine established in 1865 as a weekly, becoming a monthly in 1870 – serialised the most Australian novels. The other major periodical publishers of such titles at this time were all weekly companions to daily newspapers, long recognised by literary historians and bibliographers as the 'earliest group of Australian colonial newspapers to publish serial fiction'.[58] The *Sydney Mail*, launched in 1860 as a weekly companion to the *Sydney Morning Herald*, was the second largest publisher, with 33 titles. The *Australian Town and Country Journal* (established in 1870 as a companion to Sydney's *Evening News*) published 22, while the *Australasian* (founded in 1864 as a companion to the Melbourne *Argus*) published 20. The *Leader* (created in 1856

Table 2. Top ten periodical publishers of Australian novels, 1860 to 1889

Publishers	Nation	# Titles	% Titles
1. *Australian Journal*	Australian	35	8
2. *Sydney Mail*	Australian	33	8
3. *Australian Town and Country Journal*	Australian	22	5
4. *Australasian*	Australian	20	5
5. *Leader*	Australian	16	4
6. *Melbourne Quarterly*	Australian	9	2
7. *Illustrated Sydney News*	Australian	6	1
8. *Australian Monthly Magazine / Colonial Monthly*	Australian	5	1
8. *Australian Woman's Magazine and Domestic Journal*	Australian	5	1
10. *Centennial Magazine*	Australian	4	1

as a companion to the Melbourne *Age*) published 16. Including the three titles in the daily *Age*, these five periodicals were responsible for publishing 62 per cent of serialised Australian novels, and 31 per cent of all titles, between 1860 and 1889.

Three other journals stand out as serialising a high number of Australian novels in a short period. The *Australian Monthly Magazine* (1865–67) and its subsequent incarnation, the *Colonial Monthly* (1867–70), published five novels in the 1860s, while the *Australian Woman's Magazine and Domestic Journal* (1882–84) published the same number in the 1880s; despite lasting only one year, the *Melbourne Quarterly: A Family Journal of Original and Selected Fiction* (1882–83) published nine Australian novels (suggesting that serial fiction did not necessarily guarantee a publication's longevity). With the exception of the *Australian Journal*, the periodical publishers of Australian novels in this middle period reflect Morrison's description of this industry as a whole:

> For most of the nineteenth century…while there was a prolific and active local magazine press, for the most part circulations were tiny, finances precarious, and enterprises short-lived. The newspaper press, by contrast, was large, vigorous, and thriving.[59]

The high rate of serial publication of Australian novels from the 1860s to the 1880s corresponded with a period of marked growth in the overall size of this field. While the number of Australian novels increased only marginally (from 30 to 38) from the 1840s to the 1850s, the number of titles more than doubled to 84 in the 1860s, before increasing to 142 in the 1870s and 195 in the 1880s. The fact that periodicals consistently published around half of all titles, even as the size of the field increased substantially, suggests that serialisation and local periodicals in particular were major contributors to the 'rise' of the Australian novel. The circulations of these periodicals indicate the large local readership accessed by Australian serialised novels. By 1853, 20,000 copies of the *Argus* were sold daily;[60] the owner of the *Australian Journal* claimed monthly sales of 12,000 in 1870.[61] In 1888 approximately 18,000 copies of the *Australasian* (weekly) and 80,000 of the *Age* (daily) were sold.[62] For nineteenth-century newspapers the 'usual estimate' of readers for copies sold is three to five.[63] However, given the isolation of life in the colonies, the scarcity of available sources of print,[64] and the comparatively higher rates of literacy in these populations,[65] it seems likely that this estimate could be revised upward for the colonial context. In any case, these sales figures indicate a considerable (albeit potential) readership for serialised Australian novels in the colonies.

Analysis of the *AustLit* data shows that serialisation became an important avenue of publication of Australian novels at least a decade earlier than has been previously acknowledged, a finding that urges a reassessment of the origins and causes of this publishing trend. Previous studies, though few in number, identify the twelve- to fifteen-year period from the second half of the 1870s to the end of the 1880s as the major juncture for local serialisation of local fiction. This timing is linked to the arrival, in the mid-1870s, of the print and distribution technologies that – along with the removal of newspaper taxes[66] – enabled the expansion of the British periodical industry. Thus, Paul Eggert describes a window of opportunity for local periodical publication of Australian novels from the mid-1870s[67] – when colonial 'newspapers and magazines…were striving to extend their circulation in the period immediately after the introduction of the fast rotary presses' – to the late 1880s – when 'literary agents… saturated the market with imported serials'.[68] Similarly, although she deals with all novels in colonial newspapers rather than just Australian titles, Morrison locates the expansion of colonial periodicals and their publication of serial fiction in the 1870s and 1880s, arguing that this trend was

> closely related to technological developments: in printing, the high-speed, web-fed rotary press, which enabled first the *Age* and then other dailies to cater for a mass-market; in communications, the overseas cable linkage, which hooked the colonial press system to a global network [in 1872[69]]; in transport, the railways, which facilitated efficient distribution.[70]

The actual appearance of serialisation as a major mode of publication for Australian novels *before* the arrival of the technologies commonly seen as driving this process – in the early 1860s instead of the late 1870s – challenges this technological explanation of the trend. Figure 3 shows the number of serialised titles published from 1860 to 1899, with the dotted line indicating all titles and the unbroken line depicting those published locally. Two surges in publication emerge: the first from the early 1860s to the mid-1870s, preceding the boom Eggert and Morrison describe from the mid-1870s to the end of the 1880s. Admittedly, the larger number of titles in this second surge, and the obvious peak in the mid-1880s, to some extent justifies the existing critical focus on this later period. But in terms of the proportion of Australian novels published, the two periods were comparable (with 48 per cent of all Australian novels serialised between 1860 and 1874, and 51 per cent from 1875 to 1889). Instead of driving social and cultural change, it appears from the timing of these two surges that technological innovations in print, transportation and communication strengthened (or led to a resurgence in) an already prevalent approach to publishing Australian novels.

The timing of the original growth in serial publication of Australian novels means that the Australian trend predates the appearance of novels in London newspapers, which Graham Law asserts were 'rarely found…until the later 1870s'.[71] Studies by

Figure 3. Number of serialised Australian novels, published in Australia and total, 1860 to 1899 (two-yearly totals)

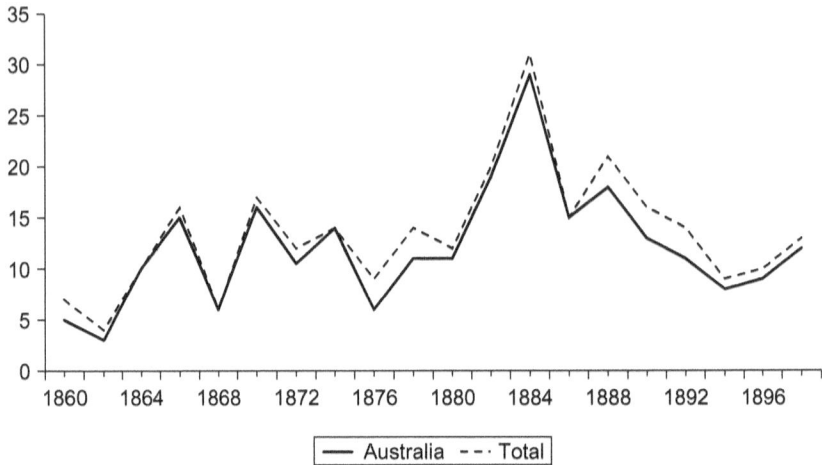

Law and William Donaldson show that, as in the colonies, novels were prominent in regional English and Scottish newspapers from the early 1860s, a trend attributed to the repeal of taxes imposed on British newspapers since the eighteenth century.[72] Law argues that these changes in taxation did not lead to the immediate inclusion of fiction in London newspapers because penny weekly magazines, 'which contained no news and thus escaped the tax', already met the metropolitan market for serialised novels.[73] Colonial governments regulated the press; but they did not impose the heavy taxes levied by the British government to inhibit radical publications. As such, the growth of fiction publication in Australian newspapers cannot be attributed to changes in taxation.

The rise of local serialisation of Australian novels did occur in the immediate aftermath of the strongest period of population growth in Australia's history. From 1840 to 1850, the non-indigenous population of the colonies more than doubled from 190,408 to 405,356. By 1860, following the discovery of gold, it more than doubled again to 1,145,585.[74] It was in this year that the *Sydney Mail* was established as a weekly companion to the *Sydney Morning Herald*, publishing one Australian novel in its first year of operation and two in its second. Melbourne's *Leader* soon followed suit, publishing its first such title in 1863 and its second in 1864. In 1865, the *Illustrated Sydney News* started serialising Australian novels; in Melbourne, the *Australian Journal* began its first issue with a local serialisation and initiated another in its second.[75] The *Australasian*, also in Melbourne, published its first Australian novel in 1866. Sydney's *Evening News* was created in 1867, and in 1870 established its weekly companion, the *Australian Town and Country Journal*, which published three Australian novels in its first year. Even excluding this late arrival, by 1866 the two major metropolitan centres, Sydney and Melbourne, had at least two periodicals competing with each other for readers, in part by serialising local novels. As Morrison notes, 'The featuring of serial fiction in newspapers has to be understood in the context of campaigns for mass readership; these, in turn, need to be seen as part of the deeply political purposes of Australian colonial newspapers'.[76] But where Morrison associates this campaign with the late nineteenth century, the correlation between population growth and the emergence of locally serialised novels in the leading periodicals of the most populous colonies[77] suggests such competition began significantly earlier.

Existing analyses of locally serialised colonial novels (again, though few in number) align this publishing trend with growth in national sentiment or identity. Johnson-Woods describes the 'intensely local' tales of convicts, squatters and gold diggers serialised in the colonial press as new, uniquely Australian genres that 'fulfilled a literary need in Australia at a time when colonials wanted to read about their country'.[78] More broadly, she aligns the 'high percentage of local fiction in new colonial publications' with the emergence and development of 'distinctive national feeling', which she argues was strongest before the 1850s and declined (due to a bourgeois 'calm-down') by the 1870s.[79] Webby makes the same association as Johnson-Woods between growth in the serialisation of original Australian fiction and growth in '[n]ational sentiments' regarding literature. But she identifies such sentiments as 'increasingly dominant in the 1870s'.[80]

These claims resonate with the high incidence of 'Australia' in the titles of these periodicals and, more broadly, with the established association of the novel and newspaper with national space.[81] I think there are strong grounds for aligning these colonial novels with the formation of 'imagined communities', and in Chapter 4, I argue that the strong male-authorship of these titles – and of locally published novels in general – relates to their expression of explicitly male-oriented forms of identity. However, the circulations of these newspaper novels indicates that the readerships for these titles were not national but metropolitan, regional and colonial.[82] Victor Isaacs and Rod Kirkpatrick's account of the regional territorialism exhibited by newspaper proprietors and politicians alike, highlights the separation of the colonies and the explicit role newspapers played in forming and defining regional identities. The first early-morning train in the colony of New South Wales, designed specifically to meet the distribution needs of the Sydney newspapers, was introduced in May 1887 'for political reasons', with the colonial government subsidising the train to ensure that residents of the Riverina (closer to Melbourne, the Victorian colonial capital, than Sydney) did not receive Melbourne papers before Sydney ones.[83]

The late date of the establishment of this distribution system accounts for the prominence throughout the nineteenth century of small-town newspapers (some of which may include novels not yet identified). But it also gives significance to the fact that it was the weekly companions to the daily newspapers – 'designed as much for the country as the city reader'[84] – that published the most local fiction. These companions were created with colonial distances and lack of distribution infrastructure in mind; they did not go out-of-date as quickly as their daily counterparts. While similar characters (convicts, squatters and gold diggers) might have populated locally serialised Australian novels, viewed in the context of the periodicals' circulations, this publishing trend suggests a tension between colonial and national forms of identification, rather than the direct alignment of the nation, the newspaper, and the novel.

III The Cycle of Serial and Book Publishing

In Australia, then, serialised novels circulated largely within rather than across the colonies. At the same time, local serialisation played a role in the movement of Australian novels between the colonies and Britain. In the British context, the 'cycle of serial and book publication' has received significant attention, and is acknowledged as a core feature of that publishing industry in the nineteenth century. Laurel Brake argues that the 'origins' and 'authority' of many periodicals were 'predicated on their links with books… In turn, authors and publishers of books alike came to view the periodical press as an extension of their sphere.'[85] It was common, in this interlinked publishing system, for the same company to publish serial and book versions of a novel, with in-house periodicals publicising their firm's book list through serialisation as well as reviews and advertisements. In the Australian context, the importance of serialisation as a stepping-stone to book publication for certain authors, such as Ada Cambridge and Rolf Boldrewood, is generally acknowledged.[86] But there is little sense of how – or whether – this publishing cycle operated for colonial authors and works more broadly, both within the colonies and between the colonies and Britain. Analysis of the *AustLit* data shows that book publication was by no means an inevitable consequence of serialisation; however, when it did occur, it was predominantly via British publishers. This trend emphasises the role of serialisation in facilitating British publication, the prevalence of the interlinked system of serial and book publication in Britain, and the relative absence of this publishing strategy in the colonies.

There is an obvious overlap between serial and book publication of Australian novels from the 1830s to the 1850s. Half of all titles serialised in these decades were also published as books, and one in five of the titles first published in this period appeared in both forms. Once again, however, Lang's (and to a lesser extent, Rowcroft's) productivity and predilection for serial publication have a large effect on the results. More than half (60 per cent) of the novels first published in this period that appeared as serials and books were by Lang, and almost three quarters (73 per cent) were by Lang or Rowcroft. Rowcroft was implicated in the cycle of serial and book publishing that Brake describes, in that his novels were serialised in the periodicals of the publishers that subsequently issued those titles as books.[87] Lang had novels serialised in periodicals owned by British companies that published Australian novels as books,[88] and titles issued as books by publishers that produced periodicals.[89] But in each case, the process involved two different companies.

While the 1850s mark the beginning of the rise and prominence of local serialisation of local novels, for the most part, it did not lead to book publication. The exceptions to this rule were two titles published serially in the *Month: A Literary and Critical Journal* and as books by J. R. Clarke, also the publisher of that journal.[90] The fact that, of all the titles serialised locally in the 1850s, only those published in the *Month* achieved book publication, implies that this outcome was promoted by the literary group that edited the periodical, and/or by J. R. Clarke.

Given the prominence of two individuals and one local journal in the transition from serial to book publishing for Australian novels from the 1830s to the 1850s, it is hard to compare the cycle in that period with its operation from the 1860s to the 1880s, when multiple individuals, periodicals and publishers were involved. A slightly lower proportion of titles were published in both forms in these later decades (17 per cent, compared with 20 per cent before 1860). However, the prominence of Lang's and Rowcroft's titles in the earlier results makes any claim of a reduction in this cycle difficult to sustain. What can be said is that more than a third (35 per cent) of Australian novels serialised between 1860 and 1889 were also published as books. Ideally, one could compare this overlap between serial and book publication in Australia to that in Britain. But a lack of firm data on the number of nineteenth-century British novels and the form in which they appeared precludes this comparison: as Robert Colby asserts, '[t]he only safe generalisations one can make about the Victorian novel are that it was popular and that it was abundant'.[91] While serialisation is commonly described as the 'standard initial mode of publication' for 'so many' novels of the Victorian era,[92] it is not clear whether, in Britain as in Australia, there were many novels only published in periodicals, or whether this publishing cycle was such a finely tuned advertising and sales device as to capture most titles in its purview.

While the lack of British data prevents direct comparison, the significantly greater chance an Australian novel had of making the transition from serial to book in Britain implies that this practice was more frequent there than in the colonies. Of the small number of Australian novels initially serialised overseas in these middle decades, 75 per cent (15 of 20 titles) were also published as books. In comparison, of the novels serialised in Australian periodicals only 32 per cent (60 of 189 titles) were published as books, and most of these (73 per cent or 44 of 60 titles) were published overseas (predominantly in Britain). To put these results another way, a novel serialised in an Australian periodical between 1860 and 1889 had a three in ten chance of becoming a book. But it had only a one in four chance again of that occurring via a local publisher. No titles were published as books in Australia after overseas serialisation. While the high rate of local serialisation, combined with the large proportion of titles that did not make the transition from serial to book, emphasises the extent to which the primary readerships of serialised Australian novels remained within the colonies, these results show that serial publication facilitated access to a wider audience for some colonial authors.

The frequency with which serialised titles were published as books in Britain seems to support Munro and Curtain's description of the history of the book in Australia as the conversion of Australian 'stories' into 'books at the industrial heart of Empire'.[93] In other words, this cycle of local serialisation and British book publication might be understood as indicative of the relative absence of colonial book publishers in an imperial market. This interpretation is belied, however, by the surprising prevalence of local book publication in this period, especially in the 1870s and 1880s, as I will elaborate shortly. As in the earlier decades, colonial authors probably preferred British to local book publication. But Australian 'stories' did not have to travel overseas to become books.

Given the possibilities and prestige of overseas book publication, this transition from (local or overseas) serial to British book – as with initial book publication in Britain – is commonly seen to indicate a title's success and, more specifically, its quality. However, as before 1860, the correlation between the place of publication and the author's location complicates this interpretation. With three exceptions – Cambridge, Maud Jeanne Franc, and W. H. Timperley[94] authors of novels that were published as serials and books overseas, like their periodical- and book-published counterparts of the earlier decades, tended themselves to be overseas: either having returned 'home' or, as in the case of Harriett Miller Davidson, visiting England before returning to Australia. Alternatively, authors now considered part of the canon of nineteenth-century Australian literature (such as Marcus Clarke) had novels published in both serial and book form locally.[95]

These exceptions do not preclude quality as a factor in the conversion of serialised titles to British-published books. But rather than debating the relative merits of different titles, I want to highlight the systematic features of the cycle of serial and book publication in this period. I am referring, specifically, to the ways in which the British publishing industry (in contrast to local publishers) explicitly promoted this transition, and how this approach facilitated the circulation of Australian novels between the colonies and Britain (above and beyond the 'quality' of individual titles). My point is not that quality is necessarily irrelevant to whether a colonial author was published overseas. But if quality is perceived as the only determining factor in the 'conversion' of 'stories' to 'books' at the Imperial centre, we ignore the commercial processes and imperatives involved in this movement of fiction.

Serialised Australian novels that became books overseas were involved in established systems for facilitating this transition. It was common for serial and book versions of colonial novels to be published overseas by the same company. More than half of all titles published as serials and books outside the colonies were implicated in this practice, including novels by Cambridge (*Cassell's Family Magazine* and Cassell; *The Churchman's Companion* and Joseph Masters);[96] B. L. Farjeon (*Tinsley's Magazine* and Tinsley);[97] Timperley (*Boy's Own Paper* and The Religious Tract Society);[98] Franc (*Crystal Stories* and Richard Willoughby);[99] Eliza Winstanley (*Bow Bells Weekly* and John Dicks);[100] and Henry Kingsley (*Macmillan's Magazine* and Macmillan).[101] As was previously the case with the two titles by Rowcroft, these authors and their novels were part of the cycle of serial and book, wherein publishers used serialisation in the periodicals they owned as a mode of advertising for upcoming book titles.

British publishers also formed relationships with particular authors of serialised novels. For instance, Macmillan published eleven titles serialised in Australian periodicals between 1860 and 1889, eight of which were by Boldrewood,[102] Sampson Low published seven such titles, all by Franc,[103] and Heinemann published two, both by Cambridge.[104] Other British publishers with more than a passing involvement in transforming Australian novels, serialised in local periodicals between 1860 and 1889, into books include Richard Bentley (six titles),[105] Remington & Co. (three)[106] and Tinsley (two).[107] In some cases, most notably with Boldrewood, the transition to book occurred many years after initial serialisation.[108] But even this belated instance indicates how British publishers sought out serials and authors already proven popular, and how this publishing practice contributed to their business model.

The strategies used by British publishers to enable and encourage the transition from serial to book were absent in the colonial context. Only two authors are represented more than once: Clarke had three novels serialised and published as books locally, though not in the same periodical or by the same publisher;[109] Cambridge had two novels published serially in the *Australasian* and as books by Melbourne-based Melville and Mullens and London-based Heinemann (the joint publication raises the possibility that this transition from serial to book was organised by the British publisher).[110] While we might assume that an Australian author could convince a local book publisher to proceed on the basis of successful serialisation, or that a publisher might identify a locally serialised novel as a good investment, such possibilities seem to have been happenstance rather than regularly promoted procedures.

The patterns that emerge in the book publication of serialised Australian novels in Britain – in contrast with the irregularity of this process in the colonies – reinforce the centrality of this practice to the Victorian publishing industry, and to the British publication of Australian novels. They also raise the question of why local publishers did not employ this approach, particularly given the apparent popularity of serialised novels in the colonies, the local publication (as I will show) of one in three Australian novels as books in the 1870s and 1880s, and the involvement of a number of these local companies in publishing periodicals. I believe the answer to this question lies in the nature of local book publishing, including its status as a 'sideline' for companies that pursued a range of print-related and (in some cases) non-print-related activities, and the likelihood that copayment for colonial book publication was common. This 'sideline', however, was conducted with considerably more regularity than has been recognised and, viewed alongside serial publication, has important implications for understanding the readerships of Australian novels and the activities of British publishers in the 1890s.

IV Book Publishing: 1860s to 1880s

As Figure 2 shows, from the 1860s to the 1880s – as in earlier decades – British companies dominated the book publication of Australian novels. But this British dominance was not as absolute as recent Australian literary and book histories claim. While only 17 per cent of book editions of Australian novels were published in the colonies in the 1860s (compared with 64 per cent in Britain), this proportion increased significantly to 34 per cent in the 1870s and 37 per cent in the 1880s.[111] In these two decades, British publishers were responsible for 50 and 49 per cent of book editions of Australian novels respectively. If the sample is limited to only those novels that were never serialised, the proportion of titles published locally increases in the 1870s and 1880s, an outcome that reflects the greater tendency for British publishers to source their Australian novels from (predominantly colonial) periodicals. In this case, local publishers were responsible for 36 and 41 per cent of book editions of Australian novels.

It is important not to overstate the contribution of local book publishers to the history of the Australian novel: local periodicals published substantially more titles, as did British book publishers,[112] and both of these other forms of publication almost certainly enjoyed more extensive circulations. Nevertheless, the local publication of more than one in three book editions of Australian novels in the 1870s and 1880s (rising to two in five if only non-serialised titles are considered) refutes the established view that book publishing only occurred elsewhere (certainly in the nineteenth century and, as I will discuss in the next chapter, according to many commentators, until at least the 1970s).

As was the case prior to the 1860s, from this decade to the end of the 1880s, British and colonial book publishers differed markedly in their degree of specialisation. Table 3 lists the top ten book publishers of Australian novels in these decades. The major British companies involved in this field – including Sampson Low, Richard Bentley, Chapman and Hall, Tinsley, John Dicks and Macmillan, together responsible for 20 per cent of Australian novels published as books from 1860 to 1889 – were all dedicated publishers as well as major competitors in their home market. In contrast, no local companies were dedicated publishers, from the most prolific, George Robertson, down to the 34 companies responsible for only one title. Instead, these predominantly Melbourne- and Sydney-based enterprises were also booksellers, printers, bookbinders, stationers, paper merchants, newsagents, distributors, libraries, periodical publishers and, in most cases, a combination of these.

Another difference between the two groups, presumably associated with their degree of specialisation, was their connection with particular authors. As with Routledge's and Ward, Lock's earlier association with Lang, the involvement in the Australian novel field of the British presses listed in Table 3 (with the exception of Hurst and Blackett) can be tied to their connection with a particular author or authors. For instance, eleven of the fifteen titles published by Sampson Low between 1860 and 1889 were by Franc;[113] of Chapman and Hall's nine titles, five were by Rosa Praed and two were by Arthur Locker;[114] Richard Bentley's thirteen titles included two by Spence and five by Praed (including two novels she co-authored with Justin McCarthy);[115] and Macmillan's five titles included two by Mary Anne Broome and two by Kingsley.[116]

In contrast – despite often being in the same city as one another – there is little evidence of strong connections between local publishers and authors. Two of the nine titles published by George Robertson between 1860 and 1889 were by Clarke.[117] Local book publishers Alex McKinley, J. J. Moore, J. Richards and Sons, and R. Mackay also published two titles by a single author: Edmund Finn, Harold W. H. Stephen, James Richards, and William Bowley respectively (as I will show in Chapter 4, that these are all male authors is indicative of gender trends in local publishing in these decades).[118] But these were the only local examples of a connection between authors and publishers.

Table 3. Top ten book publishers of Australian novels, 1860 to 1889

Publishers	Nation	# Titles	% Titles
1. Sampson Low	British	15	4
2. Richard Bentley	British	13	3
3. Chapman and Hall	British	9	2
3. George Robertson	Australian	9	2
3. The Author	Australian	9	2
3. Tinsley	British	9	2
7. John Dicks	British	5	1
7. Macmillan	British	5	1
9. Hurst and Blackett	British	4	1
9. Kemp and Boyce	Australian	4	1
9. Remington and Co.	British	4	1
9. T. C. Newby	British	4	1
9. Ward, Lock	British	4	1

There was, moreover, an important shift in the general correlation between author location and place of publication at this time. Whereas before 1860 local publishers were virtually the only avenue of book publication for novelists who remained in Australia, after 1860 this correlation was significantly reduced: about half the Australian authors whose novels were published overseas between 1860 and 1889 were resident in the colonies at the time of publication.

While copayment for local book publication probably occurred in the early nineteenth century, there is clear evidence of this practice in these middle decades. John Holyroyd states that '[m]any' of George Robertson's books 'were published on commission, i.e., at the author's expense; other titles were issued on a profit-sharing basis'.[119] George Robertson's position as the major local force in the Australian book market, as well as the largest local publisher of Australian novels, reinforces the possibility that this company's approach was indicative of local practices generally. Indeed, given the extent to which George Robertson's output exceeded that of other local publishers, this company's practices alone made copayment for book publication common in the colonies. The prevalence of this practice in the colonies provides a likely explanation of the lack of involvement of local companies in the cycle of serial and book publication, in that presumably, most authors who paid to have their books published locally were either unsuccessful in attaining serial publication or, in the few cases where titles were originally serialised, unable to translate this initial publication into book publication in Britain. At the same time, in light of the prevalence of copayment in the colonies, the fact that one in three book editions of Australian novels was published locally is remarkable, and suggests the desire of colonial authors to engage in local literary culture (even if they did so because other avenues were blocked).

In the contemporary period, self- and subsidy publishing is often (and until recently, justifiably) associated with a lack of availability and readership. The prevalence of copayment for book publication in the colonies might lead us to suppose the same fate for these titles, particularly in contrast to the widespread perception (produced by descriptions of the mass export of British books to the colonies and maintained by claims of the importance of British books for Australian readers) that books published in Britain were readily available in the colonies. But for the decades prior to the 1880s, there are important reasons not to overestimate the availability of British published books, or to underestimate the availability of locally published titles.

Munro and Curtain's account of the publishing history of Australian 'stories' implies that the movement of books between Britain and the colonies was an established and almost inevitable process: that all Australian stories 'converted into books at the industrial heart of Empire…were then shipped back to the Antipodes'.[120] Other evidence questions this conclusion. From the 1860s to the 1880s, approximately a third (34 per cent) of Australian novels published in Britain were multivolume (predominantly three-decker). From the 1830s to the 1850s – although much fewer novels were involved – this proportion was slightly higher (at 38 per cent). Multivolume publication was designed and intended for the British subscription library market.[121] Morrison and Graeme Johanson argue that there was essentially no market in the colonies for such books, due to their greater cost (including for shipping) and the scarcity of British-style subscription libraries.[122]

Multivolume titles were unlikely to have travelled to the colonies unless reissued as single volumes by British (or colonial) publishers. This occurred with approximately two thirds of multivolume Australian novels first published in Britain from the 1830s to the 1850s, but less than half of those published in the 1860s and 1870s.[123] By contrast, 75 per cent of Australian novels initially issued in multivolume in the 1880s were republished in single volumes. Yet even in such cases – and with books initially published in single volume – the availability of these titles in the colonies is questionable. According to Johanson, colonial readers were generally 'not interested in buying…6s editions', and until the 1880s '[o]nly major wealthy publishers like Murray…Macmillan, Bell and Methuen could afford' substantial trade with the colonies.[124] As a consequence, in Morrison's words, even one-volume books had 'little chance of…finding their way to the Australian colonies without special intervention, impetus, and arrangements'.[125]

Where Australian novels 'converted into books at the industrial heart of Empire' might not have returned to the colonies, all locally published titles were at least available, even if they were author-funded. The fact that, from the 1850s, none of these titles were published in multivolume formats[126] reinforces the view that there was no market for such books in the colonies. Presence does not necessarily signify readership. But in this case, the non-specialist nature of local publishers – specifically, the involvement of many in bookselling – indicates a sales outlet for these locally published books, including for those (small number of titles) published before 1860, even if availability was limited to the city where the bookseller/publisher was located. While this probable contrast in availability does not mean that local readership was necessarily greater for titles published in the colonies than in Britain, the economics of publishing in the nineteenth century reinforce the importance of local publishing to colonial readerships.

The supposed absence of local publishing of Australian literature is generally attributed to the low price of books imported from Britain. As Dolin says:

> Because 'Australia's book trade and readers were…part of an imperial cultural space, dominated and defended by London publishers', fiction was cheaper here than almost anywhere else in the world; for the same reasons, it is held, Australian writers, publishers, and readers found it all the more difficult to establish, develop, and support a national literary culture.[127]

In fact, there is evidence to suggest that both forms of local publication of Australian novels (serials and books) were cheaper than imported fiction. This is certainly the case with serialised fiction: as Johnson-Woods writes, 'One of the attractions of colonial periodicals was the price.'[128] The *Age* cost only one penny and, as Morrison says, 'was reasonably accessible to anyone who could read'.[129] While most colonial periodicals cost sixpence,[130] these publications provided colonial readers with relatively cheap access to fiction, as well as other forms of entertainment and information.

British books, sold to booksellers on 'Colonial terms', were often cheaper in the colonies than in Britain,[131] especially after the growth in colonial editions from the mid-1880s.[132] While it is not possible to assert definitively that local books cost still less (as Johanson writes, there is an 'absence of local evidence of specific prices charged by booksellers generally'[133]), some evidence suggests this conclusion. In addition to the probability that many were author-funded, locally published books did not incur shipping costs from Britain. From the 1850s, they were not issued in multivolume formats,[134] and indeed, a number were published in instalments or parts, which spread out the cost of purchase.[135] As Eggert notes, in contrast to British readers, most colonial readers 'probably...had insufficient or inconvenient access' to lending libraries.[136] In 1895, Hobart bookseller and publisher J. Walch wrote in the *Intelligencer* that, because the 'Library system is not established' in the colonies, 'readers of books must of necessity be also their owners'.[137] Therefore, price played a substantial role in determining what fiction was purchased and read.

This issue of pricing and purchase helps in turn to explain the tension between existing studies of colonial reading practices – which assume colonial readers' lack of interest in local fiction – and the high rate of local publication of Australian novels. As noted earlier, Dolin, Lyons and Webby draw their conclusions about local reading preferences from institutional traces of reading: the holdings of lending institutions, the lists of reading programs or minutes of reading groups.[138] Webby's acknowledged 'elite' focus and the small number of readers with access to the lending libraries considered by Dolin and Lyons, suggest that these studies omit, or at least marginalise, much reading activity in the colonies. In particular, they disproportionately emphasise imported over locally produced fiction, given that the latter – particularly in serial form – was largely excluded from libraries and reading groups. This is not to say that Australian readers were primarily interested in Australian fiction. Certainly much non-Australian fiction was available in the colonies, including in local periodicals.[139] However, the widespread local publication of Australian novels and the extensive circulations of serialised titles indicate that the readerships for these works were substantially larger than studies of institutional reading practices argue.

V Book Publishing: 1890s

When serial and book publication are combined, between 1860 and 1889, 61 per cent of Australian novels were first, and in many cases only, published in the colonies.[140] In the 1890s, the publishing context changed radically. This decade witnessed a marked decline in local, and substantial growth in British, publication of Australian novels. This trend occurred in the context of growth, from 1886, in cheap colonial editions, which comprised an increasing part of British book exports to Australia.[141] From the 1880s, British publishers also increasingly reissued, in single volumes, Australian novels originally published in more expensive multivolume formats.[142] These factors point to the growing importance of the colonial market for British publishers and to the role of Australian novels in the expansion of such companies into this market. However, they may seem to negate the connections I have traced between local publishing and reading practices. In fact, this existing reading culture helps to explain these trends. Specifically, the market in Australia for Australian fiction provides a framework for interpreting British publishers' involvement in the Australian field in the 1890s as part of their response, in seeking access to the increasingly lucrative colonial market, to local reading practices.

The 1890s witnessed a dramatic reduction in the proportion of Australian novels published serially, and in local serialisation. While 51 per cent of Australian novels were serialised in the 1880s, 93 per cent in local periodicals, in the 1890s those proportions fell to 17 and 85 per cent respectively. While a small number of Australian periodicals – namely, the *Australian Journal*, the *Queenslander* and the *Australian* – published more titles in the 1890s than in the 1880s, the majority (including the *Sydney Mail*, the *Leader*, the *Australasian* and the *Australian Town and Country Journal*) reduced their output. Morrison has attributed this trend to the rise of imported literary supplements, which were increasingly prevalent through the 1880s and 'saturat[ing] the market' in the following decade.[143] Whatever the cause of this decline, the 1890s marks the end of the period when serial publication, especially in colonial periodicals, played a major role in the circulation of Australian novels.

According to Morrison, the 'damage to local colonial endeavours' caused by imported literary supplements was 'more than offset' by a series of 'fundamental changes in the modes of cultural production' at this time, including the superseding of 'the hegemony of the three-decker…by a plenitude of cheap imported books' and 'the development of Australian publishing houses'.[144] Trends in British book publication of Australian novels concurrent with this decline in serial publication reinforce Morrison's claim of a fundamental shift in modes of cultural production in the 1890s. In particular, these trends uphold the connection she describes between the decline in serial novels and the availability of cheap imported fiction. From the 1880s to the 1890s there was a four-fold increase in the number of Australian novels published in Britain (from 55 to 225 titles), in the context of a shift by British publishers away from multivolume books to cheaper single editions. Where 28 per cent of the Australian novels published in Britain in the early 1890s were multivolume, in the second half of that decade the proportion fell dramatically to 2 per cent (or 3 titles). From 1897, all of the Australian novels published in Britain were single volume.

As might be expected, this growth in British book publication of Australian novels occurred in the context of an increased separation between author location and place of publication. While some well-known authors in this period – such as Nat Gould and Guy Boothby – were in England when all (or in the case of Gould, most) of their novels were published, in the 1890s, an 'Australian' author whose novel was published in Britain was more likely to be in the colonies than in Britain at the time of publication. This separation of author location and place of publication was facilitated by the cycle of serial and book publication, which became a more pronounced route to overseas book publication in this period. Only a slightly higher proportion of Australian novels were published as both serials and books in the 1890s (31 per cent compared with 29 per cent between 1860 and 1889). However, in all but one of these cases, book publication occurred overseas, predominantly in Britain.

Although the declining 'hegemony of the three-decker' was concurrent with the demise of serial fiction in the colonies as Morrison proposes, my results do not support her association of both trends with 'the development of Australian publishing houses'. In fact, they suggest the opposite: that the increased involvement of British publishers in the Australian novel field was concurrent with a decline in local book publication.

Of the Australian novels published as books in the 1890s, only 21 per cent were published in the colonies (down from 37 per cent in the 1880s); 64 per cent were published in Britain (up from 49 per cent in the 1880s). The fact that most of these locally published titles were from a single company (George Robertson) emphasises the general reduction in local book publication suggested by these proportional results. With 22 titles (as well as 12 published jointly with British publishers, mainly Swan Sonnenschein) George Robertson was actually the most prolific publisher of Australian novels overall in this decade, as Table 4 shows; no other local company published more than three titles, and most published only one or two. At the end of the 1890s, George Robertson's involvement in this field declined rapidly, and that company never again invested so heavily in publishing original Australian novels.[145]

George Robertson's approach to Australian novel publishing in the 1890s differs from that of the major British publishers of such titles in ways that indicate the continuation of a non-specialist local print industry. As in earlier decades, the major British publishers of Australian novels (including all of those shown in Table 4) were associated with a particular author and/or with the cycle of serial and book publication. For example, 17 of the 21 Australian novels published by Routledge in the 1890s were by Gould, including one also serialised in an Australian periodical,[146] and Boothby wrote more than half of the Australian novels published by Ward, Lock.[147] In contrast, none of George Robertson's titles were previously serialised, and no two were by the same author.

For this local company, however, as for many of these British publishers, the 1890s were marked by concentrated involvement in the Australian novel field. Between 1860 and 1889, the top six British companies published around 22 per cent of all Australian novels; in the 1890s, 25 per cent were published by the top five (a result that does not even include the leading publisher of Australian novels in this decade, George Robertson). Some British publishers (Hutchinson, Cassell, Methuen and Ward, Lock) went on to publish many more Australian novels during the twentieth century. But for many (including Routledge, Remington and Co., Macmillan, F. V. White, Chatto and Windus, T. Fisher Unwin, and Digby, Long and Co.), as for George Robertson, this decade (and in some cases the next) represented a peak in publishing Australian novels.

Table 4. Top ten book publishers of Australian novels, 1890 to 1899

Publishers	Nation	# Titles	% Titles
1. George Robertson	Australian	22	6
2. Routledge	British	21	6
3. Remington & Co.	British	19	5
4. Ward, Lock	British	17	5
5. Hutchinson	British	15	4
6. F. V. White	British	14	4
7. Macmillan	British	13	3
8. Chatto and Windus	British	10	3
9. T. Fisher Unwin	British	8	2
10. Sampson Low	British	7	2
10. The Author	Australian	7	2

The publishing trends I have outlined for the 1890s – the fall in local serialisation of Australian novels, the retreat of most local companies from this field, the decline in George Robertson's publishing activities at the end of that decade, and the substantial growth in British publication of Australian novels – might seem to suggest a 'foreign invasion', with local book and periodical publishers crowded out of the Australian novel field by British companies. Beyond the growth in British publication of Australian novels, there is clear evidence of 'accelerated interest concerning Australia in the British world of print'.[148] Some firms opened branches in the colonies: Collins in Sydney in 1872 and Ward, Lock in Melbourne in 1884. According to Alison Rukavina, 'by the late 1880s, British publishers...were offering their books, often deeply discounted', to colonial distributors like George Robertson as a way of gaining 'a larger share of the booming Australian market'.[149] However, viewed in conjunction with the prior existence of a local market for Australian fiction, publishing patterns in the 1890s indicate a process distinct from blunt imperial domination of the colonial market.

As recent accounts (including Rukavina's) demonstrate, British publishers did not simply flood the colonial market with cheap imports; they also worked to understand and respond to that market. Rukavina argues that British publishers and authors believed 'their financial success depended upon their direct engagement of foreign and colonial wholesalers and distributors', and describes letters from British writers (Helen Mathers and Mary Francis Cusack) expressing a desire for good sales in the Australian colonies. Mathers made a point of 'specifically including Australian content to attract Australian readers'.[150] Luke Trainor cites the 1886 report of the British Royal Commission on the Depression of Trade and Industry, which concludes that 'our supremacy is now being assailed on all sides...we must display greater activity in the search for new markets and a greater readiness to accommodate our production to local tastes and peculiarities'.[151] In relation to this, Trainor argues that Macmillan incorporated a high proportion of popular fiction in its Colonial Library Series because, in visiting Australia in 1884 and 1885 'to explore marketing possibilities', Maurice Macmillan observed 'that there was a great interest in popular fiction, of which Macmillan had little on their list'.[152]

Rukavina and Trainor highlight ways in which British publishers responded to the Australian market, but neither relates this responsiveness to the publication of Australian fiction. Beyond the two British authors she discusses, Rukavina makes no mention of whether the books imported into the colonies by George Robertson were by British or Australian authors, nor does she explore George Robertson's role as a local publisher as well as a bookseller, wholesaler, and distributor for overseas companies. Using the case study of Macmillan, Trainor explicitly distinguishes British attention to the Australian market from the publication of Australian fiction: 'Macmillan's Colonial Library was successful and a number of other publishers followed suit, but these series were not generally a showcase for Australian writers'.[153] These analyses resonate with the claim, in recent accounts of colonial literary culture, that Australian readers had little if any interest in local writing.

However, without recourse to such interest, it is difficult to explain the four-fold increase in British publication of Australian novels, especially as this occurred in the context of British publishers' growing involvement in the Australian market and attempts to 'accommodate...production to local tastes and peculiarities'.[154] If British publishers such as Macmillan were interested enough in the colonial market to recognise the demand for popular fiction and incorporate it in their lists,[155] then the local circulation of Australian novels cannot have escaped their notice. More particularly, if British publishers were encouraging 'Australian content to attract Australian readers',[156] there is every reason to suppose that they would have welcomed Australian novels with local content for the same reason. While members of subscription libraries may not have borrowed Australian fiction[157] – and while Hobart's cultural elite may not have discussed it[158] – the large proportion of Australian novels published locally (as books and, especially, as serials) demonstrates a colonial market for such fiction. The surge in British publication of Australian novels can be seen, from this perspective, as part of British publishers' response to local conditions and another means (along with opening colonial branches, publishing popular fiction, and encouraging Australian content) of gaining entry into the lucrative colonial market. While few British publishers maintained an interest in Australian novels much beyond this decade, the proposition that Australian novels in fact facilitated their access to Australian readers presents a contrast with both the paradigm of literary nationalism that previously organised perceptions of the 1890s,[159] and the more recent view that Australian readers simply followed British trends.

The dynamics I am proposing resonate with those Eggert describes in a recent article on the demise of the three-decker in British publishing and the rise of the colonial edition as the linchpin of the book trade between Britain and Australia from the late 1880s. The shift from multi- to single-volume books (a trend, as I have shown, that was also manifested in British publication of Australian novels) has been widely attributed to conditions internal to the British book trade, especially the relationship between publishers and lending libraries like Mudies.[160] While acknowledging the importance of these conditions, Eggert argues that the colonial market also motivated this shift. Specifically, because of the importance of this market for British publishers, and the power of local companies to define and defend colonial bookselling, British publishers responded to the colonial demand for cheap fiction (created by the lack of borrowing facilities) with the colonial edition.[161] I suggest that trends in the publication of Australian novels indicate that this British response to the colonial market extended beyond price to the source and content of the fiction published.

Even if British publishing activities were a response to local conditions, their involvement in the Australian novel field in the 1890s had dramatic consequences for colonial book publishers. The high proportion of book editions of Australian novels published in the colonies – especially in the second half of the 1880s (when 40 per cent of titles were published locally) – and George Robertson's position as the major publisher of such titles in the 1890s, indicates that local publishing, while remaining a 'sideline', was extremely active. As British publishers surged into the Australian market, embraced (for a short time) the Australian novel and turned to cheaper single volume editions of these titles, local book publication dropped off, immediately for most local companies and ultimately for George Robertson as well.

There seems little doubt that the late nineteenth century was a period, as Rukavina asserts, of 'competition and negotiation as British publishing houses worked with their colonial counterparts to create a space for their publications outside Britain'.[162] Trends in the 1890s suggest that one result of this competition and negotiation was the turning away of local companies from publishing toward sales and distribution. Faced with the mass import of books – including Australian novels – from Britain, it was 'simpler and more economical for the local trade' – as Richard Nile and David Walker say of the early twentieth century – 'to organise itself to be importers and retailers rather than publishers with an eye for local talent and new forms of literary expression'.[163]

***

This conclusion may seem unremarkable, in that the configuration of local bookseller and British publisher is a well-established feature of Australian literary history. What is remarkable is that this relationship only really solidified in the 1890s, at the very end of the official 'colonial' period. We are accustomed to thinking of colonial literary culture in terms of local booksellers and readers forced to await the arrival of books shipped from the 'heart of Empire'.[164] In fact, while many Australian novels were published as books in Britain, until mid-century, local publishers provided virtually the only avenue of book publication for authors who remained in Australia, whether or not they were required to pay for the privilege; in the second half of the century – especially in the 1870s and 1880s – a surprisingly high proportion of titles were published as books in the colonies. While local book publication was more common than has been recognised, its role in the production of colonial novels was relatively minor in comparison to that of serial publication, especially in local periodicals. From the 1860s to the 1880s, colonial periodicals published a greater number of Australian novels than either local or British book publishers. The circulations of these publications indicate that the readerships for locally serialised Australian novels were substantially larger than for book sales or borrowing. The neglect of serial fiction by Australian literary scholars occludes both these readerships and the close ties between the rise of the Australian novel, print capitalism and politics in Australia.

The growing scholarly interest in the history of publishing and reading in Australia has motivated a necessary and productive internationalisation of nineteenth-century studies. But the focus on British publishers and authors (as well as the longstanding preoccupation of Australian scholars with the book as the vehicle of literary culture) has overshadowed important parts of this history. I would go so far as to say there is a pattern in existing studies of colonial publishing and reading created by a view of that culture as always and inevitably derivative of Britain. Thus local serialisation is assumed to follow the importation of printing technologies and the rise of the newspaper novel in London, when in fact it preceded both. Despite the rarity of libraries in Australia, book borrowing (far more common in Britain than Australia) is used to demonstrate colonial reading practices, and to claim colonial readers' lack of interest in local fiction. The neglect of colonial book publication might also be understood as an effect of its assumed inferiority to the British model.

I am not suggesting a move in the opposite direction, to claim all local activities as better than those in Britain; this would be a return to the cultural nationalist framework that recent scholarship has done well to challenge. But always assuming colonial practices were derivative is just as unwarranted. It is also self-perpetuating: if we only look for publishing trends in Australia after they occurred in Britain, we will only find them then; if we only attend to publishing approaches equivalent to those in Britain, we will perceive local practices as lacking or absent. Instead, what is needed is a middle ground, as I have attempted to present here. Acknowledging that local as well as British publishers and authors played an important role in the development of the Australian novel, and of colonial literary culture and its reading practices – and that influence moved in both directions – provides a standpoint from which to perceive what was distinctive – as well as derivative – about writing, publishing, and reading in Australia in the nineteenth century.

Virtually every one of the (few) commentators on periodical fiction in Australia has called for further study of the phenomenon. As Johnson-Woods asserts, the sheer prevalence of this form of publication of Australian novels indicates 'a literary landscape that is of enormous importance to our understanding of the development of Australian literature'.[165] In demonstrating the major role of serial publication, and of connections between serial and book publishers, in the history of the Australian novel, this chapter adds impetus to such calls. However, the general neglect of serialised Australian fiction seems to call for a consideration not of whether it should be studied, but why it is not, and it is by addressing this question that I want to end this chapter.

Neglect of periodical publication is not unique to Australia: research into serialised fiction in America, Britain and elsewhere is routinely prefaced by claims of critical disregard. Yet Victorianists began to 'rehabilitate' the serial from the 1950s, especially in relation to Charles Dickens' novels.[166] More recently, particularly in the British and American contexts, critics such as Law and Donaldson, as well as Linda Hughes, Michael Lund and Carol Martin, have significantly raised the profile of such fiction by demonstrating the important implications of serial publication for the formation of the novel's reading publics and genres, the professionalisation of authorship, and the representation of space and time in narrative.[167] Claims of neglect in these national contexts now tend to focus on specific aspects of serial publication, like the importance of illustrations to the consumption of serial texts,[168] or the impact of serial publication on particular forms of literature, such as 'late nineteenth- early twentieth-century proto-modernist fiction'.[169] Accordingly, while Mary Elizabeth Leighton and Lisa Surridge insist that the materiality of serial texts is often given 'mere lip service', they also argue that 'it would now be difficult to find a scholar who would not acknowledge the unique layout and rhythm of serial reading'.[170]

This is not the case in Australia, where even lip service to the existence of serialised works, let alone the specificity of their reception, is often absent. Johnson-Woods attributes this situation 'largely [to] reasons of accessibility',[171] an argument not made in the American and British contexts (where the archive is significantly larger). The neglect of serial fiction is almost certainly related, at least in part, to the 'long shadow' cast by the 1890s in Australian literary studies:[172] the way that decade – when the serial novel had declined and the book was in its ascendancy – tends to provide the focus for analyses of colonial literary culture. Morrison makes a similar point when she proposes that nineteenth-century Australian literature, as a whole, receives insufficient attention due to 'the onset of a literary nationalism that turned its back on much of the colonial culture out of which it had developed'.[173] However, she also argues that serial fiction is especially overlooked because of the 'predominantly book-oriented' approach of 'nineteenth-century literary studies in Australia',[174] a circular explanation that explains the occlusion of serial fiction by pointing to its consequences.

Eggert's description of 'the division of the kingdom that English departments entrenched in the immediate post-war period' in Australia might be seen as a contributing factor.[175] This same division – between literary theorists and critics on the one hand, and bibliographical, editorial and biographical scholars on the other – has been described as characterising national literary traditions (such as America's) where serial fiction is more widely acknowledged.[176] However, the formation of Australian literary studies as a separate field of study after this post-war trend in English departments means that most Australian literary histories have been written in the shadow of this divide. As a consequence, histories written by literary critics have perhaps been inadequately informed by research into the materiality of texts. Alternatively, historical analyses by bibliographers, scholarly editors and biographers have perhaps been overlooked by many Australian literary scholars (at the same time as these studies have arguably been inadequately engaged in the debates and questions relevant to the discipline more broadly).

Maybe these causes – the dominance of the 1890s in accounts of colonial literary culture, and the division between literary criticism and scholarship from the 1950s – are sufficient to explain the lack of attention to serial fiction in Australia literary history. However, I want to suggest another, more fundamental and insidious, reason for this neglect: the uncomfortable proximity of fiction and commodity culture that serialised works expose. Although John Frow argues that the construction of 'aesthetic culture' according to 'an opposition between mass-produced "low" culture and a "high" culture which was understood to transcend commodity production' is no longer possible,[177] this dichotomy clearly continues to structure literary studies. Its influence is apparent in the broad neglect of genre fiction (an issue I explore in detail in the next chapter) and in constructions of the discipline by critics such as Katie Trumpener. Her insistence, discussed in Chapter 1, that literary scholars attend to the 'irreducibility of authorial intention'[178] frankly denies that any work worthy of attention could be contained in and shaped by commodity culture: for instance, that 'authorial intention' might have been subject to the periodical editor's decisions about the sequencing of the work; or that the author's decision to write might have been motivated, not by artistic vision, but by the financial rewards that serial publication in nineteenth-century Australian periodicals could bring.[179]

It is one thing to realise, in the abstract, that fiction is implicated in commodity culture. It is another thing entirely to be compelled repeatedly while reading the text to acknowledge this implication. Yet studying the serial novel *in situ* – that is, on newspaper pages, the only form in which many nineteenth-century Australian novels have been published – compels just such an acknowledgement. The newspaper novel is 'nestled', in Johnson-Woods' words, 'among the news, the sporting results, the gossip columns, scientific articles, advertisements and so forth'.[180] Situated contiguously with these other texts, the serial text is at least potentially continuous with them. This positioning resists the literary critical view of the text as a pure and discrete object, and embeds that work in the world of commodity production and consumption. It also highlights the presence of other readers, with entirely different understandings, investments and value judgements from the literary critic. Indeed, the novel's position implies the primacy of these other readings, given that it was for this mass audience that the newspaper novel was intended, with the specific aim of boosting sales and circulation by providing readers with entertainment. Given the dichotomised view of literary value that still holds sway in much literary scholarship – where aesthetic achievement is negatively correlated with financial success and, by association, where 'discredit increases as the audience grows'[181] – the existence of this mass audience also challenges the possibility of defining these novels as literary. Yet it was in this newspaper form that many of the now canonical texts of the colonial literary tradition were first published. Who knows how many potentially canonical novels wait in these pages.

Significantly, the structural foundations of literary studies – while challenged and exposed by the 'nestled' situation of the serial text – are enabled and upheld by the enclosed form of the book. Where the serial novel exposes the implication of fiction in commodity culture, the form of the book allows the literary critic to ignore this; where the serial text challenges the capacity of internal modes of reading to get at the full meaning of the text, the form of the book supports this approach; and where the serial text foregrounds broader conditions of reception, the form of the book allows us to imagine the special – and specially individuated and productive – relationship between text and reader intrinsic to literary criticism. As I discussed in the Introduction, and as manifested in the cultural materialist turn in Australian literary studies since the 1980s, there is now almost routine acknowledgement by critics in this field of the implication of text and author in economic (as well as political, social and historical) systems and structures. However, given the types of engagement with the text that forms of publication enable or compel, the book-orientation of Australian literary studies, and the discipline's neglect of serial fiction, implies that these renovations are not as deep as the frequency of their exposition would suggest.

This capacity of serial texts to expose the implication of literature in the market is common across all national (and global and local) literary traditions. Yet, as I said previously, significant – and increasing – attention is paid to British and American serial fiction without the collapse of those areas of literary scholarship. I would suggest, however, that there are two features of Australian literary studies that render the serial text, and the commodification of fiction it indicates, especially threatening to this national field. In contrast to British and American novels, the Australian novel did not really exist prior to the drastic expansion of serial publication in the mid-nineteenth century. Consequently, Australian newspaper novels demonstrate not only the implication of the national tradition in the market, but its origins therein. The unsettling consequences of this historical coincidence are exacerbated by historical fears regarding the insufficiency of the Australian literary tradition. In this context, the imprint of an overseas (especially a British) publisher on book editions of Australian novels has arguably provided literary critics with a significant marker of literary value: an external seal of approval that provides a contradictory basis for assertions of national literary quality.

The growing scholarly interest in print culture in Australia is likely to motivate new research into the history of serial publication, and may suggest other reasons for the neglect of this publishing trend. However, if Australian literary studies have been built on the book, an incorporation of serial texts may do more than introduce new themes and authors. In forcing literary critics into an uncomfortable proximity with readers and markets, and in requiring them to adopt a vocabulary of commerce, distribution and industry, attention to the serial text may lead to an acknowledgement that internal – close – readings can never tell a novel's full story.

Chapter 3

NOSTALGIA AND THE NOVEL: LOOKING BACK, LOOKING FORWARD

> The golden age of Australian publishing and the promotion of Australian literature, primed by the 1972 Whitlam victory and kept going through the 1980s by the financial largesse associated with the celebration of the 1988 Bicentenary of Australia, is well and truly over.[1]

The previous chapter ended with the 1890s, described by Martyn Lyons as 'perhaps the most mythologised decade in Australian cultural history'. He identifies the 'generation of the 1950s [as] largely responsible for idealising the 1890s, as intellectuals searched nostalgically for roots that might sustain a post-war resurgence of Australian literary culture'. This generation, he argues, imagined the 1890s

> as a creative moment when a specifically Australian literary nationalism took shape, based on a democratic and fiercely independent spirit located in a mythologised version of life in the bush. The bushman was a folk-hero…questioning dependence on Britain and challenging pretensions of the powerful.[2]

This understanding of the 1890s has been widely recognised and critiqued – or as Lyons puts it, 'thoroughly contested' and 'severely punctured' – by the generation that followed that of the 1950s, commonly referred to as 'baby boomers'.[3] Indeed, one could argue that the major movements in literary studies spearheaded by this generation since the 1970s – Marxism, feminism and post-colonialism – have been articulated in the Australian context as a series of challenges precisely to this 1950s definition of 'Australian literature', and the literary nationalism underpinning it. While this process of redefinition and reinvention has profoundly altered – in particular, expanded – the category of Australian literature, I will argue in this chapter that mythologising did not end with the 1890s, nor with the generation of the 1950s. Instead, the following generation developed its own nostalgic narrative, wherein the 1970s and 1980s – the era of their own entry into the academy – are, as Elizabeth Webby writes in the epigraph to this chapter, the 'golden age of Australian publishing and the promotion of Australian literature'. While this narrative renders the local publisher – rather than the bushman – the folk hero, like the legend of the 1890s it valorises 'a democratic and fiercely independent spirit' located in an idealised past.

Webby is by no means the only – or most extreme – proponent of this view (as I will demonstrate throughout this chapter), but her account provides a neat summary of the rise and fall trajectory asserted in many descriptions of Australian literature in the decades since the Second World War. According to such histories, there was no – or very little – local publishing before the 1970s, and the Australian novel was entirely produced (as supposedly it was in the nineteenth century) by British publishers. 'Then something remarkable happened. An Australian publishing industry came into being.'[4] This – Richard Flanagan's introduction to the 1970s – is one of the more dramatic examples of a prevailing tendency to identify that decade with the beginning of local publishing. *Paper Empires*, the volume of *A History of the Book in Australia* focused on the period from 1946 to 2005,[5] challenges this position to some extent by identifying a number of local publishers operating in Australia before the 1970s. But in presenting that industry as nascent, the collection's contributors largely perpetuate the notion of local publishing before 1970 as entirely marginal to the Australian book market and its reading public.

Most literary critics associate the supposed rise of local publishing in the 1970s and 1980s with growth in government funding for the arts at this time: this funding fostered Australian publishing; the publishers, in turn, actively promoted Australian authors and writing; and the Australian reading public embraced this 'national [literary] awakening'.[6] This unprecedented expansion of local publishing, it is argued, effectively challenged the longstanding dominance of British publishers in the Australian book market, and enabled unparalleled growth in Australian literary production. But in the 1990s, this short-lived period of independence and prosperity came to an end as reduced government funding – in Webby's words, 'the doctrine of economic rationalism at the political level' – and 'ever-increasing globalisation on the world economic stage',[7] enabled multinational conglomerates to enter and dominate the Australian market. As a consequence, Australian publishers – having so recently overcome British domination of the local market – were again overwhelmed by commercial interests from beyond the nation's shores. For a number of commentators, the result of multinational involvement in the Australian book market is nothing less than the demise of Australian literature itself. Michael Wilding asks: 'When publishing decisions are made ultimately in pure cash terms by the overseas conglomerates, what protects the development and continuation of a culture of quality in Australia?'[8]

In this chapter I interrogate this widely represented narrative of contemporary Australian literature and publishing by analysing publication data on first edition Australian novels from 1945 to 2009.[9] Figures 4 and 5 present an overview of these results, with the first of these graphs showing the proportion of Australian novels by Australian, British, multinational, 'other' and self- publishers, and the second depicting the number of titles published overall and by the largest three groups of publishers (Australian, British and multinational).[10] The results displayed in these graphs directly contradict the historiography outlined above. British companies had a significant presence in the Australian novel field in the immediate post-war period, but in terms of output, local publishers dominated. The 1970s and 1980s were marked by a decline in both the proportion and number of locally published titles, and in the overall number of Australian novels. Moreover, it was during this supposed 'golden age' of local publishing (not in the

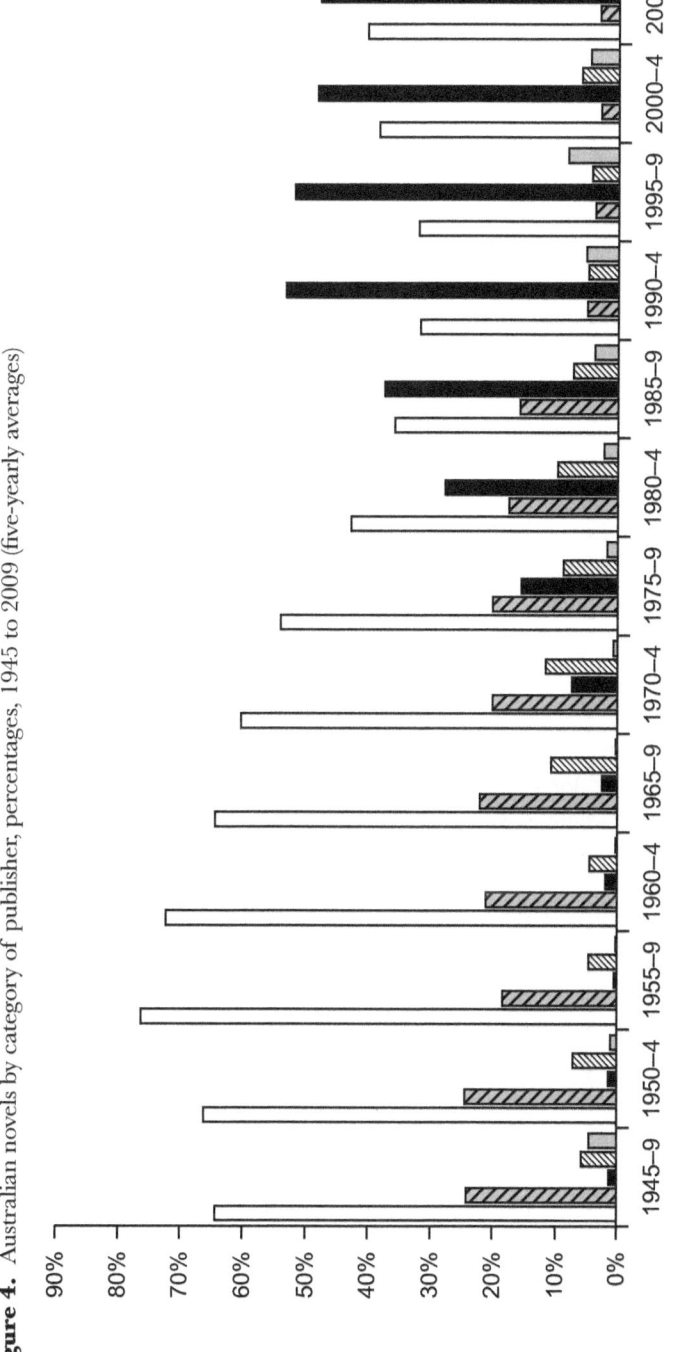

Figure 4. Australian novels by category of publisher, percentages, 1945 to 2009 (five-yearly averages)

Figure 5. Number of Australian novels, overall and by Australian, British and multinational publishers, 1945 to 2009 (five-yearly totals)

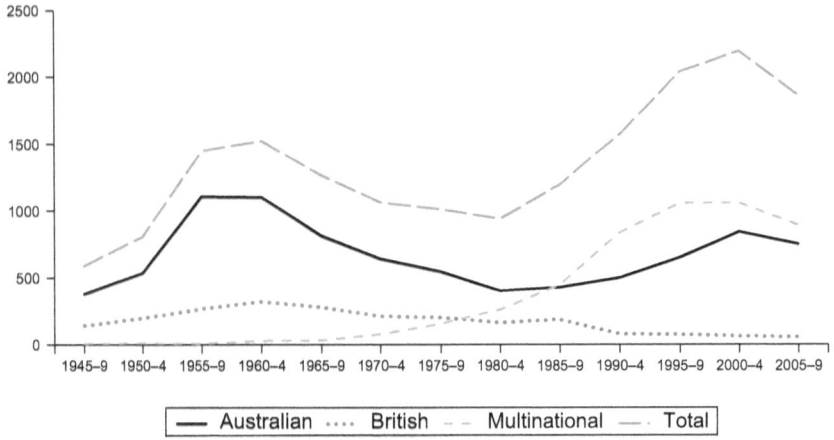

1990s and 2000s) that multinational publishers first entered the Australian novel field. Such conglomerates played a more significant role in Australian novel publishing in the 1990s. But they did not entirely dominate the field, as many commentators claim, and in the 2000s, the proportion of Australian novels published by multinationals declined in the context of growth in local publishing.

This chapter explores the relationship between the current conceptions of contemporary Australian literary history and empirical trends in publishing in four parts. The first investigates the period from the end of the Second World War until the end of the 1960s; the second considers the industry in the 1970s and 1980s; the third concentrates on multinational publishing in the 1990s and 2000s; the fourth explores continuing and emerging trends in non-multinational publishing – Australian and otherwise – in these last two decades. The trends indicated by these graphs, and explored in these sections, reveal the past and present of the Australian novel as significantly more complicated – messier, but I would suggest also more interesting – than the construction of the 1970s and 1980s as a 'golden age' can allow or express.

I also argue that misconceptions of publishing trends are to a significant extent attributable to literary nationalism. While the 'baby boomer' generation strongly criticised the version of literary nationalism embedded in the bush mythology (especially its racism and sexism), a set of aesthetic-political commitments regarding 'Australianness' and 'literariness' – and the appropriate relationship between the two – continues to organise and determine much discussion of Australian literature. This is not a new argument: the exclusion of non-literary (or popular, genre or mass-market) fiction from Australian literary studies (and literary studies in general) has often been described, as has the 'defensive nationalism' of the field (and, arguably, literary studies in general).[11] What I am interested in exploring are the particular ways in which literary nationalism – and the ideal, self-contained literary culture it constructs – underpins the prevailing narrative of contemporary Australian literary history. I consider how this narrative occludes important

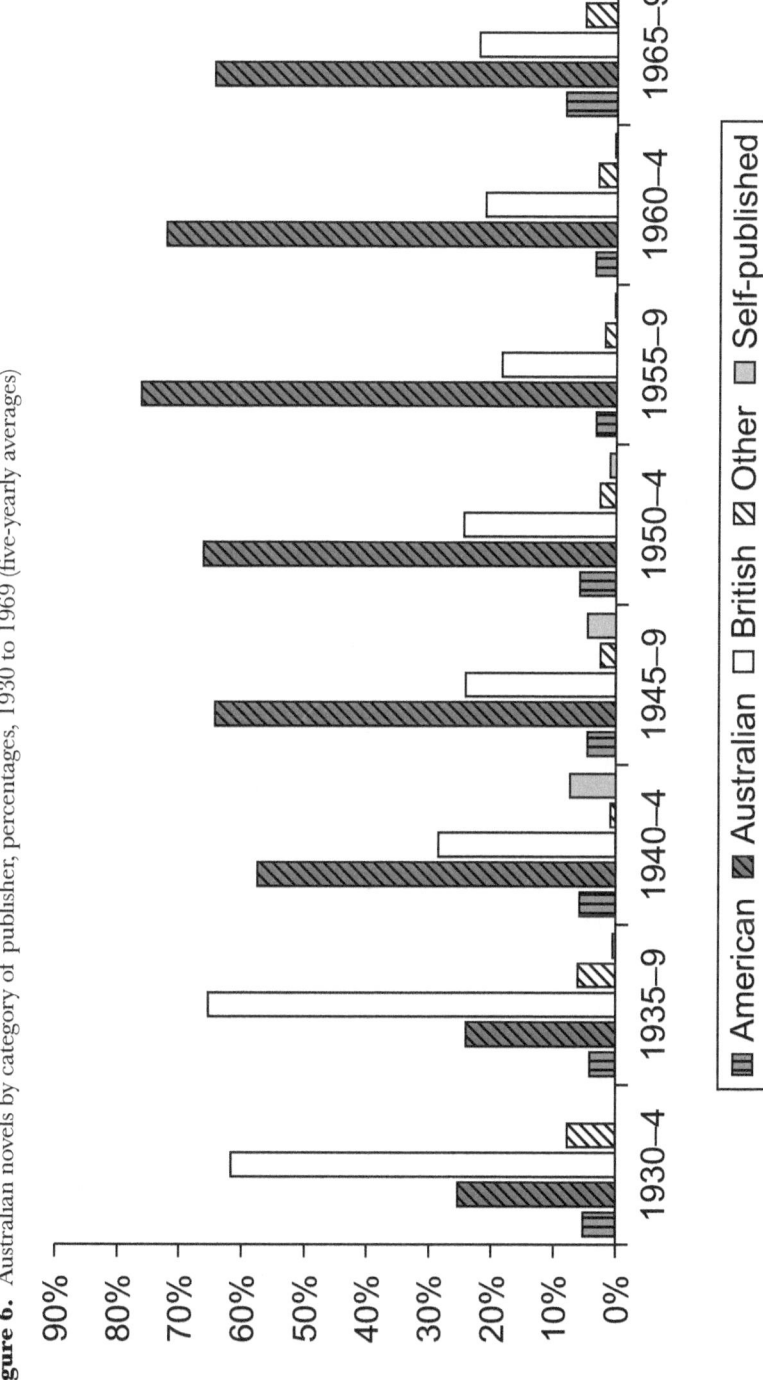

Figure 6. Australian novels by category of publisher, percentages, 1930 to 1969 (five-yearly averages)

trends within that field, and significantly inhibits our capacity to understand and theorise industry dynamics and their relationship to authorship, publishing and reading in Australia. I am also concerned with challenging the nostalgia of the established account, which seeks an image of the strength and dynamism of Australian literary culture solely in the past. This backward-looking approach can perceive recent publishing trends only negatively, and fails to provide an effective basis for understanding the past, present or future of Australian publishing, or the literary field more broadly.

I British Domination? 1940s to 1960s

In his 2007 analysis of the 'Past and Future' of Australian publishing, Flanagan supports his own sense of 'the Australian book market' before the 1970s as 'a milch cow of English publishing' by citing earlier descriptions of British domination:

> When in 1945 the federal government held a commission of inquiry into Australian publishing, it was told by Harold White, the Commonwealth Librarian, that Australia had no publishing industry... Gough Whitlam in 1964 described Australian readers as 'a captive British market, a subject people'.[12]

Flanagan's account is backed by other confident statements regarding the non-existence of a local publishing industry – such as Hazel Menehira's claim that, 'until the late 1970s an Australian novelist would still have to seek a publisher in London'[13] – as well as seemingly empirical evidence of this state. John Curtain, for instance, contends that, 'In 1953 there were only three Australian publishers – A&R [Angus and Robertson], MUP [Melbourne University Press] and F.W. Cheshire – who produced more than 10 titles per annum'.[14] Curtain restates this argument, originally presented in an article in *Logos* in 1998, in *Paper Empires* in 2006, this time with Craig Munro. In this case, the purported scarcity of local publishing is associated with British publishers' domination of the Australian book market: 'In 1953, when a quarter of all British book exports went down under, only a few Australian publishers (including Angus & Robertson, Melbourne University Press and FW Cheshire) produced more than a handful of titles each year'.[15]

My discussion in this section focuses quite substantially on essays in *Paper Empires* for two reasons: first, this collection is the most extensive recent analysis of Australian publishing in the post-war period; second, as I said in the introduction to this chapter, to some extent this book challenges the view that there was no publishing in Australia until the 1970s. My contention, however, is that *Paper Empires* maintains the broad tenets of the established historiography by describing the local industry as nascent, and dominated by Britain. The collection also proposes a parallel between the rise of this industry through the 1950s and 1960s and national sentiment. This view feeds into and supports existing accounts of the 1970s and 1980s as a 'golden age', while neglecting important features of the local industry that existed prior to these decades.

In terms of Australian novel publication, for the decades before World War Two, claims of British domination are justified. As portended by the dramatic entry of

British publishers into the Australian novel field in the 1890s (see Chapter 2), such companies were responsible for the majority of first edition titles published in the following four decades: 65 per cent in the 1900s, 55 per cent in the 1910s, 63 per cent in the 1920s and 64 per cent in the 1930s.[16] However, in contradiction of claims of Britain's post-war domination of Australian publishing, the 1940s witnessed a dramatic reversal in the distribution of Australian novels between publishers from these two nations. As Figure 6 shows,[17] 61 per cent of titles were locally published in the 1940s, increasing to 73 per cent in the 1950s. While declining slightly to 69 per cent in the 1960s, local publication remained remarkably high throughout this era of purported British domination. In respect to Australian novel publishing at least, the post-war industry was strongly Australian dominated.

In discussing local publishers before 1970, the contributors to *Paper Empires* devote their attention – and case studies – to two main groups. The first is comprised of large, established bookseller-publishers, such as A&R and Dymocks in Sydney, Cheshire in Melbourne and Rigby in Adelaide, all of which were in operation before the Second World War.[18] While A&R and Dymocks published a number of Australian works prior to the 1940s, until this decade, Cheshire and Rigby rarely produced their own titles, electing to act primarily as intermediaries between British publishers and Australian readers. The other main group of post-war publishers discussed in *Paper Empires* is comprised of smaller, dedicated book publishers, such as Lansdowne, Jacaranda, Ure Smith and Sun Books. With the exception of Ure Smith, established in 1916, these companies were formed in the late 1950s and 1960s.

A&R is repeatedly identified as the leader of this nascent or 'fledgling'[19] local publishing industry,[20] the development of which – both in the movement of large booksellers into publishing, and in the emergence of new, dedicated book publishers – is attributed to increased national sentiment in the aftermath of World War Two. Curtain and Munro describe a 'postwar phase of "national awakening"', which began to create real interest in Australia's emerging book culture'.[21] Frank Thompson refers to 'emergent nationalism' – 'which would achieve its fullest expression in the 1970s' – producing a significant shift in Australians' book buying and reading habits: 'Suddenly people wanted Australian books with Australian themes'.[22] Michael Page, Rigby's publishing manager in this period, likewise emphasises 'a tremendous demand for books about every aspect of Australia'.[23] Similar descriptions of the nationalism of post-war publishers and publishing recur throughout *Paper Empires*: the 'commitment to Australian culture and thought' shown by Andrew Fabinyi, general manager of Cheshire, is highlighted;[24] Lansdowne's list is described as 'brandish[ing] its nationalism';[25] likewise, the phenomenal success of *They're a Weird Mob* – it 'sold more copies than any other novel published in Australia, at least until Bryce Courtenay'[26] – is said to have 'exposed a rich vein of material for Ure Smith and other publishers in popular books about Australian English and Australian customs'.[27]

Certainly, both groups of post-war publishers highlighted in *Paper Empires* produced Australian novels between 1945 and 1969, with A&R's 148 titles placing that company well ahead of the other large bookseller-publishers (including Cheshire with 30 titles,[28] and Dymocks and Rigby with 23) as well as the smaller, dedicated book publishers (the most prolific of these being Ure Smith, with 13 titles).[29] *AustLit* includes other book publishers demonstrating the same commitment to Australian authors and writing that *Paper Empires* emphasises.[30] Indeed, a cooperative publisher not mentioned in that collection – the Australasian Book Society, which used members' subscriptions to finance the publication of 29 first edition Australian novels – published more titles between 1945 and 1969 than Ure Smith (or Dymocks or Rigby), despite only being created in 1952.[31] Two further examples of publishers committed to Australian writing (from the immediate post-war years, and responsible for only a small number of titles) were Dolphin Publications, which had 'a self-consciously nationalist orientation',[32] and F. H. Johnston Publishing Co., which aimed to 'publish books that will present Australia to Australians and the world'.[33] As these examples and the evidence in *Paper Empires* demonstrate, national sentiment obviously played a role in post-war Australian publishing and in the production of some Australian novel titles. Yet even combined, the outputs of the large bookseller-publishers and the smaller, dedicated book publishers (including those not mentioned in *Paper Empires*) represent a tiny proportion of the locally published titles shown in Figure 6.

Table 5. Top ten publishers of Australian novels, 1945 to 1969

Publishers	Nation	# Titles	% Titles
1. Cleveland	Australian	1476	26
2. Horwitz	Australian	1221	21
3. Calvert	Australian	296	5
4. Action Comics	Australian	256	4
5. Collins	British	199	3
6. A&R	Australian	148	3
7. Robert Hale	British	146	3
8. Hutchinson	British	98	2
9. Currawong	Australian	85	1
10. Frank Johnson	Australian	77	1

From 1945 to 1969, most Australian novels were published by an entirely different group: pulp fiction publishers. As Toni Johnson-Woods notes, pulp fiction 'correctly refers to all-fiction magazines…printed on wood-pulp paper. However, over time, the term "pulp" has become shorthand for cheap fiction',[34] especially mass-produced, formula-driven paperback novels. Such novels were the major focus of five of the six local companies in the top ten publishers of Australian novels in these decades (see Table 5), including the top four overall. Ranked in order, these five pulp fiction publishers were Cleveland, Horwitz, Calvert, Action Comics and Currawong, together responsible for 59 per cent of Australian novels from 1945 to 1969, and 83 per cent of locally published titles. Comparing the 47 per cent of Australian novels published by Cleveland and Horwitz alone, with A&R's 3 per cent of titles, demonstrates the relative size of this area of local publishing, and presents a stark contrast with prevalent descriptions, in *Paper Empires* and elsewhere, of A&R as 'the major Australian publisher before and after the war'; 'the most powerful force in Australian bookselling and publishing'; and 'so dominant that it exercised virtual monopoly power'.[35] Beyond the top five pulp fiction publishers, a number of other local companies published pulp fiction, from relatively substantial enterprises – including Frank Johnson (with 77 titles from 1945 to 1969),[36] Invincible Press (54 titles) and Webster Publications (42 titles)[37] – down to presses responsible for only a small number of Australian novels in a single decade.[38] These companies operated in what was effectively a separate industry from the publishers that are the focus of *Paper Empires*,[39] as is evident from the types of books they published (mainly westerns, war novels, crime fiction and romances); their generally much lower production values and prices; their sales outlets (newsagents, bookstalls and postal order rather than bookstores); and even the types of contracts they offered authors.[40]

Figure 7 compares the number of Australian novels by Australian and British publishers (with the local field divided to indicate the contribution and size of the pulp fiction industry). The unbroken black line depicts all locally published Australian novels; the dotted black line represents all such titles excluding those published by the large and medium-sized pulp fiction publishers (Cleveland, Horwitz, Calvert, Action Comics, Currawong, Frank Johnson, Invincible Press and Webster Publications). On the one hand, this graph shows that, at least in respect to the Australian novel, in the absence of pulp fiction publishing, claims of post-war British domination are justified. Without these publishers, the distribution of titles between Britain and Australia resembles pre-war levels, with British companies responsible for 60 and 59 per cent of Australian novels in the 1950s and 1960s respectively (compared to 21 and 22 per cent when pulp fiction publishing is included) and local presses for 22 and 15 per cent (as opposed to 73 and 70 per cent). On the other hand, in demonstrating the remarkable size of this alternative industry, Figure 7 highlights the obvious importance of pulp fiction publishing to the history of the Australian novel. In suggesting a broad shape to this publishing trend – its emergence in the Second World War; its rapid expansion in the first half of the 1950s; and the beginning of its decline in the latter part of the 1960s – the results displayed in this graph also indicate important features of the history of pulp fiction in Australia. This history, I will argue, reveals a very different relationship between national sentiment and local publishing and reading to the one emphasised in *Paper Empires*.

Figure 7. Number of Australian novels by category of publisher, 1930 to 1969 (five-yearly totals)

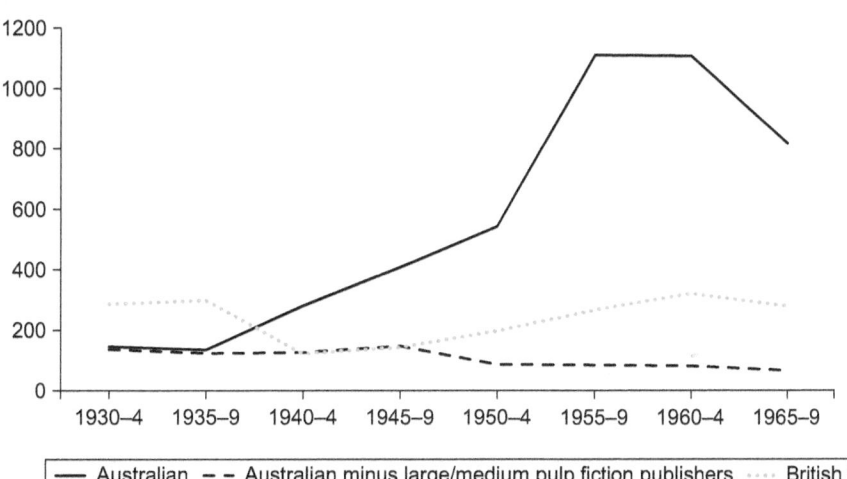

Although significantly outnumbered by those who claim the post-war Australian publishing industry was British dominated, there are scholars, such as Johnson-Woods and Graeme Flanagan, who acknowledge the prevalence of pulp fiction publishing in this period.[41] Of the minimal attention paid to this phenomenon, Horwitz has received the major part with Anthony May arguing that this publisher 'dominated', and Thompson, that it was 'the local leader in', mass-market publishing.[42] More recently, Richard Nile and Jason Ensor have demonstrated the greater novel output of Cleveland (although in this case, Horwitz's contribution is under- rather than over-stated).[43]

Two causes of the post-war surge in pulp fiction publishing have been suggested. Munro and Curtain attribute the proliferation of Australian books 'printed on anything resembling paper' to wartime 'restrictions on the importation of non-essential goods', and in particular, to the 'respite' this brought from the influx of books from Britain.[44] For Johnson-Woods, 'Australia's richest publishing decades' were the result of more specific import licensing restrictions imposed from 1939 to 1959 on any printed matter from non-sterling currency areas, mainly the United States. Designed to preserve currency reserves, these prohibitions 'effectively banned' the import of American pulps to Australia for twenty years.[45] In their recent consideration of the trend, Nile and Ensor gesture towards both causal factors in accounting for the output of Cleveland and Horwitz in the 1950s and 1960s, suggesting 'the circumstances of World War II' enabled a shift to 'a more sustainable Australian industry',[46] and noting:

> It has been suspected that pulp fiction publishers took advantage of the Australian government's moves to establish 'tariffs on American imports that effectively banned American pulps' 1939–59, but the degree to which pulp publishers were able to derive a disproportionate benefit requires further examination.[47]

It seems indisputable that both conditions (the reduced availability of British books and the absence of American books) would have influenced local publishing. And indeed, there is a clear correlation between the start of World War Two (when both conditions came into effect) and growth in Australian pulp fiction publishing. The results displayed in Figure 7 – and the trends that emerge from analysis of the companies involved and the types of novels published – maintain the possibility that a wartime respite in British books contributed to the growth in local pulp fiction. But they also indicate, I will argue, that tariffs on American fiction were a significantly more important factor in producing this local publishing trend. It is important to distinguish between, and explore the relative effects of, these two conditions because they represent significantly different ideas about the Australian book market's position in international trade. Munro and Curtain's argument, which is indicative of the emphasis in *Paper Empires* more generally, sees Australian publishers only in relation to their British counterparts. In contrast, Johnson-Woods' proposal brings into view the presence of American fiction and publishers in the Australian market.

As Figure 7 shows, World War Two witnessed a reduction in British publication of Australian novels in the context of marked growth in local pulp fiction publishing.[48] In the five years following the war, the output of local non-pulp publishers increased slightly, in step with a return to Australian novel publishing by British companies. Local pulp fiction continued to grow at a much greater rate. As growth in local pulp fiction accelerated further in the 1950s, the output of local non-pulp and British publishers of Australian novels returned to pre-war levels. The correlation between the departure of British publishers from the Australian novel field and growth in local publishing (of both pulp and, to a much lesser extent, non-pulp fiction) means it is not possible to dismiss the impact of reduced British involvement on local publishing. At the same time, the strong, and increasing growth in local pulp fiction publishing after the return of British publishers to this field, but whilst tariffs continued to be imposed on American fiction, suggests the greater impact of this latter publishing dynamic.

Trends within local pulp fiction publishing offer some further insights into influences on the book market at this time. The growth in pulp titles, shown in Figure 7, was in fact comprised of three major groups or waves of publishers. The first group – whose output began with the start of the war and declined in the early 1950s – consisted of Currawong and Frank Johnson. A second group, Horwitz and Invincible Press, began publishing Australian novels at the end of the war.[49] The decline in the 1950s of Invincible Press's output, along with the wartime pulp fiction publishers, occurred in conjunction with the return to the novel field of the British publishers of Australian novels. This conjunction suggests that Currawong, Frank Johnson and Invincible Press – as well as the local non-pulp publishers – may have been meeting the demand created by a lull in British book imports.[50] But the return of these British publishers did not seal the fate of the local pulp fiction industry. Quite to the contrary, Horwitz increased its output of Australian novels in that decade as a third group of pulp fiction publishers emerged. This included the market leader in the 1950s and 1960s, Cleveland, as well as Action Comics, Calvert and Webster Publications. The large number of novels published by Horwitz and these newer pulp fiction publishers indicates that demand for pulp fiction remained strong after the re-engagement of British publishers in the Australian novel field.

The specific types of novel published by these different groups also suggest an increasing orientation of the local pulp fiction industry to a market that would, in the absence of tariffs, probably have been met by American companies.[51] Almost without exception, local pulp fiction titles divide into explicitly Australian- and American-oriented stories. In the former category were war novels depicting the heroic actions of Australian troops overseas; romances set in Australia or featuring Australian characters in exotic locations (or in America); and crime fiction, quite often set in Kings Cross in Sydney, but also in other Australian settings (such as the race track, as is the case with the Dick Wordley mysteries published by Invincible Press). The American-oriented titles were mainly westerns or hard-boiled detective novels, and 'Americanness' is repeatedly emphasised. To use another example from Invincible Press, *West of Texandos*, by Johnnie Oxford, published in 1952, is not only set in America with American characters, but its style is clearly intended to imitate that of a traditional American western. Its first few pages include passages such as: 'now I git a bunged up eye', 'Mebbe them tenderfoot guys back East', and 'It don't look like Injun fire'.[52]

While all three groups published explicitly Australian- as well as American-style pulp novels, there was a progressive focus on American-style titles. The first group – Currawong and Frank Johnson – published American-oriented pulp novels, but their lists emphasised Australian characters and stories. Australian-style titles also tended to have higher production values (sometimes to the extent of being published in hard cover). Such fiction was also an important part of the lists of publishers in the second group. However, Horwitz and Invincible Press had cheaper production values for, and fewer, Australian-style titles than Currawong or Frank Johnson (that said, Invincible Press, like these wartime publishers, employed higher production values for its Australian- than its American-style stories). A more salacious style emerged in this second wave, both in the subject matter of the books and in the cover art (scantily clad – often unconscious – women predominate, as do men with large guns). This style continued with the third group,[53] but these pulp fiction publishers were again more strongly oriented towards American-style fiction. Two companies in the third wave – Calvert and Action Comics – published a mixture of Australian- and American-style pulps. However, Cleveland – the most prolific publisher in this third wave and in these post-war decades overall – and Webster Publications focused almost exclusively on American-style novels.[54] In most cases, it would be difficult to identify Cleveland or Webster as Australian publishers from the books they produced (a characteristic that was also increasingly true of Horwitz). This shift in local pulp fiction publishing to salacious, American-style titles strongly suggests the increasing orientation of these publishers to the gap in the Australian market left by the continuing absence of American-originated books. These companies were able, in other words, 'to derive a disproportionate benefit'[55] from tariffs applied to American fiction because they increasingly matched the type of fiction these tariffs prevented from entering the local market.

The large number of American-style titles published by these Australian companies challenges the general focus, in histories of Australian publishing, on connections between the Australian market and British publishers. Although coming into view via the activities of local companies, the prevalence of these American-style stories indicates an enormous demand – and sizeable reading market – in Australia for genres featuring American characters, themes and settings. That this demand was almost certainly created and met, before the war, by American-originated fiction challenges the prevailing view that the Australian market was predominantly formed in relation to British publishing, and even raises questions about the relative influence of fiction from America and Britain on Australian readers. The sizeable reading market in Australia for America-style pulp novels also presents a more specific challenge to the view, presented in *Paper Empires*, that local publishing arose in the post-war period because of emerging national sentiment. If anything, the output of these companies suggests a desire for American- (rather than Australian-) style stories had a greater influence on local output. At the same time, the explicit Australianness of many of these titles indicates that popular Australian genres also held strong appeal for local readers. From this perspective, trends in pulp fiction show that demand for Australian stories was greater than has been appreciated, and present a significant addition to understandings of the relationship between rising national sentiment and the 'fledgling' post-war local publishing industry described in *Paper Empires*.

In fact, the strongly Australian-oriented lists of wartime publishers, Currawong and Frank Johnson, indicate that national sentiment influenced local publishing prior to 1945. Currawong and Frank Johnson's appeal to the nationalism of their readers emerged not only in the lists of these companies, but also in their advertising. Titles in the 'Currawong First Novel' series were described as 'all "first novels" by young Australian authors',[56] and the backs of Currawong books advertised lists of 'Good Australian Books' (all published, of course, by Currawong).[57] On the back covers of books in Frank Johnson's 'Magpie Series' were the words, 'A Series of Selected Novels by Australian Authors: These stories, depicting various forms of Australian life in romance, humour, and thrilling adventure, are by far the finest and cheapest books yet issued in Australia.'[58] While these pulp fiction publishers were not the first examples of this nationalist trend in publishing,[59] their wartime emphasis on the nation suggests that, in 'brandish[ing] [their] nationalism',[60] the presses discussed in *Paper Empires* were following a trend that already existed in the pulp fiction industry.

Previous analyses of Australian pulp fiction publishing propose that this industry ended in the 1960s. According to Johnson-Woods, when prohibitions on the import of American fiction were removed in 1959, Australian pulp fiction publishing 'died overnight'.[61] For May, it is 'the rise of domestic television drama in Australia at the end of the 1960s', that had a 'devastating' effect on the local 'pulp fiction market'.[62] As I have argued, the first wave of pulp fiction publishers – and Invincible Press – essentially ceased operations in the early 1950s, in the context of the return of British publishers to the Australian book market and competition from more prolific pulp fiction publishers focused on American-style fiction. Trends among the pulp fiction publishers of the second and third wave suggest that the historical conditions noted above – the end of tariffs and the beginning of television in Australia – did have an impact: Action Comics and Webster Publications both stopped publishing in 1959, and the output of Cleveland, Horwitz and Calvert declined from this time. Nevertheless, as Figure 7 demonstrates, pulp fiction publishers continued to dominate the local industry throughout the 1960s – and, as I will show in the next section of this chapter, beyond that decade. This trend explicitly contradicts those analyses that allow for the success of local pulp fiction publishing only under limited, historical conditions: that is, before the arrival of television or while import tariffs were imposed on American fiction.

I am not suggesting that, because there was so much of it, pulp fiction should be the focus of all accounts of the Australian novel in these post-war decades. But the fact that such fiction has been all but ignored in Australian literary studies, and to a considerable extent, in histories of Australian publishing, significantly skews our understanding of authorship, publishing and reading in Australia in the 1940s, 1950s and 1960s. In particular, it indicates neglect of the role of price (and pulp fiction was primarily distinguished from other forms of book publishing by its cheapness) in shaping reading culture and local publishing in post-war Australia (as in the nineteenth century). The picture that emerges from this study – of a prolific, highly concentrated local publishing industry, producing cheap paperbacks for the mass-market and filling a gap left by the absence of American books – challenges the view that there was no publishing in Australia prior to the 1970s. It also departs from the revised narrative presented in *Paper Empires* of a market and industry dominated by Britain, where American publishers never had a presence, and where small local companies eked out an existence with nationally oriented, culture-led publishing. Neglect of Australian pulp fiction is particularly marked in comparison to the serious scholarly attention that popular genres – especially westerns and hard-boiled detective novels, and including pulp fiction – have received in America.[63] In that context, cowboys and 'private dicks' have been seen as major figures in the construction of national identity, including American masculinity.[64] We are yet to understand the basis for the appeal of these characters, or of the Australian doctors, soldiers and jockeys that also featured strongly in pulp novels, in post-war Australia.

The exclusion of pulp fiction from Australian literary and publishing histories strongly suggests the all-too-familiar operations of the high/low culture divide, where literary value is constructed via the identification and rejection of mass culture or, in Andreas Huyssen's words, 'through a conscious strategy of exclusion, an anxiety of contamination by its other: an increasingly consuming and engulfing mass culture'.[65] Seen through this paradigm, these pulp fiction publishers are uninteresting and undifferentiated, but also alarming, in the way their 'excessive' output threatens to overwhelm culturally 'valuable' forms of literature and publishing. The (perceived) sameness as well as the mass output of the pulp fiction industry is projected onto the companies responsible for that product, and onto the readers who bought such books. The resulting construction of pulp fiction publishers and readers as an undifferentiated 'mass' dispels the need for exploration of their practices and occludes the important differences between publishers and readers in this field.

As with nineteenth-century serial fiction, the neglect of post-war pulp fiction in Australia – in contrast to the attention the phenomenon receives elsewhere, in this case, in the American context – suggests a lack of confidence regarding the value of Australia's literary and cultural heritage. Somewhat paradoxically, I think this neglect also relates to the specific form of nationalism manifested in the view of the 1970s and 1980s as a 'golden age' of local publishing. As I will discuss in the next section of this chapter, the small presses lauded in such accounts stand as symbols of Australian independence from its colonial past, manifest specifically in independence from the British publishers that supposedly dominated the Australian market until this period. This nationalist narrative is compromised if local mass-market publishers – producing Australian- as well as American-style genre fiction – rather than British publishers are acknowledged as major players in the post-war Australian book market.

II The Golden Age? 1970s to 1980s

For most commentators, the 1970s and 1980s in Australia are the decades when the 'fledgling' local publishing industry spread its wings and entered, as Anne Galligan puts it, 'the golden age of Australian publishing, with the opening out of opportunities to embrace the diversity of Australian society and engage in many new public conversations'.[66] Even in *Paper Empires*, which devotes two sections to local publishing in the immediate post-war decades, the 1970s is portrayed as Australian publishing's true beginning, or 'coming of age'. Thus, Jim Hart introduces the section of that collection entitled 'New Wave Seventies' with the claim that:

> If the 1960s were the infancy of modern Australian publishing, then the 1970s was surely its adolescence – a time of life characterised by rapid growth, increased maturity

and an urge for independence, together with experimentation, recklessness, high ideals and overactive hormones.[67]

Richard Flanagan describes the industry that 'came into being' in this decade as one characterised by 'genuinely good people, book people, who believe books…matter and who seek to help writers make books that have meaning'.[68] This theme of essential goodness runs throughout accounts of Australian publishing in the 1970s and 1980s, emerging (as in Galligan's account) in descriptions of cultural diversity and/or (as in the passage from Hart) in claims of unprecedented independence, experimentation and growth. Indeed, as I will show, this idea of 'rapid growth' appears repeatedly, and is arguably the privileged claim in many such analyses, in that it is used to confirm the success of local publishing in this period.

Flanagan, 'not a believer in government protection of publishing',[69] is somewhat circumspect regarding the cause of the 'remarkable' emergence of a local publishing industry: 'The battle to build a worthwhile culture of writing and reading in a country so large with a market so small was extraordinarily difficult', he argues, '[b]ut against the greatest of odds, it *somehow* met these challenges and prospered'.[70] Most critics, however, attribute the growth and success of publishing in these decades to increased governmental and social support for Australian publishing and writing. Claiming that '[m]uch of the growth and change in publishing was a reflection of the wider social and political context', Hart describes the 1970s in terms of a 'new nationalism and a sense of independence' associated with the post-Vietnam War period and demographic changes brought by the 'first wave of baby-boomers'.[71] Ken Gelder and Paul Salzman identify the 1970s as a 'turning point in Australian writing',[72] and invoke specific instances of growth in government support for Australian publishers and authors – including state government-initiated arts programs and literary awards, and the federal government's establishment of the Literature Board in 1971[73] – to explain what they term 'an immediate and dramatic increase in the production of Australian fiction',[74] especially novels.[75] Galligan also cites the establishment of the Literature Board as a symbol of 'the changing political and cultural climate of the early 1970s…creat[ing] a sympathetic environment for Australian publishing' and producing 'an almost immediate and measurable increase in the volume and quality of work produced, and a heightened interest in publishing Australian material'.[76]

As evidence of this changing political and cultural climate, and to explain the 'rapid growth of Australian literature' in the 1970s and 1980s, other commentators invoke a gamut of social and institutional changes: from the establishment of the Australia Council and the 'easing of censorship restrictions'[77], to 'the consolidation of teaching and research in Australian literature' and 'escalating population, greater social and political complexity, widening economic structures and marked cultural diversity'.[78] Brigid Magner looks beyond these national dynamics to identify two challenges in the early 1970s to the historically unequal relationship between Australian publishers and their British counterparts – the end of the import of British colonial editions into Australia, and of the British Traditional Market Agreement (BTMA) – as important contributing factors to a 'local publishing boom'.[79] But whether conditions within or beyond the nation are seen as producing the shift, these accounts all emphasise the emergence of a self-contained and self-supporting Australian literary culture. The success, and growth, ascribed to local publishing in the 1970s and 1980s is identified with a productive symbiosis between publishers, authors, readers and government, all committed to the ideal of an authentic – independent, experimental and culturally diverse – Australian literary culture.

Data on Australian novel publishing does show evidence of the changes described in these accounts, most apparently, in growth in the number of local publishers, from 45 in the 1960s, to 88 in the 1970s and 205 in the 1980s. While not true of all such enterprises,[80] the commitment of many – if not the majority – to publishing as a cultural endeavour strongly accords with conceptions of the local industry at this time. Pursuing an agenda with obvious links to the national orientation of some Australian publishers prior to the 1970s, a number of companies demonstrated a specific commitment to writing – and in most cases, literary fiction – by Australian authors. The most prolific publishers in this group were A&R (with 58 titles in the 1970s) and the University of Queensland Press (UQP) (with 10 titles in the 1970s and 44 in the 1980s); it also included Rigby (15 in the 1970s/0 in the 1980s), Wren Books (11/0), Alpha Books (8/0),[81] Hale & Iremonger (0/18), Hyland House (4/17), Pascoe Publishing (0/8), McPhee Gribble (3/7) and Wild and Woolley (7/2). Other publishers in the 1970s and 1980s focused on experimental or counterculture writing, including Outback Press (9/1), Tomato Press (1/0), Sea Cruise Books (1/0), Experimental Art Foundation (0/2), Local Consumption Publications (0/1) and Rigmarole Books (0/1). In the 1980s, a number of local companies emerged that explicitly promoted publishing as a culturally progressive endeavour, including those focused on: regional writing, such as Fremantle Arts Centre Press (10), Boolarong (8), Artlook Books (6) and Nimrod (1); feminist or women-centred fiction, such as Dykebooks (8), Greenhouse Publications (8), Sybylla Press (2), Women's Redress Press (2) and Sisters Publishing (2); cultural diversity, such as Indra Publishing (2), Peacock Publications (2) and Dezsery Publications (1); and, in the case of Magabala Books (1), Aboriginal writing.

The appearance of these publishers and publishing agendas resonates with the descriptions I outlined above regarding changes in the local industry in the 1970s and 1980s. In Chapter 5 I discuss the important role of gender, and of the feminist movement, in this trend. However, the existing understanding of contemporary Australian literary history privileges such changes to the point where the emergence of independent, culturally dedicated local publishers comprises the totality of what is understood to have occurred in the industry at this time. As a consequence, many features of that industry are overlooked. For instance, this privileged narrative of progressive expansion omits the fragmentation in local publishing in the 1970s and 1980s. Of the publishers named above, those responsible for the most Australian novels in the 1970s – A&R, Rigby, Outback Press, Alpha Books and Wren Books – were all absent from the field by the 1980s.[82] While both Magner and Galligan note the difficult financial circumstances under which local publishers operated in these decades,[83] the prevailing narrative of unprecedented growth generally precludes acknowledgement of these difficulties and the collapse, as well as the rise, of some local companies. It also suppresses one of the main reasons for the fragmentation of the local publishing industry in this period: the acquisition,

Figure 8. Australian novels by category of publisher, percentages, 1970 to 1989 (five-yearly averages)

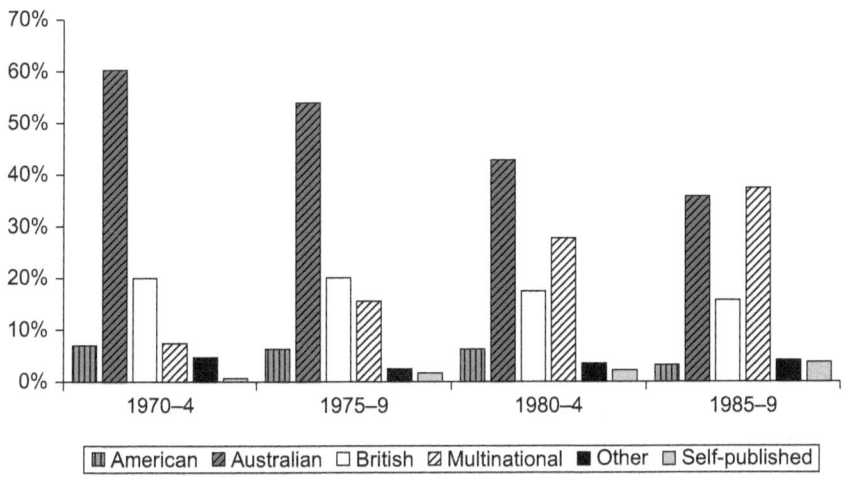

by Australian-based multinationals, of the two largest of these local publishers. James Hardie purchased Rigby in 1979, and News Limited, or News Corporation, acquired A&R in 1980. There is no place for commercial take-overs – nor, as I will discuss, the presence of multinationals in the industry – in descriptions of local publishing in the 1970s and 1980s as both prosperous and independent.

More particularly, the focus on local growth is at odds with the decline, shown in Figure 8, in the proportion of Australian novels published in Australia: from 60 per cent in the early 1970s, to 54 per cent in the late 1970s, 43 per cent in the early 1980s and 36 per cent in the late 1980s.[84] This decline was absolute as well as proportional: until the second half of the 1980s, the number of both locally published titles, and Australian novels overall, fell.[85] This downward trend can be understood in relation to the activities of two groups of publishers, each responsible for far more titles than the small local independent presses combined, but both excluded from the accounts of the 1970s and 1980s I have summarised: local pulp fiction and multinational publishers.

Table 6 depicts the top ten publishers of Australian novels in the 1970s and 1980s. It shows that the two most prolific publishers of such titles in the 1970s were Horwitz and Cleveland, which together produced nearly half (45 per cent) of that decade's titles. As in the immediate post-war decades, A&R was the only non-pulp Australian publisher in the top ten in the 1970s and 1980s; and as in these earlier decades, this local publisher was responsible for 3 per cent of Australian novels. In the 1980s, multinational publisher Torstar (owner of Harlequin/Mills & Boon) moved from third to first position. But Horwitz and Cleveland remained the second and third largest publishers of Australian novels, with a very substantial 18 per cent of titles. The output of these pulp fiction companies continued to decline through the 1990s, when they published only 3 per cent of Australian novels between them. Horwitz ceased publishing such titles in 1992, while Cleveland published its last Australian novel, *Texans Never Quit*, in 2001.[86]

Table 6. Top ten publishers of Australian novels, 1970s and 1980s

Publishers	Nation	# Titles	% Titles
1970s			
1. Horwitz	Australian	529	25
2. Cleveland	Australian	408	20
3. Torstar	Multinational	157	8
4. Robert Hale	British	91	4
5. Times Mirror Company	American	72	3
6. Collins	British	60	3
7. A&R	Australian	58	3
7. Macmillan	British	58	3
9. Thomson Organisation	Multinational	39	2
10. Wennerberg[87]	Swedish	30	1
1980s			
1. Torstar	Multinational	294	14
2. Horwitz	Australian	222	10
3. Cleveland	Australian	154	7
4. Pearson	Multinational	147	7
5. News Corporation	Multinational	88	4
6. Robert Hale	British	75	4
7. The Author	Self-published[88]	66	3
8. Collins	British	44	2
8. UQP	Australian	44	2
10. Macmillan	British	36	2

As with the post-war period, acknowledging the strong output of Horwitz and Cleveland in the 1970s and 1980s has important implications for understanding Australian publishing, authorship and reading in these decades. This output is evidence, *pace* Johnson-Woods and May,[89] that local pulp fiction publishing did not end with the 1960s. While specific historical conditions enabled the rise of this industry, these publishers were able to secure a local market and sustain it beyond the removal of tariffs and the return of American-originated fiction to Australia. It could be that Horwitz and Cleveland books were simply cheaper than the American imports, because of lower transport costs and because the publishers paid their authors less.[90] The continuation of these companies beyond the 1950s might also signal consumer loyalty or habit, with Australian readers who had bought Horwitz and Cleveland titles before 1959 simply continuing to do so once American-originated books were also available. This hypothesis is supported by the persistence of many of the more prolific authors – or author names[91] – of both publishers over many decades: in the case of Horwitz, these include Carter Brown (1950s–1980s); Marshall Grover (1960s–1990s) and J. E. Macdonnell (1960s–1980s); and for Cleveland, Larry Kent (1960s–1980s), Emerson Dodge (1960s–1990s), Kirk Hamilton (1960s–1990s) and Sundowner McCabe (1960s–2000s).

Interestingly, the ongoing success of these companies after the return of American-originated pulp fiction to the Australian market was not concurrent with a shift away from American-style fiction. Rather, in the 1970s and 1980s, Cleveland and Horwitz turned towards perhaps the most American of genres: the western. Such books always dominated Cleveland's list, but in the 1970s the company largely abandoned its secondary focus on detective fiction to concentrate on westerns. Although this genre led Horwitz's list in the immediate post-war period, from the late 1950s to the early 1970s, war novels and romances dominated. However, in the second half of the 1970s and 1980s, this company, too, returned to focusing on westerns.[92] Whatever the cause of this remarkable output of Australian-authored and published westerns in the 1970s and 1980s, as in the post-war decades, pulp fiction publishing presents a notable counterpoint to descriptions of Australian reading habits that emphasise the desire for books depicting and celebrating Australia. Flanagan, for instance, explicitly associates the success and prosperity of local publishers of the 1970s with their capacity to recognise and meet 'our right and our deepest need…to our own stories in our own voice'.[93] While the focus of many smaller local publishers on Australian stories suggests this desire was present, the size of the reading market for American-style westerns – signified (although, of course, not entirely comprised) by Horwitz and Cleveland's output – indicates that many Australian readers chose American stories (or at least, given the cheapness of these titles, selected their reading material based on price rather than national sentiment).

Although pulp fiction publishing continued to constitute a large proportion of the Australian novel field, its rapid decline during the 1970s and 1980s is also the main reason for the steepness of the fall (shown in Figure 8) in the proportion of locally published titles. The outlook is altered – though not to the extent that might be expected – if pulp fiction publishers are removed. In this case, there is numerical growth in locally published titles: in the early 1970s, non-pulp local presses published 98 Australian novels, increasing to 152 in the late 1970s, 200 in the early 1980s and 255 in the late 1980s. As Figure 9 shows, there was also some overall growth in the proportion of Australian novels published in Australia: from 19 per cent in the early 1970s to 25 per cent in the late 1970s and 27 per cent in the early 1980s. But in the late 1980s, this proportion declined to 25 per cent. The relatively strong growth in the proportion of locally published Australian novels in the 1970s was largely due to the output of Australian bookseller-publishers, A&R and Rigby. When these companies were acquired by Australian-based multinationals in the 1980s, publishers such as UQP and Hale & Iremonger filled some of the gap they left in the local non-pulp industry. But in relative as well as numerical terms, the output of these newer companies did not match that of the earlier bookseller-publishers. Certainly, the relatively flat growth in Australian publication of Australian novels from the late 1970s to the early 1980s, and the subsequent fall in this proportion, do not accord with the perception of 'rapid growth',[94] an 'immediate and dramatic increase',[95] and a 'local publishing boom'[96] at this time.

As the acquisition of A&R and Rigby signals, the main reason the steady numerical growth in non-pulp, locally published Australian novels did not translate into an overall proportional increase in local publication was the substantially increased role of multinational companies in the Australian novel field. Discussing the publishing industry in the 2000s, Magner proposes that, '[t]ransnational corporations have now begun to assume the role formerly occupied by British publishing companies'.[97] As Figure 9 indicates, this process actually occurred from the 1970s. In this decade and the next, the

Figure 9. Australian novels (excluding local pulp fiction) by category of publisher, percentages, 1970 to 1989 (five-yearly averages)

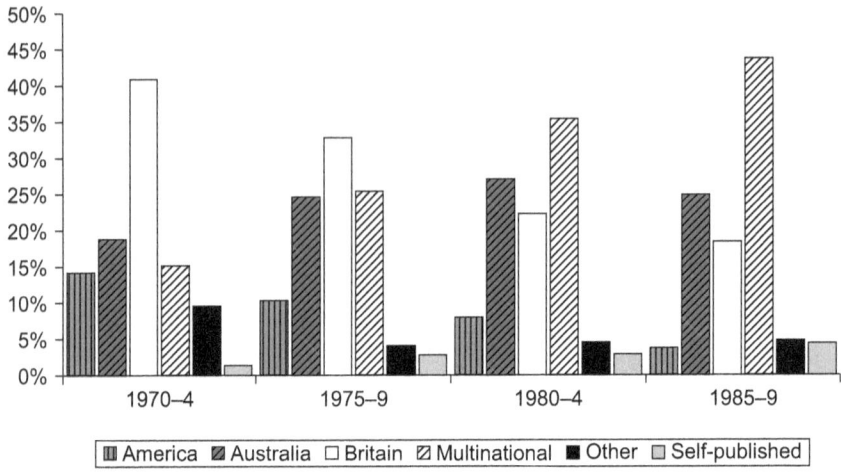

proportion of non-pulp Australian novels published by multinational companies increased from 15 per cent in the early 1970s, to 25 per cent in the late 1970s, 35 per cent in the early 1980s and 44 per cent in the late 1980s (or 7 to 15, 28 and 37 per cent, respectively, if pulp fiction is included).[98] Comparing the proportion of non-pulp Australian novels published by the two groups reveals that, in the 1980s, multinational publishers were responsible for approximately 60 per cent more titles than local publishers.[99] If we take a longer view of the field – as shown in Figure 10[100] – it is clear that what occurred in the 1970s and 1980s was an extension of earlier trends: in particular, the ongoing decline of local publishing in concert with the rise of multinational publishers.

Categorising multinational publishers is not a straightforward process. On the one hand, and although I have not done so, there are arguments for including a number of the major British publishers of Australian novels – especially those with long-established branches or offices in Australia, such as Collins, Macmillan and Hutchinson – in this category. The *OED* defines multinational as 'a company or other organization: operating in several or many countries',[101] which certainly encompasses these British presses. Moreover, in the 1970s and 1980s, these British publishers expanded through the acquisition of other publishers, a common strategy of multinational conglomerates.[102] I chose not to employ this expansive definition of multinational because of the dedication of these British presses to book publishing. In contrast, multinational conglomerates such as Torstar, Pearson and News Corporation engaged, as Galligan puts it, in 'publishing as part of the entertainment industry',[103] a lack of specialism generally perceived to reflect an economic system where the aim of maximising shareholder profits is privileged to the detriment of literary, including local literary, production. Conversely, I have categorised some companies – such as Panmacmillan, Random House and Hodder Headline – as multinational even though they focus predominantly on book publishing.

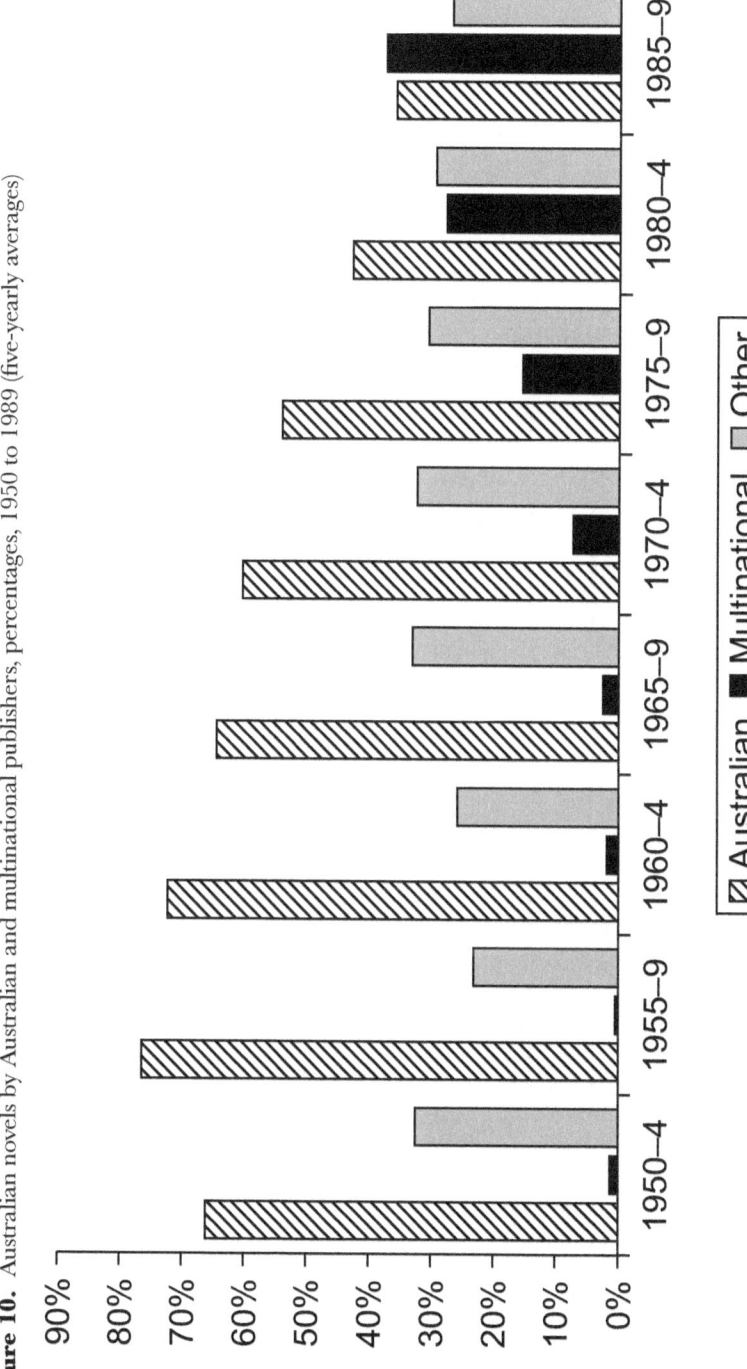

Figure 10. Australian novels by Australian and multinational publishers, percentages, 1950 to 1989 (five-yearly averages)

This approach accords with other critical descriptions of these companies,[104] and also recognises their creation via the merger or acquisition of smaller publishers: Panmacmillan was created through a merger of Pan and Macmillan; Hodder Headline is the result of the merger of Hodder and Stoughton with Headline; and Random House expanded dramatically in the 1980s through the acquisition of companies such as Crown Publishing Group, Chatto and Windus, Virago, Bodley Head, Jonathan Cape and Century Hutchinson.

Bearing in mind these complexities of definition, as Table 6 shows, the major multinational publishers of Australian novels in the 1970s and 1980s were Torstar, with 451 titles, followed by Pearson with 151, Australia-based News Corporation (or News Limited, as it was then known) with 88, and Thomson Organisation with 53; but there were many others.[105] As a reflection of the process of acquisition, these multinationals often encompass multiple imprints.[106] For instance, Pearson acquired Longman in 1968; the Penguin Group, including the Allen Lane and Puffin imprints, in 1970; Viking and Kestrel in 1975; Sphere and Hamish Hamilton in 1985; the New American Library and its holdings, including E. P. Dutton and Company, in 1987;[107] Greenhouse Publications in 1988 and McPhee Gribble in 1989. Pearson's incorporation of Greenhouse and McPhee Gribble – two of the 'small independent presses' highlighted in descriptions of local publishing in the 1970s and 1980s[108] – indicates how the multinational acquisition of the large Australian bookseller-publishers, A&R and Rigby, subsequently extended to newer, smaller independents. Tracking Pearson's acquisitions through the Australian novel field thus demonstrates the global spread of this company, as it acquired previously 'independent' British, American and Australian publishers. The same pattern occurs with Australian-based multinationals.[109]

The considerable expansion of multinational publication of Australian novels in the 1970s and 1980s presents a similar challenge to the existing historiography of these decades as the continuing presence of local pulp fiction publishers: both groups signify the incursion of companies – associated with other periods, and with commercialism and a lack of independence – into a field supposedly dominated by culture-led, government-funded publishing. Certainly, the remarkable contrast between the critical attention paid to small independent presses in histories of Australian publishing, and the proportion of titles they published (especially in comparison to local pulp fiction publishers), highlights both the critical focus on literary fiction and the small proportion of the industry considered by academic studies of book publishing. What is particularly significant about the earlier-than-acknowledged involvement of multinationals in the Australian novel field is the concurrence of this trend and the previously described growth in small independent publishers. The entry of multinational publishers into the Australian book market – supposedly in the 1990s and 2000s – is typically identified, first, as a sign of the ascendancy of neo-liberal (or economic rationalist) government policies, and second, as bringing to an end a period of local expansion and prosperity. The fact that multinational publishers were a dominant presence in Australian novel publishing when government funding for this field was at its highest suggests more complex interactions between cultural and economic influences than proposed in existing accounts of the 1970s and 1980s as a 'golden age' of Australian publishing and literature.

III Multinational Domination? 1990s to 2000s

Studies of contemporary Australian publishing routinely identify the 1990s and 2000s as a time of trade deregulation and economic rationalism, resulting in the rise and ascendancy of multinational conglomerates and the end of culturally progressive and independent local publishing. One of the most comprehensive, and cited, of these is Mark Davis's 'The Decline of the Literary Paradigm'. In using Hilary McPhee's memoir *Other People's Words* to characterise Australian publishing prior to the 1990s, Davis summarises and perpetuates what I have described as the 'golden age' view of local publishing:

> Hilary McPhee describes the Australian industry *as it was* in the 1960s, 1970s and 1980s, sparked by cultural nationalism, funded by progressive governments, the product of a nation shaking off a malaise as publishers sought to break away from the British-dominated publishing of the postwar era. This, McPhee says, was a 'creative phase'; it led to the construction of a local canon of literary authors whose titles served as flagships for most local publishers' lists, strongly supported, after 1975, by the Australia Council, founded by the Whitlam Labor government to help fund the arts.[110]

This symbiotic nurturing of Australian culture by government, publishers and authors is an ideal, I have argued, that excludes the pulp fiction and multinational publishers that actually dominated Australian novel publishing in the 1960s, 1970s and 1980s. According to Davis, this period was ended by broad 'social and governmental shifts related to globalisation': in particular, by the way 'successive Australian governments have progressively "opened up" the Australian economy to international competition, ending industry assistance schemes, eliminating remaining tariffs and encouraging exports'.[111]

Where analyses of the 1970s and 1980s list the changes in governmental policy and funding that assisted Australian publishers, Davis identifies a series of decisions arising from globalisation and deregulation in the 1990s and 2000s that negatively impacted Australian publishing. These included 'changes to the copyright law to allow the parallel import of books from the United States in 1991, and the axing by the Howard government in 1996 of the Book Bounty…[t]he introduction in 2000 of GST on all non-food retail products…[producing] for the first time, a sales tax on books' and '[l]ow levels of government funding for literature'.[112] Davis argues that, due to such changes, '[s]ince the mid-1990s the industry has globalised and consolidated to become an information-based business, beholden, in the case of nine out of ten of Australia's top companies, to global media giants'.[113] Interestingly, Davis's argument lacks the nostalgia usually associated with accounts of local publishing in the 1970s and 1980s (including McPhee's memoir). Instead, he argues that the 'literary paradigm…has always required external, non-market support to survive', and thus presents the decline of local publishing as inevitable under the new paradigm of 'neo-liberal marketisation' and globalisation. 'Quite simply', Davis concludes, 'there can be no going back, because the cultural nationalist, protectionist moment is over'.[114]

I will return to this argument, and specifically, to the association Davis draws between (purportedly new) commercialised practices in contemporary publishing and a reduction in Australian literary fiction. First I want to outline two general – overtly different – responses to the perceived ascendancy of multinationals in the current Australian book market, and the relationship of both to the prevailing constructions of local publishing in the 1970s and 1980s as a 'golden age'. While apparently in opposition both make assumptions about the state of Australian publishing in the last two decades based on a perception of multinational publishers as a new phenomenon in the industry.

Some commentators respond to the supposed dominance of multinational publishers with what might be called cautious optimism. David Carter and Anne Galligan, for example, observe that:

> There is broad agreement that there have been major transformations in the structure of publishing over the last decade or two, transformations that have made it harder in general for new Australian books to find a major publisher…and harder for smaller publishers and independent booksellers to survive.

At the same time, they note that 'mainstream publishing has always been a commercial enterprise (and we need to be sceptical of any analysis premised on the notion that publishing has suddenly become "more commercial")'.[115] With a number of other critics, Carter and Galligan also describe how the 'strong commitment to local books and to Australian culture' by editors of multinational publishers, and the movement of personnel between such publishers and local independents, blurs the boundaries between the two groups and complicates the idea that multinational involvement in Australian publishing is inevitably negative for Australian literary culture.[116]

Other commentators explicitly differentiate local from multinational publishers, and associate the presumed ascendancy of the latter with the utter destruction of an independent and culturally committed local publishing industry, and with it, Australian literature. Wilding argues that 'there are hardly any traditional independent publishers left'.[117] With 'the major part of Australian publishing…done by…the big transnational corporations',[118] the market is 'controlled by foreign interests' that are 'importing alien values', leaving the 'shaping of the national literary culture in the hands of interests that have no commitment to that culture…only [to] profit and tax minimisation'.[119] Elsewhere he writes that the 'local publishing product has to compete with a flood of imported books from the USA and England',[120] and that 'publisher after publisher [has been] swallowed by corporate giants' to the extent that '[t]he world of the gentleman publisher with a personal and idiosyncratic involvement in his editorial list, has now been replaced by the massive centralization of a score of transnational conglomerates.'[121] In similar terms, David Myers proposes that, 'With globalisation have come huge media conglomerations of multinational publishers who swamp the limited Australian market with seductive and alluring and imposing publications from the USA, the UK and Europe.'[122] Nathan Hollier argues that 'the Australian publishing industry and market is dominated by a handful of large corporations, themselves generally parts of massive, multi-national conglomerates'.[123] In this context, Hollier claims: 'Australian literature is dying, or at least disappearing; [and]…this is a bad thing, culturally and politically'.[124]

These commentators contrast local and multinational publishing, and defend the local industry, by employing a series of emotive binary oppositions, including national versus foreign, global, imported or alien values; small versus big – or more to the point, huge, massive, giants; culture versus commerce; independent versus compromised or commercial; and even good versus 'bad'. Their descriptions are highly sensational and directed towards producing dread of this foreign influence or invasion: thus, local publishers are 'swallowed by corporate giants' and 'the survival of an independent national culture' is threatened; 'huge media conglomerates…swamp the limited Australian market with seductive and alluring and imposing publications'; and 'a flood of imported books' threatens to drown a 'dying…or disappearing' Australian literature. Simone Murray identifies the 'nationalist' phase of debate about Australian book publishing as an early 1990s phenomenon, arguing that discussion now focuses on 'the future of the book publishing industry itself…in a media environment characterised by the short turnaround times of news media and digital formats'.[125] While I take Murray's point about a widening of debate, these statements from Wilding, Myers and Hollier indicate the continuation of a nationalist tone in some discussion of publishing in the late 1990s and 2000s.

I see this defensively nationalistic response to multinational publishers as the other side of the coin of the celebratory nationalism characterising the view of the 1970s and 1980s as a 'golden age' of local publishing. The dichotomies outlined above, and the clear attempt such commentary makes to limit the available positions of the debate – so that anyone who questions the idea that multinational companies are killing Australian literature is automatically positioned as a neo-liberal supporter of global capitalism – are obviously problematic. But, for my purposes, the most important thing this commentary exposes is the inadequate historicisation of conceptions of Australian publishing. The view that all local publishers are or were culturally progressive and non-commercial cannot accommodate the major historical trend of pulp fiction publishing. And in terms of current industry dynamics, the call for a return to a self-contained literary culture ignores the fact that Australian publishing has never been sealed off from the rest of the world.

While Carter and Galligan have a very different perspective on commercialism in publishing to Wilding, Myers and Hollier, their proposal that 'ownership' of the industry in Australia has shifted significantly 'over the last decade or so', to 'multinational print and/or media and entertainment conglomerate[s]',[126] reveals the same, overly simplistic periodisation of Australian publishing history. This claim of a recent change in ownership ignores the fact that, even in the 1980s, two-fifths (or 40 per cent) of all non-pulp Australian novels (and one and a half times the number produced locally) were published by multinationals. Both groups, in other words, despite their very different opinions about the implications of the trend, assume that multinationals did not publish Australian novels until the 1990s; both also assume that the rise of such companies has essentially brought an era of local publishing to an end. There is a parallel, here, with discussions of pulp fiction publishing, where even those commentators (such as Johnson-Woods and May) who acknowledge the importance of pulp fiction to the history of the Australian novel, maintain that this part of the local publishing industry disappeared

Table 7. Top ten publishers of Australian novels, 1990s and 2000s

Publishers	Nation	# Titles	% Titles
1990s			
1. Torstar	Multinational	373	10
2. Pearson	Multinational	308	9
3. Panmacmillan	Multinational	262	7
4. The Author	Self-published	247	7
5. News Corporation	Multinational	237	7
6. Reed Elsevier	Multinational	142	4
7. Random House	Multinational	132	4
8. Bertelsmann	Multinational	127	4
9. Hodder Headline	Multinational	125	3
10. A&U	Australian	114	3
2000s			
1. Torstar	Multinational	376	9
2. News Corporation	Multinational	349	9
3. Pearson	Multinational	291	7
4. Holtzbrinck	Multinational	282	7
5. Bertelsmann	Multinational	267	7
6. A&U	Australian	248	6
7. The Author	Self-published	150	4
8. Hachette Livre	Multinational	119	3
9. Zeus Publishing	Australian	93	2
10. UQP	Australian	86	2

prior to the 1970s. Both sets of claims about the history of Australian publishing are underpinned by a strict periodisation; and that periodisation itself is based on the view of the 1970s and 1980s as a period of self-contained and culturally progressive publishing activity, where other influences – whether commercial or non-national – were effectively excluded.

Multinational publication of Australian novels certainly increased in the 1990s. As Table 7 shows, with the exception of self-publishing and Allen & Unwin (A&U), all of the top ten publishers of Australian novels in the 1990s were multinationals (Torstar, Pearson, Panmacmillan, News Corporation, Reed Elsevier, Random House, Bertelsmann and Hodder Headline). In this same decade, the proportion of titles published by multinational companies increased markedly, from 33 per cent in the 1980s to 52 per cent.[127] However, this growth was not ongoing in the 2000s. While a number of multinationals remained on, or entered, the top ten publishers of Australian novels (as Table 7 shows) there were also new local publishers on this list, with self-publishers and A&U joined by Zeus Publishing and UQP. The 2000s also witnessed a decline in multinational publication of Australian novels to 48 per cent (progressive through the decade). This overall reduction of multinational publishing in the 2000s, and the rise, in that same decade, of major local publishers (discussed in the next section of this chapter), indicate a more complicated trend than the ongoing and increasing domination of the Australian market by multinational conglomerates.

A number of the multinationals involved in Australian novel publishing in the 1990s have now been subsumed by other corporations, including Random House by Bertelsmann in 1998; Panmacmillan by Holtzbrinck in 1999; and Hodder Headline by Hachette Livre in 2005. While claims of multinational domination tend to imply a homogenous group, such companies engage in the Australian book market in a number of different ways. Some have reduced their publication of Australian novels or vacated this part of the industry altogether in the 1990s and 2000s; others have held steady or increased publication of Australian novels. Both Simon & Schuster and Scholastic – corporations that, unlike most of their competitors, had no acquired stake in the Australian novel field – produced such titles for a few years but then reduced their lists drastically.[128] Other conglomerates began publishing Australian novels when they purchased a company or companies with a prior involvement in the field; but their subsequent manner of vacating, or reducing their involvement in, this aspect of the industry has differed. Reed Elsevier and particularly Torstar greatly increased production of Australian novels before reducing their lists, or losing their market share, from the mid-1990s.[129] In contrast, Hachette Livre acquired a number of companies with a significant investment in publishing Australian novels – including another multinational, Hodder Headline, and the Australian publisher Lothian – only to reduce such publishing almost instantly. Other multinationals maintained or increased production. After acquiring companies (including other multinationals) involved in Australian novel publishing, Bertelsmann and Holtzbrinck published a relatively stable number of titles. Pearson and News Corporation have gone on to publish more Australian novels than the combined output of the companies they acquired in entering the market. As this brief summary shows, the activities of many multinational conglomerates do not conform with the two approaches to publishing commonly ascribed to them: that is, the grab and smash (à la Hachette Livre), or the unstoppable incursion (as may turn out to be the case with Pearson and News Corporation). And it is not that these multinational corporations can be stopped – they may elect to depart the Australian novel field.

Such a departure would obviously please some commentators. But it would not necessarily be positive for Australian authors, nor even for all aspects of Australian publishing. Multinational publishers give Australian authors access to international markets in a way that few local publishers can: Torstar, for instance, has enabled many Australian romance novelists to attain transnational popularity and sales since the 1970s.[130] As the industry becomes increasingly globalised, there are, as Carter and Galligan argue, 'more opportunities than ever before for Australian publishers and authors to sell their books overseas, thus creating new opportunities for publication, profit and profile'.[131] In this sense, globalisation, and the presence of multinationals specifically, is fundamental to what Gelder and Salzman describe as a central characteristic of Australian literature in the 1990s and 2000s: its capacity to travel, and thus, 'to be defined by various kinds of transnationality'.[132] The Australian publishing industry has never been nationally contained, but a significant difference between its openness to British publishers in the nineteenth century (see Chapter 2) and its current openness to multinational publishers is that this latter phase allows greater access by Australian authors to the world, as well as vice versa.

Trends since the 1960s also challenge the prevalent view that multinational participation in the Australian market is concurrent with greater industry concentration. Although Wilding claims that 'sinister things are happening. More and more of the organs of communication are falling into fewer hands',[133] in fact, from the 1960s to the 1990s, the concentration of titles among the top five publishers of Australian novels has decreased in conjunction with increased multinational involvement in the field. The 70 per cent of Australian novels published by the top five companies in the 1960s declined to 61 per cent in the 1970s, 42 per cent in the 1980s, 39 per cent in the 1990s and 30 per cent in the 2000s. In this latter decade, all publishers in the top five were multinational. While 30 per cent is still a significant proportion of Australian novels for five publishers to produce, multinationals in the 2000s were responsible for nothing like the proportion of Australian novels published by local pulp fiction companies until the 1980s.

In the terms set by much existing commentary on multinational publishing in Australia, this reference to pulp fiction will undoubtedly be seen as missing the point, or unjustifiably skewing the argument. This is because such analyses predominantly focus (implicitly or explicitly) on literary (as opposed to popular genre or pulp) fiction, and associate multinational conglomeration with a specific decline in this type of publishing. Davis's work is notable among such commentaries for providing empirical evidence – as well as assertion and explanation – of this purported trend. For this reason (and because my results differ from his) I will concentrate on his study in exploring multinational involvement in the Australian novel field, specifically its relation to earlier commercial practices and its consequences for literary fiction. Davis identifies the growth of multinational conglomerates as one effect of a publishing industry driven by new commercial imperatives. The pursuit of ever-increasing profits and market share has also produced the rise of what he calls 'informationism': data-based methods, such as Nielson BookScan,[134] for tracking book sales in order to maximise profits. According to Davis, this new informationism has motivated a shift towards fast-moving, high-selling products (such as genre and non-fiction) and away from less profitable forms (such as literary fiction).[135]

Davis's description of changes in bestseller lists – pre- and post-BookScan – demonstrates a major way in which the availability of sales data is altering Australian publishing. Before BookScan, literary fiction was the 'cornerstone of the [publishing] industry's self-perception',[136] largely because the symbolically important bestseller lists were 'notoriously filtered':

> Those [publishers] contacted [for sales information] were most often independents in inner-city locations, close to universities. Genre fiction would routinely be omitted from their quick, usually anecdotal, assessment of what was moving in the shop, along with any non-fiction deemed lowbrow and unbecoming.[137]

In contrast, genre fiction and non-fiction are at the top of bestseller lists produced using sales data. Davis describes how BookScan allows booksellers 'to order on the basis of what is already selling according to the lists, creating a self-generating effect' that increases the number of sales of a small number of titles.[138] Publishers, in turn, decide whether to publish a particular book or author based on previous sales, creating a reduction in the number and range of titles published.[139] As Davis writes, 'It was only with the availability of data from sources such as BookScan that publishers began to shift away from a top-down approach to managing culture to a bottom-up, consumer driven understanding of the market.'[140]

An historical awareness of the operations of earlier pulp fiction publishers demonstrates the prior existence of these supposedly new marketing strategies, and supports Carter and Galligan's observation that 'publishing has always been…commercial'.[141] All of the approaches identified by Davis as new to contemporary publishing – including 'increased emphasis on selling books to non-traditional outlets, such as discount and variety stores'[142] – were foundational for pulp fiction publishers such as Cleveland and Horwitz, who sold their titles mainly in newsagents, bookstalls and by postal order. Branding and (as is evident from the number of titles they published) an emphasis on the frontlist and market saturation were also fundamental to their mode of operation. Even the availability of sales data, and the consumer-driven approach to the market this enables, are not new. As May notes in his discussion of Horwitz's business strategies: 'Each month the returns figures provided by Gordon & Gotch enabled Horwitz to modify its future publishing in tune with the marketplace.'[143] The activities of these pulp fiction publishers challenge Davis's view of publishing as newly commercialised – a perspective also evident, for example, in claims such as Thompson's that multinational corporations have ruined what was a 'gentlemanly' pursuit with a focus on sales.[144] Yet it is also apparent that, with the uptake of sales data by non-pulp publishers, strategies previously confined to the pulp end of the market now permeate the book trade.

Drawing on the same *AustLit* database I am using, Davis provides empirical support for his argument that the reliance on sales-data has produced a major shift away from literary to genre fiction by publishers of Australian novels. After extracting from *AustLit* details of each novel title published during three individual years by 'the top ten publishers as ranked by BookScan in 2004'[145] – that is, multinational publishers and A&U[146] – Davis removes from the results all titles ascribed a genre by *AustLit* as well as other novels he considers non-literary. Based on this dataset, Davis concludes that: 'In 1996,…Australia's multinational publishers and Allen & Unwin, the only comparably sized independent, published 60 literary novels between them. In 2004, those same publishers published 32. In 2006 they published 28.'[147] While Davis does not state the proportion of the field these titles constitute, he uses these results to indicate a significant decline in Australian literary fiction, and a paradigm shift in contemporary Australian publishing.

My analysis of the data suggests a reduction of 22 per cent,[148] as opposed to more than 100 per cent in Davis's results, in Australian literary novels published from 1996 to 2004. Moreover, while Davis's results imply a sudden decline from the mid-1990s, mine indicate that the proportion of literary novels has fallen gradually since the late 1970s. Some caution is necessary in interpreting these results. While *AustLit* identifies popular genres, it has no category for literary fiction. A spot-check of *AustLit* records against novels that would generally be considered literary indicates that such titles are simply not allocated a genre. Admittedly, this is a broad way of defining literary fiction – as those titles without a genre in *AustLit* – but it is consistent with the way that literary and genre

Figure 11. Australian genre/non-genre novels, percentages, 1970 to 2009 (two-yearly averages)

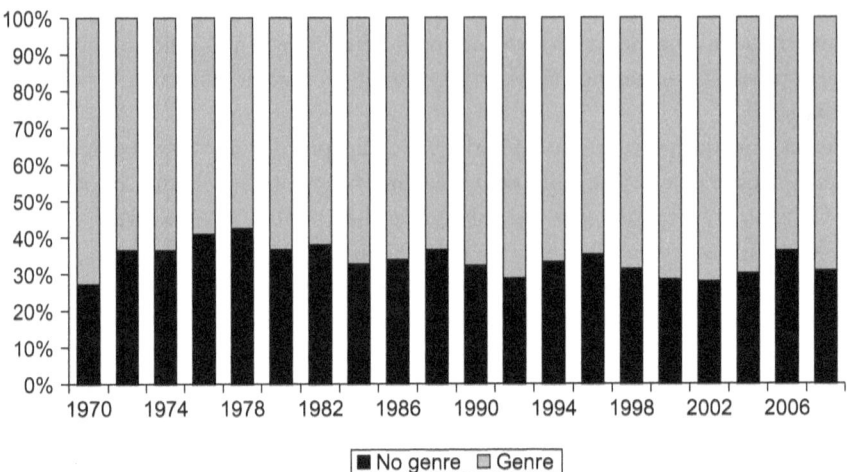

fiction are defined in opposition to one another and, more specifically, with the position of literary fiction as the invisible and normalised standard in literary studies. Figure 11 thus depicts genre novels as a proportion of total novel titles published from 1970 to 2009 (in two year moving averages), with the implication that the remainder (the non-genre titles) should represent the general trend in publication of Australian literary fiction.

The growth in the proportion of literary (or non-genre) novels until the late 1970s indicated by this graph suggests that increased government funding for, and protection of, such writing was concurrent with a fractional (rather than a field-changing) rise in the publication of literary fiction as a proportion of all novels. If an effect of government funding, this trend is neither as significant nor as sustained as accounts of these decades maintain. One might suppose that restricting the survey to Australian publishers, but excluding Horwitz and Cleveland, would reveal growth in the proportion of literary (or non-genre) novels through the 1970s and 1980s, but Figure 12 shows this is not the case. This approach simply amplifies the trends shown in Figure 11, such that there is substantial growth in the proportion of literary (non-genre) novels until the late 1970s followed by a steep decline in this proportion. In neither graph is there an acceleration of this decline since the mid-1990s, as Davis argues, or since 2000 when BookScan was introduced into Australia. In fact, in both graphs there is a slight increase in the proportion of non-genre titles in the late 2000s.

These conflicting results can be explained not only by my longitudinal approach – as opposed to Davis's focus on the years in which he assumes a decline would occur – but by the different spectrum of publishers examined:[149] while I include all novel titles, regardless of their publisher, Davis analyses the output of the top ten publishers, according to BookScan data. Davis's approach (which aims to survey what is sold, not just what is published) has the benefit of excluding self- and subsidy-published titles (the growth in which I will discuss shortly). Although they are included in *AustLit*, until very recently it was fair to presume that such titles reached a limited number of readers. I can see why

Figure 12. Australian genre/non-genre novels published in Australia (excluding Horwitz and Cleveland titles), percentages, 1970 to 2009 (two-yearly averages)

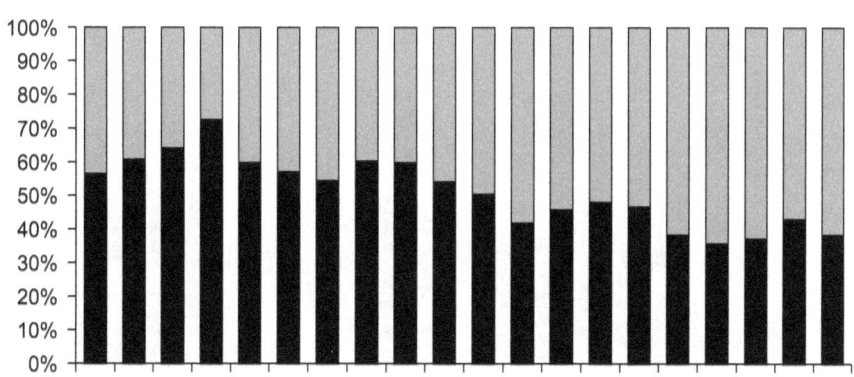

Davis wishes to limit his sample; but attempting to identify trends in the publication of literary fiction – a form that, as he demonstrates, sells fewer copies than genre fiction – by only considering the output of the ten publishers that sell the most titles, seems to me problematic.

Davis's study in fact demonstrates the declining proportion of Australian literary novels published by A&U and multinational companies, a modified conclusion that my comparison of all multinational (and A&U) and non-multinational (minus A&U) publishers supports (although my results also show this trend to have begun earlier than Davis proposes). As Figure 13 indicates, in the 1970s, genre fiction comprised a relatively similar proportion of both groups' Australian novel publications. From the 1980s through to the mid-1990s, A&U and multinationals published a greater proportion of genre titles while the rest of the field reduced theirs. From 1996 to 1999, multinational publishers and A&U were responsible for approximately 30 per cent more genre fiction than the other publishers. In the second half of the 1990s and early 2000s, both groups published an increased proportion of genre titles, but the trend was more pronounced among non-multinational publishers (an attempt, perhaps, to compete with multinationals in an increasingly 'commercialised' and 'homogenised' market). The proportion of genre titles published by both groups decreased in the 2000s. However, multinational publishers and A&U were still responsible for 16 per cent more genre titles than other publishers of Australian novels.

Davis uses trends in the output of A&U and multinationals to generalise about trends in the publication of Australian literary fiction generally because he takes for granted that these publishers have monopolised the industry.[150] However, while multinational publishers were responsible for a substantial proportion of Australian novels in the 1990s and 2000s, as I will demonstrate in the following section, only attending to their output ignores half the field, and thus overlooks important trends in both contemporary Australian novel publishing and the local industry.

Figure 13. Australian genre novels by category of publisher, percentages, 1970 to 2009 (two-yearly averages)

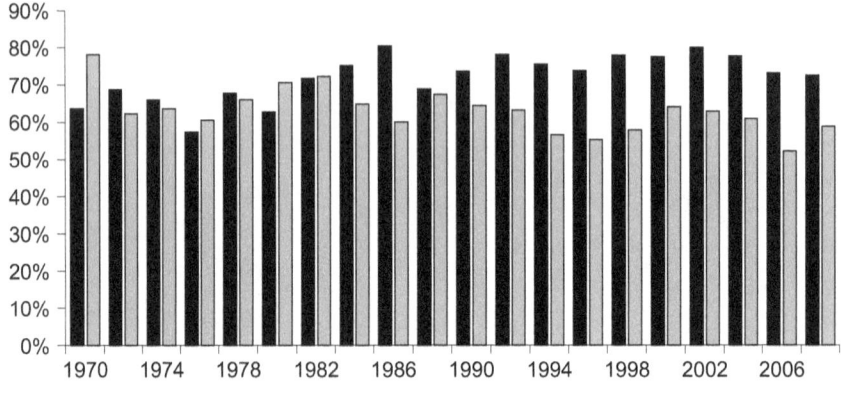

■ Proportion of genre novels published by multinationals and Allen & Unwin
□ Proportion of genre novels published by non-multinationals minus Allen & Unwin

IV The End of Local Publishing? 1990s to 2000s

In terms of Australian publishing in the 1990s and 2000s, significantly more attention is paid to multinational than to non-multinational, including local, publishing. This is a direct reversal of the critical focus in respect to the 1970s and 1980s, and an effect, I would suggest, of the narrative trajectory of contemporary Australian literary and publishing history. Specifically, the construction of the 1990s and 2000s as the fall from an earlier 'golden age' means that these decades are associated with the demise or death of local publishing and Australian literary fiction. In direct contradiction of this preconception, non-multinational presses published a substantial and increasing proportion of Australian novels: 48 per cent in the 1990s and 52 per cent in the 2000s. Perhaps even more surprisingly, given the widespread perception that publishing is globalising, the vast majority of non-multinational publishers of Australian novels were Australian-based, and the proportion of locally published titles has increased in the context of competition from multinationals. What had been a successive decline, since the 1950s, in local publication of Australian novels stabilised in the 1990s at 32 per cent of titles. In the 2000s, local publishing increased to represent 38 per cent of Australian novels published in the first half of that decade, and 40 per cent in the second. In the 1990s, the number of local publishers of Australian novels increased markedly: from 205 in the 1980s to 399 in the 1990s. But in the 2000s, as multinational publication of Australian novels declined and local publication increased, the number of Australian publishers participating in this field fell to 348.[151] In the context of these trends, other-national – including American and British – involvement in the Australian novel field declined to represent only 8 per cent of titles published in the 1990s and 2000s.

Obviously, growth in the proportion of Australian novels published locally in the 2000s challenges claims regarding the lethal effects for the local industry of multinational involvement in the Australian book market. Although multinationals continued to play a major role in the Australian novel field, with the retreat of other-national publishers and the growth in local publication of Australian novels, there is no clear trend of globalisation. At the same time, given the emphasis, in discussion of the 1970s and 1980s, on growth in the number of local publishers as a sign of that industry's prosperity, the decline in this number in the 2000s might appear to indicate a demise in local publishing.

The remainder of this chapter will look in depth at the non-multinational half of the Australian novel field, and at the local industry in particular. I begin by arguing that, despite the seemingly contradictory trends outlined above, close analysis of Australian publication of Australian novels in the 1990s and 2000s reveals a notable strengthening and consolidation of the local industry. Following this, and as a corrective to the lack of attention to non-multinational publishing in the 1990s and 2000s, I map out some of the major trajectories and dynamics in this growing area of the Australian novel field. I do this by exploring the ways in which non-multinational publishers describe their agendas and orientations in the publishing industry, particularly by drawing on self-descriptions – or publicity statements – on publishers' websites; I consider both traditional presses and the strongly emerging category of self- and subsidy publishing. While these self-descriptions are in no way disinterested, analysis of them provides insights into ongoing, as well as emerging, frameworks shaping contemporary publishing, especially regarding the relationship between national identity, literary production, aesthetic value and commodity culture.

Figure 14 concerns only locally published Australian novels. It shows the proportion published, from the 1970s to the 2000s, by companies categorised according to how many other Australian novel titles they produced per decade. This graph demonstrates the relative concentration of local publishing in the 1970s and 1980s compared with the 1990s and 2000s. The dominance (albeit declining) of Horwitz and Cleveland – the only publishers with more than 100 titles each in the two earlier decades – is apparent, and is compounded by the considerable distance between these companies and the rest of the field. In the 1980s, no local companies published between 50 and 99 Australian novels; only one published between 20 and 49 (UQP); and only three published 10 to 19 titles (Hale & Iremonger, Hyland House and Fremantle Press).[152] There was also a notable increase in this decade – from 6 to 23 per cent – in the proportion of Australian novels published by companies responsible for only one or two titles. In other words, in respect to Australian novel publishing, the local industry of the 1980s is both top and bottom heavy: pulp fiction publishers continued to dominate, and there were multiple companies with what might be called an ad hoc, or incidental, involvement in this field: they published one or two titles, but their participation was not sustained. In contrast, there was a relative absence of publishers in the middle band: companies that, with between 10 and 99 Australian novel titles in the decade, demonstrated a sustained commitment to such publishing. Indeed, in the 1980s, only 11 per cent of locally published titles came from companies responsible for between 10 and 99 titles.

The growth, in the 1980s, at the lower end of the publishing spectrum continued in the 1990s, when a third of locally published novels were by companies responsible for only one or two titles that decade. In the 2000s, however, this ad hoc element of the local

Figure 14. Proportion of locally published Australian novels by companies categorised by the number of Australian novels published per decade, 1970 to 2009 (by decade)

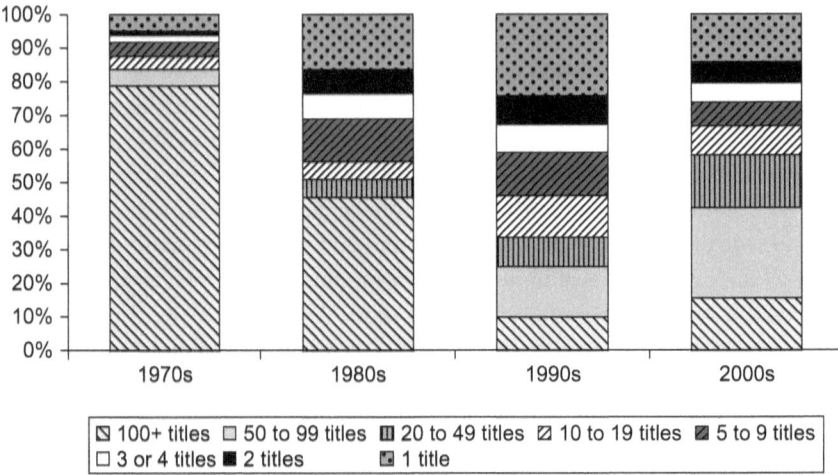

industry contracted to 20 per cent, thus constituting a less significant contribution to Australian novel publication than was the case in either the 1980s or 1990s. The fall in the number of local publishers from the 1990s to the 2000s is largely attributable to the contraction in this ad hoc portion of the industry. From this perspective, rather than a sign of multinational encroachment, the reduction in the number of local publishers of Australian novels in the 2000s – especially given its occurrence in the context of overall growth in local publication of such titles – suggests the emergence of a more established and dedicated local industry.

This understanding of contemporary publishing is reinforced by the growth, through the 1990s and 2000s, in the middle section of the local field: that is, publishers of between 10 and 99 titles. Although these decades supposedly represent the decline of the industry, the number of local publishers of between 50 and 99 titles increased from none in the 1980s to two in the 1990s (UQP and Cleveland) and six in the 2000s (Zeus, UQP, Lothian, Text Publishing, Fremantle Press and Sid Harta). In these two decades there was also considerable growth in publishers of between 20 and 49 titles, from three in the 1990s (Fremantle, Horwitz and Openbook) to ten in the 2000s (Ginninderra, Seaview, Wakefield, Jacobyte Books, Black Dog, Scribe, ABC Books, Brandl and Schlesinger, the Australian National University Press and Equilibrium Books). Eleven publishers in the 1990s and ten in the 2000s were responsible for between 10 and 19 titles, a significant increase from the three publishers in this category in the 1980s.[153] The increased number of local presses in these middle categories was accompanied by significant growth in the proportion of titles they produced: compared with 11 per cent in the 1980s, in the 1990s Australian publishers with 10 to 99 Australian novels published 36 per cent of local output; in the 2000s, this increased to 51 per cent. For both the 1990s and 2000s, A&U was the only local publisher with more than 100 titles, and the absence of other large local presses is often taken as a sign of the vulnerability of the Australian industry and literary culture. However, the considerable expansion in this middle band suggests a diverse local industry with a substantial and growing commitment to Australian literature.

As I said previously, analysis of publishers' self-descriptions or publicity statements provides insight into discursive frameworks that have currency in, and provide a structure to, the contemporary industry. In direct contrast to the widespread perception that publishing has globalised, many local publishers of Australian novels in the 1990s and 2000s express the specific commitment to Australian authors, writing and culture typically seen as characteristic of local publishing in the 1970s and 1980s. The self-descriptions of such publishers usually begin with the claim of being an 'independent Australian publisher' or 'small independent Australian publisher'. Publishers in this group include established presses such as A&U, Hale & Iremonger, Hyland House and Wakefield Press, as well as multiple, newer operations, including Text Publishing, Interactive Press, Giramondo Publishing, Otford Press, Indra Publishing, Scribe, Artemis Publishing, Ibis Books, Papyrus Press, Five Islands Press, Hunter Publishers, Bystander Press, Ackland Press, Spinifex Press, Puncher & Wattmann, Sleepers Publishing, Vanark Press and Bideena Press. Closely related to this group – and also an extension of a trend usually associated with the 1970s and 1980s in Australian publishing history – are those publishers that express dedication to the authors or writing of a particular Australian region, including Fremantle Press, Red Hill Books, Catchfire Press, Montpelier Press, Boris Books and Esperance Press.

Like these region-affiliated presses, most publishers that identify as 'Australian' also highlight their strong commitment to specifically Australian writing or authors: Hyland House 'produc[es] quality Australian titles';[154] Hale & Iremonger 'publish[es] quality Australian books';[155] Ibis 'publish[es] Australian authors';[156] Interactive Press 'specialis[es] in high quality Australian literary titles';[157] Puncher & Wattmann publishes 'quality Australian writing';[158] Bystander Press 'publish[es] both new and established Australian writers',[159] as does Sleepers Publishing, which is 'dedicated to supporting and promoting emerging and established writers in Australia';[160] Papyrus gives 'Australian authors of diverse cultural backgrounds the due recognition they deserve';[161] Bideena Publishing (with its Goanna Press imprint) is interested in 'character-driven stories about Australia by Australian authors';[162] Triple D Books is 'dedicated to the preservation of essential Australian culture';[163] and JoJo Publishing's tagline is 'Proudly supporting AUSTRALIAN authors'.[164] The publisher, Australian in Every Way, expresses its national commitment in its very name.

For the publishers that explicitly identify as 'Australian', this commitment to Australian authors and writing can extend to an alignment with a specifically national readership. The Hornets Nest [sic], for instance, describes itself as 'a small publishing/literary group which the Australian reading market is currently buzzing about';[165] Ackland Press aims to 'oppose the junk culture' by 'reinstating history within the Australian consciousness';[166] and Otford Press 'publishes titles on national and international issues of relevance to Australia'.[167] Other publishers, both large and small, that highlight their location in Australia, affiliate themselves with both national and transnational readerships: Black Dog Books' website states, 'Our outlook is unashamedly Australian, but our stories are universal';[168] Duffy and Snellgrove published writing by 'Australian and overseas writers';[169] Brandl and Schlesinger, 'one of Australia's most renowned independent publishers', publishes 'books…that appeal to both the national and international market';[170] and 'Fontaine Press…work[s] with both Australian and internationally based authors, publishing a wide range of quality publications for the Australian market, and beyond'.[171]

These explicit references to the market – on the Brandl and Schlesinger and Fontaine Press websites – are rare in the self-descriptions of 'independent Australian publishers'. Such presses tend to imply – or directly state – their commitment to culture over commerce. For most nation- or region-identified publishers, this commitment is expressed in terms of encouraging, supporting or nurturing Australian writers, especially first-time authors. Brandl and Schlesinger's appeal to the market is set alongside its aim to 'publish and nurture first time authors';[172] Text Publishing believes 'there [are] more good writers in Australia than publishers to look after them, and this would be our opportunity';[173] Giramondo 'was set up…with the aim of publishing quality creative and interpretive writing by Australian authors…and to encourage innovative and adventurous work that might not otherwise find publication because of its subtle commercial appeal';[174] Vanark Press is '[i]nterested primarily in giving innovative, young and new voices a start in literary publication';[175] and Fremantle Press aims 'to promote, encourage and provide the widest possible audience for Western Australian writers and artists'.[176] There are many more.[177] Some of these publishers make their commitment to culture over commerce even more explicit, as in Finlay Lloyd's expressed 'aim of adding a different approach to a cluttered but overly homogenised industry…publish[ing] books that excite its four collaborators without concern for whether they turn a profit';[178] Post Press's openness to submissions by 'authors of specialist works or those with intrinsic worth but for which the market is limited';[179] and Independence Jones's 'philosophy…[that] we publish books that matter to us'.[180] Despite claims of a demise in local publishing, there seems little to distinguish these nation- and region-identified publishers of the 1990s and 2000s from the celebrated, independent, culturally committed publishers of the 1970s and 1980s: except for the important fact that there are many more such publishers – publishing more novels – in these more recent decades.[181]

Most of the publishers I have discussed to this point focus on literary fiction, often referred to on their websites as 'quality' writing.[182] However, a national identification is also common among local genre fiction publishers, despite the critical perception of such writing and publishing as 'transnational'.[183] Australian-based genre fiction publishers such as Aphelion Publications, Pulp Fiction Press, Eidolon Books, MirrorDanse Books and Coeur de Lion describe themselves as specifically 'Australian', and in a number of cases, as dedicated to writing by Australian authors. MirrorDanse, for instance, 'aims to publish the best in Australian horror and science fiction',[184] while Coeur de Lion advertises itself as '[m]akers of fine Australian speculative fiction'.[185] I have found one Australian-based genre fiction publisher that does not identify as such: Eneit Press publishes 'dark fiction in its many forms'.[186] But the general tendency for such publishers to describe themselves as Australian resonates with the self-descriptions of literary publishers, and presents a marked contrast with a number of the other-national (mainly American) genre fiction publishers also involved in the Australian novel field in the 1990s and 2000s.

While larger, established American publishers in this group – namely, Dorchester and Kensington – describe themselves as 'American', this national epithet does not feature in the self-descriptions of smaller, newer American genre fiction publishers such as Mundania Press, ImaJinn, Ellora's Cave, PrimeBooks, Heartsong Presents, Hasbro/Wizards, MonkeyBrain and Active Bladder.

The lack of explicit national identifications by these smaller American genre fiction publishers seems related to their focus on a specific genre, or even specific forms within a specific genre. The following examples are all American-based romance fiction publishers responsible for Australian novels in the 1990s and/or the 2000s: Heartsong Presents (with 4 titles in these decades) publishes romance with Christian values;[187] ImaJinn (14) concentrates on romance dealing with 'the supernatural, paranormal, fantasy, futuristic and time travel';[188] and Ellora's Cave (3) specialises in romance themes such as 'ménage or more', 'capture/bondage', 'werewolf/shapeshifter' and 'interracial element'.[189] The specificity of these sub-genres – and the extensive reach of the Internet – makes it likely that an Australian author wishing to write a romance novel featuring (for instance) a werewolf, would have read other Ellora's Cave titles, and (as long as they were writing in English) be inclined to submit to that publisher regardless of where it is located. Conversely, I would suggest that most Australian-based genre fiction publishers identify as such because Australian science fiction (for example) is constructed as its own specific form of the genre within an increasingly specialised, but globally connected, market. As Aphelion Publications announces on its website, 'Australian Science Fiction is said to be in a Golden Age, and Aphelion is proud to be part of it.'[190] While this publisher may have a sincere commitment to supporting and promoting Australian science fiction, the specifically Australian form of the genre also provides a way for Aphelion Publications to distinguish its product within the large English-language market. This strategy is not restricted to genre fiction publishers.

A commitment to specifically Australian authors and writing also appears in the self-descriptions of another group of publishers whose affiliations one might also assume to be more transnational than national: presses committed to women's writing. There are local feminist presses that do not identify as Australian, such as Detour Press, which describes itself in explicitly transnational terms as:

> [A]n independent publishing house that rose from the patriarchal, capitalist arrangement called western modernity, gritted our teeth and spat all over the system that closes its gates to anyone but the white/hetero/cashed up/male. You will open we proclaim from the tops of our feminist voices and so we created the gate, the room, the house and the view.[191]

But most local publishers in this category specifically describe themselves as Australian. Although characterising its 'reach [as] from the local to the international', Spinifex Press's Australian orientation is evident in its self-description as 'an independent Australian feminist press' whose 'namesake is an Australian desert grass that holds the earth together'.[192] Likewise, Artemis Publishing 'is committed to…stories by women from all parts of Australia'.[193] While American companies dominated among the other-national publishers of Australian genre fiction in the 1990s and 2000s, most non-Australian women's or feminist publishers of Australian novels were British. As with the genre fiction publishers, the tendency for Australian-based women's presses to identify with the nation stands in contrast to these British publishers' invocation of a specifically transnational community of women. For instance, The Women's Press describes itself as 'dedicated to publishing incisive feminist fiction and non-fiction by outstanding women writers from all around the world',[194] while Black Lace identifies with 'world-leading erotic fiction written by women for women'.[195] Like the Australian companies, Poolbeg Press – marketed as 'Ireland's number one publisher of Irish fiction for women'[196] – aligns itself with a specific national category. This parallel implies that, for publishers in small English-speaking markets (like Australia and Ireland, and unlike England and America) the national identification provides a means of differentiation within the broader category of women's or feminist publishing.

Probably the largest category of non-Australian publishers of Australian novels in this period are those committed to gay and lesbian writing. In contrast to the involvement in the Australian novel local as well as overseas publishers of genre and women's writing, I have been able to identify only one dedicated Australian gay and lesbian publisher in the 1990s and 2000s: Outlaw Press, responsible for one Australian novel in the 1990s.[197] Most gay and lesbian publishers of such titles in these decades are American-based, and align themselves not with a particular nation, but with a transnational community of gay and lesbian writers and readers. They include Naiad Press (22 titles), Bella Books (11), Alyson Books (5), Green Candy (1) and Torquere Press (1) as well as British-based Gay Men's Press (8).

While it is true of many, not all local publishers of Australian novels in the 1990s and 2000s identify as Australian. Such publishers can be divided into what we might call 'traditional' and 'non-traditional' categories. I will return to the non-traditional – and significantly larger – side of this equation shortly. The traditional category is mainly comprised of small literary publishers that portray their activities as specifically opposed to multinational or mainstream publishing. For instance, Local Consumption Publications describes its 'intention…to sideswipe the low-risk, middle brow publishing climate driven by multinationals, profit margins and predictability';[198] Cottage Industry Press identifies as 'a small operation, unaffiliated with any of the global publishing monsters… No shareholders, no market-driven publishing schedule, no water cooler';[199] and 'Exisle produces the kind of books that the very big publishers do not'.[200] The most prolific publisher of Australian novels in this group, Ginninderra Press, with 4 titles in the 1990s and a substantial 42 in the 2000s, was

> set up in 1996 to provide opportunities for new and emerging authors as well as for authors writing in unfashionable genres or on non-mainstream subjects. The press recognises that there are many more worthwhile manuscripts than mainstream publishers can publish.

Interestingly, Ginninderra Press explicitly distances itself from the government-funded publishing paradigm praised in many academic analyses of Australian publishing in the 1970s and 1980s, stating that it 'chooses to operate without any direct subsidies from the public purse. The press believes that works requiring subsidies are of their nature likely to be only marginally commercially viable and subsidies encourage over-production.'[201]

Arguably, these non-nation identified local publishers have more in common with some of the (declining number of) other-national publishers of Australian literary titles – such as British-based Serpent's Tail, which aims to publish 'extravagant, outlaw voices neglected by the mainstream'[202] – than with their Australian-identified counterparts. But the alignment with independence – and against multinational or mainstream publishing – is also something that traverses the entire non-multinational publishing field, Australian and otherwise. Virtually every one of the Australian-identified literary publishers discussed above identifies as 'independent'. Sometimes this term is specifically aligned with the local industry – as is the case with Wakefield Press, which describes its twenty-first birthday celebrations in 2010 as 'mark[ing] the ongoing survival of an increasingly threatened bird, an independent Australian book publishing company'.[203] However, a number of nation-identified Australian publishers assert independence more explicitly in opposition to multinational or mainstream publishing. Brandl and Schlesinger is 'committed to publishing books that are often overlooked by the multi-national conglomerate publishers';[204] Bideena Press 'facilitate[s] publication of fresh new fiction by emerging authors who have exhausted their efforts at seeking publication from larger publishers';[205] and Finlay Lloyd 'add[s] a new voice to what we feel is a cluttered but overly homogenised industry'.[206]

Claims of independence are not restricted to literary fiction publishers. Most genre fiction publishers describe themselves as independent. For instance, Dorchester is 'the oldest independent mass market publisher in America',[207] while Pulp Fiction Press is 'an independent Australian publisher'.[208] A number of the smaller genre fiction publishers also explicitly distinguish themselves from particular manifestations of the 'mainstream': American-based Heartline Presents was created with the aim of 'fill[ing] the gap between Mills & Boon and Mainstream fiction',[209] while Australian-based MirrorDanse publishes 'genres traditionally neglected by mainstream Australian publishers'.[210]

Independence, then, emerges as a claim – or identification – that unites the spectrum of non-multinational publishers, regardless of the country in which they are based or the type of fiction they publish. It is important to acknowledge the commercial purpose of these assertions. When (the now defunct) 'independent' British publisher Aquila Books expresses the 'hope you will help us to keep the market for independent literature alive',[211] the identification this statement encourages between publisher and reader (if you buy our books you are independent) obviously aims to increase sales as well as to express a view on directions in contemporary publishing. Australian-based publisher Blackwash Press ironically highlights the promotional potential of claims of 'independence', saying on its website, 'we have nothing against big publishers based in the CBD, and indeed one day would like to become one, but for the moment we're pushing this independent schtick for all we're worth'.[212] Despite its role as a marketing strategy, this alignment with independence – and the explicit refusal of multinational publishing that often accompanies it – works against analyses of contemporary publishing that maintain a strict separation between Australian and non-Australian publishers. This widespread claim of independence, in other words, while often made with reference to the value of Australian authors, publishers and readers, also surpasses the national boundaries that some commentators retain as the basis for their discussions of this value.

As with claims of independence, the strong national identification of many local publishers – including the literary ones – needs to be understood as both a philosophical position and a marketing strategy. Just as Australian genre fiction and women's presses use their Australianness as a point of differentiation within a globalised market, national identification represents an easily deployable way for local literary publishers to carve out a space within the large, English-language book market. But even if commercial purposes are implicated, the strong, and increasingly consolidated presence of 'Australian independents' in the 1990s and 2000s contradicts the common perception that multinational conglomeration supplanted and ended the expansion of the Australian publishing industry. At least in respect to the Australian novel, the two trends are concurrent during these decades, as they were in the 1970s and 1980s.

Indeed, this survey of self-descriptions of non-multinational publishers suggests that the globalisation and consolidation of the industry, on the one hand, has motivated and enabled a foregrounding of national (and to a lesser extent, regional) identifications on the other. As is especially apparent in the publicity statements of the nation-identified presses that criticise multinational publishing, the nation functions as a concept or device for positioning publishers in the industry, one that invests a particular authority – cultural and even moral – in the commercial activities of those publishers. Independence and culture-led publishing are devices in the same sense. Although these sometimes function separately from the nation, for the most part they accrue meaning in relation to it: independence and culture-led publishing are, in other words, mobilised in support of a national culture deemed authentic in comparison with the non-culture (or contamination) multinationals are seen to represent. It seems probable that this trend extends beyond Australia, and that the reduced presence of American, British and other-national publishers in the Australian novel field in the 1990s and 2000s is at least partly the result of a concurrent national-orientation of publishers from other countries in the face of multinational conglomeration, deregulating and globalisation. However, the small proportion of titles by non-Australian, non-multinational publishers also signals the ongoing expansion of multinationals, as British companies such as Fourth Estate and Headline are subsumed into conglomerates (News Corporation and Hodder Headline respectively).

The meaning of the nation in these industry self-representations contrasts with Pascale Casanova's conception of the conservative implications of this concept in her influential book, *The World Republic of Letters*. Casanova describes a global shift, in the nineteenth and twentieth centuries, from nation-identified literary fiction (which she sees functioning as a tool and support of the nation state, and as the most conservative literary tendency) toward a world literary republic (centred on cities like Paris and the transnational literary communities and systems of acclaim they represent). Only when literature is 'freed from the obligation to help to develop a particular national identity' and authors escape 'literary spaces on the "periphery"' – such as Australia – can pure writing and literary modernisation occur.[213] For Casanova, autonomy or independence is a characteristic of literary fiction, which she sees as threatened almost as much by allegiance to a nation as by the 'rise of multinational conglomerates' and the equally transnational, but not autonomous, commercialised sphere with which these publishers are aligned.[214] The manner in which Australian literary publishers deploy national literary identifications in opposition to multinational conglomerates may, in Casanova's terms, represent a return to conservative literary nationalism. But for countries such as Australia on the periphery of world literary culture, this identification with the nation functions as a privileged expression of resistance to global capital, even as it provides a standpoint from which to engage with and operate in that market.

I want to turn, now, from 'traditional' publishers of Australian novels, located in Australia and elsewhere, to forms of non-traditional publishing – specifically, self- and subsidy publishing – responsible for an increasing proportion of Australian novels in the 1990s and 2000s. Self-publishers have had a presence in the Australian novel field throughout its history but, with the exception of the late 1940s,[215] until the 1970s such publishing represented a very small proportion of titles. Since this time, self-publication of Australian novels has grown from 1 per cent of titles (1970–4) to 2 per cent (1975–9 and 1980–4), 4 per cent (1985–9), 5 per cent (1990–4) and 8 per cent (1995–9), before declining through the 2000s, to 5 per cent (2000–4) and 4 per cent (2005–9). While these percentages may seem small, placed in the context of other trends in the Australian novel field their significance becomes apparent: for instance, in the second half of the 1980s, the 4 per cent of self-published Australian novels exceeded the 2 per cent of titles published in America.

Michael Webster describes an 'explosion' in self- (or 'vanity') publishing 'towards the end of the century', which he attributes to 'the lower cost of entry that computer technology was then offering'.[216] Its growth since the 1970s – and indeed, its appearance in the nineteenth century, as noted in Chapter 2 – shows that self-publishing is a trend with a considerably longer history and more gradual development. Nevertheless, the substantial 8 per cent of self-published Australian novels in the late 1990s supports Webster's association of this trend with new technology, as does the relatively common practice, from this time, of Australian authors creating their own websites to publicise their novels. Examples of this phenomenon include Trojan Press, Golgatha Graphics, Great Bosses, Turkey Tracks Press, Deep End Press and Blencowe Books.[217] The highly professional appearance of many of these websites means it is sometimes difficult to distinguish self-publishers from 'traditional' small presses based on their web presence. While the role of technology in enabling new publishers to enter the contemporary industry and market is frequently discussed – and indeed, features prominently in the self-descriptions of many small presses[218] – perhaps under-recognised is the extent to which technology allows self-publishers to present themselves in similar terms to other small presses. There are already examples of technology overcoming self-publishers' traditional lack of access to readers,[219] but more time is needed to see whether this phenomenon will come to characterise self-publishing more broadly.

Where the growth in self-publication of Australian novels in the 1990s lends support to the association of this practice with new technologies, its decline in the 2000s appears to contradict this argument. In fact, this apparent contradiction can be explained by the considerable growth, especially in the 2000s, in Australian subsidy publishing.

A self-publisher funds the entire production of their work, and organises every aspect of its creation and distribution. Subsidy publishing is still author-funded, but these companies provide – and charge a fee for – services such as editing, design, legal advice, printing, distribution, sales and publicity. A number of subsidy publishers describe themselves as providing a 'self-publishing service', and some produce non-subsidised as well as subsidised works. British-based publisher Janus Books – responsible for three Australian novels in the 1990s – offers subsidy, non-subsidy and self-publishing, and explains the difference between these services as follows: self-publishing is for people 'on a budget', as it allows authors to choose the services they want the publisher to provide;[220] subsidy publishing 'combines the professionalism and skill set of the trade publisher alongside the financial commitment of self-publishing';[221] access to Janus's non-subsidy publishing arm (through its Empiricus imprint) is reserved for writers with 'a literary agent'.[222] As these distinctions help to indicate, the identification of a subsidy publisher is rarely straightforward. In categorising them, I have simply tried to identify publishers that charge authors a fee.[223]

On this basis, I estimate that 2 per cent of Australian novels in the 1990s and 8 per cent in the 2000s were subsidy published; including self-published titles increases this proportion to 9 and 12 per cent respectively. These are relatively high proportions (given that other-national – including American and British – publishers were responsible for 8 per cent of Australian novels in these decades). However, it is when self- and subsidy publishing are considered in relation to the local industry that their prevalence becomes apparent. In the 1990s, 5 per cent of Australian novels published in Australia were subsidy published; in the 2000s, this proportion increased to 17 per cent. If self-published titles are included in the category of local publication (based on the presumed location of the author), the proportion of local output represented by titles where authors have contributed to or paid costs is substantial: 22 per cent in the 1990s and 25 per cent in the 2000s. The difficulty of identifying self- and subsidy publishers – and the probability that *AustLit* has not included all such titles – means these figures probably underestimate the prevalence of this practice.

As these results indicate, the vast majority of subsidy publishers of Australian novels in the 1990s and 2000s are based in Australia. This group includes a number of companies that, according to the categorisation of local publishers I outlined earlier, have a sustained involvement in the novel field (that is, they are responsible for ten or more titles in a decade). This group includes Zeus Publishing (responsible for publishing 93 Australian novels in the 2000s); Sid Harta Publishers (with 3 in the 1990s and 52 in the 2000s); Seaview Press (with 17 in the 1990s and 35 in the 2000s); and Brolga Publishing and Equilibrium Books (with 10 and 20 titles, respectively, in the 2000s). Boolarong Press (with 11 Australian novels in the 1990s and 2 in the 2000s) and Wild and Woolley (6 / 9) were, before shifting to subsidy publishing, part of the 'wave' of small independent presses that emerged in the 1970s and are highlighted in critical accounts of that era.[224] Many other Australian subsidy publishers were responsible for fewer than ten titles in the 1990s and 2000s, and the recent growth in subsidy publishing can be seen in the general increase in publishers and titles from one decade to the next. Locally based subsidy publishers in this category with titles in both decades include Black Pepper (with 5 in the 1990s/9 in the 2000s); Peacock Publications (2/8); Oracle Press (2/6); Parker Pattinson (2/1); Info Publishing (1/1) and Spectrum Publications (1/1). Book Press (2), Flame Lily Books (1) and Kingfisher Press (1) only published Australian novels in the 1990s, while in the 2000s, a substantial number of subsidy publishers entered the Australian novel field including Copyright Publishing, with three titles; A and A Books, BookBound Publishing, BookPal, Longueville, Penfolk, with two each; and with one, Aether Book Publishing, ARD Press, Copper Leife, Diane Andrews, Halbooks, Maygog, Melbourne Books, Ocean Publishing, Otmar Miller Consultancy and Pennon Publishing.

There are also overseas-based subsidy publishers of Australian novels, of which the most prolific is Trafford Publishing, previously based in Canada and now in America, and responsible for 16 Australian novels in the 2000s. The majority of overseas subsidy publishers that I have been able to identify are American and responsible for fewer than five titles in the 1990s and/or the 2000s, with output again concentrated in the latter decade.[225] For both Australian and overseas subsidy publishers, those responsible for a large number of Australian novels tend to describe themselves as specialised book publishers – often employing new technologies, such as print-on-demand and e-books to facilitate their engagement with the contemporary book market – while those with a small number of titles offer a much wider range of services, including family histories, business identity stationery and flyers (in the case of PenFolk Publishing);[226] website and commissioned writing (in the case of Diane Andrews);[227] and 'picture research, artwork or visual procurement, and intellectual property reproduction permissions' (in the case of Copper Leife).[228]

The fact that most subsidy publishers of Australian novels (large and small) are based in Australia requires an explanation, especially given the strong online presence of these companies. One might assume the Internet would make an Australian author just as likely to employ a company based in America, England or Canada, as a company in Australia. Certainly, many of the larger subsidy publishers (including Zeus Books, Seaview Press and Trafford Books) sell their titles globally online, and Sid Harta claims distributors in America, Australia, Canada, Fiji, Hong Kong, Indonesia, Malaysia, New Zealand, Singapore, South Africa, Thailand, the Netherlands and the Philippines, as well as book sales through Amazon.com and Barnes & Noble (the largest book retailer in America).[229] Other subsidy publishers make their global outlook part of their marketing: Ocean Publishing seeks authors 'no matter where in the world [they] reside';[230] Copyright Publishing describes itself as 'a Queensland enterprise with world-wide customers';[231] and Aether Book Publishing states, 'Our bookstore is global'.[232] Despite these global sales and marketing techniques, the general national correlation between authors and subsidy publishers is probably attributable to two main reasons, both rather prosaic. First, search engines tend to list companies located in the same country as the searcher at the top of the page; thus, an Australian-based author searching for a publisher online is more likely to find Australian than overseas companies. Second, and acknowledging this situation may change with growth in e-books and other forms of online publication, postage costs probably increase the likelihood of an Australian author selecting an Australian-based subsidy publisher. While Sid Harta claims outlets in a number of different countries, most subsidy publishers post books from a single country only, with substantially greater costs for international freight. I am presuming, in this respect, that a desire for readers in

Australia underpins the tendency for Australian authors to use Australian-based subsidy publishers. Both explanations suggest ways in which the global reach of the Internet is nonetheless transcribed and circumscribed by national boundaries.

Although the subsidy publishing industry is largely a national one, such presses tend to identify not with the nation but the individual. There are exceptions to this rule, especially among the larger subsidy publishers: Seaview Press advertises as 'Australian Book Publishers for Self Publishers',[233] and Zeus Books identifies as 'Australia's first e-book publisher and on line e-bookshop'. But even these publishers orient themselves primarily towards the individual customer: Zeus Books' website claims its 'goal is to meet your publishing needs and to deliver the book you've always wanted, a book you can be proud of'.[234] While most subsidy publishers describe themselves as offering a 'service' or 'solutions' to authors, some suggest a more personal relationship: Aether Book Publishing announces, 'We like authors. We talk to them';[235] Xlibris describes itself as 'created by authors, for authors', so as to better focus 'on the needs of creative writers and artists';[236] and Kingfisher Press's 'business…[is] about establishing and maintaining relationships, building trust, communication and sharing objectives'.[237] Some subsidy publishers go much further than this – promising to do nothing less than transform authors' lives: Ocean Publishing urges writers to 'take control of your destiny';[238] Spectrum asks its prospective clients to '[j]ust imagine how different your life would be when your book is published and the bookstores are selling your books like hotcakes all across the world';[239] and BookPal tells authors to 'imagine a magic cloud that takes your manuscript, turns it into a real book, and puts it in the hands of buyers…that's Bookpal'.[240]

In other ways the self-descriptions of subsidy publishers parallel those of traditional presses, including in their claims of 'independence',[241] but perhaps most markedly, in the strongly expressed opposition of many to multinational or mainstream publishing. Ocean Publishing's website asks, 'why wait for one of the faceless international publishers to notice your talents when you can self-publish your paperback book and get it out there to readers yourself?'[242] Similarly, Sid Harta offers to 'replace the big publisher's power and influence in selection of writers and success on the bookshop shelf'.[243] Yet among subsidy publishers, this rejection extends to 'traditional' – that is, non-subsidy – publishing. BookPal's website tells prospective authors, 'there is nothing quite like the feeling of seeing your very own book in print… However, traditional publishing houses created their rules for this game, making it very hard to play for most authors'.[244] Overwhelmingly, the message from these publishers is that conditions are hard for authors – as Melbourne Books puts it, for 'the increasing number of authors who find it impossible to secure a publisher'[245] – and subsidy publishing is a way of overcoming these difficulties.

While some of the self-descriptions of subsidy publishers resonate with those of traditional publishers, the growth in this part of the industry in the 1990s and especially the 2000s represents a significant new trend. As I discussed in Chapter 2, it was probably common for colonial authors to pay or contribute to the cost of local book publication. But where these books were integrated into the industry – by virtue of the involvement in bookselling of many colonial book publishers – subsidy publishers of the 1990s and 2000s exist and operate, in large part, separately from the established publishing and retail trade, particularly in their focus on online sales. The significant growth in subsidised publication of Australian novels suggests many authors are unable to gain – or are unhappy with – publication through traditional avenues. It could be that such authors have always existed, but are now turning to subsidy publishing as it becomes more prominent, accessible, or simply less shameful; alternatively, the growth in creative writing courses in the 1990s and 2000s might have increased the number of unpublished writers.[246] Myers, for instance, 'sometimes…think[s] that Australia has become a nation of neurotic, compulsive and hysterical writers, all clamouring that their precious work is worthy of commercial publication'.[247] However, the fall in the number of Australian novels in the 2000s, even with the availability of this alternative avenue of publication, contradicts this view.

Davis perceives the growth in what he calls a 'do-it-yourself [literary] culture' as a response to the increasing commercialisation and homogeneity of the contemporary industry, and the resulting difficulty for many authors to gain publication. In particular, he proposes that, as the industry orients itself towards high-selling products, self- and subsidy publishing will play an increasingly important role in the production of Australian literary fiction.[248] If this is the case, and if literary scholars wish to maintain their focus on the literary portion of the field, an engagement with this non-traditional group of publishers and their output seems imperative. But at present, self- and subsidy publishing are routinely dismissed as evidence of a lack of quality. Most critics would agree, in other words, with subsidy publisher Sid Harta's claim that, 'Publishing is a competitive and difficult business…and there is less room among the big publishers for consideration of newcomers'; however, most seem not to admit the logical extension of this argument: namely, that '[o]pportunities for good writers and many good books are lost because of this'.[249] Or rather, these lost opportunities are decried – as emphasise by the 'moral panic' that ensued when an anonymous chapter from Patrick White's *The Eye of the Storm* was refused by twelve publishers[250] – but still self- and subsidy publishing are not seen as potential sources of good writers and books.

Even if literary scholars reassess this standpoint, the question of how to engage with this part of the industry is not a simple one. Expanding our purview of eligible titles so that self- and subsidy published books are potentially included on literature courses, in criticism and reviews, as well as in awards, presents a substantial challenge for a workforce that already barely has the time to read current prize-winners. I make this point not to bemoan the pressures of an academic workload, but to highlight the deep – and largely unacknowledged – way in which critics and teachers of literature rely on the selections of the traditional publishing market, the reputation of specific publishers, and the forms of commodity production and reward the book market supports, to provide a signal of quality that precedes any literary critical or academic assessment. While some literary critics expend a lot of energy railing against the supposedly new commercialised practices in the publishing industry, neglect of self- and subsidy publishing indicates the extent to which the critical system (both general and academic) is reliant upon the systems of literary valuation that the market makes available.

My point is not that we should reject traditional publishing and turn to self- and subsidy publishing as a form of literary production somehow free from commercialised practices – this is patently not the case, as I hope my analysis of these companies has demonstrated.

However, the vehement rejection – or more commonly, the neglect or ignorance – of the implication of literary culture in commodity culture leads to a fundamentally flawed understanding of this field. We need to accept – and be concerned with and intrigued by – the way that the production and reception of literature (including 'evaluative criticism') is always already implicated in commercial systems; indeed, we need to acknowledge that the different forms of implication in such systems are constitutive of the processes of literary production and reception. This understanding is the necessary starting point for a form of literary scholarship able effectively to theorise and explore literary culture and publishing, both in the traditional, publisher-centred model, and in new, author-centred – and conceivably, in the future, reader-centred – modes.

***

In this chapter I have argued that the notion of the 1970s and 1980s as a 'golden age' – and the literary nationalism that underpins this perspective – amplifies particular aspects of contemporary Australian literary and publishing history, while minimising or ignoring others. A small group of independent, local literary publishers operating in these decades, and the fiction they produced, are seen to embody the ideal relationship between nationalism and literariness, and are thus presented as the high point, and ultimate achievement, of Australian literary culture. For the emergence of these presses to be understood in terms of national awakening and independence requires that they supplant British publishers – the cultural representatives of Australia's colonial history – rather than arise from an Australian-dominated field. There is no space in this account for the pulp fiction publishers that actually dominated the local industry from the end of the Second World War until the 1970s, and which arguably provided the lion's share of fiction available in Australia throughout these decades.

Both the fiction these companies published (oriented to the mass-market and including a significant proportion of explicitly American-style titles) and the marketing strategies they employed (usually aligned with multinational publishing in the 1990s and 2000s) contradict descriptions of local publishing prior to these recent decades. More specifically, these practices challenge the naturalised association of national location and literariness underpinning many Australian literary and publishing histories. Attention to such publishers and their substantial output demonstrates the gap between official (academic and governmental) views of what Australians were reading and the reality. Rather than a shift in the 1960s and 1970s from 'a captive British market, a subject people'[251] to an independent, culture-led reading community, publishing trends suggest that more Australian readers continued to seek popular American (as well as Australian) genres, characters and themes.

The way that even those commentators who discuss pulp fiction insist it had disappeared by the 1970s – when in fact, such publishers remained the most prolific producers of Australian novels – demonstrates the strength of the periodisation that underlies contemporary Australian literary historiography, wherein the 1970s and 1980s are a pristine moment of local literary publishing, unaffected by corrupting (popular or commercial) influences. The same point can be made about the earlier-than-acknowledged rise of multinational publishers. Even among commentators who do not view this trend as the absolute opposite of local publishing, and who acknowledge the opportunities for access to global markets these publishers represent for Australian authors, growth in multinational publishing is perceived as only occurring in the 1990s and 2000s. Multinational publication of Australian novels did become more prevalent in the 1990s, although it declined in the 2000s. But the focus on local literary publishing and fiction in the 1970s and 1980s suppresses the fact that, by the 1980s, multinational conglomerates already published 40 per cent of all non-pulp Australian novels.

What this quantitative analysis shows is that trends in Australian publishing history are significantly more continuous than has been acknowledged. The growth in local literary publishers in the 1960s and 1970s occurred despite the prevalence of local pulp fiction and continued as multinational publishers entered the Australian novel field. The ongoing growth in 'independent Australian publishers' in the 1990s and 2000s, including a substantial number of literary presses, suggests that the globalisation and consolidation of publishing is occurring in the context of – and potentially motivating a parallel shift towards – local, regional and national identifications and communities. At the same time, the recent growth in self- and subsidy publishing, and the importance of digital and online technologies to the contemporary industry, indicates the emergence of new trends with important consequences for the future of publishing and of literary studies.

The Australian literary and publishing histories I have discussed and criticised in this chapter incorporate many significant claims about the appropriate role of government in literary culture and in society more broadly, the importance of a locally based publishing industry to that society, and the role of the market in literary culture. These issues need to be debated. But because such concerns are formulated through a nostalgic narrative framework, any solutions seem to lie in the past, not the present and not the future. The established account of Australian literary and publishing history has solidified into a backward-looking approach to literary scholarship, and a backward-looking set of accounts of the book industry. Only by abandoning this narrative of a lost time that never really was can Australian literary studies develop a more critical relationship with the recent past; only on this basis can we offer an effective analysis of the present and a constructive contribution to future studies of literature and publishing in Australia and of Australian fiction.

Chapter 4

RECOVERING GENDER: RETHINKING THE NINETEENTH CENTURY

Feminist criticism has had the single greatest influence in reshaping the nature of Australian literary studies, not only in its critique of the masculinism of the nationalist tradition and the established canon, but positively in the rediscovery of mid-century women writers and the recovery of colonial romance and autobiography genres.[1]

Where feminism has clearly transformed Australian literary studies, the same cannot be said of publishing history. Despite some excellent analyses of publishing through a gendered framework,[2] for the most part, as Mary Eagleton says: 'Feminism's lack of interest in publishing history is equalled only by publishing history's similar disregard for feminism.'[3] Blackwell's recent *A Companion to the History of the Book* is a prime example of this 'disregard', including no dedicated discussion of gender in its almost 600 pages.[4] The next two chapters aim to contribute to bridging this divide between feminism and publishing history by exploring, and demonstrating the profound interconnections between, publishing and gender trends in the history of the Australian novel. This analysis will also add another layer to the revised history already presented in Chapters 2 and 3, with this chapter focusing (like Chapter 2) on the nineteenth century, and the next one (like Chapter 3) considering the decades since the end of the Second World War. The connections that emerge between publishing and gender trends extend understandings of the history of authorship, publishing and reading in these periods. They also challenge significant features of the feminist revision of Australian literary history, including the view that women will always be relegated to culturally devalued spheres, or that it is always women's writing that gets 'eclipsed from view' in critical discussion.[5]

Even to mention 'women's writing' is to confront the enormous body of discussion, mostly from a feminist perspective, regarding the essentialism of this phrase: in particular, its tendency to obscure differences between women while maintaining a rigid opposition between women and men.[6] These debates have rendered 'women's writing' a highly contested and 'unstable' term.[7] In the following two chapters I use trends in the form and place of publication and, for contemporary titles, in novel genres and the critical attention authors received, to explore differences within the categories 'men's writing' and 'women's writing'. But awareness of and attention to difference should not preclude consideration of the ways in which gender constructions shape the experiences of women as a group, as they do for men as a group. Through analysing the interconnections between trends in publishing and in the gender of authors of Australian novels, for both the nineteenth century and the decades since the end of World War Two, I argue that gender constitutively shapes men's as much as women's participation in the literary field: including the publishing avenues they have access to, the types of writing they produce, and the readerships they reach.

These next two chapters, then, take gender – not women – as their operative term. This approach avoids the tendency of many feminist accounts to only consider the female 'half of the field'. While a feminist focus on women was, as Rachel Blau DuPlessis says, 'a major cultural move for rectification and for reconstituting a culture that had formerly discounted female presence and was ignorant of the literary and artistic agency of women',[8] over time this approach has solidified into an equation of women and gender.[9] The construction of women's writing – and publishing and reading – as the site of gender analysis allows men, even if implicitly, to remain ungendered and universal subjects, and enables only a partial analysis of these areas of cultural production and reception. One of the simplest but most insidious ways in which this equation of women and gender appears is in the index of academic books that, under gender, direct the reader to 'see women'. Routledge's *The Book History Reader* makes just this association between women and gender. Although this collection – unlike Blackwell's *Companion* – includes chapters focused on gender, in making it a woman's issue, the Routledge editors overlook the ways in which gender shapes all writing, publishing and reading, not just women's.[10]

In this chapter I demonstrate that connections between gender and publishing trends are of foundational importance for understanding the history of the nineteenth-century Australian novel and locating that literary form in its transnational context. I begin by outlining and comparing gender trends in the publication of these titles with current understandings of the relationship between gender and the authorship, publication and reception of literature – especially the novel – in the colonies and in Britain and America. Through this comparison, I argue that previous studies, including those from a feminist perspective, have underestimated women's contributions to the nineteenth-century Australian novel. At the same time, men wrote the majority of such titles. This gender trend contrasts with the British and American novel fields, where women were the main authors. The significance and complexity of this male-domination of the colonial novel comes more sharply into view in light of gender differences in the place and form of publication of such titles. As I showed in Chapter 2, colonial novels were published in three main ways: as serials, predominantly in local periodicals; as books in Britain; and as books in the colonies. In this chapter I demonstrate that titles by colonial men and women were not evenly distributed across this publishing spectrum. Instead, women's novels were more likely to be serialised than men's, and men's novels were more likely to be published as books than women's. Even so, until the 1890s, colonial women novelists were markedly more successful than their male counterparts in attaining book publication in Britain, while men wrote the majority of Australian novels published as books locally.

I attribute women's overrepresentation as authors of colonial novels serialised in the colonies and, until the 1890s, as authors of titles published as books and serials in Britain, to British constructions of the nineteenth-century novel as a female-dominated form. Specifically, I discuss how these British constructions influenced both colonial publishing practices and the likelihood of British publishers accepting colonial women's novels.

In respect to the prevalent local publication of colonial men's novels – in serial and, especially, book form – I argue that novel writing had value for men in the colonies before this was the case in Britain. These different constructions of the novel, and of authorship and reading, shaped the colonial and transnational circulation of Australian novels in the nineteenth century. They also have consequences for understanding the relative success of colonial men and women novelists at this time. Arguably, local book publication had value in terms of expressing and constructing colonial or national identity. However, the greater cultural and/or economic rewards of serialisation and British book publication (areas where women were overrepresented) suggests that – while men wrote the majority of nineteenth-century Australian novels – in the cultural terms of the day, colonial women were the more successful authors.

At least, that was the case until the 1890s. In this decade, British book publication went from comprising a relatively minor to the dominant avenue of publication for colonial men novelists. This dramatic shift in gender trends in relation to the place of publication provides new insights into colonial literary culture and publishing in this seminal decade for Australian literary studies. The 1890s is widely seen as the time when a male-oriented definition of Australian culture, including literary culture, became entrenched. Existing analyses foreground gendered discourses within the colonies in this process. I demonstrate the significance of transnational constructions of authorship and the novel – and British publishing practices in particular – in shaping these colonial and national discourses, as well as gender dynamics in colonial literary culture more broadly. At the same time, I argue that earlier gender trends in colonial publishing – specifically, the prevalent local publication of colonial men's novels – underpinned British publishers' shift to colonial novels by men as they sought entry into this lucrative export market.

I Feminist Literary Criticism and the Nineteenth Century

Until the 1970s, when feminist critics began rescuing women writers from oblivion, Australian literary history was assumed to be largely, if not entirely, male dominated. As Fiona Giles writes, 'it was widely accepted that there were no [Australian] women writers in the nineteenth century'.[11] The process whereby feminist critics have rediscovered and reread women's writing has undoubtedly transformed Australian literary history. Although – I argue in Chapter 5 – critical attention is still not equally distributed between men and women authors, in contemporary histories of Australian literature, nineteenth-century women novelists (such as Ada Cambridge, Barbara Baynton, Rosa Praed and Catherine Helen Spence) are prominent. Far from absent, today it is widely accepted, as Susan Sheridan writes, that 'women have been a significant presence in the white Australian cultural scene; they were never the silenced outsiders that later historians and critics rendered them'.[12]

While the presence of women in nineteenth-century Australian literature has been acknowledged, feminist critics have tended to emphasise the prominence and importance of women writers in the early twentieth century. Drusilla Modjeska identifies this period, and the 1930s in particular, as 'remarkable years in Australian cultural history. Women were producing the best fiction of the period and they were, for the first and indeed only time, a dominant influence in Australian literature';[13] Maryanne Dever depicts the entire inter-war period as a time of 'an almost unprecedented concentration of women writers making contributions to the development of a new national literary culture';[14] Connie Burns and Marygai McNamara argue that, 'In the first half of the twentieth century women wrote almost half of the published novels and it is generally acknowledged that most of the best novelists of that period were women'.[15]

Figure 15, showing the proportion of Australian novels by men and women from 1830 to 1939, supports these claims regarding women's relative prominence in the early twentieth-century Australian novel field. While women did not write 'almost half of the published novels', they were responsible for 35 per cent of titles from 1900 to 1939 (compared with 63 per cent by men and 2 per cent by authors whose gender is unknown).[16] The overall proportion of Australian novels by women in this period was significantly increased by gender trends in authorship in the 1910s, when women wrote 43 per cent of Australian novels (and when the effects of the First World War were obviously influential).[17] However, Figure 15 also shows that women played a comparable role in the Australian novel field in the second half of the nineteenth century. Although responsible for very few titles until the mid-1850s,[18] in the following decade and a half (as the proportion of women in the colonies' non-Indigenous populations grew from 41 to 45 per cent[19]) women wrote 41 per cent of Australian novels, compared with 54 per cent by men and 5 per cent by authors whose gender is unknown. For the remainder of the nineteenth century, despite ongoing growth in the proportion of women in the colonies' populations,[20] women's authorship of such titles declined. Even so, from 1855 and 1899, women wrote 32 per cent of Australian novels (compared with 60 per cent by men and 8 per cent by authors whose gender is unknown).[21]

The prevalence of authors in the unknown gender category in the nineteenth century (9 per cent overall, compared with 2 per cent in the first four decades of the twentieth

Figure 15. Australian novels by gender of author, percentages, 1830 to 1939 (five-yearly averages)

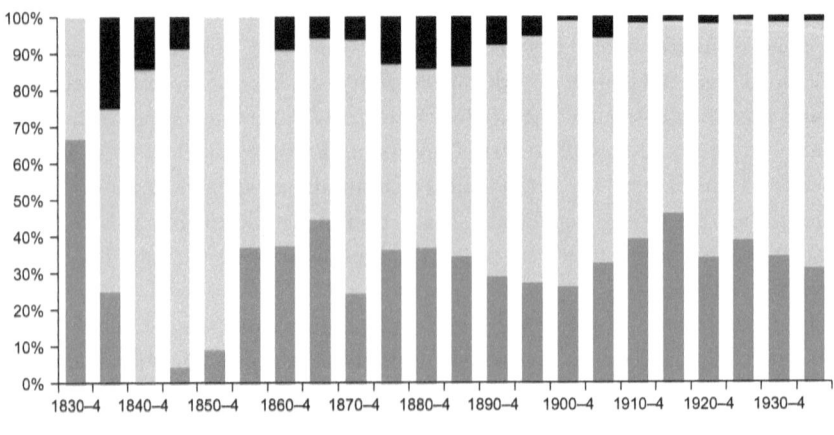

century) raises the possibility that women made a greater contribution to the Australian novel in this period than these results indicate. While there is debate over gender differences in the use of pseudonyms by nineteenth-century British and American authors,[22] most recent commentators agree that pseudonymous authors were more likely to be women. The shame associated with middle- and upper-class women earning a living – and the nineteenth-century perception of '[w]omen novelists...as inferior to male writers' – made women significantly more likely than men to assume a pseudonym, especially a male or gender-neutral one.[23] The fact that most instances where nineteenth-century Australian authors used pseudonyms or published anonymously were serial fiction[24] – given women's overrepresentation in this area – makes it likely that many novelists in the unknown gender category were actually women.

Even without the contributions of these unknown authors, the similar proportion of Australian novels by women in the second half of the nineteenth and first half of the twentieth centuries highlights a misapprehension in feminist revisions of Australian literary history. Elsewhere, I have drawn on Sheridan's argument about the occlusion of nineteenth-century women from Australian literary history to explain why feminist critics routinely single out the early twentieth century as a particularly female-dominated period.[25] As Sheridan argues, the 'colonial domestic novels' and romantic modes employed by nineteenth-century women writers were dismissed by later critics in favour of 'realist and nationalist writing' by men.[26] Early twentieth-century women writers – like Henry Handel Richardson, Miles Franklin, Katharine Susannah Prichard and Jean Devanny – responded to this male-oriented tradition, seeing 'themselves as serious writers with a social responsibility to national cultural development' and employing 'European literary modernist techniques...adapted to the requirements of social realism'.[27] I proposed that, while feminist literary criticism was instrumental in recovering nineteenth-century colonial women's writing, feminist critics have tended to focus on the 'serious' women's novels of the early twentieth century: these twentieth-century titles present a better fit with the established aesthetic and nationalist parameters of Australian literary studies than the romantic and domestic themes of nineteenth-century women's fiction. In other words, the understandable desire of feminist critics to demonstrate that women writers were just as good as their male counterparts – and to show, as a consequence, that women had been excluded from literary history because of power inequalities rather than the quality of their writing[28] – underlies the focus on, and claims of the 'unprecedented' concentration of, Australian women writers in the early twentieth-century period of 'serious' literary production.

The publishing history of Australian women's novels presents another, specifically material, reason for feminist critics' underestimation of women's contribution to the colonial novel. The recovery of early Australian women's writing involved some re-issuing of serialised novels in book editions,[29] and since that time, such works have received critical attention. However, only a small proportion of serialised novels were republished, and a sampling of those women's novels that were not – even by authors as prominent as Cambridge and Mary Fortune – shows they have been neglected by literary scholars.[30] In this light, it seems likely that the high rate of serial publication of colonial women's novels, especially of titles only published serially – combined with the book-based focus of Australian literary studies (critiqued already in this book) – has contributed to a relative lack of emphasis on women's authorship of Australian novels in the nineteenth, compared with the early twentieth, century.

In attempting to understand gender trends in the Australian novel field, it is important to compare not only different periods in the history of that form, but concurrent gender trends in different places. As well as contextualising the Australian data, this approach takes account of the circulation of Australian novels in a transnational market: one comprised of national and pre-national spaces where potentially different ideas about the relationship between gender, authorship and literature were influential. In respect to both the British and American novel fields of the nineteenth century, historians argue that women wrote the majority of titles. Nicola Thompson, for instance, proposes that, '[w]omen writers dominated the vast novel market in Victorian England',[31] a conclusion supported by Ellen Casey's analysis of novels reviewed in the *Athenaeum*.[32] Based on a study of the archives of London publisher Macmillan, from 1840 to 1917, Gaye Tuchman describes women as the main authors of British novels until at least the 1880s.[33] In America, Susan Coultrap-McQuin estimates that, '[b]y 1872 women write nearly three quarters of all novels published'.[34]

Unsurprisingly, given the close association between book and serial publishing in the nineteenth century, women are also acknowledged as the predominant authors of novels published in British and American periodicals at this time. Discussing the British context, Laurel Brake notes that, 'although the culture of newspaper journalism was… heavily male,…[w]omen…make up a higher proportion of authors of serial fiction'.[35] Michael Lund describes the same predominance of serialised novels by women in American periodicals,[36] while Anne Boyd argues that 'women were among the most prominent contributors' of fiction to such publications, including the *Atlantic Monthly*, the 'fountainhead of America's "literature"'.[37] Although women's presence in the nineteenth-century Australian novel field has been underestimated, in light of gender trends in the authorship of British and American novels of the same period, the fact that women wrote *only* a third of colonial novels (from 1855 to 1899) renders the Australian field not only male-dominated, but exceptionally so.

There has been considerable discussion of the reasons for women's dominance of the nineteenth-century British novel. It is generally recognised that women's confinement to the domestic sphere, and consequently limited social and economic roles, contributed to their overrepresentation in this profession. John Sutherland argues that middle- and upper-class women had limited opportunities for paid employment outside the home, and in this context, writing provided a possible income source that could also be combined with family responsibilities.[38] More specifically, literary historians have attributed women's dominance of the British novel to the low cultural value of that literary form: women were allowed access to the profession, in other words, because men did not see writing novels as prestigious. Tuchman's work on the relationship between the cultural value of the novel and gender trends in authorship has been particularly influential in this respect. By analysing rates of submission and acceptance of men's and women's novel manuscripts by British publisher Macmillan, Tuchman proposes a positive correlation between increased cultural value of the novel and male authorship in the nineteenth and early twentieth centuries. Before the 1880s, when 'the British cultural elite accorded little prestige to the writing of novels', women dominated the field; in the 1880s and 1890s, as 'men increasingly understood that they could achieve social and economic rewards by writing novels', they gradually 'edged [women] out' of this profession.[39] By the first decade of the twentieth century Tuchman writes, 'men's hold over the novel, particularly the high cultural novel, [had] coalesced'.[40]

As reading has become an increasingly important theme in literary studies, critics have aligned the low value accorded to the nineteenth-century British novel with the perception that its readers, as well as its writers, were predominantly women. Terry Lovell argues that, especially in the first part of the nineteenth century, 'the moral attack on the novel focused on women as readers' as well as writers.[41] Likewise, Jacqueline Pearson describes the 'anti-novel literature' of the nineteenth century as

> voluminous and repetitive: the same stereotypes, like the vulnerability of the novel-reading girl to seduction, and even the same words, like 'poison' and 'soften', recur compulsively.[42]

Analysing writing by 'men of letters' in the Victorian press, Kelly Mays demonstrates the widespread perception that reading fiction – popular serials in particular – was both dominated by women, and produced 'a feminine quality of mind'.[43] Although the view that women were the major readers of fiction was intrinsic to the devalued status of the novel, Brake argues that British periodical editors also sought out fiction – especially fiction by women – for the purposes of attracting a female audience, or as Brake puts it, as a way of 'bidding for selective reading by women readers'. In this sense, the conception of women as the major readers of fiction was an important contributor to the high proportion of serialised women's novels in British periodicals. Brake argues that other subjects dealt with in newspapers – such as politics, religion and philosophy – were considered of no interest to women readers; serial fiction, however, was seen as having the potential to greatly expand the pool of readers.[44]

In contrast with the British context, there has been relatively little attention to the influence of gender on colonial reading practices. As I discussed in Chapter 2, a number of studies propose that an 'Anglocentric reading model' dominated in Australia, with colonial readers greatly preferring British – especially popular – fiction to the local product.[45] The studies that propose this model do not consider the gender of the authors of these books, and when the gender of the reader is mentioned, it is often only in passing. For instance, Tim Dolin notes that some of the borrowers of books from the Collie Mechanics' and Miners' Institute Library were women – 46 of 392 members – and notes that '[w]omen were on average bigger readers…borrow[ing] an average of 28 books each; men 21 books each'.[46] But he does not take this discussion further.

When the gender of readers is considered in more depth, both men and women are described as participating in and producing this Anglocentric reading model. Discussing 'Australia's vigorous reading culture' in the late nineteenth and early twentieth centuries, Martyn Lyons uses the Australasian Home Reading Union – operating in New South Wales from 1892 to 1897 and designed 'to provide reading direction to country women' –

as one example of widespread attempts 'to extend and to integrate the Australian reading public even further' and to perpetuate 'a conservative and Anglocentric reading model'.[47] In her study of reading group minutes from the 1890s, Elizabeth Webby notes that 'women from Hobart's elite circles' shared the broader disregard of 'most Australian readers' for Australian fiction.[48] Webby also uses her analysis of books purchased by two elite, male-dominated organisations – the Hobart Town Book Society and Sydney's Australian Subscription Library – to refute the accuracy of 'frequent attacks in the press' claiming that 'reading of popular fiction was…confined to women, children, or others of lower educational and social status'. The records of these organisations demonstrate, she argues, that the novel – and popular British fiction in particular – 'clearly was one of the major forms of entertainment enjoyed by the male elite of both Sydney and Hobart in the first half of the nineteenth century'.[49] While this final point maintains the association of all colonial reading practices – rather than simply men's or women's – with the Anglocentric model, it also points to the currency, in the colonies, of the association of popular fiction reading with women prevalent in Britain at this time.

Although women's authorship of colonial novels has been underestimated, and while there has been relatively little exploration of gender trends in reading in the colonies, there is general critical consensus that nineteenth-century Australian women wrote different types of novels to their male counterparts. Sheridan, for instance, argues that until the late 1880s and 1890s, most novels by colonial men as well as women were in the romance genre. But where women's novels focused on the 'heroine's emotional experience and especially her quest for love' and marriage, men wrote 'stories of convicts, bushrangers and station life'.[50] Similar statements differentiating nineteenth-century Australian women's from men's writing present a clear theme in late twentieth-century feminist recoveries of colonial women's fiction.[51]

None of these arguments regarding gender trends in the authorship, publication and reception of nineteenth-century novels – in the Australian or British and American contexts – are especially controversial. Yet when viewed in relation to empirical trends in the publishing history of the Australian novel, a set of complications emerge. Given the '[l]egal, political, economic and…emotion[al] ties' between Britain and the Australian colonies,[52] one might assume that British cultural norms and constructions applied directly to life in the colonies. In terms of women's social role and domestic responsibilities, there were definite parallels between the two societies. While middle-class colonial women were able to work outside the home earlier than their British counterparts – in the 1870s and 1880s as opposed to the 1900s[53] – until that time, writing was also one of the few forms of work open to them. Even after this time, the types of employment in which women could engage were limited. These parallels between women's social and domestic responsibilities in Britain and Australia help to explain the presence of Australian women novelists. But they do not explain the male dominance of the colonial novel.

Gender trends in the nineteenth-century British novel – and the existing, Anglocentric model for colonial reading practices – make accounting for this male dominance even more challenging. We know that a great deal of British literature circulated in the colonies, including in local periodicals. Discussing the period from the mid-1870s to the end of the 1880s, Elizabeth Morrison estimates that only one fifth of the novels in colonial newspapers were by local authors.[54] This understanding of the importance of British fiction and authors for colonial readers underlies and supports the Anglocentric reading model. Yet when this circulation of British literature in the colonies is combined with women's acknowledged dominance of the British novel, another conclusion arises: at least until the late nineteenth century – when Tuchman claims men were entering the British novel field – the majority of novels available in Australia must have been by women. The fact that most locally published colonial fiction was by men contrasts with this British context, and adds another layer of complexity to the tensions that emerge from comparison of gender trends in the British and Australian novel fields.

In the next section of this chapter I consider serial publication of colonial men's and women's novels, and how the gender trends that emerge in the form and place of publication of such titles suggest a way of explaining and resolving some of these tensions. I show that, while women were overrepresented in serial publishing – and while a greater number of colonial women's novels than men's were serialised in Britain – more Australian titles by men than women were published in colonial periodicals. I associate these gender trends with constructions of authorship circulating in Britain and the colonies. In particular, I argue that British cultural norms influenced colonial publishing practices; but in the colonies there also emerged an alternative market and readership for fiction focused on colonial men's writing.

II Serial Publishing

Serialisation provided the major form of publication for colonial novels from the 1860s to the 1880s, and women's novels were clearly overrepresented in this forum. Figure 16 depicts the overall proportion of Australian novels, as well as the proportion of men's and women's novels, serialised from 1860 to 1899.[55] It shows one five-year period when a higher proportion of men's than women's novels were serialised (although, in that case, the gender difference was relatively small: in the early 1870s, 43 per cent of men's novels were published in serial form compared with 41 per cent of women's). At all other times, Australian women's novels were – often considerably – more likely to be published in periodicals. From the 1860s to the 1880s, 56 per cent of women's titles were serialised, compared with 41 per cent of men's. The proportion of women's novels only published in serial form in these decades was almost double that for men's titles (40 compared with 21 per cent).

As serial publication of Australian novels declined – from the mid-1880s – the proportion of men's novels serialised also fell, from 57 per cent of titles in the early 1880s, to 29 per cent in the late 1880s and 10 per cent in the early 1890s. The proportion of women's novels in this category also declined, but more gradually: from 63, to 52 and 35 per cent respectively. In the final five years of the nineteenth century, only a slightly higher proportion of women's than men's novels were serialised (13 as opposed to 11 per cent). Given this more gradual decline in periodical publication of women's novels, if the 1890s are included in the results already cited, the gender disparity in the likelihood of serial publication becomes even more apparent. From 1860 to 1899, 42 per cent of Australian women's novels were serialised compared with only 25 per cent of men's; and

Figure 16. Australian novels serialised, overall and by men and women, percentages, 1860 to 1899 (five-yearly averages)

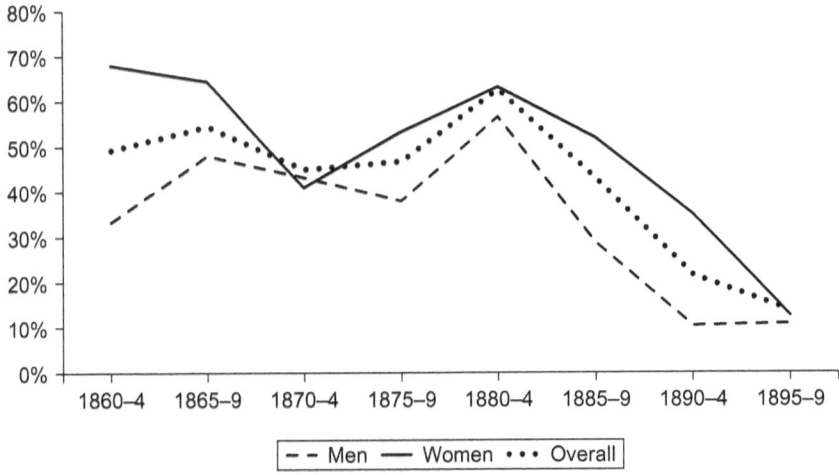

the 27 per cent of women's titles that only appeared in periodicals was more than double the 13 per cent of men's titles in this category.

Given the association, in British literary histories, of women's dominance of the nineteenth-century novel with the low cultural value accorded to such fiction, one might expect the greater likelihood of serial publication of Australian women's novels to reflect a similarly negative view of serial publication, or of novel writing and reading more broadly, in the colonies. Statements by various nineteenth-century (male) novelists certainly appear to accord local serial publication little value. For instance, only when *Robbery Under Arms* was published as a book in Britain, by Remington, did Rolf Boldrewood write in his diary, 'now I am an *author*'.[56] The statement dismisses six novels, including *Robbery*, published in Australian periodicals prior to this edition, and another serialised title issued as a book jointly by the local bookseller/publisher George Robertson and British company, S. W. Silver.[57] G. B. Barton's description, in 1889, of the poor remunerative rewards of publishing fiction in Australian periodicals suggests the low cultural value of serial publication was coupled with limited economic reward.[58] If colonial periodicals paid novelists poorly, this avenue of publication would logically be less attractive for men than women (given that women were not usually required to supply the family's income).[59]

Despite these statements, this notion that colonial women were overrepresented as authors of serialised works because this form of publication had limited social and economic rewards can be challenged on a number of fronts. Barton's claim that local serialisation was financially unrewarding contrasts with Cambridge's experience. Morrison shows that Cambridge earned significantly more from serial publication in Australian periodicals than from book publication in London with Bentley. She gives a 'cautiously conservative estimate of a total between £150 and £170' for the serialisation of Cambridge's two novels, *In Two Years' Time* and *A Mere Chance*. These amounts, Morrison writes, were 'more than double her income from the two novels in book form'.⁶⁰ The fact that the *Australian Journal* – the most prolific publisher of colonial novels in these decades – generally did not pay its authors,⁶¹ but published only one more novel by a woman than a man,⁶² suggests that economic rewards were no more important for these men than for these women in determining whether to write and where to submit their novels.

Even if, as Boldrewood's statement indicates, men sought the more culturally esteemed route of British book publication – above the potentially more financially lucrative avenue of local serialisation – women were more successful in this endeavour, as I will discuss shortly. Finally, as more than two thirds of colonial novels were by men, it is difficult to claim their lack of interest in this activity. Indeed, although women were overrepresented as authors of serialised colonial novels, because men wrote the majority of titles, the number of serialised novels by colonial men slightly exceeded the number by women (between 1860 and 1899, 119 novels by colonial men were serialised compared with 106 by women). Taken together, these factors challenge the view that men shunned serial publication, or that this outcome was economically unrewarding. Accordingly, they suggest that the relationship between gender, authorship and publishing in the nineteenth-century Australian novel field was more complex than men simply claiming and occupying a professional sphere that offered social, cultural and economic rewards, and rejecting those that did not.

Considering the number of serialised novels by colonial men and women over time, and the difference in the place of publication of such titles, provides some further context for analysing gender trends. Figure 17 depicts these results, showing the number of colonial novels by men and women in Australian and British periodicals.⁶³ In respect to local periodicals, it shows that more women's than men's novels were serialised in the 1860s, and from the late 1880s to the early 1890s (a remarkable result, given the extent to which men outnumbered women as authors of colonial novels). However, in the 1870s, early 1880s and late 1890s colonial periodicals serialised significantly more Australian novels by men than women. Although only a small number of titles were involved, the gender trend in the authorship of Australian novels published in British periodicals was quite different. With the exception of the early 1870s, late 1880s and late 1890s, more titles by women than men were serialised in Britain in each five-year period. From 1860 to 1899, 56 per cent of (or 14) Australian novels serialised in British periodicals were by women compared with 36 per cent (or 9 titles) by men.⁶⁴ To put these results another way, where 6 per cent of Australian women's novels published between 1860 and 1899 were serialised in British periodicals, this was the case with only 2 per cent of men's titles.

As well as indicating the complexity of gender trends in serial publication, Figures 16 and 17 raise three clear questions: Why were Australian women's novels both more likely to be serialised, and serialised in greater numbers, in British periodicals than men's novels? Why were titles by women generally more likely to be serialised than men's? And finally, why – in contrast to Britain and America (where most serialised novels were by women) – were more Australian men's novels than women's published in local periodicals?

Gender trends in the nineteenth-century British novel field provide a framework for answering this first question regarding the prevalence of Australian women's novels in British periodicals. As most novels in these publications were by women, the submission

Figure 17. Number of serialised Australian novels, by men and women, in Australian and British periodicals, 1860 to 1899 (five-yearly totals)

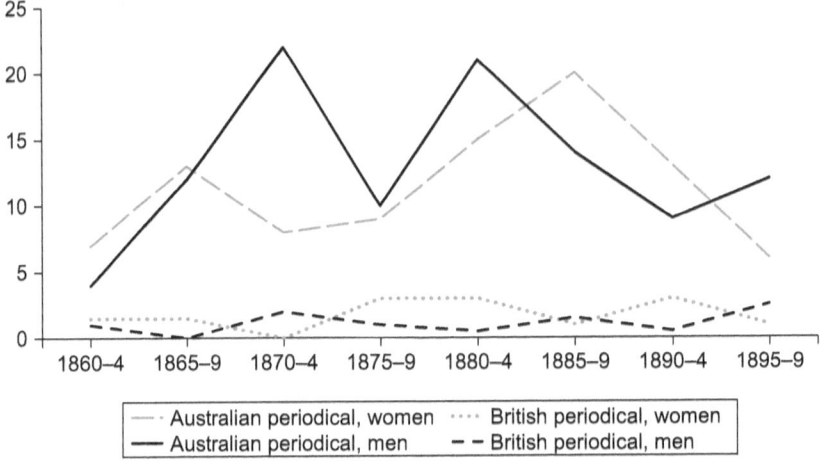

of colonial women's novels to British periodicals would have accorded with gendered constructions of the novel and of authorship in that context. The prevalence of women's novels in British periodicals, in other words, would have increased the likelihood of British editors accepting and publishing colonial women's novels. This effect would have been enhanced if, as Beverley Kingston argues, colonial women's novels were similar to those by British women. According to Kingston, the social, romantic and domestic themes dominating Australian women's writing in the nineteenth century resonated with British and American women's writing of the period, and thus

> were easily accessible to British and American readers... In contrast much masculine writing was deeply embedded in bush and outback life and idiom, and though very popular with its Australian readers, had limited appeal elsewhere.[65]

The topics depicted as well as the gender of the authors would have made colonial women's novels more accessible for overseas audiences and facilitated the entry of such titles into the British market.

Even when the colonial novels published in British periodicals are excluded, women's titles remain more likely to be serialised than men's.[66] However, in local periodicals men's novels outnumbered those by women. Considering these results, I first looked to see if any local periodicals were focused on Australian novels by one gender. While this was the case with some periodicals that published only a small number of titles,[67] it was not true of the major local periodical publishers of Australian novels. There was some variation: the *Australasian* published more novels by women, while the *Sydney Mail* and the *Leader* published more by men.[68] But the broad gender trend in serial publication – namely, the more frequent publication of men's novels in the 1870s, early 1880s and late 1890s and of women's novels in the 1860s and late 1880s and early 1890s – appeared in the lists of all major colonial periodicals, rather than being attributable to the focus of a particular publication.

While the activities of individual periodicals do not explain gender trends in local serialisation, as with British periodical publication, constructions of authorship and the novel in Britain provide a way of understanding the overrepresentation of colonial women's novels in local newspapers and journals. Earlier I noted that, as most British novels were by women and most novels serialised in Australian periodicals were British, these local periodicals almost certainly included a substantial amount of fiction by women. This is not to say that colonial readers only read novels by women. As Robert Dixon says,

> If book-sellers' catalogues and the holdings of colonial libraries are any indication, the most popular novelist in the Australian colonies during the first half of the nineteenth century was Sir Walter Scott, whose novels were imported in their thousands.[69]

Dolin's analysis of the lending records for the South Australian Institute shows that Scott's *Waverley* was still the most borrowed book in 1861–2.[70]

While Scott's popularity is clear, there are important reasons why lending library records would not necessarily reflect the fiction read in the colonies. As I argued in Chapter 2, the limited presence of such libraries meant that buying fiction, especially in its cheapest, serial form, was almost certainly the main way in which colonial readers gained access to it. And while Scott may have dominated in lending libraries, Toni Johnson-Woods identifies a woman – Mary Elizabeth Braddon – as the most-serialised author in colonial periodicals from 1872.[71] As Johnson-Woods notes, this was the year that Tillotson's Fiction Bureau opened, offering 'a cheap, dependable and consistent supply of [overseas] fiction' to colonial editors: 'given numerous authors from whom to choose', the editors of these colonial periodicals – as in Britain and America – published fiction by a woman writer,[72] and specifically, by an author of sensation novels (a genre strongly associated with the 'degenerative…reading habits' of women).[73]

The presence of non-Australian novels in colonial newspapers emphasises the importance of 'supra-national' identifications in colonial literary culture,[74] or what Morrison describes – pointing to the high proportion of overseas fiction in colonial periodicals from the mid-1870s – as 'the interconnectedness of English literatures on both sides of the Atlantic'.[75] The likely prevalence of British women's novels among the titles serialised in local periodicals, and the immense popularity of Braddon in particular, suggests that colonial editors, like their British counterparts, would have been open to submissions of fiction from women. From this perspective, as in Britain, the local serialisation of colonial women's novels would have accorded with, rather than challenged, gender trends in the periodical press. This interpretation – especially in light of Kingston's description of a close alignment between British and colonial women's writing – situates the overrepresentation of colonial women's novels in local periodicals as part of a broader, transnational trend in the authorship and readership of popular English-language novels of this period.

While critical discussions of the gendering of the novel, authorship and reading in Britain offer a way of accounting for the overrepresentation of Australian women's novels in colonial periodicals, they do not help to explain why colonial men's novels were serialised in greater numbers than women's in these publications. Indeed, if local serialisation of colonial women's novels arose from the construction of the popular English-language novel as a form predominantly written and read by women, the greater number of colonial men's novels published in local periodicals appears even less likely and explicable. What the strong presence of colonial men's novels in the periodical press from the 1860s *does* show is that novel writing had value for men in the colonies before it did for men in Britain (who, according to Tuchman, did not begin to edge women out of the profession until the 1880s and 1890s). The question then becomes: why, and from where, did this value arise?

Existing explanations of the local serialisation of colonial fiction associate this publishing trend with a growing sense of national or colonial identity.[76] Certainly, there is a correlation between expressions of colonial identity and the local serialisation of male authors: for instance, in 1870, Western Australia, Victoria, Queensland, New South Wales and South Australia all adopted state flags; the first half of the 1870s was when the greatest number of colonial men's novels were serialised in Australia. I want to be clear here. In suggesting an association between the high rate of local serialisation of colonial men's novels and the emergence and expression of colonial or national identity, I am not implying that these titles had no connection to 'supra-national' identifications in colonial literary culture. Indeed, the popularity of Scott's fiction in the colonies, and the fact that colonial men's novels were predominantly of the same adventure romance genre that Scott made popular,[77] suggests that the supra-national context influenced the emergence and reception of such titles. Equally, my argument that colonial women had increased opportunities to publish in colonial – as in British – periodicals because of British constructions of the novel as a female-authored form need not preclude the possibility that an emerging sense of colonial identity also played a role in motivating the creation and publication of such titles (particularly those depicting colonial settings and characters). Nevertheless, the strong local serialisation of colonial men's novels – given the prevalence of women's novels in British and American periodicals at this time – emphasises, and calls for an explanation of, the local conditions producing this unique gender trend in colonial publishing.

An association of the prevalence of colonial men's novels in local periodicals with the expression or representation of colonial or national identity finds support in descriptions of the content of such titles. Men's novels were focused, Sheridan proposes, on 'convicts, bushrangers and station life', or in Kingston's words, on 'bush and outback life and idiom'.[78] These accounts of colonial men's writing resonate with Johnson-Woods' description of the 'intensely local' tales of convicts, squatters and gold diggers serialised in the colonial press. Although she does not specify the gender of the authors, Johnson-Woods proposes that these titles 'fulfilled a literary need when colonials wanted to read about their country'.[79] Also not specifying – but in her case definitely implying – a male author, Spence gives a rather more negative description of the male characters that she argued 'fill[ed] the foreground' of nineteenth-century Australian writing as 'the "deadbeat"':

> the remittance man, the gaunt shepherd with his starving flocks and herds, the free selector on an arid patch, the drink shanty where the rouseabouts and shearers knock down their cheques, the race meeting where high and low, rich and poor, are filled with the gambler's ill luck.[80]

Taken together with the high rate of local serialisation of colonial men's novels, these accounts suggest that Australian periodicals incorporated a distinctly local form of fiction, focused on male characters and experiences and – according to Sheridan and Kingston at least – written by male authors.

The question of whether colonial men's novels were targeted at male readers, and women's novels at women, is one that can only be speculated upon. On the one hand, descriptions of nineteenth-century British reading practices as structured by gender – and the common cultural heritage of readers in the colonies and Britain – gives licence to the possibility that a gendered reading model operated in Australia. This possibility is reinforced by Webby's description of attacks in the press implying that reading popular fiction was not an appropriate activity for men, and specifically, by the association the evidence of these attacks implies between constructions of authorship and reading in Britain and in the colonies. On the other hand, any understanding of reading based entirely on divisions between men and women almost certainly obscures the reality of reading practices. Such obstruction is, perhaps, especially true of the colonial context, given that the 'conservative and Anglocentric reading model' presents men and women as interested in the same fiction. Indeed, this model implies that men as well as women read women's writing, in that the predilection of Australian readers for popular British fiction would have involved at least some orientation towards writing by women. Webby's description of the preference, by elite male members of Hobart and Sydney society, for popular British fiction implies just such a cross-gendered reading practice.[81]

There is, however, some evidence that a gendered model of reading operated in the colonies. A connection between women's writing and reading is supported by the fact that all five colonial novels serialised in the *Australian Woman's Magazine and Domestic Journal* appeared under female pseudonyms: Vera, Ruby L. and Chloe.[82] This exclusive use of female pseudonyms for colonial novels published in a periodical aimed at women readers suggests, as Brake argues was the case in Britain, that women's fiction was directed at women readers. It seems likely that this practice would also have influenced the inclusion of women's fiction in the weekly companions to the daily newspapers, where most colonial novels were published. While the news, politics, stock and shipping prices in these publications were presumably considered only of interest to male readers, women's novels – detailing, as Sheridan says, the 'heroine's emotional experience' and her 'quest for love' and marriage[83] – would presumably have been seen as appealing to a specifically female audience.

In contrast, an anecdote about the reception of *Robbery Under Arms*, the most-well known Australian adventure romance story of the nineteenth century, published – in the

Sydney Mail in the early 1880s – in the second major peak in local serialisation of men's novels, definitely implies a male audience for this title.⁸⁴ As Dixon writes:

> Looking back on the success of *Robbery Under Arms*, Rolf Boldrewood proudly recalled that a squatter from the Queensland border once told him, 'the mail comes in of a Saturday, y'know, and the station hands used to gather to hear me read the weekly chapter'.⁸⁵

It is hard to imagine a more homosocial image of fiction writing and reading: a male author composes a story focused on a male character; the male squatter reads the story to his male station hands and then tells the author of the experience; the author, in turn, relates the story to the male journalist. The reading community this anecdote indicates also highlights the role of these stories in enunciating ideas about colonial identity and culture, 'making real' or 'imagining' precisely that community of men so persuasively depicted in Boldrewood's story of male adventure.

To this point I have proposed that colonial women's novels were more likely to be serialised (and were serialised in greater numbers in British periodicals) because of the British construction of the novel as a form written and read by women; and that colonial men's novels were serialised in greater numbers in Australia (than in Britain) because of a colonial market and readership for titles depicting explicitly colonial, and specifically male-oriented, forms of identity. Based only on gender trends in serial publication, the empirical basis for the argument is somewhat oblique. It is, after all, problematic to assert that different constructions of the novel – one British, the other colonial – motivated publication of women's and men's novels when the majority of titles under consideration were published in local periodicals. Gender trends in book publication, to which I now turn, provide greater context and support for these propositions.

III Book Publishing: 1860s to 1880s

While serialisation could bring financial rewards and enable wide circulation of colonial novels – within a colony and/or overseas – there were also 'disadvantages to this ephemeral mode of publication. One might clip and assemble the newspaper columns', Morrison writes, 'but this was hardly the same as a book for the shelves of a bookseller, library, or family home'.⁸⁶ At the same time, not all forms of book publication were judged equal. In particular – due to its greater economic and, especially cultural, rewards – book publication in Britain was preferred to local publication. From this perspective, as well as providing new insights into the circulation of Australian novels in the nineteenth century, gender trends in the place of book publication – specifically women's greater success in attaining publication in Britain, and the prevalent local publication of men's novels – raise compelling questions about the operations of cultural value in a transnational context.

Overall, colonial men's novels were more likely to be published as books than colonial women's novels. From 1860 to 1889, 79 per cent of men's titles were published as books compared with 63 per cent of women's. A similar gender disparity occurred in respect to those novels never serialised, which comprised 60 per cent of titles by men compared with 44 per cent by women. Importantly, however, although less likely to have their novels published as books, women were much more likely to gain book publication in Britain: almost half (48 per cent) of all colonial women's novels were published as books in Britain from the 1860s to the 1880s, compared to 27 per cent of men's. Limiting the sample to titles published as books – that is, excluding the colonial novels that only appeared in serial form – highlights women's disproportionate success in this area of publication: in this case, between 1860 and 1889, 76 per cent of colonial women's titles were published in Britain, compared with only 34 per cent of men's.

In Chapter 2, I established that approximately half of the authors whose novels were published as books overseas in these decades were themselves overseas at the time of publication. This correlation makes it necessary to consider whether the higher rate of British publication of Australian women's than men's novels simply (if improbably) indicates women's greater willingness or ability to travel. In fact, men whose novels were published as books in Britain were almost twice as likely as women to be in Britain at the time of publication. So high is the incidence of British book publication for women in these decades that – although they constituted a lower proportion of the novel field (and of the colonial population) than men, although their novels were less likely (overall) to be published as books, and although women were more likely to be resident in the colonies at the time of publication – more Australian novels by women than men were published in Britain in these three decades.[87]

By contrast, local book publication was significantly more common for colonial men than women. From 1860 to 1889, 28 per cent of men's novels were published as books in Australia compared with 10 per cent of novels by women.[88] These low percentages reflect the relatively low incidence of local book publication in the nineteenth century. Considering the proportion of locally published colonial novels by men and women highlights the extent to which male authors dominated this arena: in these decades, 75 per cent of Australian novels published as books in Australia were by men, compared with only 17 per cent by women (8 per cent were by authors whose gender is unknown).

This gendered division in the place of book publication of colonial novels lends significant support to the framework I have outlined. Previously, I argued that colonial women's novels were more likely to be serialised in Australian periodicals because of the broader English-language construction of the novel in this period. The high rate of British book publication for colonial women's novels indicates the direct impact of this framework: as was the case with their submission to British periodicals, women were more successful in gaining book publication in Britain because, in that context, the novel was constructed as a form authored and read by women. The challenges for colonial authors of gaining book publication in Britain while resident in the colonies are widely recognised. Webby, for instance, notes that

> Australian writers of the second half of the nineteenth century experienced...difficulties in getting their novels published. If they remained in Australia, it was possible to gain fairly extensive publication in local magazines and newspapers, but much more difficult to move to book publication without themselves physically moving to Britain.[89]

Especially as women novelists were more likely to remain in the colonies than men, gender trends in the place of book publication demonstrate that these well-rehearsed barriers to British book publication were significantly greater for colonial men than women.

Alternatively, the fact that the vast majority (75 per cent) of novels published as books in the colonies were by men reinforces and extends my claim, regarding serial publication, of a local market and readership for Australian stories by men. In Chapter 2 I argued that not all Australian novels published in Britain travelled back to Australia, although novels published locally were definitely available. I also proposed that copayment for book publication was significantly more common in the colonies than in Britain. This first point, regarding circulation, gives the prevalence of local book publication of colonial men's novels added significance in terms of understanding the market for fiction in the colonies: not only were men's novels significantly more likely to be published as books locally, but as a result, they were more likely to circulate in the colonies than novels by women (which were predominantly published, and may have only been available, in Britain). The second point, regarding the likelihood of authors having to contribute to the costs of colonial book publication, demonstrates the desire of Australian men to engage in the novel field (in that they were willing to pay for the privilege). However, it also suggests that the economic returns of novel publication for colonial men were, on average, not only lower than for colonial women novelists, but more likely to be negative. These distinctions, in turn, point to important questions about the relative success of colonial men and women novelists in Australian and international literary culture in the nineteenth century.

Morrison's account of the consequences, for Cambridge, of '[b]eing taken up in London' – as opposed to the likely outcomes had her novels been published as books locally – emphasises the rewards of British book publication for colonial authors, and portrays local book publication as demonstrably inferior. Cambridge did not contribute to the costs of publication, as Morrison insists was frequently the case for authors whose novels were published as books in the colonies. While the income she received from book publication by Bentley, of *Two Years' Time* and *A Mere Chance*, was significantly less than for the newspaper serialisation of both works, her returns were 'almost three times Bentley's total net profit'.[90] In addition, where novels published as books in the colonies 'rarely could expect organised distribution or large sales',[91] British book publication offered a 'gateway to a network of domestic and international outlets', including the United States. It also enabled publication in 'many guises'. Cambridge's *A Marked Man* was published

> in England as a three-decker, a reset single volume with subsequent reprinting and a newspaper serial; in the United States as a reset single volume with multiple reprints, and in Australia as a 'Colonial edition' that may have circulated in New Zealand and other British colonies also.[92]

This international exposure and multiple reprintings substantially enhanced the potential economic rewards of British book publication for Cambridge and, we can assume, for colonial authors in general. Given its rewards, the greater number, and substantially greater proportion, of colonial women's than men's novels published in Britain presents women as the more successful colonial novelists. The greater likelihood of serial publication for colonial women's novels reinforces this point. Although potentially lacking cultural prestige – and sometimes unpaid – serial publication was often highly lucrative.

Women's overrepresentation as authors of colonial novels published serially and as books in Britain has important implications. On the one hand, the greater economic and cultural rewards of authorship received by women – individually and as a group – at the time of initial publication emphasises the transformation of Australian literary history wrought by later critical accounts. As feminist critics have argued, until the 1970s, the nineteenth-century novel field was constructed as largely, if not entirely, dominated by men. This male-dominated canon backgrounds those authors who, in the nineteenth century, received the greatest rewards of publication. Although displacing this canon, the feminist revision of Australian literary history – in focusing on the early twentieth century – arguably perpetuates this neglect of colonial women novelists' success by underestimating their contribution to the history of the Australian novel. On the other hand, the success of colonial women novelists challenges the view, foundational to Tuchman's association of male authorship with cultural value, that men will always concentrate in the most culturally and economically rewarded professions. This challenge arises, however, not from women's capacity to define the Australian novel (the cause of men's progressive domination of the British novel, according to Tuchman), but from the different regimes of value, operating in Britain as opposed to the colonies.

While colonial men began writing novels before their counterparts in Britain, when seeking access to the culturally esteemed and economically rewarding avenue of British book publication, these men were forced to submit their work in a British context that defined the novel as a form written and read by women. From this perspective, the desire of colonial men to write novels was at odds with the regime of value operating at the imperial centre. This relative failure of colonial men to access book publication in Britain probably explains the high rate of local publication of men's novels: rejected by publishers in Britain (where they would be less likely to have to pay for publication and would have the potential benefit of international circulation and multiple imprints) colonial male novelists were forced to resort to local publication to have their stories read.

At the same time, the barriers to the importing of British-published Australian novels until the 1880s raises the possibility that the overwhelming local publication of colonial men's novels reflected a choice on the part of these authors. Some male novelists, in other words, may have aimed for local book publication because they were more interested in gaining literary attention (or in giving their version of colonial society) in the colonies than in Britain. From this perspective, Susan Magarey's description of Spence's lack of success in gaining book publication in Australia is significant. Approaching publishers in Sydney, Spence – who had a number of novels published as books in Britain in the 1850s, 1860s and 1880s[93] – was told that, 'the only novels worth publishing in Australia were sporting or political novels'. As Magarey comments, such titles, like '[t]hose to which the critics have awarded places in the Great Tradition of Australian Fiction were...concerned with the public sphere and predominantly masculine adventures and heroics'.[94] This anecdote reinforces my claim of a readership in Australia oriented towards distinctly local, male-authored novels, focused on male characters and experiences. It also suggests that, in some cases, colonial publishers sought out – and perhaps did not require a fee for – Australian fiction. Finally, it raises the possibility that colonial women might have been compelled – by a lack of interest from local publishers – to seek publication overseas.

Although the high rate of local publication of men's novels may have been more than simply the overflow from rejections by British publishers, the greater economic and international cultural rewards of British book publication – combined with the limited distribution, and financial obligations, of local book publication – make it hard to believe British book publication was an avenue that colonial women novelists were forced to resort to. The dramatic growth in British publication of colonial men's novels in the 1890s reinforces this view, as it suggests that, given the choice, colonial men – like their female counterparts – elected for book publication in Britain. It is to this shift in gender trends in publishing, and its implications for understanding both colonial literary culture and British publishing in the 1890s, that this chapter now turns.

IV Gender and the 1890s

The 1890s are widely recognised as the decade when Australian literary culture was prominently redefined as masculine. Analyses that make this argument concentrate on discourses of gender circulating in the colonies. In this section, I use gender trends in the place of publication of Australian novels to reorient this discussion. Specifically, I demonstrate the influence of factors external to Australia on shifts in colonial literary culture, including its gender dynamics. But I also show how aspects of this local literary culture, particularly the existing reading market for Australian novels by men, was influential beyond the boundaries of the colonies, especially for British publishing activities and agendas.

To some extent, gender trends in the authorship and publication of colonial novels in the 1890s were a continuation of those I have already discussed. Previously I noted that women's novels remained more likely to be serialised than men's in the 1890s, as the role of periodicals in publishing Australian novels declined. As would be expected from this trend, the incidence of book publication for colonial men and women novelists increased, though to a lesser extent for women than men: 95 per cent of men's titles were published as books in the 1890s, compared with 88 per cent of women's. The gradual decline in the proportion of colonial novels by women since the late 1860s – shown in Figure 15 – continued, with women writing 28 per cent of titles in the 1890s (down from 35 per cent in the 1880s) compared to 66 per cent by men (up from 51 per cent in the previous decade).[95] Significantly, however, this progressive decline in the proportion of Australian novels by women – which was ongoing through the 1890s[96] – resulted not from a fall in the number of titles by women (which in fact increased slightly) but from substantial growth in publication of Australian men's novels. From the 1880s to the 1890s, the number of titles by men more than doubled (from 99 to 245), with more limited growth in titles by women (from 69 to 103). To put these results another way, publication of colonial women's novels increased by 49 per cent; but publication of men's grew – from a higher base rate – by a substantial 147 per cent.

It is unlikely that many familiar with Australian literary history – and in particular, with the gendering of that history in feminist criticism – will be surprised by this growth in Australian novels by men, and by the fall in the proportion of titles by women towards the end of the nineteenth century. Since Marilyn Lake's influential 1986 analysis of the 1890s in terms of conflict between masculinists and feminists 'for control of the national culture',[97] an understanding of this decade as a time when Australian culture (including literary culture) was masculinised – and 'cultural and political concerns designated feminine' were correspondingly marginalised and denigrated[98] – has formed a central tenet of Australian literary history.[99] The association of nationalism, realism and mateship in the *Bulletin* is seen as fundamental to this process, and to what Sheridan describes as the 'explicit and insistently masculine – indeed masculinist – tenor of th[e] cultural nationalism which became the dominant discourse constructing "Australianness" during the 1890s and which has survived in some quarters ever since'.[100]

While both men and women wrote (different styles of) romance prior to the 1890s, in this decade Sheridan argues the genre was 'gendered feminine' and constructed as 'inferior' – conventional, derivative, class-bound, domestic and colonial – in comparison to a masculine 'Australian literary tradition associated with serious, realist and nationalist writing'.[101] The denigration of women's writing that occurred in the pages of the *Bulletin* was, Sheridan argues, a 'local version' of the European and North American redefinition of the novel in terms of realism (rather than romance) and art (as opposed to popular entertainment). But in the colonies, this transnational process was shaped to specifically national and nationalist ends. In the case of the *Bulletin*, Sheridan proposes that the 'segregation…[of] serious cultural capital' represented by men's writing, from 'the devalued commercial product associated, in *Bulletin* rhetoric, with British colonial power' and with women's writing, supplied a framework for the emergent and male-dominated nationalism that periodical championed.[102]

In light of these descriptions of the male-orientation of Australian literary culture, one would expect a distinct fall in local publication of Australian women's novels during the 1890s, combined with growth in the local publication of men's novels. Figure 18 shows that the opposite occurred. From the 1880s to the 1890s, the proportion of book editions of Australian women's novels published locally increased – albeit only slightly, from 20 to 21 per cent – in the context of a substantial fall in local publication of men's titles, from 48 to 20 per cent. Rather than shift away from women's writing, for the first time in the nineteenth century local presses published a relatively equal proportion of colonial men's and women's novels (and in fact, women authors were slightly overrepresented). Figure 18 also shows that, while the proportion of book editions of women's novels published in Britain fell from 80 per cent in the 1880s to 58 per cent in the 1890s, this proportion of men's titles increased from 28 to 68 per cent respectively. Publication at the imperial centre thus goes from comprising a relatively insignificant (and unlikely) outcome for Australian male novelists, to providing the major avenue of publication.

The numbers underlying these proportional changes bring the dramatic shift in gender trends in the place of publication in the 1890s – and specifically, the growth in British publication of Australian men's novels – more sharply into view. From the 1880s to the 1890s, there was a four-fold increase in the number of Australian novels published

Figure 18. Australian novels published as books in Australia and Britain, overall and by men and women, percentages, 1880s and 1890s

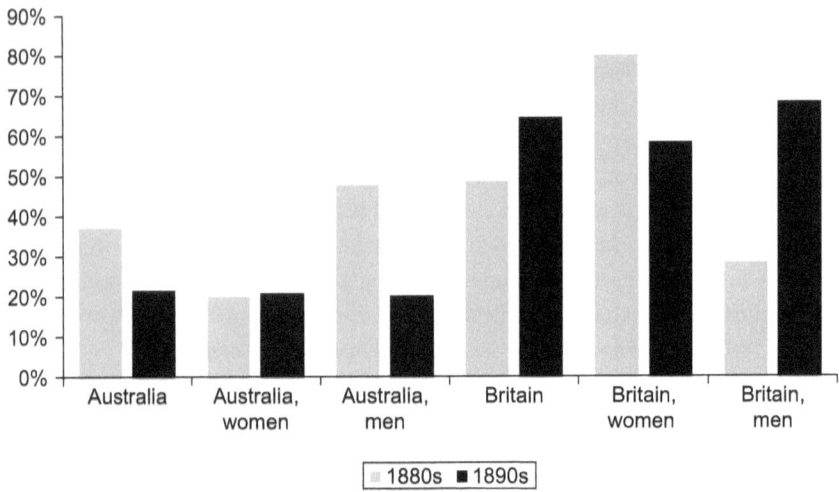

in Britain: from 55 to 225 titles. As the gender trends above would suggest, the vast majority of this growth was in publication of colonial men's novels. Where the number of colonial women's novels published as books in Britain came close to doubling from the 1880s to the 1890s (from 32 to 56 titles), this growth pales in comparison to the more than eight-fold increase in British book publication of Australian men's novels (from 19 to 166 titles). These shifts in British publication represent a complete reversal of earlier gender trends. In the first half of the 1880s, 70 per cent of Australian novels published in Britain were by women and 30 per cent were by men; by the first half of the 1890s, 72 per cent of such titles were by men, compared with 27 per cent by women;[103] in the late 1890s, 75 per cent of Australian novels published in Britain were by men compared with only 23 per cent by women.[104]

As these trends make apparent, it was the dramatic growth in the British – rather than local – publication of Australian men's novels that accounted for the predominance of male authors in the Australian novel field in the 1890s. This phenomenon urges a reassessment of earlier feminist accounts of this decade. While Sheridan's analysis locates Australian literary constructions in relation to transnational trends – namely, the redefinition of the novel as a realist and high cultural form – the emphasis she and others give to the *Bulletin* in producing the male-orientation of Australian literary culture underplays the continuing, and increasing, tendency for Australian novels to be published in Britain. The majority of Australian novelists were, in other words, much more directly impacted by the (re)definitions of authorship and of the novel occurring at the imperial centre than by the *Bulletin*'s associations of women's writing with commercialism and British colonial power. Indeed, there is some sense in which the anti-imperialism embedded in the paradigm of Australian literary nationalism is present in feminist accounts of the 1890s, foregrounding the importance of national constructions of gender and obscuring the importance and influence of the relationship between the British and colonial literary cultures and publishing industries in this period.

The substantial growth in British publication of Australian men's novels instead suggests Tuchman's description of gender trends in the British novel field. As I noted earlier in this chapter, Tuchman identifies the 1880s and 1890s as a period of redefinition, during which 'men of letters, including critics, actively redefined the nature of a good novel and a great author'.[105] This process of redefinition resonates with the dramatic turn to Australian novels by men evident even at the level of individual British publishers in the 1890s. With the exception of Tinsley and Remington, all of the British companies among the top ten publishers of Australian novels from 1860 to 1889 published mostly women's novels (as was the case with Sampson Low, Richard Bentley, John Dicks, Macmillan and T. C. Newby) or an equal number of titles by men and women (as was the case with Chapman and Hall, Hurst and Blackett, and Ward, Lock). In the 1890s, all of the British publishers in the top ten – including Routledge; Remington; Macmillan; Ward, Lock; Hutchinson; F. V. White; T. Fisher Unwin and Chatto and Windus – published a majority (and in most cases an overwhelming majority) of Australian novels by men.[106]

But even Tuchman's description of the redefinition of the British novel field in the 1880s and 1890s – and by the 1900s, the 'institutionalisation' of male dominance – does not seem adequate to explaining the extent or the suddenness of the growth in British book publication of Australian men's novels in the 1890s, especially as it occurred in conjunction with numerical growth in British publication of Australian women's novels. These British publishers did not stop or reduce their publication of colonial novels by women; they just started publishing many more titles by men. Part of this growth may be attributable to increased appetite for colonial fiction among British readers, a phenomenon that spanned 'from the 1870s down to World War I'.[107] But this explanation is also at odds with the suddenness of this shift.

The main reason I would propose for the growth in British publication of colonial men's novels in the 1890s necessitates a return to the local context, and to publishing trends more broadly. In my earlier chapter on the nineteenth century, I attributed the general growth in British publication of Australian novels in the 1890s to British publishers' attempts to gain entry into this most lucrative book export market, in part, by responding to 'local tastes and peculiarities'.[108] This response included opening colonial branches, publishing popular fiction, and encouraging British authors to include colonial content in their stories; but it also included increased publication of Australian novels, for which there was an existing local readership (demonstrated by the serialisation and book publication of such titles in the colonies). Given that most locally published Australian novels were by men, this dramatic reversal in the gender of colonial authors published in Britain suggests another way British book publishers assessed and responded to local practices and tastes.

I am not arguing that the overwhelming prevalence of Australian men's novels among those published in Britain in the 1890s was entirely the result of an established local readership for such titles: 'the colonial tail' could surely not have 'wagged the imperial dog' to that extent.[109] But I do think it probable that, in the 1890s, along with the transnational redefinition of the novel as a male-authored form (and potentially, British readers' appetite for colonial fiction), this turn by British publishers to male novelists was influenced by the nature of the Australian market and the type of books enjoyed by colonial readers. In this respect, the rhetoric of the *Bulletin* described by feminist critics – wherein proper Australian literature was realist and written by men who valued mateship and the bush experience – had a more profound effect on gender trends in the Australian novel field than would be expected if considering only the place of publication of these titles. However, I am suggesting that the *Bulletin*, rather than producing this understanding of the Australian novel, was expressing tendencies in a literary culture that had been oriented towards men's writing well in advance of the creation of this periodical, or of the redefinition of the novel in Britain and America.

What we see at the end of the nineteenth century, then, is a reversal of the fortunes of colonial men and women novelists, produced by a shift in British publishing practices. But this reversal does not negate the success of women prior to this decade. And in respect to this earlier success, an intriguing question about the *Bulletin*'s denigration of women and celebration of a national literary culture emerges: Was this stance, more than a means of reflecting and proclaiming discourses of colonial and national identity? Was it also – or even primarily – a defensive response, on the part of colonial men, to women's previous success in engaging, and engaging with, the literary world beyond the colonies?

***

The clear association between gender and publishing trends that emerges in the colonial novel field demonstrates the importance of a material history of the novel, as well as analysis of content, for understanding how gender operates in literary culture. As I have shown, men's and women's novels were not equally distributed across the spectrum of nineteenth-century Australian novel publishing. Instead, women's novels were more likely to be serialised, and serialised in greater numbers in British periodicals, than titles by men. Until the 1890s, women's novels were also more likely than men's to be published as books in Britain. I have attributed this trend to the well-established British construction of the novel as a female-dominated fictional form, and to the way this construction in the imperial centre influenced publishing and reading practices in the colonies. The overrepresentation of women's novels among the titles serialised (in Australia and Britain) and published as books in Britain, and the economic and/or cultural rewards of these forms of publication, suggest that, on average, the most successful colonial novelists were women. In particular, these trends indicate that colonial women's novels would have enjoyed more extensive international circulation at the time of publication than men's. Thus, while women's contribution to the Australian novel field has been underestimated – including by feminist critics – their fiction (presuming it was recognised as colonial) would have played a greater role than men's in representing Australia to the world in the nineteenth century.

In contrast, Australian novels by men – which were more numerous than those by women in this period – were overwhelmingly published locally, both in serial and book form. This high rate of local publication of colonial men's novels almost certainly indicates their relative failure in attaining publication in Britain. At the same time, I have argued that this publishing trend points to the existence of a market and readership for men's novels in the colonies, tied to the emergence of colonial or national identity, and focused on representing male characters and experiences. The eight-fold increase in British publication of colonial men's novels in the 1890s – the decade when such publishers made other concerted efforts to enter the Australian book market – can be seen as an acknowledgement of, and response to, this local readership. But in this case, the existence of this readership requires explanation. In the period when colonial publication of Australian men's novels was most prevalent – the 1860s to the 1880s – novel writing and reading was defined in Britain as a female-dominated activity. Why was the situation different in the colonies? Why were colonial men more keen to write and, we can assume, to read novels than their British counterparts?

According to Mays, the discourse of reading that circulated in Britain at this time was deeply implicated in anxieties about class as well as gender. On the one hand, it was feared that extending 'the literary franchise' to working-class men would destroy class barriers: one essay that Mays describes drew on Darwin's theory of evolution to evoke a 'nightmarish' future dominated by working-class readers.[110] On the other hand, '[l]ike that of women, the thought of the lower orders was represented as simplistic, "sensual and concrete", and their minds as "actually or potentially *unbalanced*" and unstable'.[111] From this perspective it was feared that, if working class men were allowed to adopt women's 'desultory and omnivorous reading' practices, 'proper gender organization' would be disordered.[112] Mays points to a concerted efforts by Victorian 'men of letters' to contain both sets of fears by guiding, training and controlling working-class male reading practices. A major effect of this was the reassertion of gender as the primary boundary in the literary domain: reading popular fiction – 'worthless, contemptible, enervating trash' – was constructed as unmanly. Working-class male readers, if they scorned such writing, were 'granted a kind of inclusion' into the exclusive male club of the 'truly literate'.[113]

While Webby demonstrates the expression of these same views in the colonial press – at least in the early nineteenth century[114] – I want to propose that, in the mid-nineteenth century, preceding the major growth in local publication of colonial men's writing, changes in colonial society altered understandings of fiction reading. In the Australian colonies, the gold rushes significantly disrupted class divisions. Although '1850s gold-rush immigrants were better educated and possessed higher levels of skill than any other group of immigrants to nineteenth-century Australia',[115] prior class standing did not determine success on the goldfields. Manning Clark describes the effects of the gold rushes on Australian society in terms of a 'great confusion of the classes':

> The owners of many of the largest houses and some of the most expensive equipages to be seen on the streets of Melbourne were men from the lowest classes who had made fortunes on the diggings, while scions of noble families in England, men who had won high honours at the ancient universities, were driving cabs in which the *nouveaux riches* lolled or displayed their wealth in some incredibly vulgar manner.[116]

While Clark's account of the period is clearly coloured by his own political views, the gold rush rendered class distinctions in the colonies less absolute than in Britain.

In the British context, as Mays describes it, firm class divisions granted elite men the authority to define and proclaim appropriate reading models. With the disruption of class divisions in the colonies during and after the gold rushes, it seems possible that ideas about what was appropriate – and in particular, what was appropriately manly – reading material would become unfixed from strict class hierarchies and redefined more explicitly in terms of gender. From this perspective, the content of colonial men's fiction – its focus on male characters and themes – may have rendered those titles appropriately masculine, and made such fiction, although popular, acceptable for men to read. If this disruption of the relationship between class, gender and reading did occur in the colonies, the form in which colonial men's novels were published would have facilitated this shift.

Growth in local publication of colonial men's novels initially occurred in the periodical press, especially in the weekly companions to the daily newspapers where the majority of fiction was serialised. The content of men's novels (convicts, bushrangers, station and outback life, squatters and gold diggers) would have keenly resonated with the serious reporting in these publications. In the 1870s, the transportation of convicts to Western Australia had only just ceased (in 1868),[117] gold rushes were ongoing (and indeed only beginning in Queensland), and bushrangers were active and much reported on in the colonial press. Agriculture and farming – station life – were fundamental to the economic prosperity of the colonies for those on the land and in the cities,[118] and newspapers contained detailed information about the cost, sale and shipping of products like wheat and wool. While these fictions seem entirely imaginary today, I am suggesting that the very newsworthiness of the themes depicted in colonial men's novels – in however romantic and adventurous a form – rendered this fiction 'serious' in a way that enabled its appeal and acceptability for colonial male readers, and underpinned men's dominance of the nineteenth-century Australian – in contrast to the British and American – novel field.

It is significant, in this sense, that the periodicals responsible for more colonial novels by men than women spanned class divisions. Where the *Sydney Mail* was 'representative of the conservative squattocracy',[119] the *Leader* 'catered to a less sophisticated audience'.[120] Whatever inequalities remained between upper and working class men in colonial society, the 'deep horizontal comradeship'[121] expressed by men reading stories about men signals an understanding of citizenship, initially colonial and later national, defined by gender – specifically, masculinity – rather than by class. Whether or not colonial male authors were compelled to seek local publication because of rejection by British publishers, in these male-dominated colonial societies, it appears they were able to gain and exercise an alternative form of cultural capital, based not on acceptance at the imperial centre but on emerging interest in a new nation.

Chapter 5

THE 'RISE' OF THE WOMAN NOVELIST: POPULAR AND LITERARY TRENDS

The prominence of women's writing [in the 1980s] has been such that the WACM (as Elizabeth Webby dubs the white Anglo-Celtic male who has been the icon of Australian literary traditions and patronage) has suffered considerable anxiety.[1]

I began Chapter 3 – which, like this one, explores the Australian novel in the post-war period – with Webby's description of the 1970s and 1980s as a 'golden age of Australian publishing and the promotion of Australian literature'.[2] What I did not discuss in that chapter were the specific connections Webby draws between the rise and fall of this 'golden age' and gender trends in Australian authorship. According to Webby, Australian literature in the decades prior to 1970 was dominated not only by publishing interests external to the nation, but by male authors, or the 'WACM – WHITE, ANGLO-CELTIC MALE'. Progressive cultural politics of the late 1960s and 1970s, 'from the student, feminist and black power movements', as well as animating an independent local publishing industry, fundamentally undermined the institutional and social structures that had maintained 'the former supremacy of the white, heterosexual, Anglo male'. In altering the 'stories we...tell about ourselves', and the subjects 'able to assert their... subjectivity', these political changes sponsored a proliferation of authors other than white men, of whom women were the major group. The economic shifts of the 1990s and 2000s, which supposedly brought an end to the 'golden age' of local publishing by enabling multinationals to enter and dominate the Australian market, also signalled the resurrection of 'WACM power'. White men may have lost their dominance on 'English courses and publishers lists' Webby writes:

> [B]ut the real game lay elsewhere. As the 'greed is good' decade of the eighties gave way to the belt tightening and down-sizing of the nineties, the WACMs reasserted control via the doctrine of economic rationalism at the political level...combined with...ever-increasing globalisation on the world economic scene.[3]

In her analysis of gender trends prior to the 1990s, Webby's study parallels many feminist accounts of contemporary Australian literary history. Specifically (as I will discuss in detail in this chapter) the associations she draws between, on the one hand, the male dominance of Australian literature prior to the 1970s and patriarchal cultural authority and, on the other, growth in women's writing in the 1970s and 1980s and women's political and social liberation, are repeated in a number of studies. Webby's account differs from most others in considering gender trends in the 1990s and 2000s. Although a small number of analyses do the same, there has been a notable decline in discussion of recent gender trends in Australian literature.

I devoted Chapter 3 to contesting the accuracy and periodisation of the 'golden age' narrative in contemporary Australian literary and publishing histories. Given the parallels that Webby's analysis signals between that account and the feminist one, it might seem inevitable that this chapter will likewise reject the accuracy and periodisation of contemporary feminist literary history. In fact, I devote much of this chapter to supporting – based on empirical data on gender trends in the authorship and publication of Australian novels – Webby's and others' contention that, around the 1970s, Australian literature underwent a profound shift from a strongly male-dominated and male-oriented field to one where women played an important and increasingly prominent role. This shift is clearly demonstrated in Figures 19 and 20, with the first graph depicting the five-yearly average proportions of Australian novels by men and women from 1945 to 2009, and the second showing the yearly number of titles by men and women over this same period.

However, I demonstrate that this gender shift also occurred – and actually occurred more dramatically or intensely – beyond the literary and critical sphere that is the explicit or implicit focus of feminist analyses of contemporary Australian literary history.[4] Genre, and specifically pulp, fiction was the most male-dominated section of the Australian novel field in the 1940s, 1950s and 1960s, and genre (specifically romance) fiction was the most female-dominated in the 1970s and 1980s. The appearance of these gender trends in authorship beyond the literary novel extends the scope of feminist arguments regarding the male domination of Australian literature before the 1970s. Specifically, these results demonstrate that the orientation towards the cultural values and ideas of male authors and readers encompassed the spectrum of Australian novel production and reception. The growth in the proportion of both Australian literary and genre novels

Figure 19. Australian novels by gender of author, percentages, 1945 to 2009 (five-yearly averages)

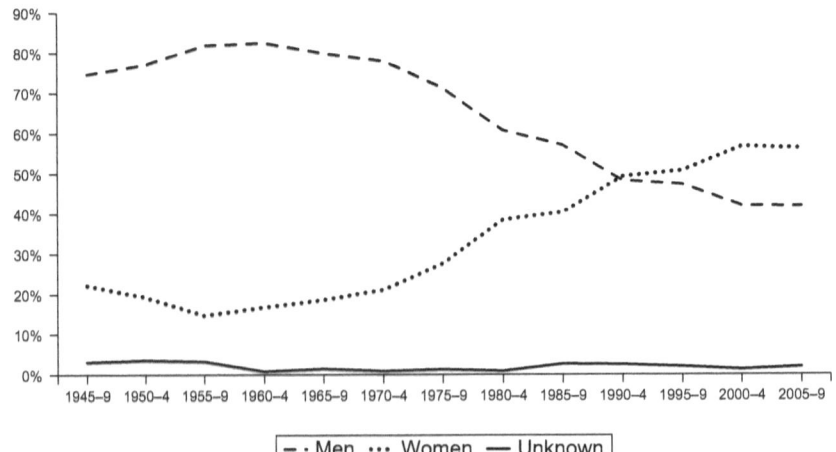

Figure 20. Number of Australian novels by gender of author, 1945 to 2009 (yearly totals)

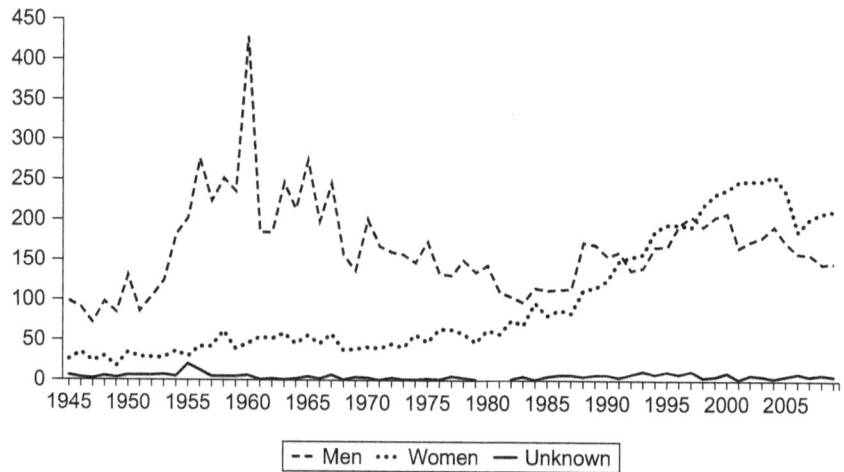

by women from the 1970s likewise extends the scope of feminist arguments. But it also challenges the meaning commonly attributed to women's writing in this decade and the next.

As Webby's account suggests, and as I will demonstrate more broadly, an emancipatory framework organises feminist analyses of growth in women's writing in the 1970s and 1980s. In particular, because women's writing is constructed as the expression of women's voices and identities, and because feminist literary criticism celebrates such expressions as signs of women's political and social power, women's increased presence in the literary field is taken to indicate – and indeed, is equated with – the success of feminism. My argument is not that feminism had no effect: trends in local literary publishing and critical discussion of Australian literature in the 1970s, and especially the 1980s, support this association of politics and authorship. Nevertheless, the parallel growth in women's literary and romance fiction complicates the direct association of women's writing, women's emancipation and the expression of feminist politics described in many feminist studies. I argue that understanding women's increased presence in the Australian novel field requires an explanation that acknowledges the influence of feminism, but recognises the importance – and almost certainly the pre-eminence – of the market in this gendered shift.

In direct contrast to the widespread discussion of women's writing in the 1970s and 1980s, there has been little – I would even go so far as to say no – acknowledgement, and certainly no explanation, of what Figures 19 and 20 also show: the ongoing growth in women's authorship of Australian novels in the 1990s and 2000s, to the extent that women now write the majority of such titles. While critical discussion of the influence of gender on the Australian novel field has diminished, gender trends in authorship and publishing – in both literary and genre fiction – in the 1990s and 2000s were in many ways a continuation and solidification of those that emerged and were influential in the 1970s and 1980s. I argue, however, that the ongoing growth in women's writing has been concurrent with a devaluing of the Australian novel. In this context, despite – and

I suggest, because of – women's current dominance of this field, recent critical attention has increasingly refocused on male authors. These results reinforce the importance of continuing attention to gender trends in authorship and publishing. But they also show the need for a more nuanced understanding of the meaning and implications of growth in women's writing since the 1970s than is allowed by the current framework of male domination yielding to female liberation.

As with Figures 19 and 20, I refer to the following two graphs throughout this chapter, so have placed them at the beginning for ease of reference. Figure 21 shows gender trends in the authorship of locally published non-pulp Australian novels from 1945 to 2009.[5] Figure 22 depicts the proportion of men and women among the top twenty

Figure 21. Australian novels (excluding pulp fiction) published in Australia by gender of author, percentages, 1945 to 2009 (five-yearly averages)

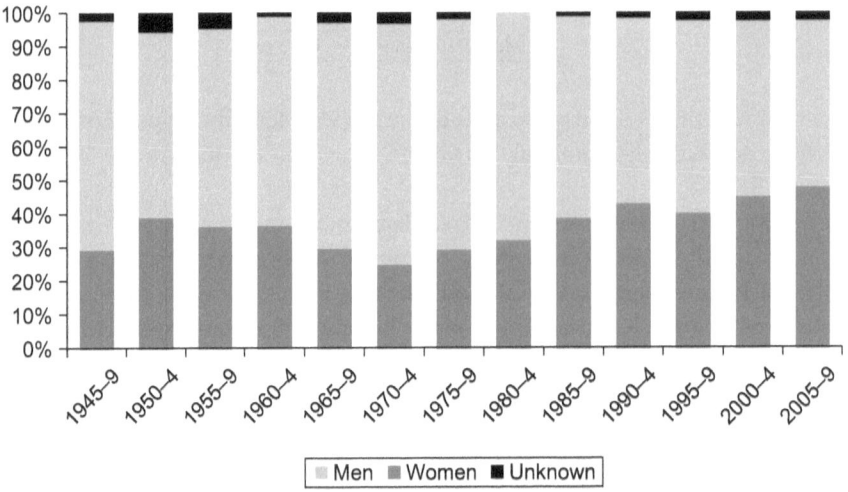

Figure 22. Men and women in the top twenty most critically discussed Australian authors, percentages, 1945 to 2006 (by decade)

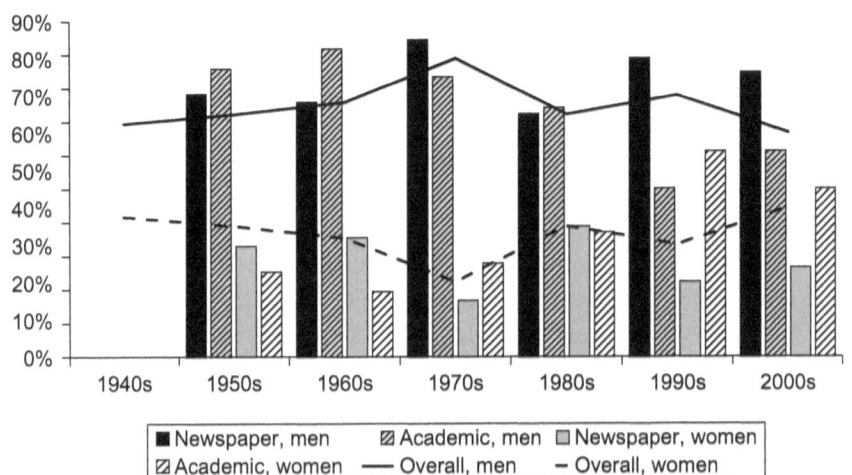

most critically discussed Australian novelists per decade from 1945.[6] For these first five years, it gives only the overall results. From the 1950s to the 2000s I have divided critical attention into two further categories of publication: newspapers and academic journals.[7] The dataset underlying this second graph is not without problems, particularly (due to the original search parameters used) its inclusion of authors not primarily known as novelists;[8] also, because of the size of this dataset, and the difficulty of extracting search results of over 1,000 records from *AustLit*, it has not been updated since the initial search in late 2007, and extends only to 2006. Despite these difficulties – and arguably, even better because of its inclusion of authors other than novelists – Figure 22 provides a useful indication of how discourses of gender shape critical debate about, as well as publication of, Australian literature.

I Male Domination? 1940s to 1960s

Men's domination of Australian literature in the immediate post-war decades is widely accepted, as indicated by Webby's confident invention of the 'WACM' acronym 'to describe th[is]…dominant influence in Australian story writing'.[9] Compared with the 1970s and 1980s, there are far fewer feminist analyses of Australian literature in this earlier period – an absence I would attribute, precisely, to the perception of these decades as male dominated, combined with the prevailing feminist focus on women's writing as definitive of gender issues. However, the studies that do explore gender trends in these decades maintain the association I noted in the introduction: between patriarchal social and cultural authority and the male domination of the authorship of Australian novels.

An important recent feminist study of this period – one that brings together and elaborates on a number of the arguments that have been made about the gendering of literature and literary debates in this period – is Sheridan's work on the 'lost' generation of women: those 'who came to writing in the 1940s and 1950s'. Sheridan points to a series of factors (material and psychological as well as discursive) that privileged men's and inhibited women's participation in post-war Australian literary culture. 'As many of the women attest', Sheridan writes,

> it was hard to find time to write – family responsibilities and economic insecurity worked against them, not to mention psychological barriers to asserting themselves as serious writers. And when they did produce, they found it hard to get published – impossible, in some instances – because of the patriarchal nature of literary institutions: the little magazines, the publishers, the funding bodies, the universities, and the forms of publicity and visibility they make possible.[10]

Sheridan perceives the male-oriented construction of Australian literature, including the novel, and the marginalisation of women it produced as having both national and transnational dimensions. Like Delys Bird, she argues that literary debates in Australia were constructed in ways that privileged the concerns of men and 'eclipsed' women's contributions.[11] The 'leading literary men of this period', Sheridan states, 'saw themselves…as engaged in battles against, variously, the communists, the modernists, the philistines…[that] did not include women as protagonists'.[12] Like David Carter, Sheridan describes the institutionalisation and professionalisation of Australian literary criticism from the 1950s as playing an important role in women's exclusion from literary culture. This process built on national literary debates, but also occurred with reference to broader traditions, with Australian literature – as part of its incorporation into universities at this time – articulated in relation to thoroughly male-dominated, transnational literary traditions: especially modernism and, later, postmodernism.[13]

The gender trends depicted in Figures 19 and 20 for the period before 1970 appear overwhelmingly to support these arguments regarding women's marginalisation within the Australian literary field. As these graphs show, male authors dominated the Australian novel in the post-war period, writing an astonishing 80 per cent of titles from 1945 to 1969. In contrast, only 18 per cent of Australian novels were by women (with 2 per cent by authors whose gender is unknown). Indeed in no other period since women began writing Australian novels in the mid-1850s do they constitute such a low proportion of authors, for such an extended period, as they did from the mid-1940s through to the late 1960s (and even into the 1970s).

Yet in considering the relationship between these empirical trends and the critical accounts, it is important to note that Sheridan's analysis (like Bird's and Carter's) is specifically concerned with literary fiction and its critical construction, whereas – as I demonstrated in Chapter 3 – at least 60 per cent of Australian novels published between 1945 and 1969 were locally published pulp fiction. In exploring gender trends in the authorship of Australian novels in this period, I begin with pulp fiction publishing before considering the remainder of the field (with a focus on the literary novel) and finally, critical discussion of Australian literature. The overwhelmingly male authorship of pulp fiction titles means that when this area of publishing is removed the field remains male dominated, but not strongly so, and not even relative to other periods in Australian literary history when critics describe a high proportion of women novelists. Gender trends in critical attention, however, definitely support the view that Australian literary culture was male oriented and dominated in these post-war decades.

Presuming that the pulp fiction novels included in *AustLit* are representative in terms of the gender novelists,[14] this area of publishing was overwhelmingly focused on male authors. From 1945 to 1969, men wrote an astonishing 93 per cent of Australian novels published by large and medium-sized pulp fiction publishers (Cleveland, Horwitz, Calvert, Action Comics, Currawong, Frank Johnson, Invincible Press and Webster Publications). Only 5 per cent of titles were by women, with 2 per cent by authors whose gender is unknown. The gendered connections between author, genre and reader that emerge in this intensely male-dominated area of Australian publishing provide insights into the operations of the local pulp fiction industry, while also indicating a gendered model of cultural production that influences publishing well beyond post-war pulp fiction.

Although Sheridan describes the difficulties in combining authorship and domestic responsibilities for women writers of the 1950s and 1960s, as I noted in Chapter 4 writing is generally seen as a profession relatively open to women because it can be done from the home.[15] Australian pulp fiction publishers, however, seem to have promoted a mode of authorship or way of working particularly suited to men. The extensive use of pseudonyms makes it difficult to determine a precise ratio of pulp fiction titles to authors, but it was not uncommon for a single novelist to write more than 20 novels. Some individuals – such as Carter Brown, J. E. Macdonnell and Keith Hetherington – wrote hundreds of novels for pulp fiction publishers, and the most prolific author, Leonard Frank Meares, published over 600 novels with Cleveland and Horwitz, mostly under the pseudonym Marshall Grover.[16] The unusually large number of titles per author suggests – as Toni Johnson-Woods discusses in relation to Carter Brown's contract with Horwitz[17] – that relations between pulp fiction publishers and authors were highly formalised, with authors often contracted to produce a certain number of titles per month or per year. This arrangement shifted writing from an activity that could be performed between other responsibilities – a model suited to women – to a high-pressure career, more befitting the traditional male breadwinner model of the period.[18]

While this mode of professionalisation of authorship seems an important factor in the prevalence of male authors of pulp fiction, the gendering of the most prevalent genres produced by this industry appears more influential. Of the novels published by large and medium-sized pulp fiction companies between 1945 and 1969 that are allocated a genre in *AustLit*,[19] 51 per cent were westerns, 20 per cent were crime or detective novels, 11 per cent were war novels and 10 per cent were romances.[20] John Cawelti singles out these genres as having long 'been thought of as distinctly gender oriented', with 'the popular romance…primarily a woman's genre…[and] action-adventure genres like the hard-boiled detective story, the western, and the war novel…produced with the image of a male audience in mind'.[21] Cawelti's comment refers to audience; my data show that authorship of Australian pulp fiction novels was strongly gendered along the same lines, with the prevalence of male authors reflecting the high proportion of genres aimed at a male audience. Although the majority of romance titles were also by men – thus reinforcing the extent to which the industry operated according to a male-oriented labour model – the small number of women authors of pulp fiction novels were concentrated in this traditionally female-oriented genre. More telling, perhaps, was the use of pseudonyms in the instances where the gender of author and gendering of genre did not align. With the notable exception of doctor/nurse stories – a subset of the romance genre that I believe was targeted at a male readership[22] – male authors of romance novels almost always employed female pseudonyms.[23] Likewise, the small number of women who published in male-oriented genres used male author names.[24]

This connection between the gendering of genre, author and reader indicates the presence, in twentieth-century popular fiction, of a similar essentialist model of cultural production and consumption to the one I discussed for the nineteenth century: where it is assumed that men and women wrote different types of fiction, and that only a male author would interest a male audience, while only a female author would interest – and deign to write for – female readers. This same privileged association of men's writing with men's concerns is, of course, central to Sheridan's description of the literary novel in this period, with men seeing themselves as 'engaged in battles' with or against other men.[25] In respect to pulp fiction, the consistent use of female pseudonyms by male authors of romances (and male pseudonyms by female authors of westerns and detective novels) indicates the enormous strength of this gendered model. At the same time, the presumed success of these pseudonyms – the capacity, in other words, for women successfully to masquerade as male authors and vice versa – provides a neat demonstration of the fallacy of this essentialist model of reading and writing.

Although performative, this gendered model of cultural production enables reflection on the readerships of these titles. If we accept that pulp westerns, hard-boiled crime and war novels were targeted at, and predominantly read by, men then the prominence of these genres in local pulp fiction publishing – and in the Australian book market – brings into view a substantial male readership. As with pulp fiction generally, in the American context the male characters of popular and pulp fiction (especially the private eye and the cowboy) – and their meaning for a male readership – have received significant critical attention. Cawelti identifies 'hard-boiled and western heroes' as private, stoic, independent and tough men, and in this sense, as 'appropriate for the heroic archetype of a democratic society'.[26] Alternatively, Joanne Tompkins describes the rigidity of gender roles depicted in the western as one of the means by which American men reclaimed cultural territory from women.[27] The extent to which these contrasting interpretations of masculinity in American genre fiction resonate with established themes in Australian literary history – such as Russel Ward's 'Australian legend',[28] and Marilyn Lake's account of the 'battle' between masculinists and feminists for cultural authority[29] – suggests fruitful avenues for future research into Australian pulp fiction and its relationship to mid-century constructions of national identity and Australian masculinity.

The predominance of male-oriented genres in the post-war Australian book market also raises the question: where were the women readers? The importance of this question comes sharply into focus if we accept, as Sheridan and others argue, that the literary novel was also male oriented. Sheridan's analysis of the *Australian Women's Weekly* (*AWW*) offers what I think is an important part of the answer to this question of what women were reading, while also helping to explain gender and genre trends in pulp fiction publishing. This publication, explicitly targeted at women, was at the peak of its considerable popularity and influence from 1946 to 1971, the period when local pulp fiction publishing also was at its height.[30] Along with 'humour, advice, columns, celebrity stories, informative features, photo series, editorials and advertising',[31] Sheridan notes that *AWW* readers were offered a substantial amount of fiction. This fiction included serialised Australian novels,[32] but condensed novels and short stories – often by overseas authors – were most common.[33] In the 1950s, the majority of stories published in the *AWW* were romance fiction by American authors.[34] The availability of such fiction in the *AWW* contrasts with the general restrictions on the import into Australia of America-originated fiction until the end of the 1950s. In Chapter 3 I argue that the publishing data supports Johnson-Woods' and others' identification of import tariffs on American print culture as the main cause of growth in Australian pulp fiction.[35] The fiction published in this major, female-oriented Australian magazine indicates that Australian women continued to have access to American fiction despite these tariffs. As well as offering some insight into what women were reading, the prevalence of American romance fiction in the *AWW* helps to explain why there was relatively little pulp romance published in Australia: as such fiction remained available, there was no gap in the market for local pulp fiction publishers to fill.[36]

The gendered connection between authorship, genre and target readership that shaped Australian pulp fiction publishing also influenced popular fiction publishing more broadly, producing a slight national trend – among American and British publishers of Australian novels in this period – towards the fiction of men or women. Specifically, where major American publishers of pulp and popular fiction – Doubleday, Bantam and Ace Books – focused on both male authors and male-oriented genres (crime, westerns and science fiction, respectively),[37] major British presses – Collins and Mills & Boon – published a high proportion of both Australian novels by women and romance fiction.[38] The connection between the gendering of genres and of authorship in pulp and popular fiction in these post-war decades, and the high proportion of Australian novels published by these companies, indicates how gender influences the novel field well beyond the literary fiction that remains the focus of most feminist analyses in the Australian context.

Where pulp – and much popular – fiction was clearly male dominated in these post-war decades, for the literary novel, evidence of this gender trend is less apparent. Male novelists were clearly overrepresented in the lists of non-Australian publishers of Australian novels known for literary fiction, including Cassell, Faber and Faber, and Hamish Hamilton (from Britain), and Farrar, Straus and Giroux (from America).[39] With the exception of Cassell, however, these companies published only a small number of titles, so had little effect on overall gender trends. Based on the studies discussed previously – by Sheridan, Bird and Carter – one would expect local non-pulp publishing to be the arena where the male domination of the Australian literary novel was most apparent: these publishers were the most directly impacted by the organisation of national literary debates around issues relevant to men, and the institutionalisation and professionalisation of Australian literary studies. Yet in respect to this group of publishers, gender trends in authorship are ambiguous. On the one hand, as Figure 21 shows, men wrote 69 per cent of locally published, non-pulp Australian novels from 1945 to 1969, compared with 27 per cent by women and 4 per cent by authors whose gender is unknown; so male novelists clearly dominated local publishing. This local industry was also slightly more male dominated than non-pulp publishing overall in this period (when 62 per cent of titles were by men, compared with 36 per cent by women and 2 per cent by authors whose gender is unknown). On the other hand, women authors had a relatively strong presence in the local non-pulp novel field for much of this period. Although only 29 per cent of such titles were by women in the late 1940s, in the early 1950s, this proportion increased considerably to 39 per cent, and remained relatively high (at 36 per cent) in the late 1950s and early 1960s, before falling to 30 per cent in the late 1960s and 25 per cent in the early 1970s. Although the overall trend is a decline, local non-pulp publishers did not again produce such a high proportion of Australian novels by women until the late 1980s and early 1990s: that is, at the peak of the period – as I will discuss in the next section – when the feminist 'rise' of the woman writer is deemed to have occurred. This relatively high rate of local publication of Australian women's novels conflicts with both the notion of a male-dominated literary culture prior to the 1970s, and the emphasis on growth in women's writing in this decade and the following one.

Focusing on individual publishers also yields no clear evidence of a definitive local shift to male authors. Leaving aside Angus and Robertson (A&R), two of the top five most prolific local presses – Australasian Book Society and Ure Smith – mainly published novels by men,[40] while two – Dymocks and, in the 1950s, Cheshire – published mostly women's novels.[41] Rigby, which only started publishing Australian novels in the 1960s, was responsible for an approximately equal number of titles by men and women in that decade.[42] Of these publishers, Dymocks was arguably the most focused on popular fiction, especially traditionally female-oriented genres such as family sagas and young adult fiction. From this perspective, it would be possible to identify a substantial part of the local publication of women's writing in the 1950s with popular genres. However, the focus on men's novels by Ure Smith was also largely tied to a popular genre, specifically humour fiction. In terms of local non-pulp publishing in these post-war decades, the most notable finding in support of claims of a male orientation of Australian literary culture relates to the output of A&R – the most prolific of these publishers, responsible for more than fifteen times the number of Australian novels than any other publisher in this group. A&R is known for its focus on Australian literary fiction above and beyond profitability,[43] and as would be expected in a field where the literary novel was increasingly male dominated, the proportion of women's novels published by this company fell, from 35 per cent in the late 1940s to 29 per cent in the second half of the 1960s. But even this trend is complicated by a substantial surge in A&R's publication of women's novels in the early 1960s, when 45 per cent of titles were by women.

Between 1945 and 1969, gender trends in authorship present scant or ambiguous signs of the male orientation and domination of Australian literary culture. In respect to critical discussion, however, there is strong evidence of this phenomenon. As Figure 22 shows, men increasingly dominated among the top twenty most critically discussed Australian authors.[44] In terms of overall discussion, from 1945 and 1949, 63 per cent of these top twenty authors were men, increasing to 65 per cent in the 1950s and 68 per cent in the 1960s. Focusing on the top five most discussed authors renders the progressive decline in attention to women even more apparent. In the second half of the 1940s this group was actually female dominated, with Henry Handel Richardson the most discussed Australian author, and Eleanor Dark and Miles Franklin in equal third place (Martin Boyd was second and Joseph Furphy, writing as Tom Collins, was fifth). In the 1950s, there were only two women in the top five: Judith Wright, ranked first but discussed for her poetry rather than her two children's novels, and Katharine Susannah Prichard, ranked equal fifth (with Henry G. Lamond). By the 1960s there was only Wright, in second place.[45] Richardson had fallen to fourteenth, and Prichard to sixteenth; Franklin and Dark had disappeared from the top twenty.[46]

Academic and newspaper discussion of Australian authors also shifted towards men in the 1950s and 1960s. In these decades, academic attention was even more male oriented than overall discussion: 77 per cent of the top twenty most discussed authors in academic journals in the 1950s were men, increasing to 83 per cent in the 1960s. As with overall attention, the declining proportion of women in the top twenty for academic discussion was accompanied by the disappearance of women from the highest-ranking positions. Although the top twenty authors in this category in the 1950s were three quarters male, women featured relatively strongly in the top ten, and even in the top five: with Judith Wright and Katharine Susannah

Prichard equal second, Dymphna Cusack fifth, Miles Franklin equal seventh and Henry Handel Richardson equal ninth.[47] By contrast, in the 1960s, Richardson, Wright and Prichard – ranked equal second, fourth and fifth respectively – were the only women authors in the top ten for academic discussion.[48]

Relative to the academic arena, newspaper discussion of Australian authors was somewhat less male dominated: in the 1950s, men constituted 70 per cent of the top twenty most discussed authors in newspapers, declining slightly to 68 per cent in the 1960s. This slight proportional decline in attention to men is, however, misleading as there was actually one fewer woman in the top twenty for newspaper discussion in the 1960s than in the 1950s.[49] Certain women also ranked higher in newspaper than in academic or overall discussion (if they appeared in these latter two categories at all). For instance, Kylie Tennant was ranked fifth in terms of newspaper discussion in the 1950s and equal seventh in the 1960s, but only equal twelfth in overall discussion in the first of these decades and thirteenth in the second (she does not appear in the top twenty for academic discussion in either decade). Other women writers besides Tennant – including Thea Astley, Dorothy Cottrell, Eleanor Dark and Ethel Turner in the 1950s, and Astley, Dymphna Cusack and Miles Franklin in the 1960s – were in the top twenty for newspaper, but not academic, attention.

Given that discussion of Australian authors in academic journals was almost certainly the most focused on the literary novel, the greater attention to male authors in this forum (than in newspapers or overall) reinforces descriptions of the male domination of Australian literary culture in these post-war decades. At the same time, the way that women were marginalised in – or, to use Gaye Tuchman's phrase, 'edged out' of – both academic and newspaper criticism indicates that literary prestige, in general, was increasingly male oriented. Accordingly, while the proportion of non-pulp Australian novels by women published locally in these post-war decades was substantially higher than might be expected based on claims of male domination of Australian literary culture, these results for critical attention clearly support Sheridan's description of the 'eclipse' of women writers. As she argues:

> Most of the [women] writers of this generation were overlooked, or not taken seriously, for much of their own lifetimes... If you look at the career of one writer or artist who seems to have missed the boat of literary fashion, you may conclude that she was just unlucky. But when you see a whole cohort of women who missed out, or were only intermittently visible during their most creative years, you begin to see the value of looking at them as a group – whether or not they saw themselves that way.[50]

I certainly agree with Sheridan that, only by looking at the experiences of women – and men – 'as a group' is it possible to identify and explore the impact of gender in the literary field. Keeping with this line of thought, I want to conclude my discussion of gender trends in the authorship and publication of post-war Australian novels with two observations about particular gendered groupings.

First, I think it is important to highlight another eclipse: one that challenges the view, implicit in Sheridan's declaration above and explicitly stated elsewhere in her paper, that it is 'women [who] get eclipsed from view over and over again'.[51] The trends in critical discussion clearly indicate that women writers such as Henry Handel Richardson, Miles Franklin and Katharine Susannah Prichard lost their once prominent places in the cultural imaginary in the 1950s and 1960s, and that critical attention to newer women authors – including Kylie Tennant, Christina Stead and Thea Astley – fell far short of that paid to male authors such as Thomas Keneally, Randolph Stow and, of course, Patrick White. However, the type of writing most thoroughly eclipsed in contemporary and subsequent critical discussion of the Australian novel is pulp fiction: an industry, a profession, and a reading community overwhelmingly dominated by men. Obviously, critics do not ignore these novelists because they were men. However, there is a basis for identifying this eclipse as also gendered, not in respect to authors but to constructions of cultural value and authority.

As Sheridan and Carter recognise, in these post-war decades literary value was constructed in strongly gendered terms, specifically through a dichotomy that opposed serious, masculinised literature to trivial, feminised fiction. Although Australian pulp novels were predominantly written by men and explicitly male-oriented genres dominated, this type of fiction – mass, commercial, cheap – exists on the feminine side of this dichotomy. While the preponderance of male authors in this field shows that these gendered constructions can directly contrast with the gender of authors, the neglect of pulp fiction in Australian literary studies – and more pointedly, the automatic dismissal, by most critics, of such fiction as unworthy and uninteresting – suggests the ongoing influence of gender in structuring cultural value and literary history.

The second point I want to make moves in essentially the opposite direction: to the connections rather than the contrast between genre and literary fiction. Although mass culture is feminised, what seems to me most interesting and significant about the gender trends that emerge in respect to the post-war Australian novel is the resonance – and potential parallels – between the gender orientation of literary and pulp forms. Both categories of fiction were not only predominantly written by men, but were oriented towards a male audience. No connections between the blatant masculinity of these pulp titles and the refined aesthetic of literary fiction have been made in the Australian context. But this is not the case elsewhere. In America – along with attention to pulp fiction generally, and to its male characters in particular – there has been extended discussion of the 'relations between literary modernism and other aspects of modern culture',[52] including the hard-boiled male detective.[53]

While attention to similar resonances in the Australian novel field is needed, the male orientation of both genre and literary fiction reinforces the underlying claim of feminist accounts of the period: that a patriarchal society, which privileged the identities and concerns of men while marginalising those of women, functioned to foreground both cultural production by male authors, and a male audience for that product. What seems to me a vital focus for future research into the Australian literary field in these post-war decades is the way in which this male-orientated culture exceeded those battles with communists, modernists and philistines that Sheridan describes; or more intriguingly, perhaps, how these same battles emerged in different forms and genres, and with potentially different meanings. The next section of this chapter explores the shift away from this male-oriented paradigm. Specifically, I consider how the rise of the feminist movement – and the attention it focused on women's identities and concerns – challenged this gendering of Australian literature and produced a redefinition of fiction also extending to both popular genre and literary spheres.

II Female Liberation? 1970s to 1980s

At the start of this chapter I identified a perception of growth in women's writing in the 1970s and 1980s as foundational to feminist accounts of contemporary Australian literary history. The empirical results clearly support this perception. As Figures 19 and 20 indicate, the proportion and number of Australian novels by women increased considerably in these decades. Women wrote 21 per cent of such titles in the early 1970s, increasing to 28 per cent in the late 1970s, 38 in the early 1980s, and 40 per cent in the late 1980s. As the proportion of Australian novels by women effectively doubled, the proportion by men fell from 78 to 71, 61 and 57 per cent respectively. Without pulp fiction, women's contributions to the Australian novel field are even greater. Women wrote 33 per cent of non-pulp titles in the early 1970s, increasing to 41 per cent in the late 1970s and 48 per cent in the early 1980s, before declining slightly to 47 per cent in the late 1980s (a fall that should be seen in the context of the relatively high proportion – 3 per cent – of authors in the unknown gender category in this final five-year period). The proportion of non-pulp novels by men fell, accordingly, from 67, to 58, 51 and 50 per cent.[54]

As I said previously, Webby attributes the proliferation of authors other than white, Anglo-Celtic men in these decades to political shifts that challenged patriarchal social and institutional power and changed the authors 'able to assert their…subjectivity' and the types of 'stories' they told.[55] Other feminist analyses from the late 1980s and early 1990s associate women's writing much more explicitly with second-wave feminism, effectively constructing it as a manifestation of feminist politics. In this context, growth in women's writing in the 1970s and 1980s is presented as a sign of the cultural and critical success of feminism. Brian Matthews, for instance, identifies the 1970s with 'protest literature' generally, but claims that in the 1980s, 'probably the greatest single and coherent pressure is the voice of second-wave feminism, whose tones many women writers convey with great assurance'.[56] In her analysis of Australian women's writing from 1970 to 1990, Gillian Whitlock describes the 'flourishing feminist culture' of the 1970s as 'the seedbed for women's writing'; as the decade progressed, 'this writing was part of the women's movement', where it was associated with 'understanding women's experience', 'conscious-raising' and 'actively changing women's lives'.[57] Elsewhere, Whitlock identifies a 'wave of women's writing' in the 1980s, and attributes this transformative feature of the 'literary landscape' to 'a series of effects produced by the re-emergence of feminism', in writing, publishing, reviewing and reading.[58] In their survey of Australian fiction from 1970 to 1988, Ken Gelder and Paul Salzman propose: 'it would be possible to trace a history of women's writing in the 1970s that paralleled the political developments of the women's movement'.[59] The focus, in Salzman's chapter on women's writing, on two themes – 'the attempt to capture certain areas of female experience, and the attempt to find a language or…narrative structure, that stretches the form of fiction away from certain conservative conventions seen as patriarchal'[60] – presents such fiction as a direct response to, even an expression of, the feminist movement.

These analyses, from the late 1980s and early 1990s, manifest the political tenor of the time. More recently, this association of women's writing and feminist writing has been subject to significant criticism. For instance, Rosalind Coward, and following her, Jennifer Strauss – focusing on Australian literature – argued that conflating 'feminist writing and writing by women' obscures important differences between women writers while promoting a depoliticised version of feminism.[61] In response to such criticism, more recent surveys tend specifically to distinguish women's writing from feminist writing: Bird, for example, identifies feminist writing as only one subset of writing by Australian women.[62] Without wanting to underplay the importance of this distinction, in what follows I contend that neither the understanding of all women's writing as an expression of feminist politics, nor this limiting of the connection between feminism and women's writing to one subset of fiction, accurately encapsulates the relationship between feminism and growth in Australian women's writing in the 1970s and 1980s, or since.

I agree with the broad premise that the feminist movement had a transformative effect on the Australian novel field and, more specifically, played a substantial role in producing the conditions for growth in women's writing. However, a focus on literary writing misapprehends the nature of that growth and the relationship between politics and fiction. Growth in women's writing occurred in the literary and political fiction that is the focus of much feminist literary criticism in the Australian context. However, the most substantial growth was in Australian women's romance fiction, a form of writing ignored in the discussion above, and often viewed as antithetical to feminism. I propose that, in the case of both literary and romance fiction, growth in women's writing – and the relationship between such writing and feminism – needs to be understood in relation to the market: specifically, to a conceptualisation, by publishers of both types of writing, of fiction by women as a clearly defined and lucrative area of publishing. Feminism played an important role in motivating recognition of writing by women as, precisely, 'women's writing'; but this recognition produced such a substantial increase in women's presence in the Australian novel field because of the ways it was translated by publishers into a series of markets for women's writing. Though linked to the focus instituted by feminism on women's lives and identities, the major market for such writing – in romance fiction – did not express the political aims of feminism. As with men's writing in the post-war decades, women's increased authorship of both literary and popular Australian novels in the 1970s and 1980s related to, and built upon, an essentialist model of cultural production, wherein – in this case – women are constructed as the only ones able (or willing) to speak to and about women.

Before discussing the areas of local and multinational publishing where the growth in women's authorship of Australian novels occurred, it is important to note that parts of the Australian novel field remained explicitly male dominated in these decades. In the local pulp fiction industry – which continued to constitute a substantial proportion of Australian novels (45 and 18 per cent of all titles in the 1970s and

1980s respectively) – gender trends were a continuation of those in the post-war decades: authorship remained intensely male dominated, with men writing 90 per cent of locally published pulp fiction in the 1970s and 98 per cent in the 1980s. Such companies also continued to focus on male-oriented genres. Of the pulp fiction titles published in the 1970s and 1980s and allotted a genre in *AustLit*,[63] 67 per cent were westerns; 13 per cent were crime or detective novels; and 9 per cent were war fiction. Only 3 per cent were in the traditionally female-oriented genre of romance fiction.[64] As in the post-war decades, the gender of the authors of these titles (or of the pseudonyms they employed) correlate strongly with the gender orientation of the genre (and, presumably, with the gender of the major audience for these books). American publication of Australian novels also became increasingly male dominated: in the 1970s, when 7 per cent of Australian novels were published in America, 92 per cent of these were by men. As with local pulp fiction, this American gender trend was a continuation and intensification of publishing trajectories of the post-war era, specifically relating to popular genres.[65]

The strong concentration of male authors in local pulp and American publishing shows the persistence of earlier, male-oriented fictional paradigms, and provides a salutary demonstration that growth in women's writing was not a universal feature of the Australian novel field from the 1970s. At the same time, the sharp decline in the output of such publishers – alone enough dramatically to increase the proportion of Australian novels by women – was part of the gendered paradigm shift towards women's writing that I want to explore. The local and multinational companies that played a growing, and by the 1990s and 2000s dominant, role in the production of Australian novels were also the two areas of the industry where publication of Australian women's novels increased from the 1970s. Figure 21 depicts this growth in local non-pulp publishing, where the 25 per cent of titles by women in the early 1970s gradually increased to 29 per cent in the late 1970s, 32 per cent in the early 1980s and 39 per cent in the late 1980s (with a corresponding fall in local publication of non-pulp titles by men from 72 to 69, 68 and 60 per cent).[66]

Given the extent to which the politically and culturally progressive energies of the 1970s are identified with the local industry, the growth in local publication of Australian women's novels, and the proportions themselves, are surprisingly low. While I believe that the results indicate that a politically progressive cultural shift did occur in Australian publishing in this decade, as in the post-war decades, gender trends in local literary publishing in the 1970s are ambiguous. As would be expected from the proportional results, the lists of most, including the major, local publishers remained focused on male authors: 44 of the 58 Australian novels published by A&R were by men, as were eight of nine by Outback Press, and eight of ten by UQP; Wren Books, Georgian House and Hyland House only published men's novels.[67] The marginal presence of novels by women on the lists of these local publishers resonates with Bird's synopsis of gender dynamics in Australian literature and literary criticism. Bird argues that, especially in the early 1970s, 'Australian fiction was a masculine territory',[68] and describes the male orientation of both the fiction and criticism in this decade. Specifically, she notes that the 'new fiction' of the early 1970s is '[n]ow often criticised as misogynist and sexist',[69] and the 'new criticism' largely ignored '[w]omen writers of the past…[and] their contemporary presence'. According to Bird, such criticism also overlooked

> the vigorous social debates about repressive gender ideologies and sexist social structures generated by feminist politics. Defining the field in those critical works is done from a male perspective and the writers dealt with are overwhelmingly male.[70]

Where the high rate of local publication of Australian men's novels in the 1970s reinforces Bird's analysis of the decade, other aspects of the data suggest that local publishers did shift towards women's writing, and literary fiction in particular. The proportion of Australian women's novels not ascribed a genre in *AustLit* (an aspect of the database that can be used, with caution, to indicate publishing trends in literary fiction) increased: in the 1960s, an equal proportion (65 per cent) of men's and women's novels were not allocated a genre; in the 1970s, the proportion of women's novels in this category increased considerably (to 70 per cent in the first part of that decade and 80 per cent in the second), while the proportion of men's declined (to 61 and 59 per cent respectively). According to these results, the major part of the growth in locally published literary fiction in the 1970s – described in Chapter 3 – occurred in women's writing. The proportion of women's non-genre novels subsequently fell to 68 per cent in the early 1980s and 61 per cent in the second half of that decade, but remained higher than the proportion of men's novels in this category for these two five-year periods (when 53 and 54 per cent of titles by men, respectively, are not assigned a genre in *AustLit*). These results clearly exaggerate the likely presence of literary fiction in the Australian novel field. Nevertheless, they suggest that, despite many publishers continuing to focus on male authors, the slight growth in local publication of Australian women's novels in the 1970s was concurrent with a fostering of women's literary titles.

Gender trends in critical discussion of Australian authors in the 1970s are also somewhat ambiguous. The trends overall, and in newspapers, support Bird's description of an 'invisible orthodoxy' operating in the 1970s and defining Australian fiction as a male domain.[71] As Figure 22 demonstrates, in these two arenas the progressive critical focus on male authors through the 1950s and 1960s continued in the 1970s. In this decade, the proportion of men in the top twenty most discussed authors increased from 68 per cent in both categories in the 1960s to 80 per cent overall and 85 per cent in newspaper articles. For academic discussion, however, the 1970s were the beginning of a significant shift towards women's writing. While 83 per cent of the top twenty most discussed authors in this category were male in the 1960s, in the 1970s this proportion declined to 75 per cent. In the context of this proportional shift, women also featured strongly among the top authors discussed, occupying the third (Henry Handel Richardson), fourth (Dorothy Hewett), fifth (Judith Wright) and sixth (Christina Stead) positions (after Patrick White and Thomas Keneally in first and second place).[72]

Aspects of this proportional shift in the gender of authors in the top twenty for academic discussion, and the specific authors targeted, are relevant to Bird's discussion of the 1970s. Bird's identification of the latter part of this decade with a 'new awareness of women's writing as a lucrative publishing category and the beginnings of a feminist critical industry' raises the question of whether the shift towards academic discussion of women's writing was largely manifest in the late 1970s.[73] In fact, while individual women authors ranked higher in the top twenty in this five-year period,[74] there was one fewer woman in this category in the second than the first half of that decade. Bird also identifies Christina Stead and Thea Astley as 'the only women writers regularly cited as worthy of mention by the new critics of the 1970s, although little attention was given them'.[75] The names cited previously suggest a wider range of authors were discussed (although Dorothy Hewett and Judith Wright, at least, would have received attention predominantly for their poetry). Nonetheless, Astley's absence from this list for the decade as a whole (despite ranking thirteenth in the early 1970s)[76] is surprising. Whatever the trends in academic discussion within the decade, and although the shift to women's writing in this arena is by no means overwhelming, these results – combined with what appears to be an orientation by local publishers to women's literary fiction – suggest that the 'invisible orthodoxy' of earlier decades was beginning to erode in the 1970s, if unevenly.

The effects of this erosion are more apparent in the 1980s. The stronger proportional growth in local publication of Australian women's novels in this decade (compared to the 1970s) was created by a clear shift, by a wide range of local literary presses, towards women's writing: 21 of 44 Australian novels published by UQP in the 1980s were by women, as were 9 of 18 by Hale & Iremonger; 5 of 10 by Fremantle Arts Centre Press; four of eight by Boolarong; and four of seven by McPhee Gribble. As would be expected, the presses identified with feminist or women-centred fiction that emerge in this decade – although publishing a limited number of titles – concentrated on women's novels: all eight titles published by Dykebooks were by women, as were five of eight by Greenhouse Publications and two of two by Sybylla Press, Sisters Publishing and Women's Redress Press. Nevertheless, there were still local publishers in the 1980s that focused on men's novels, including Hyland House (with 15 of 17 titles by men) and Pascoe Publishing (eight of nine).[77]

This incorporation of women's writing by most local literary publishers in the 1980s was mirrored by gender trends in critical attention. As Figure 22 shows, the growth in academic attention to women's writing in the 1970s continued in the 1980s, when 67 (down from 75) per cent of the top twenty most discussed authors were men. Gender trends in overall and newspaper discussion moved in the same direction as for academic debate, with the proportion of male authors in the top twenty falling (from 80) to 65 per cent overall, and (from 85) to 65 per cent in newspapers.

The women ranked in the top twenty for critical discussion in the 1980s constitute a clearly recognisable canon of contemporary Australian women's writing. Four women writers were in the top twenty across all categories: Elizabeth Jolley, the most discussed woman writer, occupied third place overall, as well as fourth in academic and fifth in newspaper discussion; Christina Stead was eighth, fifth and eleventh, respectively; Thea Astley was eleventh, seventeenth and seventh; and Dorothy Hewett was twelfth, eighteenth and nineteenth. Two other women writers were in the top twenty for both overall and newspaper discussion – Kate Grenville (thirteenth and fifteenth respectively) and Barbara Hanrahan (seventeenth and twelfth) – while Katharine Susannah Prichard was in the top twenty for overall and academic attention (appearing nineteenth and thirteenth respectively). There was also a number of women who only appeared in one category: for academic attention, Henry Handel Richardson was ninth and Shirley Hazzard sixteenth; Marion Halligan appeared in nineteenth place for newspaper attention. Of the women listed here who were writing in the 1980s, the majority of their novels were published by local literary presses, especially UQP, Fremantle Arts Centre Press and A&R (although American presses also play a significant role); interestingly, none were published by the local feminist presses that arose in this decade.

On the one hand, this shift in critical attention, and the rate of local publication of Australian women's novels, were not as pronounced as might have been anticipated by feminist descriptions of the 1980s as the 'decade of the women writer',[78] the 'moment of glory' for such authors,[79] or a time of 'radical revis[ion]' in '[c]ritical ignorance of the ways gender functions in writing, publishing and reading'.[80] Local presses, after all, still published mostly men's novels, and male authors still attracted the majority of critical attention. On the other hand, especially given the timing and concurrence of these shifts, as well as the particular women authors that received critical attention, the impact of the feminist movement on definitions of literature and on conceptions of literary value seems indisputable. In the 1980s, Australian women novelists were increasingly present on the lists of local literary presses and considerably more likely to receive critical attention than at any other time since the end of the Second World War.

Despite the importance of this local (and broadly literary) trend, the major growth in women's writing in this period occurred in multinational publishing, and romance fiction specifically. Figure 23 compares gender trends in local non-pulp publication of Australian novels (the same results shown in Figure 21) with those in multinational publishing. I will return to the meaning of the dotted lines shortly; the bars show that multinationals published a much higher proportion of women's novels than local publishers: 69 per cent of Australian novels published by multinationals in the early 1970s were by women, increasing to 76 per cent in the late 1970s before declining to 68 per cent in the early 1980s and 59 per cent in the second half of that decade. Even with this decline through the 1980s, multinationals published a significantly higher proportion of Australian novels by women during the 1970s and 1980s, and even in the late 1980s, than did local presses.[81]

This clear gender trend in multinational publication of Australian novels was concurrent with substantial growth in the number of such titles (overall and, obviously given the proportional results, by women). Figure 24 – depicting the numerical results underpinning the proportional ones in Figure 23 – shows that multinationals published a rapidly increasing number of novels by women in the 1970s and 1980s, and that this number was significantly greater than for local publication of women's novels.[82] In fact, multinational companies published more titles by women in the final five years of the 1980s (265) than local companies did in the entire 1970s and 1980s (228). Figure 24 also shows that multinationals published more titles by women than men in these decades and that, in the late 1970s, the number of Australian women's novels published by multinationals equalled and subsequently outstripped the number of locally published titles by men. Especially given the stronger growth in multinational

THE 'RISE' OF THE WOMAN NOVELIST   149

Figure 23. Australian novels (excluding pulp fiction) by men and women, published by Australian and multinational companies (with and without Torstar), percentages, 1965 to 2009 (five-yearly averages)

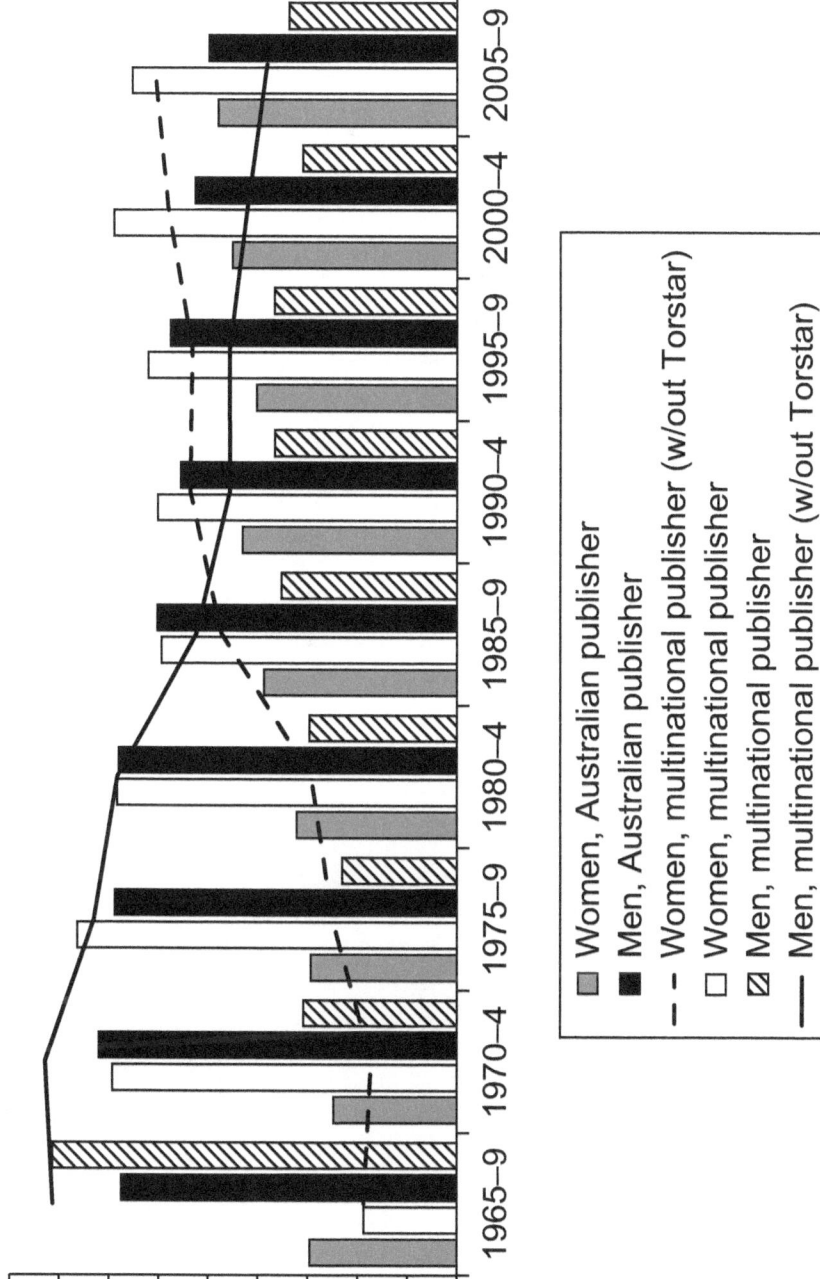

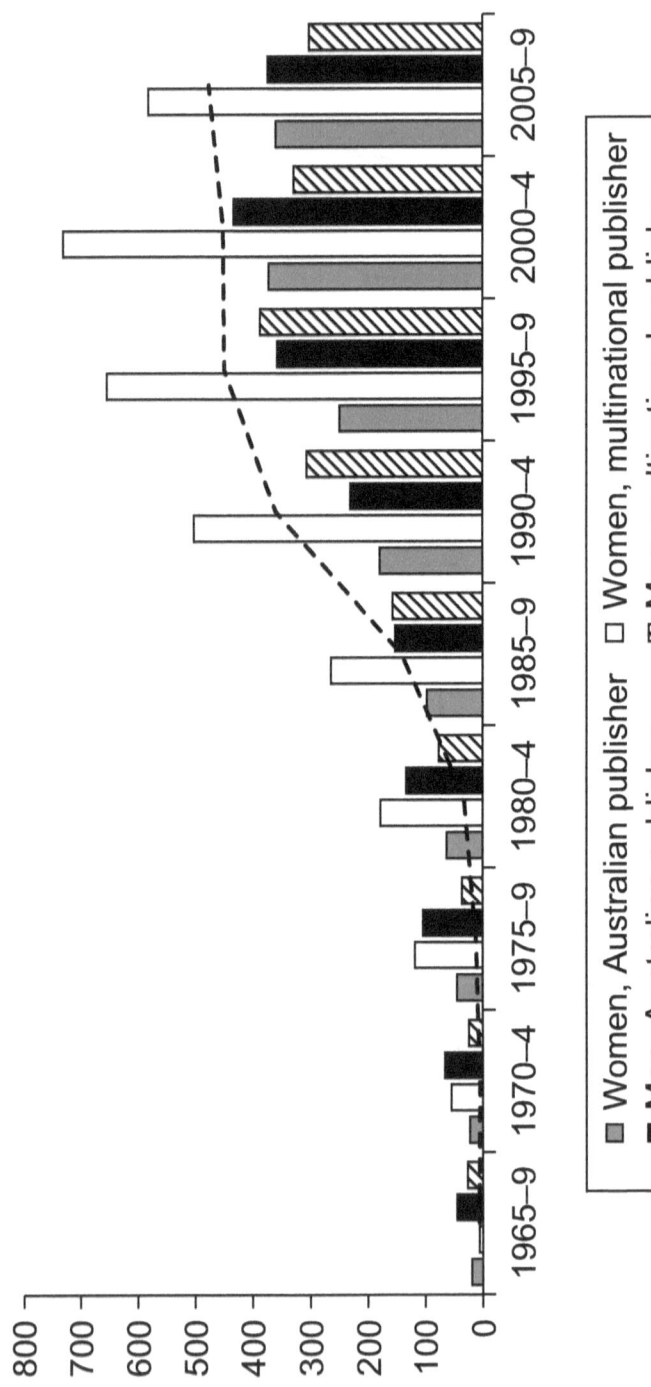

Figure 24. Number of Australian novels (excluding pulp fiction) by men and women, published by Australian and multinational companies (with and without Torstar), 1965 to 2009 (five-yearly totals)

than local publication of Australian novels in the 1970s, and the greater proportion of titles published by multinational than local presses in the 1980s,[83] these results indicate that the majority of growth in women's writing in these decades occurred in the realm of multinational publishing: specifically, as I will show, in romance fiction. As with men's writing in the post-war decades, then, growth in women's writing in the 1970s and 1980s occurred in both literary and genre fiction, with genre fiction constituting the major part of this growth.

Rather than an industry-wide focus on women's writing, this gender trend in multinational publishing – especially in the 1970s – was largely attributable to the output of a single company: Torstar, owner of Harlequin Mills & Boon and the major multinational presence in the Australian novel field in the 1970s and 1980s (responsible for 67 per cent of the Australian novels published by multinationals in the first of these decades, and 41 per cent in the second). Almost all of the titles published by this company were by women (only one in the 1970s and four in the 1980s were by men).[84] As was the case with local pulp fiction publishing, Torstar's output – focused on both romance fiction and women authors – demonstrates a strong correlation between the gendering of a genre, its authors and (we can assume) its readers.

Removing Torstar from the results has a significant effect on gender trends. The dotted lines in Figure 23 show the proportion of Australian novels by men and women published by multinational conglomerates besides Torstar; the dotted line in Figure 24 shows the number of titles by women not including this company. Based on this sample, gender proportions in local and multinational publishing followed a similar pattern through the 1970s and 1980s: incorporating an increasing proportion of women's, but still focusing on men's, novels. Indeed, without Torstar, local companies published more novels by women than multinationals until the late 1980s (another genre – young adult fiction – provided a major reason for the growth in multinational publication of women's novels in this last five-year period).[85] Even though largely attributable to the output of a single company, Australian women's romance fiction represents the leading cause of growth – not only in women's writing, but in the Australian novel field as a whole, in the 1970s and 1980s.

Romance fiction is often perceived as inimical to feminism. Stevi Jackson describes an unambiguous critique of heterosexual romance narratives, and the subjugation of women in these stories, as central to 'the early years of "second wave" feminism'.[86] Dismissive references to romance – as 'emotional manipulation' (from Kate Millet), 'dope for dupes' (from Germaine Greer) and 'the cultural tool of male power' (from Shulamith Firestone) – peppered feminist arguments from this period.[87] In *The Madwoman in the Attic*, one of the foundational texts of feminist literary criticism, Sandra Gilbert and Susan Gubar decried the 'worn-out, hackneyed stories of romance' that women are offered, and the 'glass coffin of romance' readers are encouraged and expected to accept.[88] As Susan Strehle and Mary Carden note, the 'feminist critic interested in romance of either literary or popular variety, is most inclined to regard it as an oppressive tool of patriarchy and to object to its reliance on and perpetuation of damaging stereotypes' of masculinity and femininity.[89] These descriptions of romance expose the tension between the discussion of growth in

Australian women's writing in the 1970s and 1980s – largely attributed to feminism – and the negative perception, by many feminist scholars of that period, of the romance fiction where the majority of this growth occurred. One might suggest, on this basis, that women's increased contribution to the Australian novel field at this time was largely in opposition to the feminist movement. Certainly, these trends show that feminism did not have the destructive consequences for romance fiction anticipated in the 1970s.[90]

More recent scholarship, however, claims a connection between romance fiction and feminism. Critics such as Janice Radway and Tania Modleski argue that, although women are almost always subordinated to men in their endings, romance narratives create spaces for expressing female protest and resistance, and exploring female sexuality, power and identity.[91] According to Strehle and Carden, 'romance reflects both the patriarchal oppression of women and women's strength in resisting, in forging appropriate forms of heroism', with some romances actively 'critiqu[ing]…patriarchal oppression'.[92] Authors and editors directly involved in the industry even define the genre as feminist. Romance author Jayne Ann Krentz describes romance novels as about 'female empowerment' and 'invert[ing] the power structure of a patriarchal society',[93] while former Mills & Boon editor Jay Dixon proposes that, while 'Mills & Boon romances and feminism have differing political frameworks…it may just be that under the skin they are sisters. Feminism has many faces. Perhaps romance fiction is one of them'.[94]

This notion of feminism and romance fiction as sisters 'under the skin' seems to me to stray too far into the depoliticised understanding of feminist writing (where any novel that foregrounds a female character is constituted as feminist) criticised by Coward and Strauss.[95] Nonetheless, these descriptions of romance fiction as narratives that represent and subvert patriarchal power (in however contingent a way) suggests a connection between such fiction and the women's writing celebrated in much feminist literary scholarship. The fact that both forms of fiction focus on female characters and experiences, and the correlation between the rise of romance and literary women's writing and the feminist movement, reinforces this connection. It is also significant that both types of writing – while often conceived as antithetical – operated within and are understood in relation to an essentialist model of cultural production: central to the definition of both feminist women's writing and romance fiction is women's representations of women, aimed specifically at women readers.

In terms of women's literary fiction, feminist critics have interpreted this essentialist connection between the gender of the author and reader as a political expression and ideal. However, this association of women's writing and reading simultaneously brings into view the explicitly female market for fiction that underpinned the growth in women's literary fiction, and was also implicated in the parallel, and greater, growth in romance fiction. Feminism played a major role in producing this female market for fiction. In promoting women's workforce participation and financial rights, feminism increased women's disposable income, which could be directed towards a range of non-essential items, including fiction. At the same time, literary critics who aligned themselves with feminism developed this movement's political focus on women's identities and concerns into a specific fictional category: 'women's writing'. Women's increased presence as workers in the publishing industry from the 1970s – a trend that has also been attributed to feminism[96] – presumably fostered the entry of this category of women's writing into a literary marketplace where female consumers had increasing buying power.

In light of these social trends, we can say that feminism contributed to, or even motivated, the growth in women's writing by supporting the concurrent emergence and influence of this category of women's writing, and of a market for such titles. Where I disagree with feminist interpretations of the relationship between feminism and women's writing is in their implicit assumption that all growth in women's writing – because enabled by feminism – manifests the tenets and success of that political movement. Instead, as the framework of women reading fiction by women about women ('women's writing') became an established part of the publishing industry, it exceeded the meanings ascribed to it by feminist critics. This transformation is demonstrated by the fact that, in the 1970s and 1980s, at the height of the influence of second-wave feminism, the market for romance fiction was so much larger than for any other type of Australian writing (by women or men). In overlooking this area where the major part of growth in women's writing occurred, feminist literary criticism has limited its understanding of women's presence in the Australian novel field, the meanings of women's writing for women and men, and the influence of feminism on these phenomena.

As with the concurrent orientation of pulp and literary culture to men's writing in the post-war period, the parallel growth in women's literary and romance fiction in the 1970s and 1980s demonstrates how prominent discourses of gender circulating in society influence the literary field broadly. At the same time, given the content of romance fiction, this parallel emphasises the complexity of the interactions between cultural discourses and fiction. More specifically, it challenges the emancipatory interpretation of women's writing prevalent in feminist accounts of contemporary Australian literary history, wherein growth in such writing is constructed as a sign of growth in women's political and social power.

While foundational to feminist conceptions of women's role in the Australian literary field in the 1970s and 1980s, there are clear historical arguments against this understanding of women's writing as an indicator of women's social and political liberation. As I discussed in Chapter 4, the nineteenth century is widely acknowledged as a time when most American and British novels were written by women. Yet their dominance of this field in no way reflected their social power. Rather, as Tuchman and others argue, most novels were by women because the novel was perceived as having low cultural value; it was seen as such because it was associated with women writers and readers. This self-perpetuating construction left the profession relatively open to women because men did not seek access to it.[97] It is this sense of a field that is lacking – or, in relation to recent Australian literary culture, declining – in prestige that I relate, in the next section, to the ongoing growth and eventual dominance of the Australian novel by women writers in the 1990s and 2000s.

III Beyond Gender? 1990s to 2000s

While there is no shortage of discussion of gender trends prior to the 1990s, this is not the case for the most recent two decades. The reorientation of feminist criticism, since the late 1980s, from the similarities to the differences between women writers, seems to have produced a general reluctance to identify or comment on how gender operates broadly in the literary field, including the Australian one. Gender-alert readings of particular texts or authors are still relatively common; and one encouraging feature of recent Australian literary criticism is that such analyses are no longer always limited to women's writing.[98] To some extent, this focus on particular authors is an understandable reaction against the overly homogenising statements about women's writing, and its relationship to feminism, in earlier criticism. Nevertheless, this critical shift has produced a widespread lack of attention to the ways in which gender continues to shape the literary field, constructing the publishing avenues open to men and women, the writing they produce, and the readerships they access.

The association of women's writing and political liberation – which is the paradigm and legacy of earlier feminist analyses – hampers the few studies that do comment on gender trends in contemporary Australian literature. As I discussed at the start of this chapter, Webby associates the 1990s and 2000s with the resurrection of 'WACM' power due to economic rationalism and globalisation, and the resulting entry of multinational publishers into the national market. In making the publishing industry 'the real game' in her analysis of recent gender trends, Webby turns discussion away from the type of writing being published, and its authors and readers, to the power dynamics surrounding its production. At the same time, in suggesting that the political changes of the late 1960s and 1970s have forever changed 'English courses and publishers lists', Webby implicitly allows the ongoing presence of non-'WACM' authors in the Australian novel field to continue to stand for some form of political and social emancipation.

Gelder and Salzman's *The New Diversity* was one of the books I cited, at the start of the previous section, that directly associated Australian women's writing in the 1970s and 1980s with the expression of feminist politics. Their more recent survey of Australian literature *After the Celebration*, discussing the field from 1989 to 2007, expresses clear discomfort with this approach. The introductory remarks to Salzman's chapter on women's writing – and its title, 'Is There A Woman's Chapter?' – challenge previous (including their own) homogenising treatments of this category:

> What was taken for granted as an end in itself during the height of second wave feminism – the need to focus on women's writing as a marker of female experience – was subjected to intense criticism by those who called attention to reductive assumptions about the category 'women'.

In the context of these debates, Gelder and Salzman had 'initially decided not to have a separate chapter on women's fiction': it seemed to them in 2007 'that such a category made no real sense any more'.[99] Ultimately, they proceeded with one because 'there are still various genres that are regarded as women's fiction by publishers, writers and readers'.[100] Where *The New Diversity* treated women's writing as a direct reflection of feminist politics, here it is presented as a construction by participants in the book market.

Despite this explicit disassociation of women's writing from feminism, Salzman proceeds by discussing such fiction almost entirely in relation to this political movement.

The invariable question he asks, as he proceeds through the multiple authors, novels and genres included in his chapter on women's writing, is 'Are these works feminist?' Some are determined to be so; others are not; still others are described as post-feminist or even 'post-post-feminist'.[101] Although Salzman no longer conceives of women's fiction as an emanation of feminism, the longstanding critical association of such writing with political emancipation continues to inform his analysis to the extent that, as in *The New Diversity*, feminism remains the key framework through which women's writing is assessed, or at least, positioned.[102] Both Webby's and Gelder and Salzman's discussions of gender trends in Australian literature in the 1990s and 2000s indicate the lack of alternative ways to understand and explain women's presence in the literary field beyond the framework of emancipation that feminist criticism in the 1980s and early 1990s proposed. There is, particularly in Gelder and Salzman's book, a clear sense of the inadequacy of this framework, but no other is deployed.

Even in these studies that attempt to discuss broad gender trends, there is no direct acknowledgement – let alone explanation – of the continuing growth in publication of Australian novels by women, such that, in the early 1990s, women surpassed men as the predominant authors of Australian novels. Although, as Figure 20 shows, there was a decline in the number of titles by women from 2004, the earlier fall in men's novels (from 2000) – and the lower base from which that decline began – means that women have retained this dominant position to the present. In proportional terms, as depicted in Figure 19, the 40 per cent of Australian novels by women in the late 1980s increased to 50 per cent in the 1990s and 57 per cent in the 2000s. For these same periods, titles by men fell from 57, to 47 and 42 per cent.[103] Although – in direct contrast to analyses of the 1970s and 1980s – no studies recognise it, in the last two decades women are far more than 'a well-established presence in Australian literature', as Bird argued in 2000;[104] they are consistently writing and publishing more novels than men.

Despite the radically different critical perceptions of the two periods, gender trends in the authorship and publication of Australian novels in the 1990s and 2000s were, in many ways, a continuation and solidification of those that emerged in the 1970s and 1980s. As in those earlier decades, both local and multinational publishers were increasingly oriented towards women's writing, with multinationals publishing many more Australian women's novels than local presses. The connection between gender trends in literary and popular genre fiction was also ongoing although, due to the progressive erosion of a clear separation between mass-market and literary publishers, it was less distinct. These trends demonstrate that the shift in publishers' attention to women's writing that began in the 1970s and 1980s continued in the 1990s and 2000s, and to some extent, this reorientation was also apparent in critical discussion. I will argue, however, that this gender trend does not indicate or produce women's increased political and social power (as the feminist approach to contemporary Australian literary history would seem bound to imply). Instead, the growth in women's writing has been concurrent with a devaluing of both novel writing as a profession and of the novel as a literary form. This devaluing has facilitated growth in women's writing, while paradoxically producing the conditions for resurgence in critical attention to male authors.

The results depicted in Figure 21 indicate that, apart from a slight decline in the late 1990s, the proportional growth in locally published non-pulp Australian novels by women in the 1970s and 1980s continued in the 1990s and 2000s. Compared with 39 per cent in the late 1980s, women wrote 43 per cent of such titles in the early 1990s, 40 per cent in the late 1990s, 45 per cent in the early 2000s and 48 per cent in the late 2000s. The proportion of such titles by men fell accordingly: from 60, to 55, 57, 52 and 50 per cent.[105] Given the high proportion of Australian novels by women overall, and the construction of local publishing as a site of culturally progressive activity, it is notable that, still in the 2000s, local presses published slightly more titles by men than women. The high proportion of women's novels in the lists of multinational publishers provides part of the explanation for this difference between local and overall results, and I will turn to this area shortly. But there are a number of other factors, relating to local publishing, which help to contextualise this growth and emphasise the extent to which established Australian publishers (as opposed to the alternative, emerging subsidy industry) have reoriented their lists towards women's writing in the 1990s and 2000s.

Excluding subsidy publishing from the results increases the proportion of locally published Australian novels by women to 48 (instead of 45) per cent in the early 2000s and 50 (instead of 48) per cent in the late 2000s. In contrast, men wrote 49 (instead of 52) and 48 (instead of 50) per cent, respectively, of the non-subsidised Australian novels published in Australia. Although not dramatic, this shift in gender proportions reflects men's overrepresentation in this alternative part of the local industry in the 2000s, when 63 per cent of locally published, subsidised Australian novels were by men (compared with 33 per cent by women).[106] Interestingly, men were also overrepresented as authors of self-published titles. This has been the case since the end of World War Two.[107] But due to the relatively low numbers of self-published novels before 1990, this difference had little effect on gender trends. In the 1990s, however, when 7 per cent of all Australian novels were self-published, men wrote 67 per cent of titles in this category (compared with 31 per cent by women). This gender difference moderated somewhat in the 2000s, as the proportion of self-published Australian novels declined to 4 per cent. But men remained the predominant authors of such titles, responsible for 57 per cent (compared with 38 per cent by women).[108] Especially as self- and subsidy publishing are often dismissed in explicitly feminised terms – as 'vanity' publishing – the strong presence of male authors in this part of the industry is notable. Given my estimate in Chapter 3 of the proportion of the local industry constituted by self- and subsidy publishing – 22 per cent in the 1990s and 25 per cent in the 2000s – men's overrepresentation in both areas is certainly significant for understanding gender trends in local publishing.

The extent to which subsidy publishing is male dominated helps to explain why – although women do not write a clear majority of locally published Australian novels – there is such an evident shift, in the lists of many local publishers, to women's writing in the 1990s and 2000s. This shift encompasses the largest local publishers as well as a number of smaller literary enterprises. Allen & Unwin (A&U), the most prolific Australian publisher of Australian novels in these recent decades, went from publishing substantially more titles by men than women as a British-owned company in the 1980s (17 of 22), to publishing an increasing majority of Australian novels by women: 64 of 113 titles (57 per cent) in the 1990s and 152 of 246 titles (62 per cent) in the 2000s. While Fremantle Press published a relatively equal proportion of Australian novels by both genders,[109] like A&U, the University of Queensland Press (UQP) published more titles by women than men in the 1990s and 2000s, as did Lothian and Spinifex Press.[110] More broadly, among the top twenty non-subsidy (and non-pulp) local publishers of Australian novels per decade, there is marked growth from the 1980s to the 2000s in the proportion publishing either a majority of titles by women or a relatively even proportion of titles by men and women, with a corresponding fall in the proportion publishing mostly men's novels.[111]

At the same time as local publishers have focused increasingly on women's novels, there has been a decline in the presence and relative output of feminist presses in recent decades. This reduction suggests a turning away of the local industry from specifically literary and political women's writing. However, as I argued in Chapter 3, a shift by local publishers towards genre fiction – and often by association, away from literary and political writing – has characterised the Australian novel field as a whole.[112] Indeed, *AustLit*'s allocation of genres to Australian novels suggests that, as in the 1970s and 1980s, locally published genre novels were more likely to be by men than women.[113] In the 1990s, 61 per cent of locally published men's novels are categorised as genre fiction, compared with 46 per cent of women's; this gender difference increased in the 2000s, when 65 per cent of locally published men's novels were in this category compared with 41 per cent of women's.

The focus of local literary publishers, such as A&U, UQP and Spinifex, on women's writing, combined with the strong local publication of men's genre novels, appears to contradict my claim of parallel gender trends in popular and literary fiction in the 1990s and 2000s. In fact, while men wrote a greater proportion of locally published genre novels than women – and featured strongly in certain genres (including adventure, fantasy, mystery and science fiction)[114] – in the three most prevalent (and presumably popular) genres, women's authorship increased. According to *AustLit*'s categorisation of Australian novels published by local companies, the three leading genres in these decades were young adult fiction (representing 18 per cent of titles), and crime and historical fiction (each constituting 9 per cent of this field). Where women wrote 47 per cent of locally published young adult fiction in the 1980s, in the 1990s and 2000s this increased to 51 and 59 per cent. Although women wrote a higher proportion of the other two genres in the 1990s than in the 2000s, in comparison to the 1980s, their authorship of both increased markedly: compared with 20 per cent of locally published crime novels in the 1980s, women wrote 40 and 39 per cent in the 1990s and 2000s respectively; alternatively, compared with 26 per cent of historical novels in the 1980s, in the 1990s and 2000s, women wrote 48 and 39 per cent respectively. While men remained the predominant authors of crime and historical novels, in all three genres (especially young adult fiction) the presence of women writers increased. These trends – the orientation of well-established, as well as small literary, local publishers to women's writing, and the growth in women's authorship of these prominent popular genres – have occurred in concert, and have contributed to the growth in local publication of Australian women's novels in the 1990s and 2000s.

Although these trends in local publication are significant, in the 1990s and 2000s, as in the 1970s and 1980s, the majority of growth in Australian novels by women occurred in multinational publishing. Figure 23 shows this growth, with titles by women increasing as a proportion of Australian novels published by multinationals from 60 per cent in the early 1990s, to 62 per cent in the late 1990s and 69 per cent in the early 2000s, with a slight decline to 65 per cent in the late 2000s. Over this same period, the proportion of men's titles in this part of the industry fell from 37 per cent in the 1990s to 31 per cent in the early 2000s, before increasing to 34 per cent in the second part of that decade.[115] The corresponding growth in the number of titles by women, until the late 2000s, is depicted in Figure 24, which shows that multinational companies have published almost double the number of Australian novels by women as local publishers. It also indicates that the number of Australian novels by women published by multinationals has greatly exceeded the number by men published locally and by multinationals.

As in the 1970s and 1980s, and although declining both numerically and proportionally in the 1990s and 2000s, romance fiction remained the most prevalent genre published by multinationals, and a major reason for the strong publication by such companies of Australian novels by women. Romance constituted 22 per cent of Australian novels published by multinationals in the 1990s and 20 per cent in the 2000s;[116] women authors wrote 93 and 99 per cent of these titles respectively. Once again, Torstar published the majority of these titles. This company was responsible for 88 per cent of the Australian novels published by multinationals and categorised by *AustLit* as romance in the 1990s, and 86 per cent in the 2000s. Authorship of these Torstar titles was especially female dominated: none of the 373 Australian novels published by this conglomerate in the 1990s, and only 2 of 385 in the 2000s, were by men.

Given the company's prominent role in the Australian novel field, excluding Torstar's output obviously impacts gender trends. But where, in the 1970s and 1980s, this exclusion radically reduced both the proportion and number of Australian women's novels published by multinationals, this is not the case in these two more recent decades. As Figure 23 shows, when Torstar's titles are removed, novels by women decline as a proportion of multinational publication; however, women's representation in this area remains substantially higher than for local publication, and there is no proportional decline in multinational publication of Australian novels by women in the 2000s. In numerical terms, without Torstar, there is no strong growth in multinational publication of women's novels in the late 1990s and 2000s, and in fact, the number of locally published men's novels exceeds the number of multinational women's titles until the second half of the 2000s. But there is also no numerical decline in multinational publication of Australian women's novels in the late 2000s:[117] a decline that, as Figure 24 shows, characterised local publication of Australian novels by men and women, as well as multinational publication of titles by men.

The strong multinational publication of Australian novels by women, even without Torstar, indicates that, in this part of the industry – as with local publishing – the shift to women's writing was widespread in the 1990s and 2000s. There were other multinational companies, besides Torstar, involved in the Australian novel field in the 1970s and 1980s that published more titles by women than men (namely, Pearson and Australian

Consolidated Press).[118] But the majority concentrated on male authors.[119] In the 1990s and 2000s, almost all multinational publishers of Australian novels produced more titles by women than men. This was the case for many in the 1990s, including Pearson, Panmacmillan, Random House, Hodder Headline and Bertlesmann.[120] However, two of the most prolific multinational publishers of Australian novels in that decade – News Corporation and Reed Elsevier – published slightly more novels by men than women.[121] In the 2000s, Reed Elsevier was the only multinational publisher of more than one Australian novel with more titles by men than women;[122] and it was responsible for only nine titles by men compared with eight by women. Alongside Torstar, the multinational companies that published more Australian novels by women than men in the 2000s included News Corporation (65 per cent by women), Pearson (53 per cent), Holtzbrinck (57 per cent), and Bertelsmann (58 per cent).[123]

With the exception of Torstar, the proportion of women's novels published by these multinationals is not especially high; but the overall shift to women's writing is clear. In Chapter 3 I discussed the negative critical response to growth in multinational publishing in some quarters, including the use of explicitly gendered dichotomies to describe the expansion of this industry. According to these accounts, Australian literature is threatened by a foreign other that is depicted as engulfing and abject, with the 'world of the gentleman publisher' both 'swallow[ed]' and 'flood[ed]' by multinational conglomerates.[124] Given that multinational publication of Australian novels has predominantly been of women's titles, it is interesting to consider the extent to which the tone, what might even be called the hostility, of such responses relates to gender trends in cultural production. Would the concern about the threat to an authentic Australian literary culture be as strong if multinational companies published mostly men's novels?

As in the local industry, this overall growth in multinational publication of Australian novels by women correlates with growth in the prevalence – and presumably the popularity – of particular genres with a high proportion of women authors. As I have said, romance fiction remained the most prevalent genre published by multinationals in the 1990s and 2000s. It was followed, closely, by young adult fiction and, more distantly, by historical, crime and fantasy fiction.[125] In all of these genres, women either wrote the majority of titles in both decades, or substantially increased their authorship. In the 1990s and 2000s, respectively, women were responsible for 68 and 61 per cent of Australian young adult novels published by multinationals; 60 and 59 per cent of historical fiction; 23 and 54 per cent of crime fiction; and 52 and 68 per cent of fantasy fiction. Australian women novelists also played an increasingly prominent role in a number of traditionally male-oriented genres, including adventure, horror, humour, mystery, science and thriller fiction.[126] These results indicate that, as with local publishing, the ongoing growth in multinational publication of Australian women's novels in the 1990s and 2000s was related to genre fiction; but the range of genres involved suggests an important shift. Rather than a traditionally female-oriented genre becoming more prominent, as was the case with romance fiction in the 1970s and 1980s, we are witnessing growth in female authorship of a range of genres, including those traditionally authored (and read) by men.

Also in parallel to local publishing, there is some evidence that the growth in multinational publication of women's genre fiction has been concurrent with an increase in women's literary fiction. Women wrote an increasing majority of the Australian novels published by multinationals and not allocated a genre in *AustLit*: from 45 per cent in the 1980s, to 51 per cent in the 1990s and 66 per cent in the 2000s (compared with 53, 49 and 33 per cent by men during this same period).[127] These results are strongly influenced by overall growth in multinational publication of Australian women's novels. But this shift cannot be entirely explained on this basis, because such titles have also increased (albeit with a slight fall in the 1990s) as a proportion of women's novels: where 20 per cent of Australian women's novels published by multinationals in the 1980s were not allocated a genre in *AustLit*, in the 1990s and 2000s, respectively, this proportion was 19 and 23 per cent. In contrast, although the proportion of men's novels in this category has remained higher than for women's, it has fallen dramatically: from 44 per cent in the 1980s, to 30 per cent in the 1990s and 24 per cent in the 2000s.

It is certain, as I said earlier, that not all of these non-genre titles were literary. Nonetheless, the growth in multinational publication of women's genre and non-genre novels – given the same trend in local publishing – indicates a continuation (if more muted) of earlier parallels between gender trends in genre and literary fiction, as well as a broad orientation of publishers of Australian novels to women's writing. Put simply, these trends suggest that the reorientation of the Australian novel field towards women's writing, which began in the 1970s, has continued in the 1990s and 2000s. Over these four decades, in other words, the Australian novel has been increasingly redefined as a female-authored form.

Although the feminist movement contributed to this redefinition, this gender trend does not signal or produce increased prestige for women novelists. Instead, I would suggest that this orientation of the Australian novel field to women's writing has occurred in the context – and has contributed to – the devaluation of the novel. Before elaborating on this argument, I want to look at one further set of gender trends that emerges in relation to the Australian novel in the 1990s and 2000s: in critical discussion. These trends – which, in newspaper criticism particularly, demonstrate a move away from women's writing – contrast with the broader shift to women's writing by publishers, and may seem to complicate this notion of a redefinition or reorientation of the Australian novel field. In fact, I will argue that these critical trends provide important context for, and insights into, the meaning and consequences of the ongoing growth in women's authorship of Australian novels in the 1990s and 2000s.

As Figure 22 indicates, in academic discussion, the increased focus on Australian women writers that began in the 1970s continued in the 1990s, when the proportion of women in the top twenty increased from 33 to 55 per cent. Although this proportion declined in the 2000s, to 45 per cent, still 9 of the top 20 authors discussed in academic journals were women. That said, there was only one woman in the top five: Dorothy Hewett was ranked fifth in both decades, behind nearly the same four male authors (Patrick White, David Malouf, Peter Carey and Mudrooroo in the 1990s; and Carey, Malouf, White and Les Murray in the 2000s). Notably, while most of the women in the top twenty in the 1990s were relatively contemporary authors – including Elizabeth

Jolley, Helen Darville/Demidenko, Janette Turner Hospital, Thea Astley, Beverley Farmer, Helen Garner, Kate Grenville and Barbara Hanrahan – in the 2000s, earlier women writers – including Christina Stead, Judith Wright, Miles Franklin and Henry Handel Richardson – figured more prominently.[128]

This shift away from contemporary women writers to those of earlier periods could be interpreted as a consequence of the discomfort regarding the relationship between feminism and women's writing I discussed at the start of this section. I identified this discomfort in Salzman's chapter on women's writing – which continues to discuss contemporary women's writing in relation to feminism, even as he describes most such fiction as not feminist (or as post-feminist or 'post-post-feminist').[129] Arguably, the shift to historical women's writing in academic discussion allows critics to embed their feminism (given the perception that discussing women's writing is a, or the, means of doing this form of criticism), while avoiding the disassociation of contemporary women's writing and feminist politics that Salzman grapples with. If this is the cause of the academic focus on historical women's writing, then the root of the problem is the construction of feminism not as a mode of gender-alert analysis, but as an emancipatory framework. This construction can only conceptualise women's writing as either good or bad for women or for feminism.

Even with this change in focus (from contemporary to historical) – and the predominance of men in the leading five positions – the strong representation of women in the top twenty authors for academic discussion in the 1990s and 2000s tallies with what I have been describing thus far: the shift in the Australian novel field towards women's writing. This same trend is apparent in overall critical discussion. While there was a slight increase in the proportion of men in the top twenty in this category from the 1980s to the 1990s (from 65 to 70 per cent, or from 13 of 20 to 14 of 20 authors), in the 2000s, this proportion fell to 60 per cent (or 12 of 20 authors). As in academic discussion, the top five, for both decades, was dominated by (essentially the same) male authors: Patrick White, David Malouf, David Williamson, and Les Murray were first, third, fourth and fifth, respectively, in the 1990s (Helen Darville/Demidenko was second); Peter Carey, Malouf, Williamson, Murray and White were first to fifth in the 2000s. Many of the same women in the top twenty for academic discussion in the 1990s were in the top twenty overall, including Helen Darville/Demidenko, Elizabeth Jolley, Helen Garner, Dorothy Hewett and Janette Turner Hospital.[130] However, the incorporation into the overall top twenty for the 2000s of authors such as Jackie French, Sonya Hartnett, Kerry Greenwood and Marion Halligan indicates that discussion of contemporary women's writing, while not prominent in academic journals, was occurring more broadly.[131]

In contrast, and despite demonstrating the same shift towards women's writing in the 1980s as these other two categories of critical attention, in the 1990s and 2000s, newspaper discussion of Australian literature returned to focusing predominantly on male authors. Indeed, the proportion of men in the top twenty for newspaper discussion in these two recent decades – 80 and 76 per cent, respectively – was higher than in the 1950s and 1960s. Interestingly, in both these decades, women were higher in the top five for newspaper than for academic or overall discussion: Helen Darville/Demidenko was the most discussed Australian author in newspapers in the 1990s while Helen

Garner was fourth; Kate Grenville was fourth in the 2000s. These cases involve specific controversies surrounding books by these authors – Darville/Demidenko for *The Hand That Signed the Paper*, Garner for *The First Stone* and Grenville for *The Secret River*.[132] It is an open question why the major literary controversies of the past two decades have focused on women writers. But the role of controversy in these cases also marks them as identifiable exceptions to the overall shift to male authors in newspaper discussion of Australian novelists.

Other women writers did appear in the top twenty for newspaper discussion in these decades: namely, Elizabeth Jolley and Marion Halligan in the 1990s, and Halligan, as well as Sonya Hartnett, Kerry Greenwood and Geraldine Brooks in the 2000s. However, the overwhelming impression of these results is of a paucity of women compared with a remarkable range and number of men. Male authors ranked in the top twenty for newspaper discussion in these decades ranged from prominent historical figures (including Patrick White and Banjo Paterson) to authors of young adult fiction (such as Morris Gleitzman, Matthew Riley and John Marsden), popular or genre fiction writers (including Peter Corris, Bryce Courtenay, Garry Disher, Nick Earls and Morris West), a substantial number of literary authors (namely, Peter Carey, Richard Flanagan, Peter Goldsworthy, Thomas Keneally, David Malouf, Alex Miller, Frank Moorhouse, DBC Pierre and Tim Winton) as well as playwrights and poets.[133]

These results for newspaper discussion indicate that the progressive and broad-ranging growth in women's authorship of Australian novels since the 1970s was accompanied, in the 1990s and 2000s, by a reversion – in this most public and widely read forum for discussion of Australian literature – to a focus on men. Although academic and overall attention was more evenly spread between men and women authors, the focus on male authors in newspapers finds its echo in the fact that, in both of these other fields, the top five authors in the 1990s and 2000s were either entirely or predominantly men.

Another dataset, from Vida, an advocacy group for women writers, shows the same prevailing focus on male authors in the book reviews of a wide range of major American and European newspapers and magazines in 2010, including the *Atlantic*, the *Boston Review*, *Harper's Magazine*, the *London Review of Books*, the *New Republic* (*NR*), the *New York Review of Books* (*NYRB*), the *New York Times Book Review*, the *Paris Review*, and the *Times Literary Supplement* (*TLS*). Vida also analysed the gender of the book reviewers for these publications, demonstrating that most were men. For instance, the *TLS* reviewed works by 1,366 authors in 2010, of which 1,036 (or 76 per cent) were men; of the 1,241 people who wrote these reviews, 900 (or 73 per cent) were men. In the *NR*, 86 per cent of authors reviewed were men, as were 79 per cent of reviewers; and in the *NYRB*, these proportions were 83 and 84 per cent respectively.[134]

There has been significant discussion of Vida's findings, with most commentators expressing dismay at the figures and noting the complexity of gender relations in the literary field. However, one strong thread in discussion has been the claim that women do not write as many of the types of books reviewed in these publications as men. Ruth Franklin surveyed gender proportions in the output of thirteen publishers and, after excluding titles unlikely to be reviewed, such as self-help and cookery books, found that only Riverhead (an imprint of Penguin) 'came close to parity, with 55 percent of its books by men and 45 percent by women. Random House came in second, with 37 percent by women.' Women authors were significantly less represented in publications by small independent presses such as Graywolf (25 per cent by women), Melville House (20 per cent) and Verso (11 per cent).[135] Along the same lines, but in a tone dismissive of both women writers and readers, editor of the *TLS* Peter Stothard defended his publication's lack of attention to books by women by saying: 'I'd be very surprised if the authorship of published books was 50/50. And while women are heavy readers, we know they are heavy readers of the kind of fiction that is not likely to be reviewed in the pages of the *TLS*.'[136]

A number of studies indicate that Stothard is wrong in his assessment of women's reading habits. Recent research shows that American women are significantly more likely than American men to read fiction, including literary fiction.[137] These findings are reinforced by studies showing women's dominance of the membership of reading groups and the audience at writers' festivals.[138] In respect to authorship of literature, perhaps Stothard and Franklin are correct to argue that novels – especially literary novels – are predominantly written by men; in other words, perhaps the Australian novel field represents an exception, internationally, because more than half of all recent titles – including literary titles – are by women. The fact that this information on gender trends in authorship is not known, and the difficulty this creates for interpreting gender disparities in reviewing, presents an excellent argument for more quantitative research into the relationship between publishing and gender. However, it does not explain why, despite writing a declining proportion of Australian novels in the 1990s and 2000s, male authors dominated newspaper discussion of Australian literature, as they did for discussion of literature in the various publications investigated by Vida.

In a previously published article, considering only the overall growth in Australian novels by women, and the social and economic context in which this occurred, I drew on the sociological theory of occupational gender segregation to explain this gender trend in publication.[139] This established sociological paradigm – which I also discussed in Chapter 4 – proposes that men tend to enter occupations when they are valued, whether that value is in the form of social prestige or economic reward, and leave them when they are devalued, or when more desirable jobs become available. As I discussed in this earlier article, a series of factors suggest the declining cultural value and financial rewards of novel writing for Australian authors in the 1990s and 2000s. The continuing growth in publication of genre fiction by local and multinational publishers points to a redefinition of the Australian novel as a popular rather than a prestigious literary form. Although the concurrent rise of the celebrity author has introduced a new form of prestige within the profession, it is allocated to only a very small group of writers. Meanwhile, the growth in self- and subsidy publishing, and in creative writing courses, has reduced the cultural prestige of authorship. While self- and subsidy publishing are often perceived as culturally worthless enterprises, writing courses – in presenting writing as something that can be taught and learned rather than an innate artistic gift – highlight the importance of effort rather than skill in becoming an author. Reductions in government funding for the arts in these same decades, discussed in Chapter 3, further suggest the declining cultural value ascribed to writing fiction, while also reducing the potential remunerative rewards of the profession, particularly of literary authorship. Finally, the growing prevalence of non-fictional genres (such as autobiography, biography and history) by Australian authors[140] suggests that opportunities in publishing, and perhaps cultural capital as well, are transferring to non-fiction. Based on these factors, I proposed a reduction in the cultural importance and value of the novel (and of the profession of novelist) as the reason for the growth in women's authorship of Australian novels: men were abandoning the field for this reason – as indicated by the significant decline in the number of Australian novels by men since 2000 – and leaving the profession open for women.

I still think that this association between the declining cultural and economic value of novel writing on the one hand, and the growth in the proportion of Australian novels by women on the other, underpins gender trends in authorship and publication in the 1990s and 2000s. But there are aspects of the data presented in this chapter – and two findings in particular – that complicate this explanation and call for a more nuanced assessment. The first issue is the high proportion of subsidy-published novels by men in the 2000s: if men were evacuating the field because of the reduced cultural and economic rewards of novel writing, as I have proposed, why were a disproportionate number paying to have their novels published? The second issue relates to the focus on male novelists in newspaper discussion, as well as men's dominance of the top five positions for academic and overall criticism: if the novel was devalued, and if the authorship of these titles was increasingly female dominated, why did male authors receive the majority of critical attention?

The first of these questions is a difficult one, because it is impossible to know if men will remain disproportionately represented as authors of subsidy-published novels, and/or if authors chose this avenue because of rejections by non-subsidy publishers. In terms of the proportion of men's novels published by subsidy, the recent trend is of growth until 2004, followed by a decline (although the publication of a greater proportion of men's than women's novels continued to be subsidised in the late 2000s). Assuming that authors are choosing subsidy publication following rejection by non-subsidy publishers, this trend supports two key conclusions: first, that publishers are rejecting a higher proportion of men's than women's novels; second, that there are still Australian men (albeit at a declining rate since 2004) who wish to be published novelists, even if this means paying for the privilege. While this second point seems at odds with my claim that men are turning away from writing novels because the form has been devalued, the first point provides a framework for explaining this process.

I argued previously that feminism provided the conditions for the growth in women's writing in the 1980s by focusing attention on women's identities, by creating awareness of writing by women as 'women's writing' (that is, as a category in itself, and mainly, if not exclusively, of interest to women) and finally by initiating changes in workforce participation and economic rights that gave women more control over their finances. However, I also proposed that this relationship between feminist politics and the growth in women's writing only occurred because publishing houses – also staffed predominantly by women, and recognising women as the major book buyers and readers – realised the potential lucrativeness of this category and sought fiction for this market. This process underpinned growth in women's writing, and the redefinition of the novel as a form written and read predominantly by women; but it also made it likely that men would experience reduced success in securing a publisher. From this perspective, the correspondence between the decline in the number of men's novels and the rise in men's subsidy publishing might be seen as the fall-out from this shift: these are the men who still want to be published novelists, but are unable to find a publisher without paying one. However, if my hypothesis regarding the cultural and economic rewards of novel writing is correct, we should see – as trends in subsidy publishing since 2004 suggest – an ongoing decline in this group of male novelists unable to secure a traditional publisher as novel writing becomes increasingly identified with women writers and, as a consequence, less valued and less appealing to men.

This logic of a feedback loop between growth in women's authorship and the devaluation of the Australian novel might seem to render the critical focus on male authors – especially in newspapers – even less explicable. Yet a strong male presence in the top echelons of female-dominated professions is common. Where women in male-dominated professions encounter the 'glass ceiling', Christine Williams coined the term 'glass escalator' to describe the tendency for men to gain 'the most prestigious, better paying' roles in female-dominated professions such as nursing, librarianship, elementary school teaching and social work.[141] Williams concludes, 'Each of these occupations is "still a man's world" even though mostly women work in them'.[142] This 'glass escalator' phenomenon is one that Albert Greco, Clara Rodríguez and Robert Wharton also identify in the publishing industry worforce where men occupy 'the highest positions in disproportionate numbers' despite women filling more than 60 per cent of all positions.[143]

The 'glass escalator' provides a framework for understanding why male authors dominate in newspaper discussion of Australian literature. Specifically, as male authorship of Australian novels becomes less common, it becomes more likely that men will be singled out for critical acclaim, and that literary quality will be redefined as a trait of male authors. In terms of academic criticism, the roughly equal proportions of men and women among the top twenty most discussed authors might appear to differentiate those who write for academic journals from this phenomenon. However, the fact that men predominate not only in the top five positions for each decade, but also among the contemporary authors discussed, challenges this interpretation. In the 2000s, three times as many contemporary male than female authors appeared in the top twenty for academic attention. Janette Turner Hospital, Gail Jones and Helen Darville/Demidenko were the only women writers in this category compared with a long list of men, including Peter Carey, David Malouf, Tim Winton, Christos Tsiolkas, Brian Castro, Robert Drewe, Richard Flanagan and Kim Scott. This result suggests that, as in newspaper discussion, the declining authorship of contemporary Australian novels by men has been concurrent with increased, and increasingly disproportionate, academic attention to male authors.

In the epigraph to this chapter I quoted Whitlock's claim that 'the WACM…suffered considerable anxiety' due to the 'prominence of women's writing' in the 1980s and the decline in his cultural profile and prestige.[144] If it was felt at that time, presumably men's dominance of recent critical discussion has helped to alleviate this anxiety and to reassure the WACM that the literary field is still 'a man's world'. To some extent, then, I agree with the overall tenor of Webby's analysis of gender trends in Australian literature in the 1990s and 2000s: namely, that the positive valuation of women's writing that occurred in the 1970s and 1980s has diminished in the context of a reassertion of power dynamics beneficial to men.[145] However, I do not see this reassertion occurring, as Webby does, at a meta-level in the realm of multinational publishing, economic rationalism and globalisation. Nor do I think that the continuing growth in women's writing – what Webby describes as white men losing their dominance on 'English courses and publishers lists' – is expressive or indicative of political change or liberation. The 'real game' is not the entry of supposedly commercially driven enterprises into a field where aesthetic modes have fundamentally changed in response to feminism, but a reassertion of traditional modes of valuation, where literary quality is identified with male authors.

**

This is not a particularly heartening place to conclude my chapter on contemporary gender trends in the Australian novel field. Far from seeing women's increased authorship of Australian novels as a sign of their political and social emancipation, I have associated it with the devaluing of that literary form, and of novel writing as a profession, and with a refocusing of critical attention on male authors. Hopefully, however, this might be a galvanising place to conclude, in that it may encourage some resumption of interest in the ways gender has and continues to influence the literary field, not only the meaning of particular works, but the wider operations of production, reception and valuation. Of course, it is important that critics do not overlook the significant differences between writers of either gender; but nor should we ignore the ways in which gender influences all engagements in the literary field, including critical ones. However different women writers may be from one another, their opportunities are shaped by their gender, as are the opportunities of male authors.

This chapter has demonstrated how gendered constructions of literature, authorship and reading influence the publication and reception of contemporary Australian novels. The empirical trends in authorship strongly support feminist claims of a profound shift, around 1970, from an explicitly male-dominated and male-oriented literary field to one where women play an increasingly prominent part. However, neither the initial male-dominance, nor the subsequent shift to women's writing, was limited to the literary and political fiction that is the focus of most scholarship. In the immediate post-war decades, the male-orientation of literary culture and criticism was paralleled by the overwhelming male authorship of pulp fiction titles, and the focus of this industry on genres aimed at male readers. Likewise, the growth in the 1970s and 1980s in local publication of and critical attention to women's literary fiction occurred in the context of a major expansion in Australian romance fiction by and for women.

In both periods, the relationship between authors and readers was structured by what I have called an essentialist gender model, wherein men are understood as writing fiction for men, and women for women. This gendered connection between readers and writers is not a new idea: as I discussed in the previous chapter, it is widely understood as organising the literary field in the nineteenth century. I have highlighted the existence of this framework for the production and reception of literature in the twentieth century, in both literary and genre fiction, and in the critical arena. Thus, the male authorship and readership of the prevalent pulp fiction genres (such as the western and the war novel) resonate with the privileged connection between men's writing and men's concerns described by Sheridan in respect to the post-war literary novel. Similarly, the category of women's writing – as in women writing about women for women – underpinned the growth in women's literary and romance fiction in the 1970s and 1980s. Such connections – between gender trends in the literary and popular genre realms – indicate that dominant conceptions of gender circulating in a culture at any one time have an influence well beyond the pocket of commodity culture that is the literary novel.

In many respects, gender trends in the 1990s and 2000s were a continuation of shifts initiated in the 1970s and 1980s. The growth in women's authorship of Australian novels was ongoing, and apparent in both multinational and local publishing contexts, and in genre and non-genre fiction. In terms of genre fiction, Australian women writers played an increasingly prominent role, including in previously male-dominated genres. Given that women are the major readers of fiction, including literary fiction, this continuing growth in women's authorship of Australian novels – including literary ones – does not necessarily depart from the essentialist relationship between authors and readers that emerged in publishing trends of earlier decades. In contrast to the 1970s and 1980s, however, growth in women's authorship of Australian novels in the 1990s and 2000s has not brought increased critical regard. Instead, as novels by women have become increasingly prevalent, critical attention has shifted back to men. It would be interesting, in respect to this shift, to know whether – as in the data Vida has collected – men also dominated the reviewing of Australian novels: whether they stand as the arbiters as well as the exemplars of cultural value in the contemporary field.

The impact of gender on authorship, publishing and reading highlights the continuing importance of feminist and gender-alert analyses. However, the ways in which gender plays out in these areas signals that its effects are significantly more complex and varied than is allowed by the dominant feminist framework for contemporary Australian literary history of male domination yielding to female liberation. Acknowledging and coming to terms with this complexity – and formulating a language for discussing it that extends beyond the traditional celebration of women's authorship – is necessary if feminist criticism is to maintain and pursue what has always been its main objective: exploring the operations of gender in the literary field and contesting the inequalities that field manifests. More specifically, the empirical trends that have emerged in this study challenge the scope of existing feminist analyses of gender in Australian literary history. To understand the ways in which gender influences the production and reception of literature it is necessary to look beyond both women's writing and literary fiction. Gender is not restricted to women, and gendered ideas do not exist in enclaves but spread across society. This wider view enables exploration of this spread of influence – the ways in which gender shapes the content and context for all types of fiction – and a deeper understanding of the complex interactions of cultural and political discourses, literature and the market.

Conclusion

LITERARY STUDIES IN THE DIGITAL FUTURE

The next big idea in language, history and the arts? Data.[1]

This epigraph – from an article in the recent series by the *New York Times*, 'Humanities 2.0' – reflects growing interest in the way data and data-mining, and digital tools more broadly, are changing humanities scholarship. In 'The Digital Future is Now: A Call to Action for the Humanities', Christine Borgman similarly identifies 'data- and information-intensive…research' as a major future direction for the humanities. Just as the 'availability of large volumes of data has enabled scientists to ask new questions in new ways', she argues that increased existence and awareness of humanities data – largely in the form of cultural records and 'especially as more records are digitised and made available to the public' – will enable new approaches to, and perspectives on, research questions across the humanities.[2] The editors of *A Companion to the Digital Humanities* agree, identifying data-mining as a common feature of the contributions to that collection, and a central component of future humanities research:

> This method, or perhaps we should call it a heuristic, discovers a new horizon for humanities scholarship, a paradigm as powerful as any that has arisen in any humanities discipline in the past – and, indeed, maybe more powerful, because the rigor it requires will bring to our attention undocumented features of our own ideation.[3]

Despite the prognostic tenor of such claims, quantitative and digital methods have a long history in the humanities. In the digital humanities (or humanities computing) these approaches have been deployed to analyse large datasets, particularly text-based ones, since the 1950s.[4] More recently, scholars in book history have used quantitative methods to bring 'the larger cultural field into sharper focus'[5] in ways that would not otherwise be possible. An awareness of this history of data-rich humanities research is important because it brings into view, and allows us to learn from, existing scholarship on the methodological, epistemological and theoretical challenges – as well as the benefits – of quantitative approaches. An engagement with this existing body of work was the focus of my first chapter. I argued that book history's pragmatic approach to the nature and use of data, combined with the digital humanities' method of computer modelling as a speculative and experimental practice, enable a productive integration – rather than dichotomisation – of empirical analysis and humanities inquiry. Instead of simply embracing (or rejecting) data-based approaches, a critical attitude towards such methods is necessary to ensure that this 'next big thing' is not simply a passing phase, but makes a productive and effective contribution to humanities scholarship.

Although data-rich approaches are not new, their increasing prominence does signal – as the authors I cite at the start of this chapter recognise – new and exciting avenues for research in the humanities. I especially agree with the editors of *A Companion to the Digital Humanities* that data mining and analysis have significant potential, not only to enable new insights and knowledge across the humanities, but to challenge existing, and dearly held, ideas. The recent – and certainty of future – growth in online cultural data and archives is central to the opportunities presented by data-rich humanities research. As Jerome McGann writes: 'In the coming decades – the process has already begun – the entirety of our cultural inheritance will be transformed and reedited in digital forms'.[6]

Australian literature is a forerunner in this respect. The considerable investment of scholarly energy and funding in *AustLit* over more than a decade, combined with the relatively recent origins of Australian literature, mean that Australia now boasts the most comprehensive online bibliographical archive of a national literature. The existence and scope of this digital resource has allowed me to experiment with quantitative and computational approaches to cultural data – with mining, visualising and modelling this dataset – in ways that will soon be viable and productive with a range of digital archives in the humanities. A core aim of this book is to demonstrate how data-rich scholarship can enhance humanities research, and our understanding of the past in particular, by enabling us to ask new – and old – questions in new ways.

My specific intention has been to provide a new history of the Australian novel – concentrating on the nineteenth century and the decades since the end of the Second World War, and considering this literary form in its transnational context. This new history does not focus on particular texts or authors, but considers the Australian novel as a field or system. Such an approach deliberately backgrounds the scholarly constructions of value that are frequently used to define and delimit the scope of literary histories, and the possibilities of reception of literary forms. My analysis reveals that the history of the Australian novel is comprised of a much greater variety of authors, publishers, genres and readers than any previous account has acknowledged. I have been concerned, throughout this book, with exploring the relationships between these different elements of the Australian novel field, and considering how the connections – or disconnections – between them shaped the history of this literary form. At the same time as this book departs from earlier histories, it also accords with and builds upon the cultural materialist emphasis in Australian literary studies since the 1980s. By enlarging understandings of the social, cultural, political and economic contexts in which Australian novels have been produced and consumed, this book aims to support and enable studies of individual authors and texts, as well as to motivate future data-rich and digital analyses in this field, and literary and humanities research broadly.

A quantitative, computer-enabled analysis of the *AustLit* database has enabled me to discover previously unrealised features of, and to propose new ideas about, the history of the Australian novel. Regarding the nineteenth century, I show that the relationship between Australian booksellers and British publishers usually deemed colonial – that is, with local booksellers acting as importers and retailers rather than publishers – only solidified in the 1890s, as British publishers dramatically increased their output of Australian novels in order to gain entry into the lucrative colonial book market. This strategy of British publishers was a response to the established market for Australian novels in the colonies, as demonstrated by the high rate of local publication of such fiction prior to the 1890s. Before that decade, a significant number – and from the 1860s to the 1880s, the majority – of Australian novels were published locally, especially in colonial periodicals. As well as showing connections between the emergence of the Australian novel and print capitalism and politics in the colonies, the reading communities indicated by this local publishing activity challenge the prevailing view that colonial readers had no interest in Australian fiction.

My analysis of gender trends in authorship of Australian novels in the nineteenth century, in demonstrating a clear difference in the place of publication of colonial men's and women's titles, provides insight into constructions of the novel, authorship and cultural value at this time. I attribute the overrepresentation of colonial women's novels published as books in Britain and as serials – in the colonies and Britain – to British constructions of the novel as a female-dominated form. At the same time as these British constructions shaped the colonial – and transnational – circulation and reception of Australian novels, colonial literary culture did not simply follow British practices. Instead, and in contrast to the female domination of the British and American novel fields in this period, there was a distinct focus in Australia on novels by colonial male authors. Regardless of what produced these gender trends, the greater cultural and economic rewards of publication in Britain suggest that, in the cultural terms of the day, colonial women were more successful novelists than their male counterparts. This situation changed in the 1890s, when British publication went from a rare, to the major, avenue of publication for colonial men. I identify this dramatic shift in British publishing practices as another way in which such companies, in their attempts to gain access to the colonial book market, identified and responded to local conditions.

More generally in respect to the nineteenth century, I highlight the neglect of serial fiction in Australian literary studies, and show how our understanding of Australian literary history changes when such fiction is incorporated. Recovering previously neglected forms of the Australian novel – particularly pulp and genre fiction – is likewise central to the revised history I present for the decades since the end of the Second World War. My analysis of publishing trends in this period challenges the periodisation that dominates most accounts of contemporary Australian literary and book history. In particular, I argue that the widespread perception of the 1970s and 1980s as a 'golden age' for Australian literature obscures the importance of local publishing for the production of Australian novels in the 1940s, 1950s and 1960s, as well as in the 1990s and 2000s. Where the established historiography emphasises discontinuities in Australian publishing since World War Two, I demonstrate the continuities between this supposed 'golden age' and the production, circulation and reception of Australian novels in the decades before and since. In that process I challenge the nostalgia of accounts of contemporary Australian literary history and highlight the strength and diversity of local publishing in recent decades, as well as the critical and disciplinary challenges presented by the growth in author-funded publishing.

As with the nineteenth century, my analysis of gender trends in the authorship of Australian novels in the post-war period shows how gender has profoundly shaped the history of the Australian novel. The results of this analysis support feminist claims that, around 1970, Australian literature shifted from a field dominated by men to one where women writers were increasingly prevalent. However, I also demonstrate that this shift was not restricted to literary fiction (the implicit or explicit focus of most existing feminist analyses), and was in fact more pronounced in popular genres. The parallel in gender trends in literary novels and criticism, and in popular genres, reinforces the importance of feminist or gender-alert analyses of literary culture; but it also challenges the perception – particularly pronounced in feminist analyses from the 1980s and early 1990s – of growth in women's writing as a manifestation of feminist politics and a sign of women's emancipation. While no alternative has been proffered, this framework is particularly inadequate for understanding gender trends in the 1990s and 2000s: specifically, the fact that women now write the majority of Australian novels. Far from a sign of women's social and political power, this dominance has been concurrent with – and I argue, has produced – a devaluing of the Australian novel as well as a refocusing of critical attention on male novelists.

Although I have used data-rich, computer-enabled methods to write this literary history, this is not *the* quantitative or digital history of the Australian novel. This book does not exhaust what the data in *AustLit* makes possible; indeed, it only scratches the surface. For instance, I have not considered the relationship between novels and other forms (from poetry to short stories, anthologies to diaries) also included in this online archive. It is also possible – and highly likely if, as I hope, quantitative approaches to literary history become more widespread – that future scholars will analyse and experiment with the data on Australian novels in *AustLit* to show aspects of this history I have missed or misinterpreted. Moreover, with its focus on 'Australian Literature', *AustLit* does not encompass all the writings produced by Australians, and certainly not all that is read in Australia. Recent analysis of BookScan data, for instance, shows that books about sport and cooking are the most regularly purchased.[7] Given all these avenues for future research, I see this book as a first step towards, rather than a fulfilment of, the possibilities of data-rich research for Australian literary studies.

In this book, and earlier in this conclusion, I emphasised how important it is that, when employing quantitative and computational methods, literary scholars acknowledge the specific epistemological, methodological, theoretical and rhetorical issues such approaches raise. I want to insist, to end, that it is just as important for scholars in the digital humanities to maintain a connection with, and a commitment to, humanities approaches to knowledge and inquiry. In other words, as we move towards what some are calling a 'computational turn',[8] and others 'data-driven research'[9] or a 'new empiricism',[10] it is vital that such methods are employed with the aim of contributing to debates and questions of interest to the wider humanities.

In the past, digital humanities – or humanities computing – has frequently been criticised (including by those within that community) for failing to have a significant impact on humanities scholarship. According to Mark Olsen, this failure arose from 'the view that simply counting and measuring, a rather naïve empiricism...could eliminate problems posed by theory, through verifiability of results'.[11] More recently, Alan Liu pondered, 'Where is Cultural Criticism in the Digital Humanities?' He insisted that if 'digital humanists' are to play a productive role in humanities research, they will need to find ways to 'embed their analytical methods within frames of cultural analysis'.[12] Like these commentators, I am concerned that, in this time of excitement about the potential of data-rich approaches for humanities scholarship, people pursuing such methods may let the aim of asking questions relevant to humanities research – and as Liu emphasises, of analysing operations of power– slip from view. If engagement with such issues is supplanted by a rush only to count and visualise, there is the real danger that this current 'computational turn' will simply become another chapter in what McGann calls the historic and 'persistent failure of computers to make important appointments with humanities scholarship'.[13]

I hope this book has demonstrated some of the ways that quantitative and computer-enabled methods can make relevant and significant interventions into current humanities debates, in this case, regarding literary and book history. Key to my intervention has been maintaining a focus on the nuances and interoperations of history, culture, theory and power, and through this, engaging with debates and ideas relevant to all literary and book historians, not just those interested in digital and quantitative methods. In addition, I have sought to outline and enact a methodological framework where the results of data-rich analysis are explicitly presented as contributions to, rather than replacements for, the processes of debate and theorisation that makes humanities scholarship vital. Or to put this another way, despite the rhetoric of objectivity that surrounds them, quantitative and computational analyses *are* arguments, underpinned by interpretation and theorisation. It is from this position that quantitative, computer-enabled research can and should take its place in the humanities. The strength of humanities scholarship has always been in its investigation of, and mode of engagement with, the human world in all its complexity. Digital humanities research only retains the potential to enable insights into this world – and to justify the label, humanities – if critical and cultural analysis is its core agenda, and if the fundamental humanities skills of scholarship, interpretation and argumentation remain central to the approach taken by such investigations.

NOTES

Introduction. A New History of the Australian Novel

1. Caesar, 'Franco Moretti', 135–136.
2. McGann, 'Culture and Technology', 72. See also McGann, 'A Note'.
3. *AustLit: The Australian Literature Resource*. http://www.austlit.edu.au
4. Frow, 'Thinking the Novel', 139.
5. Schreibman, Siemens and Unsworth, 'The Digital Humanities', xxvi.
6. For discussion and criticism of the national focus of literary studies and the humanities see Bender, 'The Boundaries'; Dimock, 'Scales of Aggregation'; Harpham, 'Between Humanity'.
7. Gelder and Salzman, *The New Diversity*.
8. Webby, 'Introduction', 5.
9. Carter, 'After Post-Colonialism', 118. See also Bode and Dixon.
10. See Eggert, 'The Book' and Hetherington, 'Old Tricks'.
11. See for example, Dixon, 'Tim Winton'; Carter, 'Structures, Networks'.
12. Finkelstein and McCleery, 'Introduction', 1.
13. Rose, 'An Introduction', ix.
14. Examples of such work include Bode, 'Along Gender'; Bode, 'From British'; Bode, 'Graphically Gendered'; Carter, 'Boom, Bust'; Davis, 'The Decline'; Dolin, 'First Steps'; Dolin, 'The Secret'; Eggert, 'Australian Classics'; Ensor, 'Is a Picture Worth'; Ensor, 'Reprints, International'; Indyk, 'Magical Numbers'; Lamond and Reid, 'Squinting at a Sea'; Lyons, 'Bush Readers'; Nile and Ensor, 'The Novel'; Thomson and Dale, 'Books in Selected'; Webby, 'Not Reading'.
15. Lever, 'Criticism and Fiction', 67.
16. Elizabeth Webby identifies *The Oxford History of Australian Literature*, edited by Leonie Kramer, and first published in the early 1980s, with this canonical, elitist focus (Kramer, *The Oxford History*; Webby, 'Introduction', 2–3).
17. Bird, 'New Narrations'.
18. Obviously, even mentioning less than five per cent of the authors responsible for Australian novels in the 1970s, 1980s and 1990s leaves Bird little space for any detailed commentary on, or evaluation of, individual works (especially given that many of these authors wrote multiple titles).
19. Lyons, 'Bush Readers', 17. See also Dolin, 'The Secret Reading'; Webby, 'Not Reading'.

Chapter 1. Literary Studies in the Digital Age

1. Morize, *Problems and Methods*, 3.
2. In addition to the book historical approaches that I will discuss in detail in this chapter – and which, I think, are becoming increasingly familiar to literary scholars – quantitative approaches to literature include relatively new research in Literary Darwinism, as well as established research paradigms in computational stylistics and the social sciences. For quantitative studies in Literary Darwinism see: Carroll, *Reading Human Nature*; Gotteschall, *Literature, Science*; Gottschall, 'Quantitative Literary Study'; Kruger, Fisher and Jobling, 'Proper Hero'; Salmon, 'Crossing the Abyss'. Studies in computational stylistics use large amounts of

data, mainly to explore authorial attribution: see, for example, Craig and Kinney, *Shakespeare, Computers*; Hoover, 'Statistical Stylistics'. Quantitative methods are also frequently employed in Empirical Literary Studies, which includes research in psychology and sociology: see Janssen and Dijk, *The Empirical Study*; Zyngier et al., *Directions in Empirical*.
3 Joshi, 'Quantitative Method', 264.
4 Moretti, 'Conjectures'; Moretti, *Graphs*.
5 Just to give some sense of the tenor of the discussion Moretti has generated: Rachel Serlen describes him as 'arguably the most controversial figure working in English and Comparative Literature today', and claims that he 'courts controversy'. 'This is a man', she notes, 'whose own jacket copy' for *Graphs, Maps, Trees* 'twice calls his work "heretical"' (Serlen, 'The Distant', 214). Similarly, Jonathan Arac calls Moretti's method of 'distant reading' 'a deliberately scandalous agenda' (Arac, 'Anglo-Globalism?', 37), while William Deresiewicz goes considerably further, criticising Moretti as 'a very ambitious man' driven by a desire 'to place himself at the center of global novelistic study' (Deresiewicz, 'Representative Fictions'). Almost inevitably, Harold Bloom dismisses Moretti and his methods as an 'absurdity' (cited in Serlen, 'The Distant', 218). The volume, as well as the tenor, of commentary Moretti's work motivates is remarkable. For instance, Moretti's book has been the subject not only of multiple articles and reviews by academics, such as those above, but of newspaper articles in the *New York Times* and the *Guardian*, numerous blogs and even an entire edited collection. For these newspaper articles see Sutherland, 'The Ideas Interview'; Eakin, 'Studying Literature by the Numbers'. Two of the more thought-provoking of a great many blogs on Moretti's book are Paul Ford, 'Tufte vs. Bloom 1', *Ftrain.com*, blog, accessed 23 April 2011. http://www.ftrain.com/TufteVsBloom001.html; and Mike Johnduff, 'Franco Moretti', *Working Notes: On Literary Criticism, Philosophy, Literary Theory*, blog, accessed 15 June 2010. http://mikejohnduff.blogspot.com/2009/04/franco-moretti-and-close-reading.html. The edited collection discussing Moretti's book is Goodwin and Holbo, *Reading*.
6 Haraway, *Simians, Cyborgs*, 187.
7 Levine, 'Why Science', 175.
8 Moretti, *Signs*, 15.
9 Moretti, *Graphs*, 76, 77.
10 Ibid., 3.
11 Krzysztof Pomeian, cited in Moretti, *Graphs*, 3.
12 Moretti, *Graphs*, 4.
13 Ibid., 1.
14 Timothy Burke and Matt Greenfield also point out and refute the widespread perception that Moretti is alone in using quantitative methods in literary studies (Burke, 'Book Notes', 42; Greenfield, 'Moretti and Other').
15 Neavill, 'From Printing History', 225. Darnton locates the origins of book history in the 1960s (Darnton, 'What', 10).
16 Darnton, *The Forbidden*, xxii.
17 Darnton, cited in Daskalova, 'Book History', 3; see also Barker, 'Intentionality', 199.
18 Another example of this criticism comes from William St. Clair, who rejects the way literary historians privilege the writing of literature while ignoring how literary works circulated and were read in the past. He identifies this neglect in both the 'parade-of-authors' convention, which imagines literary history as a progression of great names, and the 'parliament of texts' model, which presents 'the printed texts of a particular historical period as debating and negotiating with one another in a kind of open parliament with all the members participating and listening' (St. Clair, *The Reading*, 2).
19 For example, Moretti attributes the rise of the novel to a shift in the 'horizon of novel-reading' and identifies reader selections as a key factor in the development of clues in detective fiction (Moretti, *Graphs*, 5, 72–76; see also Moretti, 'The Slaughterhouse').
20 Finkelstein and McCleery, 'Introduction', 1.

21 Darnton, 'What', 10–11.
22 For example, Eliot, *Some Patterns*; Darnton, *The Forbidden*; St. Clair, *The Reading*.
23 Examples of such research include Wendy Griswold's work on Nigerian novels, Priya Joshi's studies of literature in India and Jonathan Zwicker's analyses of Japanese literature (Griswold, *Bearing Witness*; Griswold, 'Nigeria, 1950–2000'; Griswold, 'Number Magic'; Joshi, 'Culture and Consumption'; Joshi, *In Another Country*; Joshi, 'Quantitative Method'; Zwicker, 'Japan, 1850–1900'; Zwicker, *Practices*; Zwicker, 'The Long Nineteenth Century').
24 Moretti, 'Style, Inc'; Moretti, 'Network Theory'.
25 There has been debate regarding the connections between Moretti's work and Literary Darwinism. As Emily Apter writes, 'Moretti's rehabilitation of evolutionary theory has been criticised as a throwback to nineteenth-century theories of natural selection (with their eugenicist baggage)' (Apter, 'Untranslatables', 591). Chad Hines distinguishes the two, arguing that Moretti uses evolutionary theory as a metaphor or analogy rather than a theoretical framework (Hines, 'Evolutionary Landscapes', 5). While there may be connections – beyond the use of fictional data – Moretti's analyses are significantly more sophisticated and less didactic than any I have come across in Literary Darwinism (for a thorough critique of this paradigm see Kramnick, 'Against Literary Darwinism').
26 See, for example, Milkman, Carmona and Gleason, 'A Statistical Analysis'; Milic and Slane, 'Quantitative Aspects of Genre'.
27 It is interesting that feminist criticism has been and still is dismissed in the same terms. Rita Felski characterises the attack on feminist literary criticism as follows: according to those who dismiss feminist literary criticism, '[a]ll literary critics worthy of the name…share a deep and abiding love of the works they read. Their response to a great work of literature is one of overpowering awe and almost painful pleasure. Feminists, however, are conspicuously lacking in such higher emotions. They are mean-spirited malcontents who only know how to debunk and denounce, who are importing sterile ideologies into a sphere that was once blessedly free of political wrangling' (Felski, *Literature After Feminism*, 1).
28 Moretti, 'Style, Inc'.
29 Trumpener, 'Critical Response', 160.
30 Tally, 'Review of *Graphs*', 134.
31 Rothberg, 'Quantifying Culture?', 321.
32 Spivak, *Death of a Discipline*, 108.
33 Haraway, 'Situated Knowledges', 584.
34 Izzo, 'Outside Where', 597.
35 Arac, 'Anglo-Globalism?', 45.
36 Spivak, *Death of a Discipline*, 108.
37 English, 'Everywhere and Nowhere', xiii. Bill Readings likewise decries the 'logic of quantification' and the 'logic of accounting' that governs contemporary universities (Readings, 'The University', 471).
38 Lever, 'Criticism and Fiction', 67.
39 Nussbaum, *Poetic Justice*; Poovey, *A History*; Merry, 'Measuring'.
40 Merry, 'Measuring', 84.
41 Eric Hayot also proposes a specifically disciplinary reason for the attention Moretti has received, suggesting that this notion of 'distant reading' has arrived just at the 'moment when the last major wave of new ideas seems to have floundered. Many people seem to want a new Theory to replace the exhausted old Theory' (Hayot, 'A Hundred', 65).
42 It is also, I would suggest, significantly easier to attack another humanities scholar than a scientist or someone in senior university management.
43 Hermanson, 'Review'. Similarly, Marc Parry notes that, 'As the humanities struggle with financial stress and waning student interest, some worry that the lure of money and technology will increasingly push computation front and center' (Parry, 'The Humanities').
44 Hermanson, 'Review'.

45 Spivak, *Death of a Discipline*, 108. For an excellent discussion of the changing role of visual representation – and the relationship of the image to 'truth' – in medical science see Kemp, "'A Perfect'".
46 English, 'Everywhere and Nowhere', xiii.
47 Hudson, 'Numbers and Words', 140.
48 Black et al., 'Geographical Information', 12–13.
49 Darnton, 'Book Production', 259.
50 Black et al., 'Geographical Information', 12.
51 Darnton, 'Book Production', 259.
52 Joshi, 'Quantitative Method', 273. Many book historians integrate both qualitative and quantitative approaches. For instance, Joshi argues that statistics often 'indicat[e] the question, but only close textual reading…can address [it]' (Joshi, 'Quantitative Method', 273). Similarly, Jonathan Zwicker uses both 'anecdotes' on individual texts and 'numbers' – statistical analysis of the fiction market – to explore nineteenth-century Japanese literature (Zwicker, 'Japan, 1850–1900', 512).
53 Zwicker, 'Japan, 1850–1900', 514.
54 Eliot, 'Very Necessary', 284.
55 Black et al., 'Geographical Information', 12–13; see also Eliot, 'Very Necessary', 283.
56 Gottschall et al., 'Are the Beautiful', 44.
57 Trumpener, 'Critical Response', 163.
58 Ibid., 164.
59 For an insightful critique of literary history's foundations 'on a claim about the importance of acquaintance' and 'how far that insistence…has made literary history look like a relatively temporary business indeed', see Ferguson, 'Planetary Literary', 661.
60 Moretti, 'Conjectures', 55.
61 Ibid., 57.
62 Moretti, *Graphs*, 2.
63 Serlen, 'The Distant', 220.
64 Burke, 'Book Notes', 41.
65 Serlen, 'The Distant', 220.
66 Moretti, 'Moretti Responds (II)', 74.
67 Moretti, *Graphs*, 4.
68 Spivak, *Death of a Discipline*, 108.
69 Frow, 'Thinking the Novel', 142.
70 Moretti, *Graphs*.
71 Moretti, 'Conjectures'.
72 Serlen, 'The Distant', 217. Moretti makes much the same comment about Literary Darwinism, disparaging the 'passion' of those in this field 'for fuzzy or crude units of analysis' (Moretti, 'Moretti Responds (II)', 73).
73 Moretti, *Graphs*, 9.
74 Serlen, 'The Distant', 219.
75 Moretti, *Graphs*, 9.
76 Serlen, 'The Distant', 219–220.
77 Spivak, *Death of a Discipline*, 108.
78 Moretti, *Graphs*, 2.
79 Moretti, 'Graphs, Maps', 63.
80 Serlen, 'The Distant', 220.
81 Friedman, 'Explanation', 5.
82 Moretti, *Graphs*, 26.
83 Ibid., 29.
84 Ibid., 5.
85 Serlen, 'The Distant', 222.

86 Moretti, *Graphs*, 29.
87 Moretti, 'Conjectures', 66.
88 Serlen, 'The Distant', 222.
89 Moretti, 'The End', 76.
90 Moretti, *Graphs*, 92.
91 Eliot, 'Very Necessary', 287.
92 Joshi, 'Quantitative Method', 269.
93 Eliot, 'Very Necessary', 289.
94 Frow, 'Thinking the Novel', 142.
95 *AustLit*, 'About AustLit', accessed 3 June 2011. http://www.austlit.edu.au/about
96 *AustLit*, 'About Scope', accessed 3 June 2011. http://www.austlit.edu.au/about/scope
97 On 31 December 2011 *AustLit* listed its content as: 737,896 works; 132,115 agents and 29,546 subjects (*AustLit*, 'AustLit', accessed 31 December 2011. http://www.austlit.edu.au/).
98 This has been the case in Australia since at least the 1920s, when the Palmers emphasised the importance of the Australian novel to the development of national and cultural identity (Carter, 'Critics, Writers' 267).
99 *AustLit*, 'About Books', accessed 3 June 2011. http://www.austlit.edu.au/about/books
100 Another modification I have made to the data extracted from *AustLit* is in my treatment of uncertain years. Approximately four per cent of the Australian novels published between 1830 and 1899 and 1945 and 2009 have as their date of publication a decade rather than a specific year (for instance, 197–). I have chosen to divide such novels evenly among the other years in the decade, even if this produces a fractional result (for instance, 124.5 Australian novels published between 1890 and 1894).
101 I created the two main datasets underpinning the analysis in this book as follows: performing guided searches in *AustLit*, asking for all 'single work' novel titles in particular year ranges; displaying these results as tagged text and copying them to a text file; and using command lines in terminal to organise the data before exporting it in CSV format. This process left me with Excel files that initially included the type, title, author, year of publication, publisher and genre/s for each Australian novel. I then looked at each publisher to determine if it was owned by another company (a task that was especially complex for data after the 1980s, due to the growing rate of acquisition and conglomeration of publishing companies). I also added information to these files as my research developed and specific questions emerged: for instance, I categorised all the authors by gender; for nineteenth-century Australian novels I differentiated the years of publication – that is, first serial and first book – and included the number of volumes in which books were published. To experiment with and visualise the data I used the pivot table and graphing functions in Excel. The only datasets used in this book that were not extracted using the process described above related to critical discussion of authors (explored in Chapter 5). Because these datasets were much larger than the others – and because *AustLit* only allows searches with less than 1,000 results to be displayed as tagged text – they were extracted through a process known as screen-scraping, performed in February 2007.
102 Most 'Non-*AustLit* Novels' are by well-known authors (such as George Eliot, Harriet Beecher Stow and Charles Dickens) deemed to have profoundly influenced particular Australian authors.
103 'Banned in Australia' is one of *AustLit*'s specialist datasets, led by Nicole Moore and including approximately 500 titles (*AustLit*, 'Banned in Australia', accessed 4 June 2011. http://www.austlit.edu.au/specialistDatasets/Banned).
104 Four print-versions of *AustLit* were published from 2001 to 2008. See Arnold and Hay, *The Bibliography: A-E*; Arnold and Hay, *The Bibliography: F-J*; Arnold and Hay, *The Bibliography: K-O*; Arnold and Hay, *The Bibliography: P-Z*.
105 The only datasets I have not updated are the ones concerning critical discussion of Australian authors.
106 *AustLit*, 'About Scope', accessed 3 June 2011. http://www.austlit.edu.au/about/scope

107 *AustLit*, 'Inclusion Criteria for Authors', accessed 3 June 2011. http://www.austlit.edu.au/about/scopepolicy#selectionCriteria
108 For discussion of these parameters and decisions in Australian bibliography see Arnold and Hay, 'Introduction', viii, xi.
109 Dever, '"Conventional Women"', 133.
110 Darnton, 'Book Production', 240.
111 Moretti, *Signs*, 15.
112 Darnton, 'Book Production', 240.
113 Joshi, 'Quantitative Method', 264.
114 Griswold, 'Number Magic', 276.
115 In presenting my results, one decision I made – based on this status of literary data as indication rather than proof of historical trends – was not to give statistics with decimal points. Given that the data is inevitably incomplete, I felt that multiple decimal points (as well as interrupting the reading process for literary scholars perhaps not accustomed to dealing with charts and numbers) implied a level of exactitude that was misleading.
116 Arthur, 'Virtual Strangers'.
117 McCarty, *Humanities Computing*, 27.
118 Rothberg, 'Quantifying Culture?', 322.
119 See also Drucker, 'Philosophy and Digital'.
120 McGann, *Radiant Textuality*, 18.
121 McCarty, *Humanities Computing*, 6.
122 Ibid., 12.
123 Davidson, 'Humanities 2.0', 710.
124 McCarty, 'Knowing...: Modeling'.
125 McCarty, *Humanities Computing*, 24.
126 Ibid., 36, 27.
127 McCarty, 'Knowing...: Modeling'.
128 *AustLit*, 'Reading by Numbers'. http://www.austlit.edu.au/ResourcefulReading/ReadingByNumbers
129 McCarty, 'Knowing...: Modeling'.
130 McCarty, *Humanities Computing*, 26–27.
131 Eliot, 'Very Necessary', 293.

Chapter 2. Beyond the Book: Publishing in the Nineteenth Century

1 Munro and Curtain, 'After the War', 3.
2 Jacklin, 'The Transnational Turn', 1.
3 Dixon, 'Boundary Work', 35.
4 Dixon, 'Australian Literature', 20; see also Carter, 'After Post-Colonialism', 114.
5 Webby, 'Not Reading', 308.
6 Johanson, *A Study*, 5; see also Lyons, 'Britain's Largest'.
7 Weedon, *Victorian Publishing*, 38–39.
8 Lyons, 'Bush Readers', 17.
9 Dolin, 'The Secret Reading', 130; see also Dolin, 'First Steps'.
10 Webby, 'Not Reading', 309, 310.
11 Webby, 'Colonial Writers', 50.
12 The 'Other' category contains a surprisingly wide array of countries where Australian novels were first published as books, including America, Belgium, Denmark, France, Germany, India, Italy, Japan, New Zealand, Sweden and Switzerland. Titles published jointly, other than in Australia and Britain, are also included in this 'Other' category (some such joint publishing arrangements involved American, Australian and British publishers; Australian and

New Zealand publishers; and British and American – or Canadian or German – publishers). The relatively high proportion of Australian novels published outside either the colonies or Britain – especially in the 1860s and 1870s (when 14 per cent of titles published as books were in this category) – challenges the prevailing understanding of colonial literary culture as formed through a direct and, for the colonies, exclusive relationship with British publishers. While this other movement of Australian 'stories' deserves attention, I concentrate on the two main sites for book publication of Australian novels in this period: Britain and the colonies.

13 John Sutherland defines serial publication – or serialisation – as 'the division of narrative into separately issued instalments, usually for commercial convenience but occasionally for art' (Sutherland, *Victorian Fiction*, 87).
14 Munro and Curtain, 'After the War', 3.
15 Five of these titles were eventually issued as books in the twentieth century (Cawthorne, *The Islanders*; Chisholm, *Little Joe*; Lang, *Lucy Cooper*; Lang, *Mazarine*; Lang, *Raymond*). Fourteen other Australian novels initially serialised from the 1860s to the 1890s were also only issued in book form in the twentieth and twenty-first centuries (mostly in the 1980s, 1990s and 2000s). Due to the long gap between serial and book publication, and my focus on the circulation of these titles in the nineteenth century, in this chapter – and Chapter 4 – I include these titles in the 'serial only' category (Atkinson, *Debatable Ground*; Atkinson, *Myra*; Atkinson, *Tom Hellicar's Children*; Atkinson, *Tressa's Resolve*; Davitt, *Force and Fraud*; De Boos, *Mark Brown's Wife*; De Boos, *The Poor Man*; Lang and Crittenden, *Ellen Wareham*; Spence, *A Week*; Spence, *Gathered In*; Swan, *The Late N. Walter*; Whitworth, *Mary Summers*).
16 Lang wrote two of the five first edition Australian novels published by Routledge in these decades (Lang, *The Ex-Wife*; Lang, *Will He Marry*), and all four of Ward, Lock's (Lang, *Captain Macdonald*; Lang, *My Friend's Wife*; Lang, *The Forger's Wife*; Lang, *Too Much Alike*).
17 Feather, *A History of British Publishing*, 82.
18 Ibid., 77.
19 Atkinson, *Cowanda*; Atkinson, *Gertrude the Emigrant*; Rowe, *Arthur Owen*.
20 Lang, *Legends of Australia*.
21 James Tegg and his brother Samuel are described as 'the first example of an attempt to exploit the colonial market through a chain of interconnected businesses with their centre in London' (Fitzhardinge, 'Tegg, James'). The centre referred to here is the publishing business of their father, Thomas Tegg, 'one of the largest publishers of his day' (Barnes and Barnes, 'Reassessing the Reputation', 58; see also Crittenden, *James Tegg*).
22 Horne, *Rebel Convicts*.
23 *AustLit*, 'George Slater', accessed 23 September 2010. http://www.austlit.edu.au/run?ex=ShowAgent&agentId=A%2cKP
24 Yarra-Guinea, *Frank Kennedy*.
25 Champion and Champion, 'The Wharf', 2–3.
26 Savery, *Quintus Servinton*; *AustLit*, 'Melville, Henry', accessed 10 November 2010. http://www.austlit.edu.au/run?ex=ShowAgent&agentId=A-7a
27 Tegg blamed the demise of the first of these magazines on 'local writers' and their 'dilatoriness in delivering copy' (Fitzhardinge, 'Tegg, James').
28 Feather, *A History of British Publishing*, 82.
29 London Online lists the population of London in 1841 as 1,948,417, while the Australian Bureau of Statistics lists the non-Indigenous population of the Australian colonies in the same year at 220,968 (London Online, 'Historical Overview'; Australian Bureau of Statistics, '3105.0.65.001').
30 David Christie Murray, cited in Johnson-Woods, 'Mary Elizabeth Braddon', 112.
31 Weedon, *Victorian Publishing*, 38.
32 Richard Tames, cited in Weedon, *Victorian Publishing*, 30.
33 Weedon, *Victorian Publishing*, 38–39.

34 Ibid., 41.
35 Weedon describes 'a series of reversals' in the British book trade from 1826 to 1869, when 'a number of companies went bankrupt or came close to it' (Weedon, *Victorian Publishing*, 47).
36 *Tegg's New South*; Darling, *Simple Rules*; Lee, *Brandy and Salt*.
37 Barnes and Barnes, 'Reassessing the Reputation', 58.
38 Fitzhardinge, 'Tegg, James'.
39 *AustLit*, 'J. R. Clarke', accessed 20 November 2011. http://www.austlit.edu.au/run?ex=Show Agent&agentId=A4Ch
40 Lea-Scarlett, 'Clarke, Jacob Richard'.
41 Morrison, 'Introduction', xi.
42 Morrison, 'More than a Case', 25.
43 London publisher Remington required author Rolf Boldrewood to contribute to the costs of publication (Eggert, '*Robbery Under Arms*', 129; see also Eggert and Webby, 'Introduction', xliii–xliv).
44 There was one self-published title in the 1830s and two in the 1850s, with an additional two in the 1860s, six in the 1870s, two in the 1880s and seven in the 1890s. Only one of these self-published titles – *Reminiscences of Australia: The Diggings and the Bush*, by W. May Howell – lists a place of publication outside the Australian colonies (An Australian Colonist, *A Victim*; Bell, *Oscar: A Romance*; Bunn, *The Guardian*; Burnage, *A Novel*; Burnage, *Bertha Shelley*; Cameron, *The Fire Stick*; Cameron, *The Mysteries*; Cameron, *Transformations*; Canmore, *Hector Beaumill*; Cohen, *Stanhope Burleigh*; Collis, *Willis of Ryde*; Dunlop, *Middle Life*; Fraser, *Melbourne and Mars*; Glenfield, *On Strike*; Healey, *The Seven Christians*; Hennessey, *A Lost Identity*; Howell, *Reminiscences*; Isaacs, *The Queen*; Leplastrier, *The Travels*; Wailes, *Me: The History*).
45 As I discussed in Chapter 1, *AustLit* classifies an author as 'Australian' if s/he is born in Australia, 'resident in Australia', or 'visiting…and engaging with Australian subjects or themes'. This latter category, which relates to a relatively small proportion of twentieth-century titles, has a significant impact in this early part of the nineteenth century, when a number of authors of novels categorised by *AustLit* as 'Australian' are visitors to the colonies (or, in limited instances, never visited but drew on documentary or anecdotal evidence to set their works in Australia). While it might be possible to exclude authors who visited the colony only briefly, or those who did not visit at all, as with any manual adjustment to a dataset, such a strategy is liable to introduce error. At the same time, it would fail to remove ambiguity: with the exception of those few (difficult to identify) authors who never visited, the condition of inclusion – being born in the colonies, or living there for a year, or ten, or thirty – remains a random constraint (*AustLit*, 'Scope Policy', accessed 17 December 2011. http://www.austlit.edu.au/about/scopepolicy).
46 For a discussion of this genre in the Canadian context see Hanson, *Emigration*.
47 See Bennett, *Cross Currents*; Eggert and Webby, *Robbery Under Arms*; Johnson-Woods, *Index to Serials*; Johnson-Woods, 'Mary Elizabeth Braddon'; Mills, *The Native Companion*; Morrison, 'Introduction'; Morrison, 'Newspaper Publications'; Morrison, 'Retrieving Colonial'; Morrison, 'Serial Fiction'; Stuart, *Australian Periodicals*; Stuart, 'Colonial Periodicals'; Stuart, *His Natural Life*; Webby, 'Before the *Bulletin*'; Webby, 'Colonial Writers'.
48 Johnson-Woods, *Index*, 5; see also Webby, 'Before the *Bulletin*', 4.
49 For example, Brake, *Print in Transition*; Hayward, *Consuming Pleasures*; Hughes and Lund, *The Victorian Serial*; Johanningsmeier, *Fiction*; Law, *Serialising Fiction*; Lund, *America's Continuing Story*; Myers and Harris, *Serials and their Readers*.
50 On the neglect of serialised Australian fiction see Morrison, 'Retrieving Colonial', 27; Eggert, '*Robbery Under Arms*', 131; Webby, 'Before the *Bulletin*', 6.
51 For instance, although Dolin notes that much of the 'Australian appetite for cheap popular fiction' was 'supplied in newspapers', in then drawing broad conclusions about colonial reading practices on the basis of book lending records, he effectively dismisses the role of newspaper

novels in such reading practices, or at least, assumes that serial fiction was essentially the same as that available in lending libraries (Dolin, 'The Secret Reading', 115).
52 The titles published in the *Mofussilite* are: Lang, *Captain Macdonald*; Lang, *Ellen Wareham*; Lang, *Livy Lake*; Lang, *Mazarine*; Lang, *My Friend's Wife*; Lang, *My Furlough*; Lang, *Passages in the Life*; Lang, *Recollections*; Lang, *The Ex-Wife*; Lang, *The Wetherbys*; Lang, *Too Clever*; Lang, *Too Much Alike*; Lang, *Violet*; Lang, *Will He Marry*. The titles by Lang published in British periodicals are Lang, *Lucy Cooper*; Lang, *Raymond*; Lang, *The Forger's Wife*.
53 Rowcroft, *Tales*; Rowcroft, *The Bushranger*.
54 Rowcroft was editor of *Hood's Magazine and Comic Miscellany* in 1845, the year *The Bushranger of Van Diemen's Land* was serialised in that periodical. He was also editor of *The British Queen and Statesman* from 1842 to 1843, during which time that periodical incompletely serialised *Tales of the Colonies* (Shattock, *The Cambridge Bibliography*, 989/990).
55 Webby, 'Colonial Writers', 50; see also Webby, 'Before the *Bulletin*', 4.
56 This novel was published first as a book edition by Routledge in 1857 and then as a serial in the *Examiner* in 1859 (Gerstaecker, *The Two*).
57 Johnson-Woods, 'Beyond Ephemera'.
58 Morrison, 'Serial Fiction', 309.
59 Ibid., 308.
60 *AustLit*, 'The Argus', accessed 12 October 2011. http://www.austlit.edu.au/run?ex= ShowWork&workId=CZj%2c
61 The reliability of this claim is brought into question by George Massina's corresponding and unlikely assertion that, when Marcus Clarke took over the editorship of the journal, monthly sales immediately fell from 12,000 to 4,000 (Campbell, *The First Ninety*, 83).
62 Morrison, 'Introduction', xxxi.
63 Johanningsmeier, *Fiction*, 2, 37.
64 Johnson-Woods, 'Mary Elizabeth Braddon', 111.
65 Nicholas and Shergold, 'British and Irish Convicts', 21.
66 Feather, *A History of British Publishing*, 85–96, 112.
67 A rotary newspaper press was installed in the *Times* in 1866 (Arnold, 'Printing Technology', 105). The *Sydney Mail* appears to have been the first colonial periodical to adopt this technology, introducing a rotary press in 1875 (O'Grady, *A Century*, 675). In the late 1870s, 'three Victory steam presses [were installed] in the *Age* office in Melbourne [and] produced a combined output of 50,000 copies of a four-page daily newspaper an hour.... [B]oth the Adelaide dailies adopted the same process in 1892' (Arnold, 'Printing Technology', 105).
68 Eggert, '*Robbery Under Arms*', 129.
69 Isaacs and Kirkpatrick, *Two Hundred*, 9.
70 Morrison, 'Retrieving Colonial', 28.
71 Law, 'Imagined Local', 188; see also Law, *Serialising Fiction*, 45–47, 51.
72 Feather, *A History of British Publishing*, 112; Law, 'Imagined Local'; Donaldson, *Popular Fiction*.
73 Law, 'Imagined Local', 188.
74 Australian Bureau of Statistics, '3105.0.65.001'.
75 Campbell, *The First Ninety Years*, 53.
76 Morrison, 'Serial Fiction', 310.
77 In 1866, New South Wales had a population of 428,167 compared with Victoria's 633,602. By 1870, New South Wales and Victoria's populations had grown to 497,992 and 723,925 respectively (Australian Bureau of Statistics, '3105.0.65.001').
78 Johnson-Woods, 'Beyond Ephemera', 211.
79 Johnson-Woods, 'Mary Elizabeth Braddon', 112.
80 Webby, 'Before the *Bulletin*', 32. In relation to this claim, Webby argues that the *Sydney Mail* – the largest newspaper publisher of Australian novels in this middle period – 'did not make a particular feature of Australian authors until the 1880s' (Webby, 'Before the

Bulletin', 6). Similarly, Morrison suggests that colonial newspapers 'did not routinely notice Australian fiction until the mid-1890s' (Morrison, 'Introduction', xlii).

81 Anderson, *Imagined Communities*, 25 (original italics). Law points to Franco Moretti's *Atlas of the European Novel* (which he says 'attempts literally to map the geographical development of national consciousness in European fiction in terms of both forms and market') as a prominent recent offspring of Anderson's theory. Both critics, Law insists, and nation-based literary studies generally, ignore 'the complexities of serial publication': Anderson 'never recognizes that news and novels often occupied the same publishing space, while Moretti seems only able to conceive of narrative fiction in the shape of the bound volume' (Law, 'Imagined Local', 185; Moretti, *Atlas*).

82 Donaldson and Law make this same argument in relation to local novels serialised in regional English and Scottish newspapers in this period (Donaldson, *Popular Fiction*; Law, 'Imagined Local').

83 Isaacs and Kirkpatrick, *Two Hundred*, 11.

84 Arnold, 'Newspapers', 256.

85 Brake, *Print in Transition*, 3.

86 Adelaide, 'How Did Authors', 86; Eggert, '*Robbery Under Arms*', 129; Morrison, 'Introduction', xiv; Webby, 'Colonial Writers', 70–71. Morrison also includes Praed and Catherine Martin in this category (Morrison, 'Newspaper Publications', 531; Morrison, 'Retrieving Colonial', 29; Morrison, 'Serial Fiction', 315).

87 *Tales of the Colonies* was serialised (incompletely) in the *British Queen and Statesman* in 1842, with Saunders and Otley releasing the book edition in 1843 (Rowcroft, *Tales*). Henry Colburn published *Confessions of an Etonian* serially in his periodical, the *New Monthly Magazine and Literary Journal*, in 1848, and as a book in 1852 (Rowcroft, *Confessions*).

88 *Raymond* was serialised in *Blackwood's Edinburgh Magazine*, founded by publisher William Blackwood (Lang, *Raymond*), and *Lucy Cooper: An Australian Tale* was serialised in *Sharpe's London Magazine*, owned by George Virtue, of Arthur Hall, Virtue and Co. (Lang, *Lucy Cooper*). In neither case did periodical publication segue into book publication; in fact, neither novel was published as a book until the late twentieth century.

89 *Violet, or, The Danseuse: A Portraiture of Human Passions and Character* was published by Henry Colburn, owner of the *New Monthly Magazine and Literary Journal* (Lang, *Violet*), and *The Wetherbys, Father and Son, or, Sundry Chapters of Indian Experience* was published by Chapman and Hall, owner of the *Bentley's Miscellany* (Lang, *The Wetherbys*). However, both novels were serialised in the *Mofussilite* rather than the periodicals owned by the book publishers.

90 Michael, *The Isle*; Rowe, *Arthur Owen*. One of these titles – James L. Michael's *The Isle of Vines: A Fairy Tale for Old and Young* (illustrated by Louisa Atkinson) – was published as a book jointly with British book publisher and distributor, Simpkin, Marshall.

91 Colby, 'Review', 566.

92 Crawford, 'No Time', 322. See also Morrison, 'Serial Fiction', 306.

93 Munro and Curtain, 'After the War', 3.

94 Cambridge, *My Guardian*; Franc, *Fern Hollow*; Timperley, *Bush Luck*.

95 Clarke and Walstab, *Long Odds*; Clarke, *His Natural Life*.

96 Cambridge, *My Guardian*; Cambridge, *The Two Surplices*.

97 Farjeon, *Bread-and-Cheese*; Farjeon, *Joshua Marvel*.

98 Timperley, *Bush Luck*.

99 Franc, *Fern Hollow*.

100 Winstanley, *For Her Natural Life*.

101 Kingsley, *Ravenshoe*; Kingsley, *The Hillyars*.

102 Boldrewood, *A Colonial Reformer*; Boldrewood, *A Sydney-Side*; Boldrewood, *My Run*; Boldrewood, *Nevermore*; Boldrewood, *Plain Living*; Boldrewood, *The Miner's Right*; Boldrewood, *The Sealskin*; Boldrewood, *The Sphinx*.

103 Franc, *Emily's Choice*; Franc, *Into the Light*; Franc, *Minnie's Mission*; Franc, *No Longer*; Franc, *Silken Cords*; Franc, *Two Sides*; Franc, *Vermont Vale*.
104 Cambridge, *A Black Sheep*; Cambridge, *A Little Minx*. In addition, Chapman and Hall and John Dicks each published two book editions of Australian novels serialised in British periodicals (Trollope, *John Caldigate*; Praed, *Zero*; Winstanley, *For Her Natural Life*; Winstanley, *Margaret Falconer*).
105 Cambridge, *A Mere Chance;* Cambridge, *In Two Years*; McCarthy and Praed, *The Ladies' Gallery*; Praed, *Miss Jacobsen's Chance*; Spence, *Mr Hogarth's Will*; Spence, *The Author's Daughter*.
106 Adams, *John Webb's End*; Boldrewood, *Robbery*; Ranken, *Windabyne*.
107 Farjeon, *The Duchess*; Meredith, *Phoebe's Mother*. These Australian novels were in addition to the two titles serialised in Tinsley's in-house magazine.
108 Eggert, 'Robbery Under Arms', 129.
109 Clarke, *Chidiock Tichbourne*; Clarke, *His Natural Life*; Clarke and Walstab, *Long Odds*.
110 Cambridge, *Not All in Vain*; Cambridge, *The Three Miss Kings*. Cambridge also had two novels serialised and published as books in Britain (Cambridge, *My Guardian*; Cambridge, *The Two Surplices*), and a number of novels published as books overseas, after initial serialisation in Australia (Cambridge, *A Black Sheep*; Cambridge, *A Little Minx;* Cambridge, *A Marriage*; Cambridge, *A Mere Chance*; Cambridge, *In Two Years Time*).
111 These results confirm John Arnold's description of the 1880s as 'a boom time for the colonial printing industry'. According to Arnold, this 'growth was a reflection of the overall development of, and investment in, manufacturing that took place in eastern Australia between 1860 and 1880' (Arnold, 'Printing Technology', 104).
112 In the 1860s, 39 Australian novels appeared in local periodicals, and 38 were published as books in Britain, compared with 11 local book publications. In the 1870s and 1880s, respectively, 57 and 92 titles were published in local periodicals, 48 and 55 by British book publishers, and 33 and 42 by local book publishers.
113 Franc, *Emily's Choice*; Franc, *Hall's Vineyard*; Franc, *Into the Light*; Franc, *John's Wife*; Franc, *Little Mercy*; Franc, *Minnie's Mission*; Franc, *No Longer*; Franc, *Silken Cords*; Franc, *The Master*; Franc, *Two Sides*; Franc, *Vermont Vale*.
114 Locker, *Sir Goodwin's Folly*; Locker, *Sweet Seventeen*; Praed, *An Australian Heroine*; Praed, *Moloch*; Praed, *Nadine*; Praed, *The Head Station*; Praed, *Zero*.
115 Spence, *Mr Hogarth's Will*; Spence, *The Author's Daughter*; Praed, *Affinities*; Praed, *Miss Jacobsen's Chance*; Praed, *Policy and Passion*; McCarthy and Praed, *The Ladies' Gallery*; McCarthy and Praed, *The Rebel Rose*.
116 Broome, *A Christmas Cake*; Broome, *Spring Comedies*; Kingsley, *Ravenshoe*; Kingsley, *The Hillyars*.
117 Clarke, *His Natural*; Clarke, *Twixt*.
118 Finn, *A Priest's Secret*; Finn, *The Hordern Mystery*; Stephen, *Saved By a Ring*; Stephen, *The Golden Yankee*; Richards, *Edwin Randolph*; Richards, *Under a Face*; Bowley, *Humanity*; Bowley, *Work or Labour*.
119 Holroyd, *George Robertson*, 44.
120 Munro and Curtain, 'After the War', 3.
121 Eggert and Webby, 'Introduction', liii.
122 Johanson, *A Study*, 6–7, 161; Morrison, 'More than a Case', 29.
123 *AustLit* shows that, in the 1860s, only 5 of the 12 multivolume Australian novels published in Britain were reissued in single volume by British or colonial publishers; in the 1870s, this was the case for only 6 of 16 titles.
124 Johanson, *A Study*, 105, 213.
125 Morrison, 'More than a Case', 29.
126 While colonial book publishers issued two- and three-volume editions (as well as single and part issue publications) in the 1830s and 1840s, from the 1850s no locally published books were multivolume.

127 Dolin, 'The Secret Reading', 115.
128 Johnson-Woods, *Index*, 4.
129 Morrison, 'Introduction', xxxii, xxxv.
130 Johnson-Woods, *Index*, 4.
131 Holroyd, *George Robertson*, 42.
132 Johanson, *A Study*, 10.
133 Johanson, *A Study*, 231.
134 For a discussion of the pricing structure of fiction in England see Eliot, '"Never Mind"'.
135 Eighty-six per cent of locally published books were issued in parts or single volume in the 1850s, 82 per cent in the 1860s, 97 per cent in the 1870s, and 100 per cent in the 1880s and 1890s.
136 Eggert, '*Robbery Under Arms*', 134.
137 J. Walch, cited in ibid., 134.
138 See Dolin, 'The Secret Reading'; Dolin, 'First Steps'; Lyons, 'Bush Readers'; Webby, 'Colonial Writers'.
139 Considering the period from the mid-1870s to the end of the 1880s, Morrison estimates that only a fifth of the novels in colonial newspapers were by local authors (Morrison, 'Serial Fiction', 315).
140 In contrast, only 30 per cent of Australian novels were first published in Britain from 1860 to 1889; 1 per cent were jointly published by Australian and British presses.
141 Colonial editions existed before this date. In 1843 Murray's Colonial and Home Library was launched, but contained no fiction and was unsuccessful outside Britain. Bentley issued its first series of colonial editions, with 16 titles, from 1878 to 1881, beginning again from 1885. However, it was in 1886, when Macmillan's Colonial Library Series was launched, that the colonial edition achieved its recognised and enduring form, and only '[f]rom the late 1890s onwards [that] the…colonial edition…became commonplace' (Johanson, *A Study*, 36).
142 Of the 19 Australian novels published in multiple volumes in Britain in the 1880s, 15 were reissued in single volume.
143 Eggert, '*Robbery Under Arms*', 129; see also Johnson-Woods, *Index*, 5.
144 Morrison, 'Serial Fiction', 319.
145 George Robertson published six Australian novels in 1898 alone (as well as four published jointly with Swan Sonnenschein), but only one title in both 1899 and 1901 (and none in 1900). No other first edition Australian novels bore the George Robertson imprint until the end of the first decade of the twentieth century. A consideration of all first edition books published by George Robertson included in *AustLit* – ranging from children's fiction to autobiography, drama and essays – reveals this same peak in production in the 1890s followed by a retreat from this activity. (The notable exception to this pattern is poetry collections: George Robertson published more of these in the 1880s and 1910s than in the 1890s or 1900s).
146 Gould, *A Gentleman*; Gould, *Banker and Broker*; Gould, *Golden Ruin*; Gould, *Harry Dale's Jockey*; Gould, *Landed at Last*; Gould, *Only a Commoner*; Gould, *Running It Off*; Gould, *Seeing Him Through*; Gould, *Stuck Up*; Gould, *The Dark Horse*; Gould, *The Doctor's Double*; Gould, *The Double Event*; Gould, *The Famous Match*; Gould, *The Magpie Jacket*; Gould, *The Miner's Cup*; Gould, *Who Did It?*
147 Boothby, *A Bid*; Boothby, *Doctor Nikola*; Boothby, *In Strange Company*; Boothby, *The Marriage*; Boothby, *The Beautiful White*; Boothby, *The Lust*.
148 Trainor, 'Australian Writers', 143.
149 Rukavina, '"This is a Wonderfully"', 92.
150 Ibid., 92–93.
151 Trainor, 'Australian Writers', 143.
152 Ibid., 144.
153 Ibid., 154.
154 Ibid., 143.

155 Ibid., 144.
156 Rukavina, '"This is a Wonderfully"', 92–93.
157 Lyons, 'Bush Readers'; Dolin, 'The Secret Reading'; Dolin, 'First Steps'.
158 Webby, 'Not Reading'.
159 Ibid., 308.
160 Eliot, 'The Three-Decker'.
161 Eggert, '*Robbery Under Arms*', 142.
162 Rukavina, '"This is a Wonderfully"', 81.
163 Nile and Walker, 'The "Paternost Row Machine"', 8.
164 Munro and Curtain, 'After the War', 3.
165 Johnson-Woods, 'Beyond Ephemera', 209.
166 Patten, 'Serialised Retrospection', 123.
167 For example, Brake, *Print in Transition*; Hayward, *Consuming Pleasures*; Hughes and Lund, *The Victorian Serial*; Jones, 'Modernism'; Johanningsmeier, *Fiction*; Keymer, 'Reading Time'; Law, *Serialising Fiction*; Lund, *America's Continuing Story*; Martin, *George Eliot's*; Myers and Harris, eds, *Serials*.
168 Leighton and Surridge, 'The Plot Thickens'.
169 Jones, 'Modernism', 103.
170 Leighton and Surridge, 'The Plot Thickens', 97.
171 Johnson-Woods, 'Beyond Ephemera', 209.
172 Ferres, 'Introduction', 1.
173 Morrison, 'Serial Fiction', 317.
174 Ibid., 320.
175 Eggert, 'The Book', 68.
176 For discussion of this division in the American context see McGann, *Radiant Textuality*, 103.
177 Frow, *Cultural Studies*, 13.
178 Trumpener, 'Critical Response', 160.
179 Morrison notes that Cambridge's instalment plan for *A Black Sheep* was largely ignored by the *Age*, which payed her 'the extremely large amount' of £197 for the Australian serial rights (Morrison, 'Introduction', xxvi).
180 Johnson-Woods, 'Beyond Ephemera', 210. Brake extends this idea, defining the periodical fictional text as 'a model of textual heteroglossia' incorporating 'coloured wrappers, customized advertisers, title pages, indices, illustrations, and juxtaposed and sequential editorial matter' (Brake, *Print in Transition*, 27).
181 Bourdieu, 'The Field', 330.

Chapter 3. Nostalgia and the Novel: Looking Back, Looking Forward

1 Webby, 'Australian Literature', 16.
2 Lyons, 'Introduction', xvii, xvi.
3 This notion of separate generations is, of course, a myth in itself. Mark Davis makes this point in *Gangland*, but also shows how this particular generation has dominated cultural and political debate in Australia since the 1970s (Davis, *Gangland*).
4 Flanagan, 'Colonies', 134.
5 Munro and Sheahan-Bright, *Paper Empires*.
6 Munro and Curtain, 'After the War', 6.
7 Webby, 'Australian Literature', 17.
8 Wilding, 'Michael Wilding', 154, 153.
9 When considering any of the results in this book, but especially those referring to publishing post–World War Two, it is important to note that many companies published under a number of imprints. Horwitz, for example, published Australian novels under the Horwitz, as well as the Transport Publishing Co., Stag, Scripts, Gold Star and Horwitz Grahame imprints.

10 In Figure 4, the category of 'other' incorporates Australian novels published first in America as well as a range of other countries (from Argentina and Austria through to Vietnam and Zimbabwe); joint publications (titles published by two or more publishers from different countries or 'categories': that is, not both from the same nation, or both multinationals or both unknown); Australian novels published in periodicals; and titles where the place of publication is unknown. I have categorised novels as 'self-published' only when the author is listed as the publisher in *AustLit*, or when the publisher is a small company established by the author to publish only that author's works: Artesian Productions, for instance, was established by Coral Hull for the purposes of self-publication (*AustLit*, 'Artesian Productions', accessed 9 December 2010. http://www.austlit.edu.au/run?ex=ShowAgent&agentId=A4e=). I have not listed titles published by subsidy presses, or by individuals publishing other individuals' novels, as self-published.

11 For a paper that makes both claims about Australian literary studies see Gelder, 'Recovering Australian'. For discussion of the allegiance of humanities disciplines, especially literary studies, to the nation-state see Harpham, 'Between Humanity'; Dimock, 'Scales of Aggregation'; and Casanova, *The World Republic*.

12 Flanagan, 'Colonies', 134.

13 Menehira, 'Review of *Nine Lives*'.

14 Curtain, 'How Australian', 143.

15 Munro and Curtain, 'After the War', 3.

16 As in the nineteenth century, Australian novel publishing in the first half of the twentieth century – indeed, until the early 1970s – was largely the province of publishers from two nations: Britain and Australia. From the 1900s to the 1930s, local book publishers were the second-highest producers of Australian novels, responsible for 26, 37, 26 and 25 per cent of titles in these four decades respectively. The remainder of Australian novels (9, 7, 11 and 12 per cent of titles, respectively) were by American, other-national (including Canadian, French, German and Italian), periodical and unknown publishers.

17 The category 'other' in Figure Six includes titles published in nations besides America, Australia or Britain; joint and periodical publications; and titles published by multinationals and unknown publishers.

18 With the exception of Cheshire – formed in 1935 – all of these bookseller-publishers were established in the nineteenth century.

19 Munro, '2001', 86.

20 For example, George Ferguson, A&R's one-time editor, states that, 'At A&R we were conscious of playing a leadership role in helping the industry and other publishers to develop' (Ferguson with James, 'Flagship Angus', 11).

21 Munro and Curtain, 'After the War', 6. In *Making Books*, Anne Galligan similarly describes how a 'new sense of nationalism' led to 'demand for Australian books' following World War Two. But she also notes that, even before the war, 'some publishers, such as A. C. Rowlandson of the New South Wales Bookstall Co. and George Robertson of A&R, did pursue a personal mission to publish books by Australian authors dealing with Australian material' (Galligan, 'The Culture', 36).

22 Thompson, 'Sixties Larrikins', 32.

23 Page, 'Rigby Limited', 43.

24 McLaren, 'Andrew Fabinyi', 20.

25 Currey, 'Lansdowne', 39.

26 Carter, '*They're a Weird Mob* and Ure Smith', 26.

27 Ibid., 28.

28 This figure combines the ten novels published by the Cheshire Group (including the imprints Cheshire, Lansdowne and Jacaranda) before 1964, and the 20 titles published under these imprints after Publishing Associates acquired the company.

29 This figure rises to 19 if the Australian novels published after Ure Smith's merger with Horwitz are included.
30 As in the nineteenth century, some Australian novels in this period were published by companies involved in a range of print-related activities, from bookselling and general printing to bookbinding and distribution. From 1945 to 1969, this group included small printers, such as Hawthorn Press (two titles) and Realist Printing and Publishing Co. (one), as well as major enterprises, such as bookseller-publisher, Robertson & Mullens (two), and printer and publisher of scholarly and historical works, The Wentworth Press (one). Companies such as National Press – a Melbourne-based printer/publisher – and C. H. Pitman – a Perth-based bookbinder/publisher – produced slightly more titles (eight and six respectively).
31 *AustLit*, 'Australasian Book Society', accessed 20 October 2010. http://www.austlit.edu.au/run?ex=ShowAgent&agentId=A%2c;Q
32 *AustLit*, 'Dolphin Publications', accessed 20 October 2010. http://www.austlit.edu.au/run?ex=ShowAgent&agentId=A%2c@u
33 *AustLit*, 'F. H. Johnston Publishing Co. Pty Ltd', accessed 20 October 2010. http://www.austlit.edu.au/run?ex=ShowAgent&agentId=A8HV
34 Johnson-Woods, 'The Mysterious', 74.
35 Ferguson with James, 'Flagship Angus', 11; Munro, 'A&R's Takeover', 13; Davis, 'Literature, Small Publishers', 6. Of course, A&R published more than novels. But even considering all titles, A&R's output does not exceed – or even come close – to Cleveland's 1,460 novels or Horwitz's 1,205, nor do these totals indicate the extent of Cleveland and Horwitz's publishing activities. Horwitz also published education titles (Thompson, 'Sixties Larrikins', 31; May, 'Horwitz', 52), while a significant proportion of Cleveland publications were novellas and magazines rather than novels.
36 Frank Johnson also published hard cover books, but pulp fiction titles were a substantial part of its list.
37 With 43 titles, Australian Consolidated Press (ACP) could arguably be included in this list of medium-sized pulp fiction publishers. I have chosen not to do so partly because the company, like Frank Johnson, also published non-pulp fiction (through the literary imprint, Shakespeare Head Press) and partly because, with this literary imprint and its media holdings, ACP was a multinational company.
38 Publishers identified by *AustLit* with 'pulp fiction', or cheap paperbacks, and responsible for between one and four titles between 1945 and 1969 include Ayers & James, Cavalcade Magazine, Emvee Publications, F. J. Thwaites, Frew Publications, J. Dennett, New-Fiction Publishing, N. S. W. Bookstall and Co. and Wyvern Press.
39 *Paper Empires* also mentions pulp fiction publishing – mainly in a case study on Horwitz and one on pulp fiction more broadly (May, 'Horwitz', 50–52; Morrison, 'Pulp Fiction', 257–260). But my point is that, in characterising the local industry in terms of non-pulp fiction publishers – and as nascent and driven by national sentiment – this collection backgrounds this major aspect of post-war Australian publishing.
40 For a discussion of Horwitz's contract with Alan Yates (who wrote as Carter Brown) see Johnson-Woods, 'The Mysterious'. A clear distinction between pulp and non-pulp publishers has all but disappeared from contemporary publishing. But this does not mean pulp fiction production values are no longer employed; only that they have been incorporated into the wider industry.
41 Johnson-Woods, '"Pulp" Fiction Industry'; Johnson-Woods, 'The Mysterious', 74; Flanagan, *Australian Vintage*; Loder, *Invincible Press*.
42 May, 'Horwitz', 50; Thompson, 'Sixties Larrikins', 31; John Loder has recently published a bibliography of Invincible Press's crime and mystery series (Loder, *Invincible Press*).
43 In 2008, Ensor noted that 'Cleveland and Horwitz produced the greatest output of novels from 1954 to 1971 (respectively 1424 and 770 novels each), establishing them as undeniably the most prolific Australian publishers for the period' (Ensor, 'Reprints, International Markets',

202). The comparatively low number of publications Ensor cites for Horwitz, compared to the results presented here, occurs because he does not include Horwitz's various imprints (such as Scripts, Stag and Transport Publishing) in his count. More recently, with Richard Nile, Ensor presented these same results, updating the number of titles published by both companies in this period to 1460 for Cleveland and 815 for Horwitz in accordance with additions to *AustLit*, but still not including Horwitz's imprints in the total (Nile and Curtain, 'The Novel', 539).

44 Munro and Curtain, 'After the War', 4.
45 Johnson-Woods, 'The Mysterious', 74; for an extended discussion of these tariffs see Johnson-Woods, 'Pulp Fiction: Governmental'; see also Zifcak, 'The Retail', 202–203; and Flanagan, 'Foreword', 6.
46 Nile and Ensor, 'The Novel', 536.
47 Nile and Ensor, 'The Novel', 539.
48 The decline in British publication of Australian novels actually began in the late 1930s – presumably due to the impact of the Great Depression on British publishing – but deepened during the Second World War.
49 Horwitz published some titles – under the Transport Publishing Co. imprint – towards the end of the war; but this company's output properly expanded after 1945.
50 The fact that many of the major British publishers of Australian novels – including Collins, Mills & Boon, Hutchinson and Robert Hale – focused on cheap, popular genre fiction increases the likelihood that their return to the Australian novel field had an impact on the (cheap, popular) local pulp fiction market.
51 The following observations are made on the basis of the large pulp fiction collection at the University of Melbourne library. For holdings see University of Melbourne Special Collections, 'Douglas Taylor Collection'.
52 Oxford, *West of Texandos*, 1–3.
53 In the 1960s, Horwitz also began publishing a number of war-torture-porn titles, such as *Terror of the Swastika* and *Butcher of Auschwitz*, both by John Slater (a pseudonym for Ray Slattery). For discussion of this phenomenon see Harrison, 'The Lurid War'.
54 Cleveland's list included a small number of Australian war stories, but the vast majority of its titles were American-style westerns and murder mysteries, a phenomenon I discuss in more detail in Chapter 5.
55 Nile and Ensor, 'The Novel', 539.
56 Minnis, *And All The Trees*, inside front cover.
57 De Wreder, *Black Male*, back cover.
58 Devanny, *The Killing*, back cover.
59 The lists and advertising material of earlier wartime publishers of Australian novels – Popular Publications and New Century Press – preceded these pulp fiction publishers in their appeal to national sentiment. Popular Publications' logo was a map of Australia inscribed with 'PP', and nationalism was an explicit part of its advertising material. This from the back cover of *Trouble Ahead* (published in 1940):

> Popular Publications deserves your patronage, as they publish the BEST BOOKS written by AUSTRALIANS, printed and bound in AUSTRALIA, by AUSTRALIANS, on AUSTRALIAN paper for AUSTRALIAN readers, the profit (if any) remains in AUSTRALIA. (Gunton, *Trouble Ahead*, back cover, original caps).

New Century Press advertised 'Well-known Australian Authors at 2/6' (Kelaher, *Apron Strings*, back page) and many of its titles explicitly considered questions of national identity. For instance, *Broad Acres: A Story of Early Australian Life on the Land*, published in 1939, includes a foreword by Dame Mary Gilmore that states: 'here is the work of one who knows Australia, whose family has helped make her history, and who, in the guise of a novel, gives life as it was lived where his people still hold their land after three generations' (Gilmore, 'Foreword', 9). While Popular Publications closed before the end of the war, New Century Press continued, a longevity that might be ascribed, at least in part, to its own shift to pulp fiction (mainly novellas of the western and hard-boiled crime variety).

60 Currey, 'Lansdowne', 39.
61 Johnson-Woods, 'The Mysterious', 74.
62 May, 'Horwitz', 52; see also Dolin, 'The Secret', 115.
63 On westerns, see McVeigh, *The American Western*; Mitchell, *Westerns: Making the Man*; Tompkins, *West of Everything*; on hard-boiled crime fiction see Abbott, *The Street Was Mine*; Breu, *Hard-Boiled Masculinities*; McCann, *Gumshoe America*.
64 Cawelti, *Mystery, Violence*; Tompkins, *West of Everything*.
65 Huyssen, *After the Great Divide*, vii.
66 Galligan, 'The Culture', 43.
67 Hart, 'New Wave', 53.
68 Flanagan, 'Colonies', 135.
69 Ibid., 137.
70 Ibid., 134 (my italics).
71 Hart, 'New Wave', 53–54.
72 Goldsworthy, 'Fiction from 1900', 118.
73 Gelder and Salzman, *The New Diversity*, 2–4.
74 Ibid., 2.
75 Ibid., 3.
76 Galligan, 'The Culture', 39.
77 Goldsworthy, 'Fiction from 1900', 131.
78 Bird, 'New Narrations', 183.
79 British colonial editions ceased being exported to Australia in 1972 (Magner, 'Anglo-Australian', 7). Shortly after this, a court decision in the United States ended the *BTMA* by allowing Australian publishers 'access to rights for local editions of many US-originated books that had previously been locked into agreements with British publishers' (Hart, 'New Wave', 55). Operating unofficially 'for many years' but 'formalised in 1947' (Osborne, 'Australian Literature', 107), the *BTMA* had previously meant that:

> Australia-owned publishing companies were not permitted to acquire separate rights to British-originated books. A British publisher buying rights from an American publisher automatically obtained rights to the whole British Empire (except Canada); the US publisher was then obliged to cease supplying the book to Australia and could not sell Australian rights to any Australian publishers. (Magner, 'Anglo-Australian', 8)

80 This local growth incorporates an emerging group of religious publishers, responsible for a small number of Australian novels in the 1970s and 1980s, including Openbook (with four titles in these decades), Joint Board of Christian Education (two) and with one title each, Methodist Overseas Missions and New Creation Publications. As in the immediate post-war decades (and the nineteenth century) some publishers of Australian novels in the 1970s and 1980s were involved in a range of print-related activities, including bookselling, general printing, bookbinding and distribution. In the category of printer-publisher, National Press (with two titles) was in operation before the 1970s and 1980s, but there were also new-comers to the field in these decades, including AIM Printing (one), CCH Australia (five), Globe Press (one) and Foot and Playstead (one).
81 Both Wren Books and Alpha Books had explicitly national agendas: Wren Books aimed to 'promote Australian writers', while Alpha Books 'published only books written by Australian residents on Australian subjects'. See Hesperian Press, 'Hesperian Press', accessed 4 October

2010. http://www.hesperianpress.com/. *AustLit*, 'Alpha Books', accessed 9 November 2010. http://www.austlit.edu.au/run?ex=ShowAgent&agentId=A%2c=8).

82 Outback Press also published one title in 'early 1980', after which the publisher ceased due to financial difficulties (Schwartz, 'Inner-Urban', 63, 66).

83 Magner, 'Anglo-Australian', 9; Galligan, 'The Culture', 42–43.

84 In Figures 8, 9 and 10, the category 'other' includes Australian novels published in countries besides America, Australia and Britain, as well as titles issued jointly and by unknown publishers.

85 This decline is a continuation of trends from the late 1960s. From the high point of publication of Australian novel titles in the late 1950s and early 1960s (when approximately 1,100 titles locally, and 1,500 overall, were published in each of these five-year periods), production falls to 815 titles locally and 1,265 overall in the late 1960s; 641 and 1,064 in the early 1970s; 546 and 1,012 in the late 1970s; and 403 and 941 in the early 1980s, before beginning to rise again in the second half of that decade, to 428 and 1,195 titles.

86 Anthony, *Texans Never Quit*.

87 Almost certainly Wennenberg did not publish 30 first edition Australian pulp novels in the 1970s. This company – along with other Scandinavian publishers, such as Winther in Denmark – tended to reprint these titles following their publication in Australia (with Horwitz) and/or America (with Signet). Presumably, the high number of first issues that *AustLit* accords to this company is a consequence of the ephemeral nature of pulp fiction, and the fact that not all editions of a title – or even all titles – remain. In other words, although these Swedish editions were not the first, these titles are the first, or only, remaining editions of these Australian pulp novels (for a brief synopsis of the practices of the Nordic publishers of Australian pulp fiction see Toni Johnson-Woods, 'Carter Brown Mystery Series: Nordic Carter Browns', blog, accessed 18 January 2012. http://carterbrownmysteryseries.blogspot.com/2010/08/nordic-carter-browns.html).

88 Only 1 per cent of self-published (or 7 of 570) titles have as their place of publication somewhere outside Australia. However, it is only at the end of this chapter – when I consider self- and subsidy published titles as a proportion of local publications – that I count self-published titles as locally published.

89 Johnson-Woods, 'The Mysterious', 74; May, 'Horwitz', 52.

90 Certainly, from the 1960s, Horwitz turned almost entirely to publishing Australian authors, due in part to their popularity but also because 'these largely unknown Australian authors cost…much less than their American counterparts'. See *AustLit*, 'Horwitz', accessed 3 December 2010. http://www.austlit.edu.au/run?ex=ShowAgent&agentId=A%2cDF

91 Not all author names represent a single individual: for instance, Cleveland authors Don Haring and Des R. Dunn wrote under the 'Larry Kent' name. Most of the other author names – including the most famous, 'Carter Brown' – were also pseudonyms.

92 Perhaps the growing success of the mass-market romance publisher, Torstar – owner of Harlequin/Mills & Boon – encouraged this shift from Horwitz.

93 Flanagan, 'Losing Our Voice', 12.

94 Hart, 'New Wave', 53.

95 Gelder and Salzman, *The New Diversity*, 2.

96 Magner, 'Anglo-Australian', 7.

97 Ibid., 9.

98 In the context of this growth in multinational publication, the proportion of non-pulp Australian novels by British publishers fell from 41 per cent in the early 1970s to 33 per cent in the late 1970s, 22 per cent in the early 1980s and 18 per cent in the late 1980s.

99 In the 1980s, multinational publishers were responsible for 708 Australian novels compared with 450 by local non-pulp publishers.

100 The category of 'other' in Figure 10 incorporates Australian novels first published in America, Britain and a host of other countries, as well as self-published titles and those where the place of publication is unknown.

101 *OED Online*. 'multinational, adj', accessed 23 February 2009. http://dictionary.oed.com/cgi/entry/00318191?single=1&query_type=word&queryword=multinational&first=1&max_to_show=10
102 For instance, in 1952, Macmillan purchased the American publisher St. Martin's Press and in 1971, the Australian publisher Sun Books. Collins acquired a series of British publishers with a prior involvement in the Australian novel field including: Geoffrey Bles (and its paperback imprint, Fontana) in 1953; Harvill in 1955; and in 1983, Mayflower Books and Grafton Books (both part of the publishing holdings of the Granada Group). Hutchinson's acquisitions were even more extensive, and included Andrew Melrose, Hurst and Blackett, Skeffington, and Stanley Paul in the 1920s, and Barrie and Jenkins, in the 1970s. The large holdings of these British publishers were presumably why they were targeted for take-overs, in the 1980s and 1990s, by even larger multinational conglomerates: in 1989, News Corporation acquired Collins while Random House purchased Hutchinson (from London Weekend Television); Macmillan was subsumed into Holtzbrinck in 1999.
103 Galligan, 'The Culture', 44.
104 See Gelder and Salzman, *After the Celebration*, 2; Carter and Galligan, 'Introduction', 5.
105 Multinational publishers responsible for a moderate number of Australian novels in the 1970s and 1980s included Elsevier then Reed Elsevier (39 titles), Bertelsmann (35), two further Australian-based multinationals, James Hardie (19) and ACP (17), and Random House (17). A number of others – incorporating many more imprints – published between 1 and 14 titles: Century Hudson; Fromm International; Granada; Harcourt; Hearst Corporation; Hodder Headline; Houghton Mifflin; McGraw-Hill; Octopus Publishing Group; Putnam; Simon & Schuster; Time Warner and Times Publishing.
106 Torstar also published Australian novels under the imprints Harlequin, Mills & Boon, Harlequin Mills & Boon, Silhouette and Laser Books; Thomson Organisation also published Australian novels under the imprints Michael Joseph, Nelson and Sphere.
107 This acquisition of E. P. Dutton and Company was actually a reincorporation of that company into the Penguin Group.
108 Galligan, 'The Culture', 39–40.
109 News Corporations' imprints included A&R (acquired along with its Sirius Books imprint) as well as the previously independent American publisher Harper & Row (acquired in 1987 and itself the result of the merger, in 1962, of Harper & Brothers and Row, Peterson & Company) and the long-established British publisher, Collins (in 1989). News Corporation also created its own Bay Book imprint in 1971 (Griffen-Foley, 'Packer Publications', 49). ACP, which published Australian novels – including pulp fiction titles – under that name from the 1940s, acquired British publishers Shakespeare Head Press, Golden Books and Frederick Muller in the 1950s, and for a short time in the 1980s owned Greenhouse Publications before selling it to Pearson. James Hardie, the notorious building products manufacturer, is multinational by virtue of its manufacturing businesses rather than its publishing holdings. In 1979 that company acquired a number of local publishing imprints: Rigby, Lansdowne and Ure Smith.
110 Davis, 'The Decline', 119 (my italics).
111 Ibid., 121.
112 Ibid.
113 Ibid., 119.
114 Ibid., 130–131.
115 Carter and Galligan, 'Introduction', 6.
116 Carter and Galligan, 'Introduction', 6. See also Flanagan, 'Colonies', 135; Gelder and Salzman, *After the Celebration*, 2; Galligan, 'The Culture', 44–46.
117 Wilding, 'Australian Literary', 60.
118 Ibid., 57.
119 Ibid., 64.

120 Wilding, 'Michael Wilding', 153.
121 Ibid., 152.
122 Myers, 'Getting Published', 66.
123 Hollier, 'Between Denial', 62.
124 Ibid., 66.
125 Murray, 'Generating Content', 53.
126 Carter and Galligan, 'Introduction', 5.
127 As I said previously, the definition of multinational is complex. In the 1990s and 2000s, there are some relatively small enterprises that cannot easily be identified with a particular nation and could arguably be included in the category of multinational. For example, Australian-originated press New Holland (which also publishes Australian novels under its Gibbes Street imprint) is much smaller than the major multinationals, but has 'offices in South Africa, UK and NZ' and a similarly wide list, '[f]rom travel, biography, sport and true crime to self-help gardening, food and natural history' (New Holland Publishers, 'About', accessed 10 November 2010. http://www.newholland.com.au/about.asp). Walker Books Australia also defies easy categorisation. On the one hand, it is a subsidiary of the parent company, Walker Books, based in the United Kingdom. But this company – which explicitly describes itself as an 'independent' that has 'spread [its] wings' – identifies Walker Books Australia not as a subsidiary but a 'sister compan[y]' (Walker Books, 'About Walker', accessed 18 November 2010. http://www.walker.co.uk/about-walker.aspx). These definitional difficulties raise questions about the meaning and usefulness of the term multinational in an increasingly global publishing industry. However, in this study I have decided to exclude these smaller 'multinational' publishers from that category to maintain its (relative) coherence.
128 Scholastic published most of its Australian novels in the mid-1990s and Simon & Schuster in the early 2000s.
129 The reduction in Australian novels published by Torstar is potentially related to the overall decline, described by George Paizis, in that company's 'sales…both in the main markets – USA and Europe – and elsewhere' since the mid-1980s (Paizis, 'Category Romance', 128). Interestingly, Paizis describes Torstar as both the product and the victim of globalisation: 'its thirty-five per cent share of world mass-paperback sales forced it to seek ever new markets: expansion into new areas is the only means of survival because a competitor will rush to fill a vacuum if and when prospects allow' (Paizis, 'Category Romance', 131).
130 A number of Australian authors published by Torstar have won the Romance Writers of America RITA Award for the year's best romance novel (Best Traditional Romance) including: Jessica Hart, in 2005; Marion Lennox, in 2006; and Barbara Hannay, in 2007. The fact that only one of Lennox's many novels appears in *AustLit* signals, as *AustLit* acknowledges, that the database's records for such titles are only representative, and that genre fiction publishers such as Torstar played an even more significant role in publishing Australian authors than the results in this chapter indicate. (See Hannay, *Claiming His Family*; Hart, *Christmas Eve Marriage*; Lennox, *Princess of Convenience*; Romance Writers of America, 'RITA Awards: Past Winners'.)
131 Carter and Galligan, 'Introduction', 6.
132 Gelder and Salzman, *After the Celebration*, x.
133 Wilding, 'Australian Literary', 57; Myers, 'Getting Published', 66; Hollier, 'Between Denial', 62.
134 BookScan is a sales database, introduced into Australia in December 2000 and now tracking sales in around 90 per cent of Australian bookstores (Davis, 'The Decline', 117).
135 Davis, 'The Decline', 122.
136 Ibid., 120.
137 Ibid., 116.
138 Ibid., 126.
139 Davis, 'The Decline', 125–126; see also Knox, 'The Ex Factor', 52–53; Hollier, 'Between Denial', 67.
140 Davis, 'The Decline', 125–126.

141 Carter and Galligan, 'Introduction', 6.
142 Davis, 'The Decline', 123.
143 Ibid., 123.
144 Thompson, 'Sixties Larrikins', 31.
145 Davis, 'The Decline', footnote 6.
146 Ibid., 120.
147 Ibid.
148 In 1996, 149 non-genre novels were published, compared with 116 in 2004.
149 The broader definition of literary fiction that I adopt in this study should not produce this difference in results. As long as literary fiction is categorised consistently *within* each study, the relative scope of the category should not greatly alter the publishing trends that are identified. Certainly, it should not produce a more than 100 per cent variation in results.
150 Davis modifies this view in a subsequent article, where he acknowledges the continuing importance and presence of local publishers (Davis, 'Literature, Small Publishers').
151 None of these results include self-published titles in the category of Australian publisher. If such titles are included, the proportion of Australian novels published in Australia increases from 32 to 39 per cent in the 1990s; from 38 to 43 per cent in the early 2000s; and from 40 to 44 per cent in the late 2000s.
152 Fremantle Arts Centre Press was renamed Fremantle Press in 2007 (*AustLit*, 'Fremantle Press', accessed 5 December 2011. http://www.austlit.edu.au/run?ex=ShowAgent&agentId=A10J).
153 In the 1990s, the publishers of between 10 and 19 Australian novels were: Seaview Press, Albatross Books, Text Publishing, Millennium Books, Wakefield Press, Hyland House, ABC Enterprises, Duffy and Snellgove, Boolarong Press, Australian Pocket Press and Eldorado Publishing. Seaview, Text Publishing, Wakefield and ABC go on to publish more than 20 titles in the 2000s. In the 2000s these publishers were: Indra Publishing, Hybrid Publishers, Interactive Publications, Cleveland, Saltwater Press, Central Queensland University Press, Duffy and Snellgove, Australian Scholarly Publishing, University of Western Australia Press and Brolga Publishing.
154 Hyland House, accessed 15 September 2010. http://www.greenweb.com.au/hyland/html/welcome.html
155 Hale & Iremonger, accessed 15 September 2010. http://www.haleiremonger.com/
156 Ibis Editions Australien, accessed 15 September 2010. http://goldbook.libraryjournal.com/CompanyInfo.aspx?CoID=3627028&Company=Ibis+Editions+Australien
157 Interactive Press, accessed 9 December 2010. http://www.ipoz.biz/IP/IP.htm
158 Small Press Underground Networking Community, 'Puncher and Wattman', accessed 6 December 2010. http://spunc.com.au/members/puncher-wattmann
159 Bystander Press, accessed 7 December 2010. http://www.bystander.com.au/index.html
160 *AustLit*, 'Sleepers Publishing', accessed 3 December, 2010. http://www.austlit.edu.au/run?ex=ShowAgent&agentId=A6dA
161 Papyrus Publishing, 'About Us', accessed 8 December 2010. http://www.papyrus.com.au/default.html
162 Goanna Press, 'About Us', accessed 8 December 2010. http://www.bideenapublishingco.com/about.htm
163 Triple D Books, 'About Us', accessed 9 December 2010. http://tripledbooks.com.au/aboutUs/aboutUs.htm
164 JoJo Publishing, 'About Us', accessed 9 December 2010. http://www.jojopublishing.com/_Information/ABOUT-US.asp
165 The Hornets Nest, 'The Hornets Nest Publishing & Literary Group', accessed 25 November 2010. http://home.vicnet.net.au/~hornet/
166 Ackland Press, 'Ackland Press', accessed 25 November 2010. http://www.hulskamp.com.au/~acland/
167 Danny Yee, 'Australian Publishers', *Danny Yee*, blog, accessed 25 November 2010. http://danny.oz.au/books/publishers/

168 Black Dog Books, 'About black dog books', accessed 19 November 2010. http://www.bdb.com.au/about/
169 *AustLit*, 'Duffy and Snellgrove', accessed 7 December, 2010: http://www.austlit.edu.au/run?ex=ShowAgent&agentId=A%2c=z
170 Brandl and Schlesinger, 'Brandl and Schlesinger', accessed 7 December 2010. http://www.brandl.com.au/about-Brandl-and-Schlesinger-book-publishers
171 Fontaine Press, 'Fontaine Press – About Us', accessed 7 December 2010. http://www.fontainepress.com/aboutus/
172 Brandl and Schlesinger, 'Brandl and Schlesinger', accessed 7 December 2010. http://www.brandl.com.au/about-Brandl-and-Schlesinger-book-publishers
173 *AustLit*, 'Text Publishing', accessed 8 December 2010. http://www.austlit.edu.au/run?ex=ShowAgent&agentId=A%2c@n
174 Giramondo Publishing, 'History', accessed 8 December 2010. http://www.giramondopublishing.com/history
175 Vanark Press, 'Welcome to Vanark Press and Literary Advisory Services', accessed 9 December, 2010: http://www.vanarkpress.com/
176 *AustLit*, 'Fremantle Press', accessed 9 December 2010. http://www.austlit.edu.au/run?ex=ShowAgent&agentId=A10J
177 For instance, JoJo 'endeavour[s] to create a starting block for genuine new authors with something authentic to say' and 'encourage[s] genuine new Australian authors and whenever possible offer[s] guidance to them' (JoJo Publishing, 'Our Philosophy', accessed 20 November 2010. http://www.jojopublishing.com/_Information/OUR-PHILOSOPHY.asp; JoJo Publishing, 'About Us', accessed 20 November 2010. http://www.jojopublishing.com/_Information/ABOUT-US.asp). Sleepers Publishing '[a]dvocates for new and established writers in Australia' (Sleepers Publishing, 'Sleepers', accessed 9 December 2010. http://www.sleeperspublishing.com/).
178 DCP, University of Canberra, 'Artists Talk: Storytelling by Practising Artists', accessed 27 June 2011. http://www.canberra.edu.au/dcp/news/artists-talk
179 Post Pressed, 'About Post Pressed', accessed 8 December 2010. http://www.postpressed.com.au/
180 Independence Jones, 'About Us', accessed 21 March 2011. http://www.independencejones.com/aboutus.html
181 The Vulgar Press – established in 1999 and 'dedicated to the publication of working-class and other radical forms of writing' – does not fit into this category of national/independent publishing, nor does this publisher explicitly identify with other categories I will discuss: it is 'not limited by genre' and does not describe itself as opposed to multinational publishing. At the same time, this company's commitment to working-class and radical writing resonates with the discourse of independence and cultural-commitment that I have argued characterises the self-identifications of local publishers in the 1970s and 1980s, as in the 1990s and 2000s (The Vulgar Press, 'Home', accessed 22 December 2011. http://www.vulgar.com.au/).
182 Local literary fiction publishers that invoke 'quality' in their self-descriptions include Text Publishing, Hyland House, Hale & Iremonger, Brandl and Schlesinger, Local Consumption Publications, Hybrid Publishers, Five Mile Press, Giramondo, Puncher & Wattmann, Crumplestone Press and Fontaine Press.
183 For example Gelder, 'Recovering Australian', 115.
184 Small Press and Independent Publishing Community, 'MirrorDanse Books', accessed 9 December 2010. http://spunc.com.au/members/mirrordanse-books
185 Small Press and Independent Publishing Community, 'Coeur de Lion', accessed 9 December 2010. http://spunc.com.au/members/coeur-de-lion
186 Eneit Press, 'About Us', accessed 9 December 2010. http://www.eneitpress.com/index.php?page=9
187 Heartsong Presents, 'Your Christian Romance Book Club', accessed 9 December 2010. http://www.heartsongpresents.com/

188 abc directory.com, 'ImaJinn Books', accessed 8 December 2010. http://www.abc-directory.com/site/713481. See also ImaJinn, 'Imajinn Books', accessed 8 December 2010. http://www.imajinnbooks.com/mm5/merchant.mvc
189 Ellora's Cave, 'Ellora's Cave Romantica Publishing', accessed 18 September 2010. http://www.jasminejade.com/default.aspx
190 Aphelion Publications, 'Aphelion Publications', accessed 9 December 2010. http://www.eidolon.net/aphelion/aphelion.htm
191 Detour Press, 'About Detour', accessed 9 December 2010. http://www.rubbingmirrors.com/
192 Spinifex Press, 'About Us', accessed 9 December 2010. http://www.spinifexpress.com.au/About_Us/
193 *AustLit*, 'Artemis Publishing', accessed 9 December 2010. http://www.austlit.edu.au/run?ex=ShowAgent&agentId=A1Wf. This publisher should not be confused with Artemis Press.
194 The Women's Press, 'About', accessed 9 December 2010. http://www.the-womens-press.com/aboutthewomenspress.htm/
195 Black Lace, 'Welcome to Black Lace', accessed 9 December 2010. http://nt6744.vs.netbenefit.co.uk/
196 Poolbeg, 'About Us: Who Are We?' accessed 9 December 2010. http://www.poolbeg.com/
197 Triffitt, *Cheap Thrills*. Michael Hurley describes Outlaw Press as '[a] major entrepreneurial force in Australian gay publishing' (Hurley, *A Guide*, 72). While Spinifex Press identifies as feminist, it publishes a substantial number of titles in its 'lesbian' category.
198 Local Consumption Publications, 'Local Consumption', accessed 9 December 2010. http://www.localconsumption.com/
199 Cottage Industry Press, 'Cottage Industry Press: No Water Cooler', accessed 9 December 2010. http://www.timsinclair.org/cip.htm
200 Exisle Publishing, 'About Us', accessed 9 December 2010. http://www.exislepublishing.com/about-us.html
201 Ginninderra Press, 'Ginninderra Press', accessed 9 December 2010. http://www.ginninderrapress.com.au/
202 This is the publisher's original claim, and the one cited on most websites (for example, WireAdventures in Sound and Music, 'Links: Organisations + Resources', accessed 20 December, 2011: http://www.thewire.co.uk/links/organisations-resources/s/). However, the Serpent's Tail website now carries a modified 'commitment to publishing voices neglected by the mainstream' (Serpent's Tail, 'About Us', accessed 9 December 2010. http://www.serpentstail.com/about-us). This shift in self-description is perhaps explained by the fact that authors published by Serpent's Tail won the Nobel Prize for Literature, in 2004, and in 2005, the Orange Prize for Fiction and the John Llewellyn Rhys Prize.
203 Wakefield Press, 'About Us', accessed 12 December 2010. http://www.wakefieldpress.com.au/pages.php?pageid=1
204 Brandl and Schlesinger, 'Brandl and Schlesinger', accessed 7 December 2010. http://www.brandl.com.au/about-Brandl-and-Schlesinger-book-publishers.
205 Goanna Press, 'About Us', accessed 8 December 2010. http://www.bideenapublishingco.com/about.html
206 *AustLit*, 'Finlay Lloyd', accessed 9 December 2010. http://www.austlit.edu.au/run?ex=ShowAgent&agentId=A8XP
207 *AustLit*, 'Dorchester Publishing', accessed 9 December 2010. http://www.austlit.edu.au/run?ex=ShowAgent&agentId=A3WV
208 Pulp Fiction Press, 'News', accessed 14 June 2011. http://pulpfictionpress.com.au/
209 Fantastic Fiction, 'About Mary Lyons', accessed 9 December 2010. http://www.fantasticfiction.co.uk/l/mary-lyons/
210 Small Press and Independent Publishing Community, 'MirrorDanse Books', accessed 9 December 2010. http://spunc.com.au/members/mirrordanse-books

211 Aquila Books, 'Aquila Books', accessed 29 October 2009. http://www.aquilabooks.co.uk/noframes/index.htm
212 Blackwash Press, 'About', accessed 9 December 2010. http://blackwashpress.com/newblack_003.htm
213 Casanova, *The World Republic*, 200.
214 Ibid., 171.
215 Figure 4 shows that approximately 4 per cent of Australian novels were self-published in the late 1940s. The majority of these titles are by Lionel Birnberg, and as they are listed in *AustLit* with the publication date 194–, may have been published during rather than after the Second World War.
216 Webster, 'Into the Global Era', 82.
217 Trojan Press, 'About Trojan Press', accessed 8 December 2010. http://www.trojanpress.com.au/about.htm; Golgatha Graphics, 'Golgatha Graphics', accessed 8 December, 2010: http://www.golgotha.com.au/; Great Bosses, 'Great Bosses', accessed 8 December, 2010: http://www.greatbosses.com/index.html; Turkey Tracks Press, 'Turkey Tracks Press', accessed 8 December 2010. http://www.turkeytrackspress.com.au/; Deep End Press, 'Deep End Press', accessed 8 December 2010. http://deependpress.com/about.html; Blencowe Books, 'Blencowe Books', accessed 8 December 2010. http://www.blencowebooks.com.au/
218 Australian examples of this phenomenon include Post Pressed, which highlights its 'use of current technology' to 'produce book runs which are not feasible for most large commercial publishers' (Post Pressed, 'About Post Pressed', accessed 8 December 2010. http://www.postpressed.com.au/); re.press, which describes its '[a]ttentive[ness] to the latest developments in contemporary technologies' as a way of making its 'publications…available globally, wherever there is access to the Internet' (re.press, 'About', accessed 8 December 2010. http://re-press.org/about/); Knocklofty Books, which is 'working to hasten the transition between conventional print publishing and the world of electronic books' (Knocklofty, 'About', accessed 8 December 2010. http://knocklofty.com/?page_id=2); DreamCraft, which is 'working in the new and innovative digital field of "POD publishing"' (Mel Keegan online, 'About Dreamcraft, accessed 8 December 2010. http://www.dreamcraft.com/melkeegan/about.htm); and Papertiger Media, which 'publishes poetry on CDROM as a challenge to orthodox methods of poetry publishing' (*AustLit*, 'Papertiger Media', accessed 8 December 2010. http://www.austlit.edu.au/run?ex=ShowAgent&agentId=A3oY). The success of this part of the industry is suggested by the acquisition, in 2005, of Jacobyte Books (the most prolific e-book publisher of Australian novels, with 22 titles in the 2000s) by American e-publishing company BeWrite Books.
219 A recent *Guardian* article outlines the well-known case of John Locke – who sold over a million Kindle books using Kindle Direct Publishing – as well as other examples of successful self-published authors (Flood, 'How Self-Publishing').
220 Janus Books, 'Self Publishing', accessed 8 December 2010. http://januspublishing.co.uk/index.php?option=com_content&task=view&id=25&Itemid=43
221 Janus Books, 'Subsidy Publishing', accessed 8 December 2010. http://januspublishing.co.uk/index.php?option=com_content&task=view&id=23&Itemid=40
222 Janus Books, 'Non-Subsidy Publishing', accessed 8 December 2010. http://januspublishing.co.uk/index.php?option=com_content&task=view&id=24&Itemid=42
223 Aether Book Publishing, for instance, claims it is 'not a vanity publisher' but 'charge[s] a publishing fee', and so I have included it in the subsidy publishing category (ACT Writers Centre website, 'Aether Book Publishing', accessed 9 December 2010. http://www.actwriters.org.au/publishing_opportunities.html). At times, there is considerable controversy over whether a publisher is 'vanity' or 'traditional'. See, for example, discussions about PublishAmerica on Wikipedia (Wikipedia, 'PublishAmerica', accessed 9 December 2010. http://en.wikipedia.org/wiki/PublishAmerica) and the 'Smaller Indiana' writers group website ('Smaller Indiana',

accessed 9 December 2010. http://www.smallerindiana.com/group/writersgroup/forum/topics/1736855:Topic:171801).

224 Boolarong Press was founded in the late 1970s to 'assist regional authors' (*AustLit*, 'Boolarong Press', accessed 8 December 2010. http://www.austlit.edu.au/run?ex=ShowAgent&agentId=A%2cBt), but now offers 'self publishing service to authors (ie [sic] the author pays the costs and receives the profits)' (Boolarong Press, 'Overview: Who We Are', accessed 8 December 2010. http://www.boolarongpress.com.au/content/whoweare/). In 1991, Wild and Woolley 'developed the Fast Books system of short run book production which caters to authors who self-publish quality paperback books' (Wild and Woolley, 'Wild & Woolley', accessed 8 December 2010. http://www.fastbooks.com.au/WW.history.html).

225 Vantage Press ('America's oldest self-publishing corporation') published three Australian novels in the 1990s, but none in the 2000s (Vantage Press, 'Vantage Press', accessed 8 December 2010. http://www.vantagepress.com/). Others published such titles only in the 2000s, including: Booksurge (4 Australian novels); Virtualbookworm (3); 1st books library (3); Xlibris (2); iUniverse (2); Panache Partners (1); PublishAmerica (1); Lionheart Wallis Publishing (1); Just My Best (1); American Book Publishing (1); Authorhouse (1); and Eloquent Books (1). There are substantially fewer British-based subsidy publishers involved in the Australian novel field, but whether this reflects a lower number of such publishers in Britain than in America is impossible to say on the basis of this dataset. The British-based companies in this category include, in the 1990s, Janus Publishing (3 Australian novels) and Excalibur (2); and in the 2000s, Pen Press Publishers (1).

226 PenFolk Publishing, 'Welcome to PenFolk Publishing', accessed 8 December 2010. http://www.penfolk.com.au/

227 Hotfrog Australian Business Directory, 'About Diane Andrews', accessed 9 December 2010. http://www.hotfrog.com.au/Companies/Diane-Andrews-Publishing

228 Copper Leif, 'About Us', accessed 9 December 2010. http://www.copperleife.com/index.htm

229 Sid Harta Publishers, 'Sid Harta Publisher Distributors', accessed 11 December 2010. http://sidharta.com/distributors/index.jsp?country=showAll

230 Ocean Publishing, 'Welcome to Ocean Publishing', accessed 9 December 2010. http://www.oceanpublishing.com.au/

231 Copyright Publishing, 'About Us', accessed 9 December 2010. http://www.copyright.net.au/about.php

232 ACT Writers Centre website, 'Aether Book Publishing', accessed 9 December 2010. http://www.actwriters.org.au/publishing_opportunities.html

233 Seaview Press, 'Welcome to Seaview Press', accessed 9 December 2010. http://www.seaviewpress.com.au/

234 Zeus Books, 'About Us', accessed 11 December 2010. http://www.zeus-publications.com/about.htm

235 ACT Writers Centre website, 'Aether Book Publishing', accessed 9 December 2010 http://www.actwriters.org.au/publishing_opportunities.html

236 Xlibris, 'Self-Publishing Your Book with Xlibris', accessed 9 December 2010. http://www2.xlibris.com/

237 bizwiki, 'Kingfisher Press', accessed 18 July 2010. http://www.kingfisher-press.com/profile.htm

238 Ocean Publishing, 'Welcome to Ocean Publishing web site', accessed 9 December 2010. http://www.oceanpublishing.com.au/

239 Spectrum Publications, 'Self-publishing', accessed 9 December 2010. http://www.spectrumpublications.com.au/index.php?option=com_content&task=view&id=15&Itemid=31

240 Bookpal, 'Introducing Bookpal', accessed 9 December 2010. http://www.bookpal.com.au/Home/selfpublishing/tabid/1196/Default.aspx

241 See, for example, Ocean Publishing and Just My Best (Ocean Publishing, 'Welcome to Ocean Publishing', accessed 9 December 2010. http://www.oceanpublishing.com.au/; Just My Best,

Inc., 'Just My Best Book Publishing Company', accessed 9 December 2010. http://www.jmbpub.com/).
242 Ocean Publishing, 'Welcome to Ocean Publishing', accessed 9 December 2010. http://www.oceanpublishing.com.au/
243 Sid Harta Publishers, 'Manuscript Submission Guidelines', accessed 9 December 2010. http://publisher-guidelines.com/about/
244 Bookpal, 'Introducing Bookpal', accessed 9 December 2010. http://www.bookpal.com.au/Home/selfpublishing/tabid/1196/Default.aspx
245 Melbourne Books, 'About Us', accessed 9 December 2010. http://www.melbournebooks.com.au/mbooks/about.html
246 For an in-depth discussion of this phenomenon see Brook, 'Accounting for Creative Writing'.
247 Myers, 'Getting Published', 67.
248 Davis, 'The Decline', 130.
249 Sid Harta Publishers, 'Manuscript Submission Guidelines', accessed 9 December 2010. http://publisher-guidelines.com/about/
250 Gelder and Salzman, *After the Celebration*, 14.
251 Gough Whitlam, cited in Flanagan, 'Colonies', 134.

Chapter 4. Recovering Gender: Rethinking the Nineteenth Century

1 Carter, 'Critics, Writers', 282.
2 For example, Hughes and Lund, *Victorian Publishing*; Murray, *Mixed Media*; Poland, '"Sisterhood is Powerful"'; Tuchman, *Edging Women Out*.
3 Eagleton, 'Review of *Mixed Media*', 130.
4 Eliot and Rose, *A Companion*.
5 Sheridan, 'Generations Lost', 44.
6 See Felski for a useful overview of these debates (Felski, *Literature After Feminism*, 57–60).
7 Buck, *Bloomsbury Guide*, xi.
8 DuPlessis, 'Gender Buttons', 27.
9 Ibid., 30.
10 Finkelstein and McCleery, *The Book*; Eliot and Rose, *A Companion*.
11 Giles, *Too Far Everywhere*, 1.
12 Sheridan, *Along the Faultlines*, viii.
13 Modjeska, *Exiles at Home*, 1.
14 Dever, '"Conventional women"', 133, 141.
15 Burns and McNamara, 'Introduction', ix. See also Ferres, 'Introduction', 15; Goldsworthy, 'Fiction from 1900 to 1970', 118; Whitlock, 'From Eutopia'; Sheridan, 'Women Writers', 319.
16 *AustLit* usually indicates an author's 'gender'. When this listing was absent and I was unable to determine the author's gender – or when titles were authored by both men and women – I listed the novel in the 'unknown' gender category. Like *AustLit*, my dataset does not differentiate female authors who used male pseudonyms from the general category of 'female' author, nor male authors who used female pseudonyms from the general category of 'male' author.
17 With almost 39 per cent of the total male population aged between 18 and 44 enlisting for service (Butler, *The Official History*, 902), this conflict significantly reduced the potential pool of male authors. In the 1910s, 56 per cent of Australian novels were by men and 2 per cent were by authors whose gender is unknown.
18 Only five of the forty-eight titles published before 1855 were by women: two by Mary Grimstone (in 1832 and 1834) and one each by Anna Maria Bunn (1838), Mary Theresa Vidal (1846) and Catherine Helen Spence (1854) (Bunn, *The Guardian*; Grimstone, *Cleone*; Grimstone, *Woman's Love*; Spence, *Clara Morison*; Vidal, *Winterton*). With the exception of Bunn's self-published title, all of these novels were published as books in Britain, and none were serialised; Spence was the only

author to attain British publication while remaining in Australia. As the discussion in Chapter 2 shows, the common features of these women's novel's publishing histories – British book publication without serialisation, predominantly achieved when the author travelled to Britain – were not peculiar to women writers but characterised the early Australian novel field as a whole.
19 Australian Bureau of Statistics, '3105.0.65.001'.
20 Women increased as a proportion of the colonies' non-indigenous populations from 45 per cent in 1870 to 47 per cent in 1899 (Australian Bureau of Statistics, '3105.0.65.001').
21 These results – showing the proportion of women novelists to be slightly higher in the early twentieth than in the latter part of the nineteenth century – differ from those I presented in an earlier article (Bode, 'Graphically Gendered'). This difference is due to *AustLit*'s removal of British women writers – most notably, Mary Elizabeth Braddon – previously included in the database due to the high number of novels they published in colonial periodicals.
22 Gaye Tuchman argues that, until 1880, men were more likely to use a female pseudonym than women were to use a male or gender-neutral name (Tuchman, *Edging Women Out*, 53; see also Lovell, *Consuming Fiction*, 82; Judd, 'Male Pseudonyms').
23 Casey, 'Edging Women Out?', ftn 6. See also Sutherland, *Victorian Fictions*, 156, 159–160.
24 Of the nineteenth-century Australian novels by 'unknown' authors, 66 per cent were published as serials, and 69 per cent of these only appeared in this form.
25 Bode, 'Graphically Gendered'.
26 Sheridan, *Along the Faultlines*, 4, xi.
27 Ibid., 155.
28 Nicola Thompson makes a similar argument about feminist analyses of nineteenth-century British women's writing: namely, that in the process of uncovering such authors, feminist critics have concentrated on those whose fiction is compatible with contemporary understandings of feminism (Thompson, 'Responding', 2).
29 Louisa Atkinson has been the most prominent subject of this process. Since the 1980s, four of her novels that had only appeared as serials have been reissued as books: Atkinson, *Tressa's Resolve* and Crittenden, *Tressa's Resolve*; Atkinson, *Tom Hellicar's Children*; Atkinson, *Myra*; Atkinson, *Debatable Ground*.
30 According to *AustLit* records from 5 December 2011, none of Cambridge's novels that were only serialised have received any critical attention (see Cambridge, *Across the Grain*; Cambridge, *Against the Rules*; Cambridge, *Dinah*; Cambridge, *Missed in the Crowd*; Cambridge, *Up the Murray*). The same is true of all but one of Fortune's serialised novels (Fortune, *Bertha's Legacy*; Fortune, *Clyzia*; Fortune, *Dan Lyon's Dream*; Fortune, *Dan Lyons' Loom*; Fortune, *Dora Carleton*; Fortune, *The Secrets*). The exception is Fortune's novel *The Bushranger's Autobiography*, discussed by Lucy Sussex (Fortune, *The Bushranger's Autobiography*; Sussex, 'A Woman of Mystery'). Other women's novels only published in serial form that have received no critical attention include Franc, *Jem's Hopes*; Liston, *Auckland Marston*; Lloyd, *Retribution*; Smith, *A Woman's Battle*; Turner, *Miss Elizabeth*.
31 Thompson, 'Responding', 1.
32 Casey, 'Edging Women Out?', ftn 8. *Athenaeum* was a literary magazine published in London from 1828 to 1921.
33 Tuchman, *Edging Women Out*, 7–8.
34 Coultrap-McQuin, *Doing Literary Business*, 2.
35 Brake, 'Writing, Cultural Production', 64. See also Hughes and Lund, 'Textual/Sexual Pleasure', 144; Hughes and Lund, *Victorian Publishing*, 103.
36 Lund, *America's Continuing Story*, 26.
37 Boyd, '"What! Has She Got"', 5–6.
38 Sutherland, *Victorian Fiction*, 164.
39 Tuchman, *Edging Women Out*, 1, 204. Tuchman also describes the different contracts and pay offered to men and women authors – with 'second-ranked men' paid 'more than second-

ranked women' – and the different critical standards applied to men and women authors (Tuchman, *Edging Women Out*, 176, 204). Norman Feltes similarly argues that nineteenth-century publishers underpaid women novelists and underestimated the quality of their writing (Feltes, *Literary Capital*, 23).

40 Tuchman, *Edging Women Out*, 7–8.
41 Lovell, *Consuming Fiction*, 9–10.
42 Pearson, *Women's Reading*, 196.
43 Mays, 'The Disease of Reading', 178; see also Brantlinger, *The Reading Lesson*, 32; Chavez, 'Wandering Readers', 126–127.
44 Brake, 'Writing, Cultural Production', 61.
45 Lyons, 'Bush Readers', 17. See also Dolin, 'The Secret Reading'; Dolin, 'First Steps'; Webby, 'Colonial Writers'; Webby, 'Not Reading'.
46 Dolin, 'The Secret Reading Life', 118–119.
47 Lyons, 'Bush Readers', 17.
48 Webby, 'Not Reading', 309, 310.
49 Webby, 'Fiction, Readers', 373.
50 Sheridan, *Along the Faultlines*, 45, 27.
51 See, for example, Adelaide, 'Introduction', 1–8; Kingston, 'Women in Nineteenth Century'; Sheridan, *Along the Faultlines*; Spender, 'Introduction'. In *Writing a New World*, xi–xvi; Spender, 'Introduction'. In *Her Selection*, 1–3.
52 Johanson, *A Study*, 20.
53 Nugent, *Women's Employment*, 31. Women in the Australian colonies also had higher rates of literacy than women in Britain (Oxley and Richards, 'Convict and Free', 33).
54 Morrison, 'Serial Fiction', 315.
55 This approach – measuring the proportion of each gender's novels serialised, as opposed to the proportion of serialised titles by men or women – provides a means of assessing men's and women's relative participation in different areas of publishing; that is, it allows for the greater number of nineteenth-century Australian novels by men than women.
56 Boldrewood, cited in Eggert and Webby, 'Introduction', xxvii.
57 Boldrewood, *A Colonial Reformer*; Boldrewood, *Babes in the Bush*; Boldrewood, *My Run Home*; Boldrewood, *Robbery Under Arms*; Boldrewood, *The Miner's Right* and Boldrewood, *The Squatter's Dream*. This final title was the one issued jointly by George Robertson and S. W. Silver. This British company published two other titles authored anonymously by Boldrewood: *S. W. Silver & Co.'s Australian Grazier's Guide* and *S. W. Silver & Co.'s Australian Grazier's Guide: No. II – Cattle*. The fact that Boldrewood does not acknowledge either of these book publications – as well as his adoption of anonymity and their non-literary content – gives some further clues as to how Boldrewood defined being 'an *author*'.
58 Barton, 'The Status of Literature', 238.
59 Cambridge, for instance, claims she began writing novels for newspapers to 'add something to the family resources when they threatened to give out' (cited in Morrison, 'More than a Case', 25). There are, of course, notable exceptions to this rule, such as Mary Fortune, who, after the failure of her marriage, 'supported her family with proceeds from her writing' (*AustLit*, 'Fortune, Mary', accessed 24 January 2011. http://www.austlit.edu.au/run?ex=ShowAgent&agentId=ATy).
60 Morrison, 'More than a Case', 25.
61 Campbell, *The First Ninety*, 56.
62 Between 1860 and 1899, the *Australian Journal* serialised 22 titles by women, 21 by men and 12 by authors whose gender is unknown.
63 The number of serialised Australian novels by unknown authors were: two (1860–4); one (1865–9); four (1870–4); five (1875–9); eleven (1880–4); eleven (1885–9); seven (1890–4); and six (1895–9).

64 Eight per cent of Australian novels serialised in British periodicals – or two titles – were by authors whose gender is unknown.
65 Kingston, 'Women in Nineteenth Century', 91.
66 Thirty-six per cent of Australian women's novels were serialised locally between 1860 and 1899, compared with 22 per cent of men's; 38 per cent of the Australian novels in colonial periodicals were by women compared with 43 per cent by men (19 per cent were by authors whose gender is unknown).
67 The *Queenslander* published four novels, all by men; of the nine novels first published in the *Melbourne Quarterly*, seven were by men, with one by a woman and one by an author whose gender is unknown; the *Adelaide Observer* published three novels, all by women; the *Australian Evangelist* and the *South Australian Temperance Herald* published two titles each, all by women. (None of these totals include novels published concurrently in two or more periodicals; including such titles changes the results for the *Queenslander* to five novels by men and one by a woman; and for the *Adelaide Observer*, to six titles by women).
68 Of the Australian novels published from 1860 to 1899: in the *Australasian*, 27 per cent (6 titles) were by men, 59 per cent (13 titles) were by women and 14 per cent (3 titles) were by authors whose gender is unknown; in the *Sydney Mail*, 41 per cent (12 titles) were by men, 28 per cent (8 titles) were by women and 31 per cent (9 titles) were by authors whose gender is unknown; in the *Leader*, 48 per cent (11 titles) were by men, 35 per cent (8 titles) were by women and 17 per cent (4 titles) were by authors whose gender is unknown. Two other titles – one serialised concurrently in the *Australasian* and the *Fortnightly Review*, another in the *Leader* and the *Queenslander* – were by men.
69 Dixon, *Writing the Colonial*, 15.
70 Dolin, 'The Secret Reading', 282.
71 Johnson-Woods, 'Mary Elizabeth Braddon'.
72 Ibid., 112.
73 Mays, 'The Disease of Reading', 177.
74 Law, 'Imagined Local', 185.
75 Morrison, 'Serial Fiction', 319–320.
76 Johnson-Woods, 'Beyond Ephemera', 211; Johnson-Woods, 'Mary Elizabeth Braddon', 112; Webby, 'Before the *Bulletin*', 32.
77 Sheridan, *Along the Faultlines*, 27.
78 Sheridan, *Along the Faultlines*, 27; Kingston, 'Women in Nineteenth Century', 91.
79 Johnson-Woods, 'Beyond Ephemera', 211.
80 Spence, *Ever Yours*, 131.
81 Webby, 'Fiction, Readers'.
82 Chloe, *Mrs Lyndon's Governess*; Ruby L., *Hope Morton*; Vera, *Adele*; Vera, *A Life's Sacrifice*; Vera, *Harold Dane's Legacy*.
83 Sheridan, *Along the Faultlines*, 45.
84 Boldrewood, *Robbery*.
85 Dixon, *Writing the Colonial*, 38. In this passage Dixon cites Brissenden, '*Robbery Under Arms*', 38.
86 Morrison, 'More than a Case', 26.
87 Between 1860 and 1889, 71 Australian novels published as books in Britain were by women compared with 62 titles by men. This figure does not take into account novels produced jointly by British and other (usually colonial) publishers. When such titles are included, the number by men increases by 10 to 72, but the number by women remains constant. While men thus outnumber women, this disproportionate growth in men's titles also supports the broader argument I am making: that colonial men's novels were perceived as having a particular audience in the colonies.
88 Of the colonial novels published as books between 1860 and 1899, a considerable 17 per cent of men's titles were published in 'Other' countries, compared to only 1 per cent of women's.

This result shows that the surprisingly high proportion of Australian novels published outside Australia or Britain – noted in Chapter 2 – was also a gendered phenomenon.

89 Webby, 'Colonial Writers', 70.
90 Morrison, 'More than a Case', 25.
91 Ibid., 5–6.
92 Morrison, 'Introduction', xI. *A Marked Man* was actually published by Heinemann in 1890 – so one year after the period under consideration. But the example still provides an accurate indication of the possibilities of British – and limitations of local – book publication in the earlier decades.
93 Spence, *An Agnostic's Progress*; Spence, *Clara Morison*; Spence, *Mr Hogarth's Will*; Spence, *Tender and True*; Spence, *The Author's Daughter*.
94 Magarey, *Unbridling the Tongues*, 48.
95 In these two decades, 14 and 6 per cent of Australian novels, respectively, were by authors whose gender is unknown.
96 In five yearly increments from the early 1880s to the late 1890s, the proportion of Australian novels by women, men, and unknown authors, respectively, was as follows: 37, 49 and 14 per cent; 34, 52 and 14 per cent; 29, 63 and 8 per cent; and 27, 67 and 5 per cent.
97 Lake, 'The Politics of Respectability', 264.
98 Sheridan, *Along the Faultlines*, 27.
99 See also Martin, 'Relative Correspondence', 56; Allen, '"Mundane Men"', 618. There are, however, those who reject Lake's conclusions. John Docker argues that the 'Feminist Legend', as he terms Lake's account, 'is in danger of overlooking and denying the ambivalences and pro-women and pro-feminist aspects of Nineties male writing', even in the *Bulletin* (Docker, 'Postmodernism, Cultural History', 131–132). Alternatively, Chris McConville contends that the battle for control over the national culture in the 1890s proceeded along class, not gender, lines (McConville, 'Rough Women, Respectable Men', 433).
100 Sheridan, *Along the Faultlines*, 34.
101 Ibid., xi.
102 Ibid., 39.
103 In the second half of the 1880s, 50 per cent of Australian novels published as books in Britain were by women compared with 37 per cent by men.
104 The proportion of Australian novels published in Britain by authors whose gender is unknown was zero in the early 1880s, 11 per cent in the late 1880s, 1 per cent in the early 1890s and 2 per cent in the late 1890s.
105 Tuchman, *Edging Women Out*, 7–8.
106 Specifically, male authors are responsible for 19 of 21 titles by Routledge; 14 of 19 by Remington; 12 of 13 by Macmillan; 11 of 17 by Ward, Lock (one of the 17 was by an unknown author); 10 of 15 by Hutchinson; 12 of 14 by F. V. White; 5 of 8 by T. Fisher Unwin; and 7 of 10 by Chatto and Windus.
107 Dixon, *Writing the Colonial*, 5.
108 Trainor, Australian Writers', 143.
109 Eggert, '*Robbery Under Arms*', 142.
110 Mays, 'The Disease of Reading', 180.
111 Ibid., 179.
112 Ibid., 178.
113 Ibid., 182, 181.
114 Webby, 'Fiction, Readers', 373.
115 Martin, 'Immigration Policy', 39.
116 Clark, *A Short History*, 315.
117 Transportation of convicts to the eastern colonies ceased by 1852 (Shaw, 'English Convicts', 279).
118 Henzell, *Australian Agriculture*, ix.

119 Dixon, *Writing the Colonial*, 7.
120 *AustLit*, 'The Leader,' accessed 30 June 2011. http://www.austlit.edu.au/run?ex=ShowWork&workId=CZxI
121 Anderson, *Imagined Communities*, 7.

Chapter 5. The 'Rise' of the Woman Novelist: Popular and Literary Trends

1 Whitlock, 'Eight Voices', xi.
2 Webby, 'Australian Literature', 16.
3 Ibid., 17.
4 Throughout this chapter, when I refer to literary fiction I am discussing not only those novels that might be aligned with high or elite literary culture (such as work by Patrick White or Christina Stead) but the broader category of middlebrow fiction as discussed by David Carter: 'the "good books", the books we find in the "good book stores"' (Carter, 'The Mystery', 173).
5 The results displayed in this graph exclude titles by the large and medium-sized Australian pulp fiction publishers identified in Chapter 3 (namely, Cleveland, Horwitz, Calvert, Action Comics, Currawong, Frank Johnson, Invincible Press and Webster Publications).
6 It is important to realise, in interpreting these results, that one instance of critical attention to an Australian novelist is recorded whether the author is the subject of an entire monograph or is just mentioned in passing in a newspaper article. While this approach obviously collapses variation within the critical field, I would argue that it best captures the essence of literary attention and reputation by bringing into sharp relief – indeed amplifying – the existence of those authors who emerge as reference points, or touchstones, for discussion of (Australian) literature. For another example of a quantitative approach to critical attention to authors aimed at exploring canon formation see Damrosch, 'World Literature'.
7 I categorised academic journals retrospectively, based on the publications that were peer reviewed in 2007. A separate category, of non-peer reviewed literary journals or magazines was also created, but is not discussed in this chapter. The authors who receive significant critical attention in this category of literary journals or magazines are quite different to those who appear in the top twenty rankings for academic or newspaper articles, mainly because so many of these non-peer reviewed literary journals and magazines cater to English teachers, and focus on children's and young adult fiction.
8 As I defined a novelist as anyone who had published at least one novel, there are authors included in these results who are not primarily known for writing novels (such as David Williamson, Dorothy Hewett, Judith Wright and Les Murray). Notably, fewer such authors appear in the top twenty for critical discussion as the century progresses, suggesting the increasing importance of the novel to Australian literature. Although extracting data on commentary about novels rather than novelists would have produced a more accurate picture of critical success in respect to this fictional form, for capturing gender trends in critical attention, there is a sense that the form for which authors are discussed is secondary to the broader way discourses about gender shape critical attention.
9 Webby, 'Australian Literature', 17.
10 Sheridan, 'Generations Lost', 44; see also Sheridan, *Nine Lives*.
11 Sheridan, 'Generations Lost', 44; see also Bird, 'New Narrations', 196.
12 Sheridan, 'Generations Lost', 44.
13 Sheridan, 'Generations Lost', 44; see also Carter, 'Critics, Writers', 270–276.
14 One reason this might not be the case is because, more than for other forms of Australian fiction, bibliographical lists of pulp fiction tend to be composed from the personal collections of individuals (see, for example, Flanagan, *The Australian Vintage*; Loder, *Invincible Press*). It is possible that, following their own preferences, the original collectors of these titles focused

on male-oriented genres, problematically shaping the current archive and our understanding of this ephemeral component of Australian print culture. This possibility presents a salutary warning of the dangers of assuming an archive reflects print culture of the past, unmediated by earlier and undocumented selection processes. At the same time, the extensiveness of *AustLit*'s pulp fiction archive, and the ongoing bibliographical work of scholars keenly aware of the gatekeeping consequences of private collections (Johnson-Woods et al, 'Pulp Fiction'), provides support for assuming that the prevalence of male-authored, male-oriented genres does not simply reflect individual readers' collections.

15 Sutherland, *Victorian Fiction*, 164.
16 In total, Meares published an astonishing 746 novels, mainly westerns, from 1954 to 2000 (an average of more than 16 titles a year) (*AustLit*, 'Grover, Marshall', accessed 11 February 2011 http://www.austlit.edu.au/run?ex=ShowAgent&agentId=A%2b-7).
17 Johnson-Woods, 'The Mysterious Case'.
18 There is debate about the extent to which the male breadwinner remained the dominant cultural model in Australia in the 1950s and 1960s (see McQueen, '"Breadwinning"'; Nolan, 'The High Tide'). But according to John Murphy and others, the economic prosperity of this period 'gave, for a time, the norms, privileges and pressures of male breadwinning a distinctive salience' (Murphy, 'Reply', 103; see also Probert, '"Grateful Slaves"').
19 *AustLit* allocates a genre to 3126 of 3504 (or 89 per cent of) of such titles.
20 In the majority of cases, *AustLit* gives a novel a single genre; however, some titles are allocated two or three genres. In the latter cases, I have simply divided the novel between the categories: for instance, a title designated action and mystery, will end up signifying half an action title and half a mystery title (or a third when there are three genres listed). Beyond westerns, crime or detective, war and romance novels, the proportion of different genres published by local pulp fiction companies was: adventure (4 per cent); historical, humour, mystery and thriller (1 per cent each); fantasy, horror, science fiction and young adult (less than 0.5 per cent each).
21 Cawelti, *Mystery, Violence*, 107.
22 Based on Melbourne University's pulp fiction collection, I would say that male-authored doctor/nurse romances focus on the (male) doctor's rather than the (female) nurse's experiences – as is the case with titles by J. E. Macdonnell – and/or depict such relationships under combat conditions – as with Shane Douglas's novels. Arguably, such 'romance' novels are more closely related to the traditionally male-oriented war genre than to the majority of female-oriented romances.
23 The most prominent example of this practice is R. Wilkes Hunter, who wrote around one hundred romance novels, many published with Horwitz, under female pseudonyms including Caroline Farr, Sheila Garland, Fiona Ashton, Diana Douglas, Lucy Waters, Leslie Wilkes, Shauna Marlowe, Alison Hart and Kerry Mitchell. A number of these pseudonyms were also used by other male authors, such as Carl Ruhen, Lee Pattinson and J. E. Macdonnell. Significantly, the only romance novels where Hunter uses male pseudonyms are doctor/nurse titles.
24 The 22 detective novels by Audrey Armitage and Muriel Watkins, published by Horwitz in the 1950s, appeared under the pseudonym 'K. T. McCall'; all but one of Marie Ford's 12 westerns, published by Currawong in the 1940s, are inscribed, 'by M. Ford'.
25 Sheridan, 'Generations Lost', 44.
26 Cawelti, *Mystery, Violence*, 184.
27 Tompkins, *West of Everything*.
28 Ward, *The Australian Legend*.
29 Lake, 'The Politics of Respectability'.
30 Sheridan, 'Generations Lost', 41.
31 Sheridan et al., *Who Was*, 8.
32 Between 1945 and 1959 eight crime novels by Margot Neville (a pseudonym used by two sisters, Margot Goyder and Ann Neville Goyder Joske) were serialised in, or published as a

free supplement to, the *AWW* (Neville, *Murder and Gardenias*; Neville, *Murder and Poor*; Neville, *Murder Before*; Neville, *Murder of a Nymph*; Neville, *Murder of the Well-Beloved*; Neville, *Murder to Welcome*; Neville, *Sweet Night*; Neville, *The Seagull*).

33 *AustLit*, 'The *Australian Women's Weekly*', accessed 4 February 2011. http://www.austlit.edu.au/run?ex=ShowWork&workId=CZkV

34 Sheridan et al., *Who Was*, 73.

35 Johnson-Woods, 'The Mysterious'; Johnson-Woods, 'Pulp Fiction: Governmental'; Zifcak, 'The Retail', 202–203; and Flanagan, 'Foreword', 6.

36 Such availability also offers a way of explaining an interesting connection between economics, gender and nationalism I observed in Action Comics' list. The cheaper titles (including the magazines) of this publisher – ranging in price from eight or nine pence to two or three shillings – tended to be American-style pulps in traditional male-orientated genres (westerns and hard-boiled detective stories). In contrast, the upper end of Action Comics' list – longer novels priced at five shillings and five shillings and six pence – was mainly comprised of romances explicitly aimed at women readers. These more expensive, longer novels also tend to depict Australian rather than American characters and settings. As women readers had access to cheap, American-style romance fiction in magazine format, it makes sense that pulp fiction publishers such as Action Comics would have marketed their romance titles as less disposable – that is, as luxury items involving an investment of time as well as money – as well as distinctively national.

37 Of Doubleday's 27 titles, 93 per cent were by men, as were all of the 25 titles published by Bantam and the 14 by Ace Books. Among the American publishers, the major exception to this connection between a focus on male authors and on male-oriented genres was Times Mirror – the most prolific American publisher of Australian novels with 44 titles, all by men and all published in the 1960s, mostly through its Signet and New American Library imprints. While approximately half of these titles were by Carter Brown (in the traditionally male-oriented mystery and detective genres) most of the rest were romance fiction. This contradiction between the gender of authors and the gender orientation of the genre is resolved by the fact that, with only one exception (Vader, *Battle of Sydney*), the Australian authors published by Times Mirror were also associated with the Australian pulp fiction publisher Horwitz. This phenomenon suggests that the contract Times Mirror signed with Horwitz for the distribution of Carter Brown titles (see Johnson-Woods, 'The Mysterious Case', 76) was more widespread. As with locally published pulp fiction, these male authors (including Macdonnell, Ruhen and Hunter) employed female pseudonyms when writing romance novels, thereby maintaining the illusion of an essentialist relationship between the gendering of author, genre and reader.

38 Of the titles published by Collins ascribed a genre in *AustLit* (160 of 199 titles or 80 per cent), more than half (53 per cent) were romance novels by women, as were essentially all (71 of 72 or 99 per cent of) titles published by Mills & Boon.

39 Of the top ten British publishers of Australian novels in these post-war decades, Cassell was responsible for the highest proportion of male authors (81 per cent, or 38 of 47 novels) and was the only company with a predominantly literary publishing schedule. Of the Australian novels published by Faber and Faber between 1945 and 1969, 9 of 13 were by men, as were all 7 titles published by Hamish Hamilton, and eight of ten by Farrar Straus and Giroux.

40 All eight titles published by ABS in the early 1950s were by men, as were three of four in the late 1950s, seven of seven in the early 1960s and seven of ten in the late 1960s. Ure Smith published five of five titles by men in the late 1950s and six of seven in the early 1960s.

41 Fourteen of the 16 Australian novels published by Dymocks in the 1950s, and one of one in the 1960s were by women (one of the titles in the 1950s was by an author whose gender is unknown). Two of three titles published by Cheshire in the 1950s were by women; however, in the 1960s, five of six were by men.

42 Nine of the 14 Australian novels published by Rigby in the 1960s were by women.

43 Ferguson with James, 'Flagship Angus', 10–11; see also James, '"Basically"', 11.
44 Authors are positioned in the top twenty for critical attention based on the number of mentions of their work recorded in *AustLit*. For the period from 1945 to 1969, my dataset for overall critical discussion includes 7,014 secondary works, of which 3,265 relate to the first twenty positions for each year (a result that does not take into account those years when, because some authors received the same number of mentions, there are more than twenty authors in the top twenty). For the other categories of critical attention, the overall figures are lower, but still large enough to justify quantitative analysis. From 1950 to 1969, for academic and newspaper discussion, respectively, there are 1,447 and 1,320 secondary works in total, of which 744 and 740 refer to the first twenty positions for each year of these decades. These substantial figures emphasise the scale of the *AustLit* database. Even so, they pale in comparison with the number of secondary works for later decades. In the 1990s, for instance, the dataset for critical discussion includes 26,114 works overall (5,903 referring to the top twenty positions in each year of that decade); 2,708 academic works (921 for the top twenty positions); and 11,639 newspaper works (3,024 for the top twenty positions).
45 Wright published one of these novels in the 1950s and one in the 1960s (Wright, *Kings of the Dingoes*; Wright, *Range the Mountains High*). The other authors in the top five in the 1950s were Randolph Stow, Patrick White, Martin Boyd and Henry G. Lamond.
46 The other authors in the top five overall for the 1950s were Randolph Stow, Patrick White and Martin Boyd; and for the 1960s, White, Hal Porter, Donald Horne and Morris West.
47 The male authors in the top ten for academic attention in the 1950s were: Vance Palmer, first; Judah Waten, fourth; Patrick White, sixth; Norman Lindsay, equal seventh; and William Gosse Hay, equal ninth.
48 The male authors in the top ten for academic attention in the 1960s were: Patrick White, first; Randolph Stow, equal second (with Henry Handel Richardson); Hal Porter, sixth; David Martin, seventh; Thomas Keneally, eighth; and in equal ninth place, Geoffrey Dutton, Norman Lindsay, Martin Boyd, Kenneth Mackenzie and Peter Cowan.
49 The proportional decline occurs because eight novelist are equal twentieth in the 1950s – with four mentions each in newspapers – thus significantly extending the number of novelists in the top twenty.
50 Sheridan, 'Generations Lost', 40–41.
51 Ibid., 44.
52 North, *Reading 1922*, 9.
53 See, for example, Cawelti, *Mystery, Violence*, 141; Christianson, 'A Heap of Broken Images', 144–145; Holquist, 'Whodunit and Other Questions', 150; Kennedy, 'Black Noir', 44.
54 Whether or not local pulp titles are included, the proportion of Australian novels by authors whose gender is unknown is 1 per cent from the early 1970s to the early 1980s and 3 per cent in the late 1980s.
55 Webby, 'Australian Literature', 17.
56 Brian Matthews, cited in Whitlock, 'Eight Voices', xii.
57 Whitlock, 'Graftworks', 236.
58 Whitlock, 'Eight Voices', xii–xiv.
59 Gelder and Salzman, *The New Diversity*, 54–55.
60 Ibid., 55.
61 Strauss, 'Are Women's', 35; see also Coward, '"This Novel"', 57.
62 Bird, 'New Narrations', 197.
63 *AustLit* allocates a genre to 1062 of 1314 (or 81 per cent of) pulp fiction titles published in the 1970s and 1980s.
64 In descending order, the genres of the other pulp fiction titles published in the 1970s and 1980s were: adventure (5 per cent); horror, humour, thriller (1 per cent each); and historical, mystery, science fiction and young adult (less than 0.5 per cent each).

65 As in the immediate post-war decades, and especially the 1960s, this gender trend is largely attributable to two factors: first, the close association between the most prolific American publisher of Australian novels – Times Mirror – and the Australian pulp fiction industry (all 72 Australian novels published by Times Mirror in the 1970s were by men, and most were by authors with a prior association with Horwitz); second, the focus of a number of other American publishers of Australian novels on male-oriented genres – including Doubleday, publishing mainly crime fiction with 22 of 33 Australian novels by men, and Putnam, publishing 14 titles, mostly science fiction and all by men. In subsequent decades, as the proportion of Australian novels published in America declined, the authorship of such titles also became progressively less male-dominated.

66 In five-yearly averages from the early 1970s to the late 1980s, the proportion of locally published novels by authors whose gender is unknown was 3, 2, 0 and 1 per cent.

67 Three publishers that showed more of an orientation towards women writers in this decade were Rigby, also the second largest local publisher in this decade, with 6 of 15 titles by women; Alpha Press, with 4 of 8 titles; and Wild and Woolley, with 3 of 7.

68 Bird, 'New Narrations', 196.

69 Ibid., 187.

70 Ibid., 196.

71 Ibid.

72 Katharine Susannah Prichard, equal eleventh with David Williamson, is the other woman author in the top twenty for academic discussion in this decade.

73 Bird, 'New Narrations', 187.

74 In the first half of the 1970s, women authors in the top twenty for academic discussion were Henry Handel Richardson (equal second with Marcus Clarke), Dorothy Hewett (fifth), Katharine Susannah Prichard (seventh), Judith Wright (equal eighth with Hal Porter) and Thea Astley (thirteenth); in the second half of that decade, they were Christina Stead (second), Wright (equal third with Thomas Keneally), Hewett (fifth) and Richardson (seventh).

75 Bird, 'New Narrations', 186.

76 Astley receives attention in only three academic works of the late 1970s, with the result that she was equal forty-fifth (along with many other authors) for academic discussion in this five-year period.

77 Other local publishers, with approximately the same output as the largest of the feminist- or women-oriented local presses, focused entirely on male authors, including Animo Publishing, Rastar and Cory and Collins (all with seven of seven titles by men).

78 Bird, 'New Narrations', 204.

79 Elizabeth Jolley, cited in Whitlock, 'Eight Voices', xi.

80 Bird, 'New Narrations', 196.

81 Across both decades, women wrote 65 per cent of Australian novels published by multinationals, compared with 33 per cent of titles published by local, non-pulp presses. For the late 1980s, these proportions were 59 and 39 per cent respectively.

82 Multinational companies published 54 titles by women in the early 1970s, increasing to 119 in the late 1970s, 178 in the early 1980s and 265 in the late 1980s. For these same five-year periods, multinationals published 24, 36, 77 and 157 titles by men, and local non-pulp presses published 22, 45, 63 and 98 titles by women and 65, 105, 133 and 153 titles by men.

83 In Chapter 3, I showed that, excluding pulp fiction, a larger proportion of Australian novels were published by local than multinational companies in the 1970s, but that growth in multinational publication was stronger, such that, in the 1980s, these companies published a greater proportion of Australian novels than local companies. The proportion of Australian novels published by local and multinational companies, respectively, was as follows: in the early 1970s, 19 and 15 per cent; in the late 1970s, 25 and 25 per cent; in the early 1980s, 27 and 35 per cent; and in the late 1980s, 25 and 44 per cent.

84 Torstar also published 3 novels in the early 1980s and 23 in the late 1980s (in addition to 22 titles in the 1990s) by an 'author' whose gender I have listed as unknown until 1995. All of these titles are by Emma Darcy, a pseudonym used by husband-and-wife writing team Wendy and Frank Brennan until Frank's death in 1995. Since that time Wendy has continued writing for Torstar under this pseudonym.
85 In the late 1980s, 17 per cent of Australian novels published by multinationals (or without Torstar, 25 per cent) are categorised by *AustLit* as young adult. Authorship of such titles was not as female-dominated as romance fiction, and in local publishing the proportion of young adult Australian novels by men and women was relatively even. However, of the young adult titles published by multinationals, more than twice the number were by women than men.
86 Jackson, *Heterosexuality*, 98.
87 Millet, *Sexual Politics*, 37; Germaine Greer, cited in Jackson, *Heterosexuality*, 114; Firestone, *The Dialectic*, 139.
88 Gilbert and Gubar, *The Madwoman*, 158, 68.
89 Strehle and Carden, 'Introduction', xvi.
90 In 1976, Cawelti predicted that 'the coming of age of women's liberation will invent significantly new formulas for romance, if it does not lead to a total rejection of the moral fantasy of love triumphant' (Cawelti, *Adventure, Mystery*, 42).
91 Radway, *Reading the Romance*; Modleski, *Loving with a Vengeance*.
92 Strehle and Carden, 'Introduction', xviii.
93 Krentz, 'Introduction', 5.
94 Dixon, *The Romance Fiction*, 195.
95 Strauss, 'Are Women's'; Coward, '"This Novel"'.
96 Barbara Reskin discusses this process in relation to publishing generally, and editing in particular. Among the factors she identifies as responsible for the decline in male editors are reduced editorial autonomy, job security and wages (Reskin, 'Culture, Commerce', 107). Albert Greco, Clara Rodríguez and Robert Wharton report that in 2002 women comprised '60.6 percent of all book-publishing employment' in the American publishing industry (Greco et al., *The Culture and Commerce*, 167).
97 Tuchman, *Edging Women*, 10–12, 205–206.
98 This shift is particularly apparent in recent analyses of masculinity in Australian fiction, for example, Morris, '"Growing up an Australian"'; Randall, 'Charismatic Masculinity'.
99 Gelder and Salzman, *After the Celebration*, 179.
100 Ibid., 180.
101 Ibid., 212.
102 Given the extent to which this inherited feminist critical framework has limited gender to women's writing, it is not incidental that Salzman discusses the gendering of particular genres, but only in relation to women authors. More specifically, Salzman ends the chapter by saying:

> The work of the women writers in this chapter crosses a variety of genres, and the fact that they are read here as 'women writers' is not intended to restrict other reading possibilities, but rather to reflect how gender remains a powerful category within contemporary Australian society.

Although clearly stating that women's writing can be read through frameworks besides gender (as is the case in the rest of the book), Salzman constructs fiction by women as the only type of fiction impacted by 'gender [as] a powerful category' in Australian society and literary studies, ignoring the role of gender in shaping men's engagement in the literary field (Gelder and Salzman, *After the Celebration*, 212–213).
103 I have given the decade averages because there is relatively little change in gender proportions within the decades. In five-year moving averages, from the early 1990s to the late 2000s, the proportion of Australian novels by women is 49, 51, 57 and 56 per cent; for men, these

proportions are 48, 47, 42 and 42 per cent. Pulp fiction titles comprised a relatively small proportion of Australian novels in the 1990s, and were essentially absent in the 2000s. When pulp titles are removed, the proportion of Australian novels by women increases slightly in the 1990s to 52 per cent (with the proportion of titles by men falling to 46 per cent). The proportion of titles by authors whose gender is unknown, with and without locally published pulp fiction, is: 2 and 3 per cent in the early 1990s; 2 and 2 per cent in the late 1990s; 1 and 2 per cent in the early 2000s; and 2 and 2 percent in the late 2000s.

104 Bird, 'New Narrations', 196.

105 In five-year moving averages, from the early 1990s to the late 2000s, the proportion of locally published novels by authors whose gender is unknown is: 2, 2, 3 and 2 per cent.

106 Four per cent of subsidy-published titles in the 2000s were by authors whose gender is unknown. In the 1990s, before subsidy publishing became a significant presence in the local industry, men wrote 57 per cent of these titles compared with 38 per cent by women (5 per cent of titles were by authors whose gender is unknown). This result roughly accords with overall rates of local publication of Australian novels by men (57 per cent) and women (41 per cent) in that decade.

107 Very nearly all of the Australian novels self-published between 1945 and 1969 were by men (of the 45 self-published titles in this period, only two were by women and four by authors whose gender is unknown); in the 1970s, 20 of the 24 (or 83 per cent of) self-published titles were by men; in the 1980s, this was the case for 42 of 66 (or 64 per cent of) such titles.

108 In the 1990s and 2000s, respectively, 3 and 2 per cent of self-published titles were by authors whose gender is unknown.

109 Fremantle Press published 20 titles by women in the 1990s compared with 21 by men, and 25 titles by women in the 2000s compared with 30 by men.

110 UQP published 50 titles by women compared with 47 by men in the 1990s, and 45 titles by women and 40 by men in the 2000s; Lothian published 4 titles by women compared with 3 by men in the 1990s, and 49 by women and 28 by men in the 2000s; all of Spinifex Press's titles (9 in the 1990s and 8 in the 2000s) were by women.

111 For the purpose of this anlaysis, I consider that publishers with between 40 and 60 per cent of titles by men or women are responsible for a relatively equal amount of titles by both genders. In the 1980s 29 per cent of the top twenty most prolific local publishers of Australian novels published a relatively equal number of titles by men and women; this proportion increased to 48 per cent in the 1990s and 2000s. Over these same three decades, the proportion of the top twenty local publishers of Australian novels that published a majority (over 60 per cent) of titles by women increased from 18 to 22 and 29 per cent, while the proportion that published a majority (over 60 per cent) of titles by men fell from 54 to 30 and 24 per cent. The same overall trend is apparent if only the top ten local (non-subsidy/non-pulp) publishers of Australian novels are considered: in this case, by decade from the 1980s to the 2000s, the proportion of local presses that published a majority of titles by men declined from 46 to 27 and 10 per cent; the proportion that published a relatively even number of novels by men and women increased from 38 to 55 per cent before declining slightly to 50 per cent, while the proportion that published mostly women's novels increased from 15 to 18 to a substantial 40 per cent.

112 For discussion of this phenomenon see Gelder, 'Politics and Monomania' and McCann, 'How to Fuck', 23–24.

113 Fifty-eight per cent of (or 1529 of 2618) Australian novels published locally in the 1990s and 2000s are allocated a genre in *AustLit*.

114 Two per cent of locally published Australian novels in these decades are categorised as adventure fiction by *AustLit*; this is also the case with mystery and science fiction; 3 per cent of titles are fantasy.

115 Authors whose gender is unknown wrote 3 per cent of Australian novels published by multinationals in the early 1990s, 1 per cent in the late 1990s, less than 0.5 per cent in the early 1990s, and 1 per cent in the 2000s.

116 Although the decline in romance fiction as a proportion of multinational publication is relatively minimal over these two decades, it is a major decline from the 1980s, when 40 per cent of Australian novels published by multinationals were romance fiction.
117 According to *AustLit* records, Torstar's output of Australian novels more than halved in the 2000s (from 278 titles in the first half of the decade to 107 in the second). Removing Torstar from the results also removes this substantial decline, with the effect that multinational publication of Australian women's novels increases through the 1990s and 2000s (albeit only slightly from the late 1990s to the late 2000s).
118 Besides Torstar, Pearson was the most prolific multinational publishers of Australian novels in the 1970s and 1980s with more titles by women than men: 81 of 151, or 54 per cent. Other multinational companies – responsible for a relatively small number of Australian novels – that also published a majority of women's titles were ACP (13 of 17) and Random House (10 of 17).
119 Multinational publishers of Australian novels in the 1970s and 1980s that published a majority of men's titles included: News Corporation (58 of 88 titles by men); Thomson Organization (38 of 53); Reed Elsevier (24 of 37); Bertelsmann (28 of 35); Panmacmillan (13 of 20); James Hardie (15 of 19) and Hearst Corporation (9 of 11).
120 Of Pearson's 309 titles, 181 (59 per cent) were by women, as were 141 (54 per cent) of Panmacmilan's 262; 68 (52 per cent) of Random House's 132; 66 (53 per cent) of Hodder Headline's 125 titles; and 68 (54 per cent) of Bertelsmann's 127 titles.
121 News Corporation published 237 Australian novels in the 1990s, of which 119 (just over 50 per cent) were by men; Reed Elsevier published 142, of which 77 (54 per cent) were by men.
122 The two multinational publishers with only one Australian novel – by a man – in the 2000s were Amazon and www.1stbooks.
123 News Corporation published 231 of 355 Australian novels by women; Pearson published 158 of 298; Holtzbrink published 162 of 282; and Bertlesmann published 156 of 267. Other multinational publishers of a substantial number of Australian novels in the 2000s with a majoirty of titles by women included: Hachette Livre, with 72 (60 per cent) of 120 titles; Hodder Headline, with 50 (64 per cent) of 78 titles; Simon & Schuster, with 30 (54 per cent) of 56 titles; Scholastic, with 16 (53 per cent) of 30 titles; and Time Warner, with 18 (75 per cent) of 24 titles.
124 Wilding, 'Michael Wilding', 152, 153.
125 In the 1990s and 2000s, multinational companies published 812 romance titles; 755 young adult; 292 historical; 277 crime or detective; and 261 fantasy fiction. These totals represent 21, 20, 8, 7 and 7 per cent, respectively, of the Australian novels published by multinationals in these decades.
126 In the 1980s, 11 per cent of the Australian adventure novels published by multinationals were by women, in the 1990s and 2000s, respectively, this proportion increases to 22 and 43 per cent; in these same decades, women authored 0, 29 and 59 per cent of horror fiction; 22, 46 and 63 per cent of humour fiction; 20, 71 and 47 per cent of mystery novels; 27, 40 and 39 per cent of science fiction; and 5, 18 and 22 per cent of thrillers published by multinationals. As a proportion of Australian novels published by such companies, these genres each represent 1 (adventure and horror), 2 (mystery), 3 (science fiction and thriller) and 5 (humour) per cent of the total in the 1990s and 2000s.
127 Authors whose gender is unknown wrote 2 per cent of such titles in the 1980s, less than 0.5 per cent in the 1990s and 1 per cent in the 2000s.
128 This is not to say there were no women authors from earlier periods among the top twenty for academic discussion in the 1990s (Christina Stead and Henry Handel Richardson featured) or no contemporary women writers in the list for the 2000s: Janette Turner Hospital and Elizabeth Jolley were there again, as was the new-comer to the list, Gail Jones. However, there is certainly a shift in the weighting over these two decades – from contemporary to historical – in academic discussion of women writers. Leaving aside the top five for both decades, the male authors who attracted the most academic attention were: in the 1990s,

Les Murray, Tim Winton, David Foster, Gerald Murnane and Michael Wilding; and in the 2000s, Winton, Christos Tsiolkas, Brian Castro, Marcus Clarke, Robert Drewe, Kim Scott and Richard Flanagan.
129 Gelder and Salzman, *After the Celebration*, 212.
130 Beyond the top four in the 1990s, the male authors who featured in the top twenty for overall discussion were: Peter Carey, Thomas Keneally, Tim Winton, Louis Nowra, Gary Crew, Mudrooroo, John Marsden, Geoffrey Dutton, Garry Disher and Peter Goldsworthy.
131 The other women in the top twenty for overall discussion in the 2000s are familiar from academic discussion, and include Kate Grenville, Judith Wright, Helen Garner and Dorothy Hewett. Beyond the top five, the men in this list for the 2000s were Thomas Keneally, Tim Winton, Frank Moorhouse, Gary Crew, Morris Gleitzman, John Marsden and Louis Nowra.
132 Darville, *The Hand*; Garner, *The First*; Grenville, *The Secret*.
133 The playwrights and poets who featured prominently in newspaper discussion in the 1990s and 2000s were David Williamson, Louis Nowra and Les Murray; Geoffrey Dutton also appeared in the top twenty in the 1990s.
134 Vida, 'The Count 2010'. Recently updated figures for 2011 show essentially the same gender trends (Vida, 'The Count 2011').
135 Franklin, 'A Literary Glass Ceiling?'
136 Peter Stothard, cited in Page, 'Research Shows Male Writers'.
137 Based on survey data, and 'controlling for socio-demographic characteristics, like education', Steven J. Tepper describes women as '2.3 times more likely to read a book of fiction in the past year compared to men' (Tepper, 'Fiction Reading', 256). A 2004 study reports similar findings for literary fiction (Greco et al., *The Culture and Commerce*, 173). This gender trend was also noted in the early twentieth century, with William Gray and Ruth Munroe arguing in 1929 that 'women read almost twice as many books, on the average, and they do it in less time as a rule' (Gray and Munroe, *The Reading Interests*, 32).
138 See, for example, Long, *Book Clubs*, xiii; Stewart, 'We Call Upon', 9.
139 Bode, 'Along Gender Lines', 92–93.
140 Bode, 'Publishing and Australian', 36–38.
141 Williams, 'The Glass Escalator', 256.
142 Williams, *Still a Man's World*, 4.
143 Greco et al., *The Culture and Commerce*, 167.
144 Whitlock, 'Eight Voices', xi.
145 Webby, 'Australian Literature', 17.

Conclusion. Literary Studies in the Digital Future

1 Cohen, 'Digital Keys for Unlocking'.
2 Borgman, 'The Digital Future is Now'.
3 Schreibman et al., 'The Digital Humanities', xxvi.
4 As a growing number of histories of the digital humanities – or humanities computing – assert, the first data-rich, computational humanities project was produced in the early 1950s, shortly after the creation of electronic computers, when Roberto Busa created a 'machine-generated and machine-printed concordance' of the poetry of St. Thomas Aquinas (Winter, 'Roberto Busa', 8. See also Aarseth, 'From Humanities Computing'; Hockey, 'The History of Humanities Computing', 3; McGann, *Radiant Textuality*, 3).
5 Joshi, 'Quantitative Method', 271.
6 McGann, 'Culture and Technology', 72. See also McGann, 'A Note'. Already there is a considerable range of digital projects, not only presenting cultural data but providing tools, strategies and spaces with, and in, which to explore and analyse such collections: for example, MONK, offering 'a digital environment designed to help humanities scholars discover and analyse patterns in the

texts they study' (MONK, 'Metadata Offer New Knowledge', accessed 8 April 2011. http://www.monkproject.org/). The possibilities for literary studies represented by Google Books (Google Books, accessed 23 June 2011. http://books.google.com/), and Google's Ngram Viewer (Books Ngram Viewer, accessed 23 June 2011. http://ngrams.googlelabs.com/) – which claims to enable text mining of over five million books in Google Books – have received significant attention (see, for example, Parry, 'The Humanities'). However, there is also pertinent and timely debate about the utility and reliability of digital collections and the tools available to search them. Matthew Jockers, for instance, cautions humanities scholars to be wary of the reliability of Google's Ngram viewer for research purposes (see Jocker's, 'Unigrams, and Bigrams').

7 Davis, 'The Decline', 118.
8 David M. Berry, 'The Computational Turn'. Workshop, Swansea University, accessed 8 April 2011. http://www.thecomputationalturn.com/
9 Hedges, 'Grid-enabling'.
10 Bode and Dixon, 3.
11 Olsen, 'Critical Theory', 396. For other studies, by scholars within the literary or humanities computing community, expressing disappointment at the net outcomes and impact of their collective project see Corns, 'Computers in the Humanities'; Milic, 'Progress in Stylistics'; Olsen, 'Signs, Symbols'; Potter, 'Statistical Analysis'; Potter, 'Preface', xviii; Prescott, 'Consumers'.
12 Liu, 'Where is Cultural'.
13 McGann, *Radiant Textuality*, 103. Similarly Olsen decries the failure of digital humanities scholars 'to capture the support and imagination of colleagues who do not use computers...[and to] have a significant impact on the research community as a whole' (Olsen, 'Signs, Symbols', 309).

BIBLIOGRAPHY

Aarseth, Espen. 'From Humanities Computing to Humanistic Informatics: Creating a Field of Our Own'. Department of Humanistic Informatics, University of Bergen, Norway. Accessed 28 June 2011. http://www.iath.virginia.edu/hcs/aarseth.html
Abbott, Megan E. *The Street Was Mine: White Masculinity in Hardboiled Fiction and Film Noir*. New York: Palgrave Macmillan, 2002.
Adams, Francis. *John Webb's End: Australian Bush Life*. Serialised by *Centennial Magazine*, 1889; London: Remington, 1891.
Adelaide, Debra. 'How Did Authors Make a Living?' In *A History of the Book in Australia, 1891–1945: A National Culture in a Colonised Market*, edited by Martyn Lyons and John Arnold (St Lucia: University of Queensland Press, 2001), 83–103.
———. 'Introduction'. In *A Bright and Fiery Troop: Australian Women Writers of the Nineteenth Century*, edited by Debra Adelaide (Ringwood: Penguin, 1988), 1–14.
Allen, Judith. '"Mundane" Men: Historians, Masculinity and Masculism'. *Historical Studies* 22.89 (1987): 617–628.
An Australian Colonist. *A Victim of Circumstantial Evidence: A Sensational Story, Full of Thrilling and Startling Incidents*. Sydney: The Author, 1893.
Anderson, Benedict. *Imagined Communities: Reflections on the Origin and Spread of Nationalism*. London: Verso, 1991.
Anthony, Clay. *Texans Never Quit*. Brookvale: Cleveland, 2001.
Apter, Emily. 'Untranslatables: A World System'. *New Literary History* 39 (2008): 581–598.
Arac, Jonathan. 'Anglo-Globalism?' *New Left Review* 16 (2002): 35–45.
Arnold, John. 'Newspapers and Daily Reading'. In *A History of the Book in Australia, 1891–1945: A National Culture in a Colonised Market*, edited by Martyn Lyons and John Arnold (St Lucia: University of Queensland Press, 2001), 255–281.
———. 'Printing Technology and Book Production'. In *A History of the Book in Australia 1891–1945: A National Culture in a Colonised Market*, edited by Martyn Lyons and John Arnold (St Lucia: University of Queensland Press, 2001), 104–112.
Arnold, John and John Hay. 'Introduction'. In *The Bibliography of Australian Literature: A–E*, edited by John Arnold and John Hay (Kew: Australian Scholarly Publishing, 2001), vii–xiii.
———, eds. *The Bibliography of Australian Literature: A–E*. Kew: Australian Scholarly Publishing, 2001.
———, eds. *The Bibliography of Australian Literature: F–J*. St Lucia: University of Queensland Press, 2004.
———, eds. *The Bibliography of Australian Literature: K–O*. St Lucia: University of Queensland Press, 2007.
———, eds. *The Bibliography of Australian Literature: P–Z*. St Lucia: University of Queensland Press, 2008.
Arthur, Paul. 'Virtual Strangers: e-Research and the Humanities'. *Australian Cultural History* 27.1 (2009): 47–59.
Atkinson, Louisa. *Cowanda, the Veteran's Grant: An Australian Story*. Sydney: J. R. Clarke, 1859.
———. *Debatable Ground, or, The Carlillawarra Claimants*. Serialised by *Sydney Mail*, 1861; Canberra: Mulini Press, 1992.

———. *Gertrude the Emigrant: A Tale of Colonial Life*. Sydney: J. R. Clarke, 1857.
———. *Myra*. Serialised by *Sydney Mail*, 1864; Canberra: Mulini Press, 1988.
———. *Tom Hellcar's Children*. Serialised by *Sydney Mail*, 1871; Canberra: Mulini Press, 1983.
———. *Tressa's Resolve*. Serialised by *Sydney Mail*, 1872; Canberra: Mulini Press, 2004.
AustLit: The Australian Literature Resource. http://www.austlit.edu.au
Australian Bureau of Statistics. '3105.0.65.001 – Australian Historical Population Statistics'. Accessed 9 April 2010. http://abs.gov.au/AUSSTATS/abs@.nsf/ProductsbyCatalogue/632CDC28637CF57ECA256F1F0080EBCC?OpenDocument
Barker, Nicolas. 'Intentionality and Reception Theory'. In *A Potencie of Life: Books in Society*, edited by Nicolas Barker (London: British Library, 1993), 195–202.
Barnes, James L. and Patience P. Barnes. 'Reassessing the Reputation of Thomas Tegg, London Publisher, 1776–1846'. *Book History* 3 (2000): 45–60.
Barton, G. B. 'The Status of Literature in New South Wales: III. How the Newspaper Proprietors Look at It'. *Centennial Magazine* 2.3 (October 1889): 238–240.
Bell, Alfred Bernie. *Oscar: A Romance of Australia and New Caledonia*. Brisbane: The Author, 1894.
Bender, Thomas. 'The Boundaries and Constituencies of History'. *American Literary History* 18.2 (2006): 219–228.
Bennett, Bruce, ed. *Cross Currents: Magazines and Newspapers in Australian Literature*. Melbourne: Longman, 1981.
Bird, Delys. 'New Narrations: Contemporary Fiction'. In *The Cambridge Companion to Australian Literature*, edited by Elizabeth Webby (Cambridge: Cambridge University Press, 2000), 183–208.
Black, Fiona A., Bertrum H. MacDonald and J. Malcolm W. Black. 'Geographic Information Systems: A New Research Method for Book History'. *Book History* 1 (1998): 11–31.
Bode, Katherine. 'Along Gender Lines: Reassessing Relationships Between Australian Novels, Gender and Genre from 1930 to 2006'. *Australian Literary Studies* 24.2 (2009): 79–95.
———. 'From British Domination to Multinational Conglomeration? A Revised History of Australian Novel Publishing, 1950 to 2007'. In *Resourceful Reading: The New Empiricism, eResearch and Australian Literary Culture*, edited by Katherine Bode and Robert Dixon (Sydney: Sydney University Press, 2009), 194–219.
———. 'Graphically Gendered: A Quantitative Study of the Relationships between Australian Novels and Gender from the 1830s to the 1930s'. *Australian Feminist Studies* 23.58 (2008): 435–450.
———. 'Publishing and Australian Literature: Crisis, Decline or Transformation?' *Cultural Studies Review* 16.2 (2010): 24–48.
Bode, Katherine and Robert Dixon. 'Resourceful Reading: A New Empiricism in the Digital Age?' In *Resourceful Reading: The New Empiricism, eResearch and Australian Literary Culture*, edited by Katherine Bode and Robert Dixon (Sydney: Sydney University Press, 2009), 1–27.
Boldrewood, Rolf. *A Colonial Reformer*. Serialised by *Australian Town and Country Journal*, 1876–7; London: Macmillan, 1890.
———. *A Sydney-Side Saxon*. Serialised by *Centennial Magazine*, 1888–9; London: Macmillan, 1891.
———. *Babes in the Bush*. Serialised by *Australian Town and Country Journal*, 1877–9; London: Macmillan, 1900.
———. *My Run Home*. Serialised by *Australian Town and Country Journal*, 1874; London: Macmillan, 1897.
———. *Nevermore*. Serialised by *Centennial Magazine*, 1889–90; London: Macmillan, 1892.
———. *Plain Living: A Bush Idyll*. Serialised by *Australasian*, 1884; London: Macmillan, 1898.
———. *Robbery Under Arms*. Serialised by *Sydney Mail*, 1882–3; London: Remington, 1888.
———. *S. W. Silver & Co.'s Australian Grazier's Guide*. London: S. W. Silver, 1879.
———. *S. W. Silver & Co.'s Australian Grazier's Guide: No. II – Cattle*. London: S. W. Silver, 1881.
———. *The Miner's Right: A Tale of the Australian Goldfields*. Serialised by *Australian Town and Country Journal*, 1880; London: Macmillan, 1890.
———. *The Sealskin Cloak*. Serialised by *Sydney Mail*, 1884–5; London: Macmillan, 1896.

———. *The Sphinx of Eaglehawk: A Tale of Old Bendigo*. Serialised by *Australasian*, 1887; London: Macmillan, 1895.

———. *The Squatter's Dream: A Story of Australian Life*. Serialised by *Australian Town and Country Journal*, 1875; London and Sydney: S. W. Silver and George Robertson, 1878.

Boothby, Guy. *A Bid for Fortune, Or, Dr Nikola's Vendetta*. Serialised by *Windsor Magazine: An Illustrated Monthly for Men and Women*, Unknown; London: Ward, Lock and Bowden, 1895.

———. *Across the World for a Wife*. London: Ward, Lock, 1898.

———. *Doctor Nikola*. London: Ward, Lock and Bowen, 1896.

———. *In Strange Company: A Story of Chili and the Southern Seas*. London: Ward, Lock and Bowden, 1894.

———. *The Beautiful White Devil*. London: Ward, Lock and Bowden, 1896.

———. *The Lust of Hate*. Serialised by *Queenslander*, 1897; London: Ward, Lock, 1898.

———. *The Marriage of Esther: A Torres Strait Sketch*. London: Ward, Lock and Bowden, 1895.

Borgman, Christine. 'The Digital Future is Now: A Call to Action for the Digital Humanities'. *Digital Humanities Quarterly* 3.4 (2009). Accessed 15 April 2011. http://www.digitalhumanities.org/dhq/vol/3/4/000077/000077.html

Bourdieu, Pierre. 'The Field of Cultural Production, or: The Economic World Reversed'. *Poetics* 12 (1983): 311–356.

Bowley, William. *Humanity: A Romance of Melbourne Life*. Melbourne: R. Mackay, 1872.

———. *Work or Labour of Love: A Philosophical Romance, Illustrative of the Phases of Australian Life*. Melbourne: R. Mackay, 1873.

Boyd, Anne E. '"What! Has She Got Into the '*Atlantic*'?" Women Writers, the *Atlantic Monthly*, and the Formation of the American Canon'. *American Studies* 39.3 (1998): 5–36.

Brake, Laurel. *Print in Transition, 1850–1910: Studies in Media and Book History*. Basingstoke: Palgrave, 2001.

———. 'Writing, Cultural Production, and the Periodical Press in the Nineteenth Century'. *Writing and Victorianism*, edited by J. B. Bullen (London and New York: Longman, 1997), 55–72.

Brantlinger, Patrick. *The Reading Lesson: The Threat of Mass Literacy in Nineteenth Century British Fiction*. Bloomington: Indiana University Press, 1998.

Breu, Christopher. *Hard-Boiled Masculinities*. Minneapolis: University of Minnesota Press, 2005.

Brissenden, Alan. '*Robbery Under Arms*: A Continuing Success'. In *The Australian Experience: Critical Essays on Australian Novels*, edited by W. S. Ramson (Canberra: Australian National University Press, 1974), 38–55.

Brook, Scott. 'Accounting for Creative Writing'. *Preliminary Report of the Accounting for Creative Writing Student Survey (May 2008)*, School of Culture and Communication, The University of Melbourne, October 2009. Accessed 12 December 2010. http://aawp.org.au/files/Preliminary%20report%20of%20the%20Accounting%20for%20Creative%20Writing%20survey.pdf

Broome, Mary. *A Christmas Cake In Four Quarters*. London: Macmillan, 1871.

———. *Spring Comedies*. London: Macmillan, 1871.

Buck, Claire. *Bloomsbury Guide to Women's Literature*. London: Bloomsbury Publishing, 1992.

Bunn, Anna Maria. *The Guardian: A Tale*. Sydney: The Author, 1838.

Burke, Timothy. 'Book Notes: Franco Moretti's *Graphs, Maps, Trees*'. In *Reading Graphs, Maps, Trees: Responses to Franco Moretti*, edited by Jonathan Goodwin and John Holbo (Anderson: Parlor Press, 2011), 41–48.

Burnage, William Aubrey. *A Novel Without a Name*. Newcastle: The Author, 1878.

———. *Bertha Shelley, the Lily of the Hunter Valley!: An Australian Story of Forty Years Ago*. Newcastle: The Author, 1876.

Burns, Connie and Marygai McNamara. 'Introduction'. In *Eclipsed: Two Centuries of Australian Women's Fiction*, edited by Connie Burns and Marygai McNamara (Sydney: Imprint, 1988), ix–xvii.

Butler, A. G. *The Official History of the Australian Army Medical Services in the War of 1914–1918: The Western Front*, vol. 2. Canberra: Australian War Memorial, 1940.

Caesar, Michael. 'Franco Moretti and the World Literature Debate'. *Italian Studies* 62.1 (2007): 125–135.

Cambridge, Ada. *A Black Sheep.* Serialised by *Age*, 1888–9; London: Heinemann, 1890.

———. *A Little Minx: A Sketch.* Serialised by *Sydney Mail*, 1885; London: Heinemann, 1893.

———. *A Marriage Ceremony.* Serialised by *Australasian*, 1884; London: Hutchinson, 1894.

———. *A Mere Chance.* Serialised by *Australasian*, 1880; London: Richard Bentley, 1882.

———. *Across the Grain.* Serialised by *Australasian*, 1882.

———. *Against the Rules.* Serialised by *Australasian*, 1885–6.

———. *Dinah.* Serialised by *Australasian*, 1879–80.

———. *In Two Years Time.* Serialised by *Australasian*, 1879; London: Richard Bentley, 1879.

———. *Missed in the Crowd.* Serialised by *Australasian*, 1881–2.

———. *My Guardian: A Story of the Fen Country.* Serialised by *Cassell's Family Magazine*, 1876–7; London: Cassell, 1878.

———. *Not All in Vain.* Serialised by *Australasian*, 1890–1; Melbourne: Melville, Mullen and Slade, 1892.

———. *The Three Miss Kings.* Serialised by *Australasian*, 1883; Melbourne: Melville, Mullen and Slade, 1891.

———. *The Two Surplices.* Serialised by *Churchman's Companion*, Unknown; London: Joseph Masters, 1865.

———. *Up the Murray.* Serialised by *Australasian*, 1875.

Cameron, Donald. *The Mysteries and Miseries of Scripopolis: An Account of a Week in Sandhurst.* Melbourne: The Author, 1872.

———. *Transformations; or Scenes and Seances: A Sequel to 'Scripopolis'; Being Raps from the Spirit of Demonax.* Melbourne: The Author, 1873.

Cameron, John. *The Fire Stick: Incidents in the Shearers Strike. A Tale of Australian Bush Life.* Brisbane: The Author, 1893.

Campbell, Ronald G. *The First Ninety Years: The Printing House of Massina, Melbourne, 1859 to 1949.* Melbourne: Massina, 1950.

Canmore, Luscar. *Hector Beaumill.* Serialised by *Penny Melbourne Journal*, circa 1860; Melbourne: The Author, 1865.

Carroll, Joseph. *Reading Human Nature: Literary Darwinism in Theory and Practice.* Albany: State University of New York Press, 2011.

Carter, David. 'After Post-Colonialism'. *Meanjin* 66.2 (2007): 114–119.

———. 'Boom, Bust or Business as Usual? Literary Fiction Publishing'. In *Making Books: Contemporary Australian Publishing*, edited by David Carter and Anne Galligan (St Lucia: University of Queensland Press, 2007), 231–246.

———. 'Critics, Writers, Intellectuals: Australian Literature and its Criticism'. In *The Cambridge Companion to Australian Literature*, edited by Elizabeth Webby (Cambridge: Cambridge University Press, 2000), 258–293.

———. 'Structures, Networks, Institutions: The New Empiricism, Book History and Literary History'. In *Resourceful Reading: The New Empiricism, eResearch and Australian Literary Culture*, edited by Katherine Bode and Robert Dixon (Sydney: Sydney University Press, 2009), 31–52.

———. 'The Mystery of the Missing Middlebrow'. In *Imagining Australia: Literature and Culture in the New New World*, edited by Judith Ryan and Chris Wallace-Crabbe (Harvard: Harvard University Press, 2004), 173–202.

———. 'They're a Weird Mob and Ure Smith'. In *Paper Empires: A History of the Book in Australia, 1946–2005*, edited by Craig Munro and Robyn Sheahan-Bright (St Lucia: University of Queensland Press, 2006), 24–30.

Carter, David and Anne Galligan. 'Introduction'. In *Making Books: Contemporary Australian Publishing*, edited by David Carter and Anne Galligan (St Lucia: University of Queensland Press, 2007), 1–14.

Casanova, Pascale. *The World Republic of Letters.* Cambridge: Harvard University Press, 2004.

Casey, Ellen Miller. 'Edging Women Out?: Reviews of Women Novelists in the *Athenaeum*, 1860–1900'. *Victorian Studies* 39.2 (1996): 151–171.

Cawelti, John G. *Adventure, Mystery, and Romance*. Chicago: University of Chicago Press, 1976.

———. *Mystery, Violence, and Popular Culture*. Madison: The University of Wisconsin Press, 2004.

Cawthorne, W. A. *The Islanders*. Serialised by *Illustrated Adelaide Post*, 1854; Adelaide, Rigby, 1926.

Champion, Shelagh and George Champion. 'The Wharf at Little Manly'. *Manley Library Local Studies*. Accessed 12 July 2010. www.manly.nsw.gov.au/downloaddocument.aspx?DocumentID=3120

Chavez, Julia M. 'Wandering Readers and the Pedagogical Potential of *Temple Bar*'. *Victorian Periodicals Review* 40.2 (2007): 126–150.

Chisholm, Caroline. *Little Joe*. Serialised by *Empire*, 1859–60; Ashgrove: Preferential Publications, 1991.

Chloe. *Mrs Lyndon's Governess*. Serialised by *Australian Woman's Magazine and Domestic Journal*, 1884.

Christianson, Scott R. 'A Heap of Broken Images: Hardboiled Detective Fiction and the Discourse(s) of Modernity'. In *The Cunning Craft: Original Essays on Detective Fiction and Contemporary Literary Theory*, edited by Ronald G. Walker and June M. Frazer (Macomb: Western Illinois University Press, 1990), 135–148.

Clark, Manning. *A Short History of Australia*. Carlton South: Melbourne University Press, 1997.

Clarke, Marcus. *Chidiock Tichbourne; or, the Catholic Conspiracy*. Serialised by *Australian Journal*, 1874–5; Melbourne: E. W. Cole, 1893.

———. *His Natural Life*. Serialised by *Australian Journal*, 1870–2; Melbourne: George Robertson, 1874.

———. *Twixt Shadow and Shine*. Melbourne: George Robertson, 1875.

Clarke, Marcus and George A. Walstab. *Long Odds: A Novel*. Serialised by *Colonial Monthly*, 1868–9; Melbourne: Clarson, Massina and Co., 1869.

Cohen, Isaiah Reginald. *Stanhope Burleigh: A Novel*. Sydney: The Author, 1872.

Cohen, Patricia. 'Digital Keys for Unlocking the Humanities' Riches'. *New York Times*, 16 November 2010. Accessed 15 April 2011. http://www.nytimes.com/2010/11/17/arts/17digital.html?_r=1

Colby, Robert A. 'Review of *The Cambridge Companion to the Victorian Novel*, edited by Deirdre David and *A Companion to Victorian Fiction*, edited by William Baker and Kenneth Womack'. *Studies in the Novel* 35.4 (2003): 566–569.

Collis, Walter. *Willis of Ryde*. Stanmore: The Author, 1899.

Corns, Thomas N. 'Computers in the Humanities: Methods and Applications in the Study of English Literature'. *Literary and Linguistic Computing* 6 (1991): 127–130.

Coultrap-McQuin, Susan. *Doing Literary Business: American Women Writers in the Nineteenth Century*. Chapel Hill: University of North Carolina Press, 1990.

Coward, Rosalind. '"This Novel Changes Lives": Are Women's Novels Feminist Novels? A Response to Rebecca O'Rourke's Article "Summer Reading"'. *Feminist Review* 5 (1980): 53–64.

Craig, Hugh and Arthur F. Kinney, eds. *Shakespeare, Computers, and the Mystery of Authorship*. Cambridge: Cambridge University Press, 2009.

Crawford, Shawn. 'No Time To Be Idle: The Serial Novel and Popular Imagination'. *World & I* 13.11 (1998): 322–333.

Crittenden, Victor. *James Tegg: Early Sydney Publisher and Printer: The Tegg Brothers, the Australian Arm of the Book Empire of Thomas Tegg of London*. Canberra: Mulini Press, 2000.

———, ed. *Tressa's Resolve*. Canberra: Mulini Press, 2004.

Currey, John. 'Lansdowne and Lloyd O'Neil'. In *Paper Empires: A History of the Book in Australia, 1946–2005*, edited by Craig Munro and Robyn Sheahan-Bright (St Lucia: University of Queensland Press, 2006), 38–41.

Curtain, John. 'How Australian Publishing Won its Way Against the Odds'. *Logos* 9.3 (1998): 143–146.

Damrosch, David. 'World Literature in a Postcanonical, Hypercanonical Age'. In *Comparative Literature in an Age of Globalization*, edited by Haun Saussy (Baltimore: The John Hopkins University Press, 2006), 43–53.

Darling, Lady Eliza. *Simple Rules for the Guidance of Persons in Humble Life*. Sydney: James Tegg, 1837.

Darnton, Robert. 'Book Production in British India, 1850–1900'. *Book History* 5 (2002): 239–262.
_____. *The Forbidden Best-Sellers of Pre-Revolutionary France*. New York: Norton, 1995.
_____. 'What is the History of Books?' In *The Book History Reader*, edited by David Finkelstein and Alistair McCleery (London: Routledge, 2002), 9–26.
Darville, Helen. *The Hand That Signed the Paper*. St Leonards: Allen and Unwin, 1994.
Daskalova, Krassimira. 'Book History, the State of Play: An Interview with Robert Darnton'. *SHARP News* 3 (1994): 2–4.
Davidson, Cathy N. 'Humanities 2.0: Promise, Perils, Predictions'. *PMLA* 123.3 (2008): 707–717.
Davis, Mark. *Gangland: Cultural Elites and the New Generationalism*. St Leonards: Allen and Unwin, 1999.
_____. 'Literature, Small Publishers and the Market in Culture'. *Overland* 190 (2008): 4–11.
_____. 'The Decline of the Literary Paradigm in Australian Publishing'. In *Making Books: Contemporary Australian Publishing*, edited by David Carter and Anne Galligan (St Lucia: University of Queensland Press, 2007), 116–131.
Davitt, Ellen. *Force and Fraud: A Tale of the Bush*. Serialised by *Australian Journal*, 1865; Canberra: Mulini Press, 1993.
De Boos, Charles. *Mark Brown's Wife: A Tale of the Gold-Fields*. Serialised by *Sydney Mail*, 1871; Canberra: Mulini Press, 1992.
_____. *The Poor Man: Being Some Account of the Extraordinary Adventures Met with, of the Strange Sights Seen, and the Curious Things Heard, by Mr. Redde Pepper, in His Search after that Much Injured Individual*. Serialised by *Sydney Mail*, 1864; Melbourne: Australian Scholarly Publishing, 2005.
De Wreder, Paul. *Black Male*. Sydney, Currawong, 1945.
Deresiewicz, William. 'Representative Fictions'. *The Nation* 4 December, 2006. Accessed 7 September 2010. http://www.thenation.com/article/representative-fictions
Devanny, Jean. *The Killing of Jacqueline Love*. Sydney: Frank Johnson, 1942.
Dever, Maryanne. '"Conventional women of ability": M. Barnard Eldershaw and the Question of Women's Cultural Authority'. In *Wallflowers and Witches: Women and Culture in Australia 1910–1945*, edited by Maryanne Dever (St Lucia: University of Queensland Press, 1994), 133–146.
Dimock, Wai Chee. 'Scales of Aggregation: Prenational, Subnational, Transnational'. *American Literary History* 18.2 (2006): 219–228.
Dixon, Jay. *The Romance Fiction of Mills & Boon, 1909–1990s*. London: University College London Press, 1999.
Dixon, Robert. 'Australian Literature – International Contexts'. *Southerly* 67.1–2 (2007): 15–27.
_____. 'Boundary Work: Australian Literary Studies in the Field of Knowledge Production'. *Journal of the Association for the Study of Australian Literature* 3 (2004): 27–43.
_____. 'Tim Winton, *Cloudstreet* and the Field of Australian Literature'. *Westerly* 50 (2005): 240–260.
_____. *Writing the Colonial Adventure: Race, Gender and Nation in Anglo-Australian Popular Fiction, 1875 to 1914*. Oakleigh: Cambridge University Press, 1995.
Docker, John. 'Postmodernism, Cultural History, and the Feminist Legend of the Nineties: *Robbery Under Arms*, the Novel, the Play'. In *The 1890s: Australian Literature and Literary Culture*, edited by Ken Stewart (St Lucia: University of Queensland Press, 1996), 128–149.
Dolin, Tim. 'First Steps Toward a History of the Mid-Victorian Novel in Colonial Australia'. *Australian Literary Studies* 22.3 (2006): 273–293.
_____. 'The Secret Reading Life of Us'. In *Readers, Writers, Publishers: Essays and Poems*, edited by Brian Matthews (Canberra: Australian Academy of the Humanities, 2004), 115–133.
Donaldson, William, *Popular Fiction in Victorian Scotland: Language, Fiction and the Press*. Aberdeen: Aberdeen University Press, 1986.
Drucker, Joanne. 'Philosophy and Digital Humanities: A Review of Willard McCarty, *Humanities Computing*. London and New York: Palgrave, 2005'. *Digital Humanities Quarterly* 1.1 (2007). Accessed 5 September 2011. http://digitalhumanities.org/dhq/vol/1/1/000001/000001.html
Dunlop, James. *Middle Life: A Tale*. Adelaide: The Author, 1871.
DuPlessis, Rachel Blau. 'Gender Buttons'. *Australian Literary Studies* 24.2 (2009): 20–38.

Eagleton, Mary. 'Review of *Mixed Media: Feminist Presses and Publishing Politics*, by Simone Murray'. *Feminist Review* 85 (2007): 130–131.

Eakin, Emily. 'Studying Literature by the Numbers'. *New York Times*, 10 January, 2004. Accessed 15 April 2011. http://www.nytimes.com/2004/01/10/books/studying-literature-by-the-numbers.html

Eggert, Paul. 'Australian Classics and the Price of Books: The Puzzle of the 1890s'. *Journal of the Association for the Study of Australian Literature*, Special Issue: The Colonial Present (2008): 130–157.

———. '*Robbery Under Arms*: The Colonial Market, Imperial Publishers, and the Demise of the Three-Decker Novel'. *Book History* 6 (2003): 127–146.

———. 'The Book, Scholarly Editing and the Electronic Edition'. In *Resourceful Reading: The New Empiricism, eResearch and Australian Literary Culture*, edited by Katherine Bode and Robert Dixon (Sydney: Sydney University Press, 2009), 53–69.

Eggert, Paul and Elizabeth Webby. '*Robbery Under Arms*: Introduction'. In *Robbery Under Arms*, by Rolf Boldrewood, edited by Paul Eggert and Elizabeth Webby (St Lucia: University of Queensland Press, 2006), xxiii–lxxxix.

———, eds. *Robbery Under Arms*, by Rolf Boldrewood. St Lucia: University of Queensland Press, 2006.

Eliot, Simon. '"Never Mind the Value, What About the Price?": Or, How Much Did Marmion Cost St. John Rivers?' *Nineteenth-Century Literature* 56.2 (2001): 160–197.

———. *Some Patterns and Trends in British Publishing, 1800–1919*. London: Bibliographical Society, 1994.

———. 'The Three-Decker Novel and its First Cheap Reprint, 1862–94'. *Library* 7 (1895): 38–53.

———. 'Very Necessary But Not Quite Sufficient: A Personal View of Quantitative Analysis in Book History'. *Book History* (2002): 283–293.

Eliot, Simon and Jonathan Rose, eds. *A Companion to the History of the Book*. Malden: Wiley-Blackwell, 2009.

English, James F. 'Everywhere and Nowhere: The Sociology of Literature After "the Sociology of Literature"'. *New Literary History* 41.2 (2010): v–xxiii.

Ensor, Jason. 'Is a Picture Worth 10,175 Australian Novels?' In *Resourceful Reading: The New Empiricism, eResearch and Australian Literary Culture*, edited by Katherine Bode and Robert Dixon (Sydney: Sydney University Press, 2009), 240–273.

———. 'Reprints, International Markets and Local Literary Taste: New Empiricism and Australian literature'. *Journal of the Association for the Study of Australian Literature* Special Issue: The Colonial Present (2008): 198–218.

Farjeon, B. L. *Bread-and-Cheese and Kisses*. Serialised by *Tinsley's Magazine*, 1872; London: Tinsley, 1873.

———. *Joshua Marvel*. Serialised by *Tinsley's Magazine*, 1870–2; London: Tinsley, 1871.

———. *The Duchess of Rosemary Lane*. Serialised by *Sydney Mail*, 1876–7; London: Tinsley, 1876.

Feather, John. *A History of British Publishing*, 2nd ed. New York: Routledge, 2006.

Felski, Rita. *Literature After Feminism*. Chicago: University of Chicago Press, 2003.

Feltes, Norman N. *Literary Capital and the Late Victorian Novel*. Madison: University of Wisconsin Press, 1993.

Ferguson, Frances. 'Planetary Literary History: The Place of the Text'. *New Literary History* 39 (2008): 657–684.

Ferguson, George with Neil James. 'Flagship Angus & Robertson'. In *Paper Empires: A History of the Book in Australia, 1946–2005*, edited by Craig Munro and Robyn Sheahan-Bright (St Lucia: University of Queensland Press, 2006), 10–12.

Ferres, Kay. 'Introduction: In the Shadow of the Nineties'. In *The Time To Write: Australian Women Writers 1890–1930*, edited by Kay Ferres (Ringwood: Penguin, 1993), 1–16.

Finkelstein, David and Alistair McCleery. 'Introduction'. In *The Book History Reader*, 2nd ed., edited by David Finkelstein and Alistair McCleery (London: Routledge, 2009), 1–4.

———, eds. *The Book History Reader*, 2nd ed. London: Routledge, 2009.

Finn, Edmund. *A Priest's Secret: Under Seal of Confession*. Melbourne: Alex McKinley, 1888.

———. *The Hordern Mystery*. Melbourne: Alex McKinley, 1889.
Firestone, Shulamith. *The Dialectic of Sex: The Case for Feminist Revolution*. London: Women's Press, 1979.
Fitzhardinge, L. F. 'Tegg, James (1808–1845)'. *Australian Dictionary of Biography. Online Edition*. Accessed 16 April 2010: http://adbonline.anu.edu.au/biogs/A020465b.htm?hilite=James%3BTegg
Flanagan, Graeme. *The Australian Vintage Paperback Guide*. New York: Gryphon Books, 1994.
Flanagan, Richard. 'Colonies of the Mind; Republics of Dreams: Australian Publishing Past and Future'. In *Making Books: Contemporary Australian Publishing*, edited by David Carter and Anne Galligan (St Lucia: University of Queensland Press, 2007), 132–148.
———. 'Losing Our Voice'. *Sydney Morning Herald*, 30–31 May, 2009: 12–13.
Flood, Alison. 'How Self-Publishing Came of Age'. *Guardian*, 12 November 2011. Accessed 12 November 2011: http://www.guardian.co.uk/books/2011/jun/24/self-publishing
Fortune, Mary. *Bertha's Legacy*. Serialised by *Australian Journal*, 1866.
———. *Clyzia the Dwarf: A Romance*. Serialised by *Australian Journal*, 1866–7.
———. *Dan Lyon's Dream*. Serialised by *Melbourne Quarterly*, 1885.
———. *Dan Lyons' Loom*. Serialised by *Gippsland Mercury*, 1884–5.
———. *Dora Carleton: A Tale of Australia*. Serialised by *Australian Journal*, 1866.
———. *The Bushranger's Autobiography*. Serialised by the *Australian*, 1871–2.
———. *The Secrets of Balbrooke: A Tale*. Serialised by *Australian Journal*, 1866.
Franc, Maud Jeanne. *Emily's Choice: An Australian Tale*. Serialised by *Australian Evangelist*, 1865–6; London: Sampson Low and Company, 1867.
———. *Fern Hollow, or Old Days in New Lands*. Serialised by *Crystal Stories*, 1885; London: Richard Willoughby, 1885.
———. *Hall's Vineyard*. London: Sampson Low and Company, 1875.
———. *Into the Light*. Serialised by *Christian Colonist*, 1880–4; London: Sampson Low and Company, 1885.
———. *Jem's Hopes and What They Grew To*. Serialised by *South Australian Temperance Herald*, 1872.
———. *John's Wife*. London: Sampson Low and Company, 1874.
———. *Little Mercy: or, For Better, for Worse*. London: Sampson Low and Company, 1877.
———. *Minnie's Mission: An Australian Temperance Tale*. Serialised by *South Australian Temperance Herald*, 1866–70; London: Sampson Low and Company, 1869.
———. *No Longer a Child*. Serialised by *Leader*, 1878–9; London: Sampson Low and Company, 1882.
———. *Silken Cords and Iron Fetters: An Australian Tale*. Serialised by *Gawler Times and Goldfields Reporter*, 1869–70; London: Sampson Low and Company, 1870.
———. *The Master of Ralston*. London: Sampson Low and Company, 1885.
——— *Two Sides to Every Question: From a South Australian Standpoint*. Serialised by *Illustrated Adelaide News*, 1876–7; London: Sampson Low and Company, 1876.
———. *Vermont Vale: or Home Pictures in Australia*. Serialised by *Australian Evangelist*, 1863–4; London: Sampson Low and Company, 1866.
Franklin, Ruth. 'A Literary Glass Ceiling? Why Magazines Aren't Reviewing More Female Writers'. *New Republic*, 7 February 2011. Accessed 19 June 2011: http://www.tnr.com/article/books-and-arts/82930/VIDA-women-writers-magazines-book-reviews
Fraser, Joseph. *Melbourne and Mars: My Mysterious Life on Two Planets: Extracts from the Diary of a Melbourne Merchant*. Melbourne: The Author, 1889.
Friedman, Michael. 'Explanation and Scientific Understanding'. *Journal of Philosophy* 71.1 (1974): 5–19.
Frow, John. *Cultural Studies and Cultural Value*. Oxford: Oxford University Press, 1995.
———. 'Thinking the Novel. Review of *The Novel*, edited by Franco Moretti'. *New Left Review* 49 (2008): 137–145.

Galligan, Anne. 'The Culture of the Publishing House: Structure and Strategies in the Australian Publishing Industry'. In *Making Books: Contemporary Australian Publishing*, edited by David Carter and Anne Galligan (St Lucia: University of Queensland Press, 2007), 34–50.
Garner, Helen. *The First Stone: Some Questions About Sex and Power*. Chippendale: Picador, 1995.
Gelder, Ken. 'Politics and Monomania: The Rarefied World of Contemporary Australian Literary Culture'. *Overland* 184 (2006): 48–56.
_____. 'Recovering Australian Popular Fiction: Towards the End of Australian Literature'. In *Australian Literary Studies in the 21st Century: Proceedings of the 2000 ASAL Conference held at the University of Tasmania*, edited by Philip Mead (Hobart: Association for the Study of Australian Literature, 2000), 112–120.
Gelder, Ken and Paul Salzman. *After the Celebration: Australian Fiction, 1989–2007*. Carlton: Melbourne University Press, 2009.
_____. *The New Diversity: Australian Fiction, 1970–88*. Melbourne: McPhee Gribble, 1989.
Gerstaecker, Friedrich. *The Two Convicts*. Serialised by *Examiner and Melbourne Weekly News*, 1859–60; London: Routledge, 1857.
Gilbert, Sandra M. and Susan Gubar. *The Madwoman in the Attack: The Woman Writer and the Nineteenth-Century Literary Imagination*. New Haven: Yale University Press, 2000.
Giles, Fiona. *Too Far Everywhere: The Romantic Heroine in Nineteenth-Century Australia*. St Lucia: University of Queensland Press, 1998.
Gilmore, Mary. 'Foreword'. In *Broad Acres: A Story of Australian Early Life on the Land*, by W. M. Fleming. Sydney: New Century Press, 1939.
Glenfield, Edric. *On Strike, or, Where Do the Girls Come In?* Sydney: The Author, 1890.
Goldsworthy, Kerryn. 'Fiction from 1900 to 1970'. In *The Cambridge Companion to Australian Literature*, edited by Elizabeth Webby (Cambridge: Cambridge University Press, 2000), 105–133.
Goodwin, Jonathan and John Holbo, eds. *Reading Graphs, Maps, Trees: Responses to Franco Moretti*. Anderson: Parlor Press, 2011.
Gottschall, Jonathan. *Literature, Science, and a New Humanities*. New York: Palgrave Macmillan, 2008.
_____. 'Quantitative Literary Study: A Modest Manifesto and Testing the Hypotheses of Feminist Fairy Tale Studies'. In *The Literary Animal: Evolution and the Nature of Narrative*, edited by Jonathan Gottschall and David Sloan Wilson (Chicago: Northwestern University Press, 2005), 199–224.
Gottschall, Jonathan, with Christine Callanan, Nicole Casamento, Natalie Gladd, Dristen Manganini, Tanya Milan-Robertson, Patrick O'Connell, Kimberly Parker, Nathan Riley, Valerie Strucker, Adam Tapply, Christopher Wall and Alexis Webb. 'Are the Beautiful Good in Western Literature?: A Simplified Illustration of the *Necessity* of Literary Quantification'. *Journal of Literary Studies* 23.1 (2007): 41–62.
Gould, Nat. *A Gentleman Rider*. London: Routledge, 1898.
_____. *Banker and Broker*. London: Routledge, 1893.
_____. *Golden Ruin*. London: Routledge, 1898.
_____. *Harry Dale's Jockey 'Wild Rose'*. London: Routledge, 1893.
_____. *Jockey Jack*. London: Routledge, 1892.
_____. *Landed at Last*. London: Routledge, 1898.
_____. *Only a Commoner*. London: Routledge, 1895.
_____. *Running It Off; or Hard Hit*. London: Routledge, 1892.
_____. *Seeing Him Through*. London: Routledge, 1897.
_____. *Stuck Up*. London: Routledge, 1894.
_____. *The Dark Horse*. London: Routledge, 1899.
_____. *The Doctor's Double: Anglo-Australian Sensation*. London: Routledge, 1896.
_____. *The Double Event: A Tale of the Melbourne Cup*. Serialised by *Sydney Referee*, circa. 1890; London: Routledge, 1891.
_____. *The Famous Match*. London: Routledge, 1898.
_____. *The Magpie Jacket: A Tale of the Turf*. London: Routledge, 1896.

———. *The Miner's Cup: A Coolgardie Romance*. London: Routledge, 1896.
———. *Thrown Away or, Basil Ray's Mistake*. London: Routledge, 1894.
———. *Who Did It?* London: Routledge, 1896.
Gray, William S. and Ruth Munroe. *The Reading Interests and Habits of Adults: A Preliminary Report*. New York: Macmillan, 1929.
Greco, Albert N. Clara E. Rodríguez and Robert M. Wharton. *The Culture and Commerce of Publishing in the 21st Century*. Stanford: Stanford University Press, 2007.
Greenfield, Matt. 'Moretti and Other Genre Theorists'. *The Valve*, 12 January 2006. Accessed 24 June 2009. http://www.thevalve.org/go/valve/article/moretti_and_other_genre_theorists/
Grenville, Kate. *The Secret River*. Melbourne: Text Publishing, 2005.
Grimstone, Mary Leman. *Cleone: A Tale of Married Life*. London: Effingham Wilson, 1834.
———. *Woman's Love*. London: Saunders and Otley, 1832.
Griswold, Wendy. *Bearing Witness: Readers, Writers, and the Novel in Nigeria*. Princeton: Princeton University Press, 2000.
———. 'Nigeria, 1950–2000'. In *The Novel: Volume 1, History, Geography, and Culture*, edited by Franco Moretti (Princeton: Princeton University Press, 2006): 509–520.
———. 'Number Magic in Nigeria'. *Book History* 5 (2002): 275–282.
Gunton, Eric. *Trouble Ahead*. South Melbourne: Popular Publications, 1940.
Hannay, Barbara. *Claiming his Family*. Chatswood: Harlequin Mills & Boon, 2006.
Hanson, Carter F. *Emigration, Nation, Vocation: The Literature of English Emigration to Canada, 1825–1900*. East Lansing: Michigan State University Press, 2009.
Haraway, Donna. *Simians, Cyborgs and Women: The Reinvention of Nature*. New York: Routledge, 1991.
———. 'Situated Knowledges: The Science Question in Feminism and the Privilege of Partial Perspective'. *Feminist Studies* 14.3 (1988): 575–599.
Harpham, Geoffrey Galt. 'Between Humanity and the Homeland: The Evolution of an Institutional Concept'. *American Literary History* 18.2 (2006): 245–261.
Harrison, John. 'The Lurid War Paperbacks of Horwitz Publications'. In *Sin Street Sleeze: The Lurid Pulp and Pop Culture Writings of John Harrison*. Accessed 6 December 2010. http://john-harrison.blogspot.com/2007_03_01_archive.html
Hart, Jessica. *Christmas Eve Marriage*. Chatswood: Harlequin Mills & Boon, 2004.
Hart, Jim. 'New Wave Seventies'. In *Paper Empires: A History of the Book in Australia, 1946–2005*, edited by Craig Munro and Robyn Sheahan-Bright (St Lucia: University of Queensland Press, 2006), 53–57.
Hayot, Eric. 'A Hundred Flowers'. In *Reading Graphs, Maps, Trees: Responses to Franco Moretti*, edited by Jonathan Goodwin and John Holbo (Anderson: Parlor Press, 2011), 64–70.
Hayward, Jennifer. *Consuming Pleasures: Active Audiences and Serial Fiction from Dickens to Soap Opera*. Lexington: The University Press of Kentucky, 1997.
Healey, Daniel. *The Seven Christians of Championdom: A Tale of the Times*. Sydney: The Author, 1885.
Hedges, Mark. 'Grid-Enabling Humanities Datasets'. *Digital Humanities Quarterly* 3.4 (2009). Accessed 14 June 2011. http://digitalhumanities.org/dhq/vol/3/4/000078/000078.html
Hennessey, David. *A Lost Identity*. Sydney: The Author, 1897.
Henzell, Ted. *Australian Agriculture: Its History and Challenges*. Collingwood: CSIRO Publishing, 2007.
Hermanson, Scott. 'Review of *A Companion to Digital Literary Studies*, edited by Ray Siemens and Susan Schreibman'. *Electronic Book Review* 2 May (2009). Accessed 31 May 2011. http://www.electronicbookreview.com/thread/fictionspresent/authoritative
Hetherington, Carol. 'Old Tricks for New Dogs: Resurrecting Bibliography and Literary History'. In *Resourceful Reading: The New Empiricism, eResearch and Australian Literary Culture*, edited by Katherine Bode and Robert Dixon (Sydney: Sydney University Press, 2009), 70–83.
Hines, Chad Allen. 'Evolutionary Landscapes: Adaptation, Selection and Mutation in Nineteenth-Century Literary Ecologies'. PhD diss., University of Iowa, 2010. Accessed 13 June 2011. http://ir.uiowa.edu/etd/514/

Hockey, Susan. 'The History of Humanities Computing'. In *A Companion to the Digital Humanities*, edited by Susan Schreibman, Ray Siemens and John Unsworth (Oxford: Blackwell Publishers, 2004), 3–19.

Hollier, Nathan. 'Between Denial and Despair: Understanding the Decline of Literary Publishing in Australia'. *Southern Review* 40.1 (2007): 62–77.

Holquist, Michael. 'Whodunit and Other Questions: Metaphysical Detective Stories in Post-War Fiction'. *New Literary History* 3.1 (1971): 135–156.

Holyroyd, John. *George Robertson of Melbourne: Pioneer, Bookseller and Publisher*. Melbourne: Robertson and Mullens, 1968.

Hoover, David L. 'Statistical Stylistics and Authorship Attribution: An Empirical Investigation'. *Literary and Linguistic Computing* 16.4 (2001): 421–444.

Horne, R. H. *Rebel Convicts: An Australian Novel*. Melbourne: George Slater, 1858.

Howell, W. May. *Reminiscences of Australia: The Diggings and the Bush*. London: The Author, 1869.

Hudson, Pat. 'Numbers and Words: Quantitative Methods for Scholars of Texts'. In *Research Methods for English Studies*, edited by Gabriele Griffin (Edinburgh: Edinburgh University Press, 2005), 131–155.

Hughes, Linda K. and Michael Lund. 'Textual/Sexual Pleasure and Serial Publication'. In *Literature in the Marketplace: Nineteenth-Century British Publishing and Reading Practices*, edited by John O. Jordan and Robert L. Patten (Cambridge: Cambridge University Press, 1995), 143–164.

———. *The Victorian Serial*. Charlottesville and London: University Press of Virginia, 1991.

———. *Victorian Publishing and Mrs Gaskell's Work*. Charlottesville and London: University Press of Virginia, 1999.

Hurley, Michael. *A Guide to Gay and Lesbian Writing in Australia*. St Leonards: Allen and Unwin, 1996.

Huyssen, Andreas. *After the Great Divide: Modernism, Mass Culture, Postmodernism*. Bloomington: Indiana University Press, 1986.

Indyk, Ivor. 'Magical Numbers'. In *Resourceful Reading: The New Empiricism, eResearch and Australian Literary Culture*, edited by Katherine Bode and Robert Dixon (Sydney: Sydney University Press, 2009), 142–155.

Isaacs, George. *The Queen of the South: A Colonial Romance: Being Pictures of Life in Victoria in the Early Days of the Diggings*. Gawler: The Author, 1858.

Isaacs, Victor and Rod Kirkpatrick. *Two Hundred Years of Sydney Newspapers: A Short History*. North Richmond: Rural Press Ltd. with the assistance of the Printing Industries Association of Australia, 2003. Accessed 17 June 2010. espace.library.uq.edu.au/eserv/UQ:11092/sydnews.pdf

Izzo, Donatello. 'Outside Where? Comparing Notes on Comparative American Studies and American Comparative Studies'. In *American Studies: An Anthology*, edited by Janice A. Radway, Kevin K. Gaines, Barry Shank and Penny Von Eschen (Chichester: Blackwell Publishing, 2009), 588–603.

Jacklin, Michael. 'The Transnational Turn in Australian Literary Studies'. *Journal of the Association for the Study of Australian Literature* Special Issue: Australian Literature in a Global World (2009): 1–14.

Jackson, Stevi. *Heterosexuality in Question*. London: Sage, 1999.

James, Neil. '"Basically We Thought About Books": An Interview with George Ferguson'. *Publishing Studies* 5 (2007): 8–16.

Janssen, Susanne and Nel van Dijk, eds. *The Empirical Study of Literature: Its Development and Future*. Rotterdam: Barjesteh van Waalwijk van Doorn & Co's Uitgeversmaatschappij, 1998.

Jockers, Matthew. 'Unigrams, and Bigrams, and Trigrams, Oh My'. Accessed 15 April 2011. http://www.stanford.edu/~mjockers/cgi-bin/drupal/node/53

Johanningsmeier, Charles A. *Fiction and the American Literary Marketplace: The Role of Newspaper Syndicates in America, 1860–1900*. Cambridge: Cambridge University Press, 1997.

Johanson, Graeme. *A Study of Colonial Editions in Australia, 1843–1972*. Wellington: Elibank Press, 2000.

Johnson-Woods, Toni. 'Beyond Ephemera: The *Australian Journal* (1865–1962) as Fiction Publisher'. PhD diss., University of Queensland, 2000.

———. *Index to Serials in Australian Periodicals and Newspapers. Nineteenth Century*. Canberra: Mulini Press, 2001.

———. 'Mary Elizabeth Braddon in Australia: Queen of the Colonies'. In *Beyond Sensation: Mary Braddon in Context*, edited by Marlene Tromp, Pamela Gilbert and Aeron Haynie (New York: SUNY Press, 2000), 111–125.

———. 'Pulp Fiction: Governmental Controls of Cheap Fiction, 1939–1959'. *Scripts & Print* 30.2 (2006): 103–119.

———. '"Pulp" Fiction Industry in Australia 1949–1959'. *Antipodes* (June 2006): 63–67.

———. 'The Mysterious Case of Carter Brown: or, Who Really Killed the Australian Author?' *Australian Literary Studies* 21.4 (2004): 74–88.

Johnson-Woods, Toni, Joanne Sawyers and Michelle Dicinoski. 'Pulp Fiction', *AustLit Research Communities*. Accessed 18 January 2012. http://www.austlit.edu.au/specialistDatasets/PulpFiction

Jones, Susan. 'Modernism and the Marketplace: The Case of Conrad's *Chance*'. *College Literature* 34.3 (2007): 101–119.

Joshi, Priya. 'Culture and Consumption: Fiction, the Reading Public, and the British Novel in Colonial India'. *Book History* 1 (1998): 196–220.

———. *In Another Country: Colonialism, Culture, and the English Novel in India*. New York: Columbia University Press, 2002.

———. 'Quantitative Method, Literary History'. *Book History* 5 (2002): 263–274.

Judd, Catherine A. 'Male Pseudonyms and Female Authority in Victorian England'. In *Literature in the Marketplace: Nineteenth-Century British Publishing and Reading Practices*, edited by John O. Jordan and Robert L. Patten (Cambridge: Cambridge University Press, 1995), 250–268.

Kelaher, Mary. *Apron Strings*. Sydney: New Century Press, 1939.

Kemp, Martin. '"A Perfect and Faithful Record": Mind and Body in Medical Photography Before 1900'. In *Beauty of Another Order: Photography in Science*, edited by Ann Thomas (New Haven: Yale University Press, 1997), 120–149.

Kennedy, Liam. 'Black Noir: Race and Urban Space in Walter Mosley's Detective Fiction'. In *Criminal Proceedings: The Contemporary American Crime Novel*, edited by Peter Messent (London: Pluto Press, 1997), 42–61.

Keymer, Tom. 'Reading Time in Serial Fiction Before Dickens'. *Yearbook of English Studies* 30 (2000): 34–45.

Kingsley, Henry, *Ravenshoe*. Serialised by *Macmillan's Magazine*, 1861–2; London: Macmillan, 1862.

———. *The Hillyars and the Burtons: A Story of Two Families*. Serialised by *Macmillan's Magazine*, 1863–5; London: Macmillan, 1865.

Kingston, Beverley. 'Women in Nineteenth Century Australian History'. *Labour History* 67 (1994): 84–96.

Kirschenbaum, Matthew. 'Poetry, Patterns, and Provocation: The nora Project'. *The Valve: A Literary Organ* 12 January (2006). Accessed 27 January 2008. http://www.thevalve.org/go/valve/article/poetry_patterns_and_provocation_the_nora_project/

Knox, Malcolm. 'The Ex Factor: BookScan and the Death of the Australian Novelist'. *The Monthly* May (2005): 51–55.

Kramer, Leonie, ed. *The Oxford History of Australian Literature*. Melbourne: Oxford University Press, 1981.

Kramnick, Jonathan. 'Against Literary Darwinism'. *Critical Inquiry* 37 (2011): 315–347.

Krentz, Jayne Ann. 'Introduction'. In *Dangerous Men and Adventurous Women: Romance Writers on the Appeal of the Romance*, edited by Jayne Ann Krentz (Philadelphia: University of Pennsylvania Press, 1992), 3–9.

Kruger, Daniel J., Maryanne Fisher and Ian Jobling. 'Proper Hero Dads and Dark Hero Cads: Alternate Mating Strategies Exemplified in British Romantic Literature'. In *The Literary Animal: Evolution and the Nature of Narrative*, edited by Jonathan Gottschall and David Sloan Wilson (Chicago: Northwestern University Press, 2005), 225–243.

Lake, Marilyn. 'The Politics of Respectability: Identifying the Masculinist Context'. *Historical Studies* 22 (1986): 116–131.
Lamond, Julieanne and Mark Reid. 'Squinting at a Sea of Dots: Visualising Australian Readerships Using Statistical Machine Learning'. In *Resourceful Reading: The New Empiricism, eResearch and Australian Literary Culture*, edited by Katherine Bode and Robert Dixon (Sydney: Sydney University Press, 2009), 223–239.
Lang, John. *Captain Macdonald, or, Haps and Mishaps at Capias Castle*. Serialised by *Mofussilite*, 1857; London: Ward and Lock, 1856.
_____. *Ellen Wareham*. Serialised by *Mofussilite*, 1862; Canberra: Mulini Press, 2005.
_____. *Legends of Australia*. Sydney: James Tegg, 1842.
_____. *Livy Lake*. Serialised by *Mofussilite*, 1849.
_____. *Lucy Cooper: An Australian Tale*. Serialised by *Sharpe's London Magazine*, 1846; Canberra, Mulini Press, 1992.
_____. *Mazarine*. Serialised by *Mofussilite*, 1845; Canberra, Mulini Press, 2004.
_____. *My Friend's Wife, or, York, You're Wanted*. Serialised by *Mofussilite*, 1859; London: Ward and Lock, 1859.
_____. *My Furlough by Robert Weatherly*. Serialised by *Mofussilite*, 1854, Incomplete.
_____. *Passages in the Life of an Undergraduate: Edited by One of His Friends*. Serialised by *Mofussilite*, 1846–7; Meerut: J. A. Gibbons, 1847.
_____. *Raymond*. Serialised by *Blackwood's Edinburgh Magazine*, 1840; Canberra: Mulini Press, 2004.
_____. *Recollections of the Late Jack Weatherly by His Brother Jeffrey*. Serialised by *Mofussilite*, 1845, Incomplete.
_____. *The Ex-Wife*. Serialised by *Mofussilite*, 1856; London: Routledge, 1858.
_____. *The Forger's Wife, or, Emily Orford*. Serialised by *Fraser's Magazine*, 1853; London: Ward and Lock, 1855.
_____. *The Wetherbys, Father and Son, or, Sundry Chapters of Indian Experience*. Serialised by *Mofussilite*, 1853; London: Chapman and Hall, 1853.
_____. *Too Clever by Half, or, The Harroways*. Serialised by *Mofussilite*, 1847–8; London: Nathaniel Cooke, 1853.
_____. *Too Much Alike, or, The Three Calendars*. Serialised by *Mofussilite*, 1847; London: Ward and Lock, 1855.
_____. *Violet, or, The Danseuse: A Portraiture of Human Passions and Character*. Serialised by *Mofussilite*, 1848; London: Henry Colburn, 1836.
_____. *Will He Marry Her?* Serialised by *Mofussilite*, 1858; London: Routledge, 1858.
Lang, John and Victor Crittenden. *Ellen Wareham*. Serialised by *Mofussilite*, 1862; Canberra: Mulini Press, 2005.
Law, Graham. 'Imagined Local Communities: Three Victorian Newspaper Novelists'. In *Printing Places: Locations of Book Production and Distribution since 1500*, edited by John Hinks and Catherine Armstrong (New Castle and London: Oak Knoll Press; British Library, 2005), 185–203.
_____. *Serialising Fiction in the Victorian Press*. Basingstoke: Palgrave, 2000.
Lea-Scarlett, E. J. 'Clarke, Jacob Richard (1822–1893)'. *Australian Dictionary of Biography. Online Edition*. Accessed 16 April 2010. http://adbonline.anu.edu.au/biogs/A030390b.htm?hilite=Jacob%3BRichard%3BClarke
Lee, William, *Brandy and Salt; Being an Effectual Remedy for Most of the Diseases Which Afflict Humanity*. Sydney: James Tegg, 1842.
Leighton, Elizabeth and Lisa Surridge. 'The Plot Thickens: Toward a Narratological Analysis of Illustrated Serial Fiction in the 1860s'. *Victorian Studies* 51.1 (2008): 65–101.
Lennox, Marion. *Princess of Convenience*. Richmond: Mills & Boon, 2006.
Leplastrier, Henry John. *The Travels and Adventures of Mr Newchamp*. Melbourne: Stringer, Mason (for the author), 1854.

Lever, Susan. 'Criticism and Fiction in Australia'. *Overland* 193 (2008): 64–67.
Levine, George. 'Why Science Isn't Literature: The Importance of Differences'. In *Rethinking Objectivity*, edited by Allan Megill (Durham: Duke University Press, 1994), 65–79.
Liston, Ellen. *Auckland Marston: An Australian Story*. Serialised by *Leader*, 1879–80.
Liu, Alan. 'Where is Cultural Criticism in the Digital Humanities?' *Alan Liu*. Accessed 12 January 2012. http://liu.english.ucsb.edu/where-is-cultural-criticism-in-the-digital-humanities/
Lloyd, Jessie Georgina. *Retribution*. Serialised by *Illustrated Sydney News*, 1884–5.
Locker, Arthur. *Sir Goodwin's Folly: A Story of the Year 1795*. London: Chapman and Hall, 1864.
———. *Sweet Seventeen: A Home and Colonial Story*. London: Chapman and Hall, 1866.
Loder, John. *Invincible Press Pulps: Crime and Mystery Series. Together with The Thriller Club, True Crime Series, Invincible Detective Magazine and American Sleuth*. Melbourne: The Author, 2008.
London Online. 'Historical Overview of London Population'. Accessed 25 June 2010. http://www.londononline.co.uk/factfile/historical/
Long, Elizabeth. *Book Clubs: Women and the Uses of Reading in Everyday Life*. Chicago: The University of Chicago Press, 2003.
Lovell, Terry. *Consuming Fiction*. London: Verso, 1987.
Lund, Michael. *America's Continuing Story: An Introduction to Serial Fiction, 1850–1900*. Detroit: Wayne State University Press, 1993.
Lyons, Martyn. 'Britain's Largest Export Market'. In *A History of the Book in Australia, 1891–1945: A National Culture in a Colonised Market*, edited by Martyn Lyons and John Arnold (St Lucia: University of Queensland Press, 2001), 19–26.
———. 'Bush Readers, Factory Readers, Home Readers – Expanding the Australian Reading Public c. 1890–1930'. *Publishing Studies* 5 (1997): 17–23.
———. 'Introduction'. In *A History of the Book in Australia, 1891–1945: A National Culture in a Colonised Market*, edited by Martyn Lyons and John Arnold (St Lucia: University of Queensland Press, 2001), xiii–xix.
McCann, Andrew. 'How to Fuck a Tuscan Garden: A Note on Literary Pessimism'. *Overland* 177 (2004): 22–24.
McCann, Sean. *Gumshoe America: Hard-Boiled Crime Fiction and the Rise and Fall of New Deal Liberalism*. Durham: Duke University Press, 2000.
McCarthy, Justin and Rosa Praed. *The Ladies' Gallery: A Novel*. Serialised by *Leader*, 1888–9; London: Richard Bentley, 1888.
———. *The Rebel Rose: A Novel*. London: Richard Bentley, 1888.
McCarty, Willard. *Humanities Computing*. London: Palgrave Macmillan, 2005.
———. 'Knowing…: Modeling in Literary Studies'. In *Companion to Digital Literary Studies*, edited by Susan Schreibman and Ray Siemens. Oxford: Blackwell, 2008. Accessed 24 June 2011. http://www.digitalhumanities.org/companionDLS/
McConville, Chris. 'Rough Women, Respectable Men and Social Reform: A Response to Lake's "Masculism"'. *Historical Studies* 22.88 (1987): 432–440.
McGann, Jerome. 'A Note on the Current State of Humanities Scholarship'. *Critical Inquiry* 30.2 (2004): 409–413.
———. 'Culture and Technology: The Way We Live Now, What Is To Be Done?' *New Literary History* 36.1 (2005): 71–82.
———. *Radiant Textuality: Literature After the World Wide Web*. New York: Palgrave, 2001.
McLaren, John. 'Andrew Fabinyi and Cheshire'. In *Paper Empires: A History of the Book in Australia, 1946–2005*, edited by Craig Munro and Robyn Sheahan-Bright (St Lucia: University of Queensland Press, 2006), 19–21.
McQueen, Humphrey. '"Breadwinning" in the 1950s: A Response to John Murphy'. *Labour & Industry* 13.3 (2003): 99–103.
McVeigh, Stephen. *The American Western*. Edinburgh: Edinburgh University Press, 2007.
Magarey, Susan. *Unbridling the Tongues of Women: A Biography of Catherine Helen Spence*. Adelaide: University of Adelaide Press, 2010.

Magner, Brigid. 'Anglo-Australian Relations in the Book Trade'. In *Paper Empires: A History of the Book in Australia, 1946–2005*, edited by Craig Munro and Robyn Sheahan-Bright (St Lucia: University of Queensland Press, 2006), 7–10.
Martin, Alan. 'Immigration Policy Before Federation'. In *The Australian People: An Encyclopedia of the Nation, its People and their Origins*, edited by James Jupp (Oakleigh: Cambridge University Press, 2001), 39–44.
Martin, Carol A. *George Eliot's Serial Fiction*. Columbus: Ohio State University Press, 1994.
Martin, Sue. 'Relative Correspondence: Franklin's *My Brilliant Career* and the Influence of Nineteenth-Century Australian Women's Writing'. In *The Time To Write: Australian Women Writers, 1890–1930*, edited by Kay Ferres (Ringwood: Penguin, 1993), 54–70.
May, Anthony. 'Horwitz'. In *Paper Empires: A History of the Book in Australia, 1946–2005*, edited by Craig Munro and Robyn Sheahan-Bright (St Lucia: University of Queensland Press, 2006), 50–52.
Mays, Kelly J. 'The Disease of Reading and Victorian Periodicals'. In *Literature in the Marketplace: Nineteenth-Century British Publishing and Reading Practices*, edited by John O. Jordan and Robert L. Patten (Cambridge: Cambridge University Press, 1998), 165–194.
Menehira, Hazel. 'Review of *Nine Lives: Postwar Women Writers Making their Mark*, by Susan Sheridan'. *M/C Review*, 23 March 2011. Accessed 7 June 2011. http://reviews.media-culture.org.au/modules.php?name=News&file=article&sid=4658
Meredith, Louisa Anne. *Phoebe's Mother: A Novel*. Serialised by *Australasian*, 1866–7; London: Tinsley, 1869.
Merry, Sally Engle. 'Measuring the World: Indicators, Human Rights, and Global Governance'. *Current Anthropology* 52.3 (2011): 83–95.
Michael, James L. *The Isle of Vines: A Fairy Tale for Old and Young*. Serialised by *Month: A Literary and Critical Journal*, 1860; Sydney and London: J. R. Clarke and Simpkin, Marshall, 1858.
Milic, Louis T. 'Progress in Stylistics: Theory, Statistics, Computers'. *Computers and the Humanities* 25.6 (1991): 393–400.
Milic, Louis T. and Steve Slane. 'Quantitative Aspects of Genre in the Century of Prose Corpus'. *Style* 28.1 (1994): 42–55.
Milkman, Katherine L., Rene Carmona and William Gleason. 'A Statistical Analysis of Editorial Influence and Author-Character Similarities in 1990s *New Yorker* Fiction'. *Literary and Linguistic Computing* 22.3 (2007): 305–328.
Millet, Kate, *Sexual Politics*. London: Virago, 1977.
Mills, Carol, *The Native Companion: Complete Indexes*. Canberra: Mulini Press, 1999.
Minnis, A. E. *And All The Trees Are Green*. Sydney: Currawong, 1944.
Mitchell, Lee Clark. *Westerns: Making the Man in Fiction and Film*. Chicago: University of Chicago Press, 1996.
Modjeska, Drusilla. *Exiles at Home: Australian Women Writers 1925–1945*. Melbourne: Sirius Books, 1991.
Modleski, Tania. *Loving with a Vengeance: Mass-Produced Fantasies for Women*. Hamden: Archon Books, 1982.
Moretti, Franco, *Atlas of the European Novel, 1800–1900*. London: Verso, 1998.
———. 'Conjectures on World Literature'. *New Left Review* 1 (2000): 54–68.
———. *Graphs, Maps, Trees: Abstract Models for a Literary History*. London: Verso, 2005.
———. 'Graphs, Maps, Trees: Abstract Models for Literary History – 3'. *New Left Review* 28 (2004): 43–63.
———. 'Moretti Responds (II)'. In *Reading Graphs, Maps, Trees: Responses to Franco Moretti*, edited by Jonathan Goodwin and John Holbo (Anderson: Parlor Press, 2011), 73–75.
———. 'Network Theory, Plot Analysis'. *New Left Review* 68 (2011): 80–102.
———. *Signs Taken for Wonders: Essays in the Sociology of Literary Forms*. London: Verso, 1983.
———. 'Style, Inc. Reflections on Seven Thousand Titles (British Novels, 1740–1850)'. *Critical Inquiry* 36.1 (2009): 134–158.

———. 'The End of the Beginning: A Reply to Christopher Prendergast'. *New Left Review* 41 (2006): 71–86.

———. 'The Slaughterhouse of Literature'. *Modern Language Quarterly* 61 (2000): 207–228.

Morize, André, *Problems and Methods of Literary History*. New York: Biblo & Tannen Booksellers & Publishers, Inc., 1922.

Morris, Robyn. '"Growing up an Australian": Renegotiating Models of Mateship and Australianness in Hsu-Ming Teo's *Behind the Moon*'. *Journal of Intercultural Studies* 27:1–2 (2006): 151–166.

Morrison, Elizabeth. 'Introduction'. In *A Black Sheep*, by Ada Cambridge, edited by Elizabeth Morrison (Canberra: Australian Defence Force Academy and Australian Scholarly Editions Centre, 2004), xi–ixvii.

———. 'More than a Case of "Comparative Failure": The Story Behind the Premature Bentley Ventures of Anglo-Australian Ada Cambridge'. Unpublished Article. 41 pages.

———. 'Newspaper Publications of Novels by Ada Cambridge'. *Australian Literary Studies* 12.4 (1986): 530–531.

———. Retrieving Colonial Literary Culture: The Case for an Index to Serial Fiction in Australian (or Australasian?) Newspapers'. *Bibliographical Society of Australia and New Zealand Bulletin* XIII.1 (1989): 27–36.

———. 'Serial Fiction in Australian Colonial Newspapers'. In *Literature in the Marketplace: Nineteenth-Century British Publishing and Reading Practices*, 2nd ed., edited by John O. Jordan and Robert L. Patten (Cambridge: Cambridge University Press, 1998), 306–324.

Morrison, Ian. 'Pulp Fiction'. In *Paper Empires: A History of the Book in Australia, 1946–2005*, edited by Craig Munro and Robyn Sheahan-Bright (St Lucia: University of Queensland Press, 2006), 257–260.

Munro, Craig. '2001 Publishing Report Card'. In *Paper Empires: A History of the Book in Australia, 1946–2005*, edited by Craig Munro and Robyn Sheahan-Bright (St Lucia: University of Queensland Press, 2006), 85–89.

———. 'A&R's Takeover Crisis'. In *Paper Empires: A History of the Book in Australia, 1946–2005*, edited by Craig Munro and Robyn Sheahan-Bright (St Lucia: University of Queensland Press, 2006), 13–19.

Munro, Craig and John Curtain. 'After the War'. In *Paper Empires: A History of the Book in Australia, 1946–2005*, edited by Craig Munro and Robyn Sheahan-Bright (St Lucia: University of Queensland Press, 2006), 3–7.

Munro, Craig and Robyn Sheahan-Bright, eds. *Paper Empires: A History of the Book in Australia, 1946–2005*. St Lucia: University of Queensland Press, 2006.

Murphy, John. 'Reply to Humphrey McQueen'. *Labour & Industry* 13.3 (2003): 99–103.

Murray, Simone. 'Generating Content: Book Publishing as a Component Media Industry'. In *Making Books: Contemporary Australian Publishing*, edited by David Carter and Anne Galligan (St Lucia: University of Queensland Press, 2007), 51–67.

———. *Mixed Media: Feminist Presses and Publishing Politics*. London: Pluto Press, 2004.

Myers, David. 'Getting Published in Australia'. *Quadrant* December (2004): 66–67.

Myers, Robin and Michael Harris, eds. *Serials and their Readers*. Winchester: St Paul's Bibliographies, 1993.

Neavill, Gordon B. 'From Printing History to the History of the Book'. *Canadian Review of Comparative Literature-Revue Canadienne de Littérature Comparée* 23.1 (1996): 225–237.

Neville, Margot. *Murder and Gardenias*. Serialised by *Australian Women's Weekly*, 1946; London: Geoffrey Bles, 1946.

———. *Murder and Poor Jenny*. Serialised by *Australian Women's Weekly*, 1955; London: Geoffrey Bles, 1954.

———. *Murder Before Marriage*. Serialised by *Australian Women's Weekly*, 1951; London: Geoffrey Bles, 1951.

———. *Murder of a Nymph*. Serialised by *Australian Women's Weekly*, 1950; London: Geoffrey Bles, 1949.

------. *Murder of the Well-Beloved*. Serialised by *Australian Women's Weekly*, 1954; London: Geoffrey Bles, 1953.

------. *Murder to Welcome Her*. Serialised by *Australian Women's Weekly*, 1957; London: Geoffrey Bles, 1957.

------. *Sweet Night for Murder*. Serialised by *Australian Women's Weekly*, 1960; London: Geoffrey Bles, 1959.

------. *The Seagull Said Murder*. Serialised by *Australian Women's Weekly*, 1953; London: Geoffrey Bles, 1952.

Nicholas, S. and P. R. Shergold. 'British and Irish Convicts'. In *The Australian People: An Encyclopedia of the Nation, its People and their Origins*, edited by James Jupp (Oakleigh: Cambridge University Press, 2001), 16–22.

Nile, Richard and David Walker. 'The Mystery of the Missing Bestseller'. In *A History of the Book in Australia: A National Culture in a Colonised Marked*, edited by Martyn Lyons and John Arnold (St Lucia: University of Queensland Press, 2001), 235–254.

------. 'The "Paternost Row Machine" and the Australian Book Trade, 1890–1945'. In *A History of the Book in Australia, 1891–1945: A National Culture in a Colonised Market*, edited by Martyn Lyons and John Arnold (St Lucia: University of Queensland Press, 2001), 3–18.

Nile, Richard and Jason Ensor. 'The Novel, the Implicated Reader and Australian Literary Cultures, 1950–2008'. In *The Cambridge History of Australian Literature*, edited by Peter Pierce (Melbourne: Cambridge University Press, 2009), 517–548.

Nolan, Melanie. 'The High Tide of a Labour Market System: The Australasian Male Breadwinner Model'. *Labour & Industry* 13.3 (2003): 73–92.

North, Michael. *Reading 1922: A Return to the Scene of the Modern*. Oxford: Oxford University Press, 1999.

Nugent, Maria. *Women's Employment and Professionalism in Australia: Histories, Themes and Places*. Canberra: Australian Heritage Commission, 2002.

Nussbaum, Martha C. *Poetic Justice: The Literary Imagination and Public Life*. Boston: Beacon Press, 1995.

O'Grady, Patricia. *A Century of Journalism: The Sydney Morning Herald and its Record of Australian Life, 1831–1931*. Sydney: Fairfax & Sons, 1931.

Olsen, Mark. 'Critical Theory and Textual Computing: Comments and Suggestions'. *Computers and the Humanities* 27.5–6 (1993–4): 395–400.

------. 'Signs, Symbols and Discourses: A New Direction for Computer-Aided Literature Studies'. *Computers and the Humanities* 27.5–6 (1993–4): 309–14.

Osborne, Roger. 'Australian Literature in a World of Books: A Trans-National History of Kylie Tennant's *The Battlers*'. In *Resourceful Reading: The New Empiricism, eResearch and Australian Literary Culture*, edited by Katherine Bode and Robert Dixon (Sydney: Sydney University Press, 2009), 105–118.

Oxford, Johnnie. *West of Texandos*. Sydney: Invincible Press, 1952.

Oxley, Deborah and Eric Richards. 'Convict and Free Immigrant Women before 1851'. In *The Australian People: An Encyclopedia of the Nation, its People and their Origins*, edited by James Jupp (Oakleigh: Cambridge University Press, 2001), 30–34.

Page, Benedicte. 'Research Shows Male Writers Still Dominate Books World'. *Guardian*, 4 February 2011. Accessed 19 June 2011. http://www.guardian.co.uk/books/2011/feb/04/research-male-writers-dominate-books-world

Page, Michael. 'Rigby Limited'. In *Paper Empires: A History of the Book in Australia, 1946–2005*, edited by Craig Munro and Robyn Sheahan-Bright (St Lucia: University of Queensland Press, 2006), 41–43.

Paizis, George. 'Category Romance in the Era of Globalization: The Story of Harlequin'. In *The Global Literary Field*, edited by Anna Guttman, Michel Hockx and George Paizis (Cambridge: Cambridge Scholars Press, 2006), 126–151.

Parry, Marc. 'The Humanities Go Google'. *Chronicle of Higher Education*, 28 May 2010. Accessed 31 May 2011. http://wiredcampus.chronicle.com/article/The-Humanities-Go-Google/65713/

Patten, Robert L. 'Serialised Retrospection in *The Pickwick Papers*'. In *Literature in the Marketplace: Nineteenth-Century British Publishing and Reading Practices*, 2nd ed., edited by John O. Jordan and Robert L. Patten (Cambridge: Cambridge University Press, 1998), 123–142.

Pearson, Jacqueline. *Women's Reading in Britain, 1750–1834: A Dangerous Recreation*. Cambridge: Cambridge University Press, 1999.

Poland, Louise. '"Sisterhood is Powerful": Sisters Publishing and Book Club in Australia'. *Script & Print* 29.1–4 (2005): 276–289.

Poovey, Mary. *A History of the Modern Fact: Problems of Knowledge in the Sciences of Wealth and Society*. Chicago: The University of Chicago Press, 1998.

Potter, Rosanne G. 'Preface'. In *Literary Computing and Literary Criticism: Theoretical and Practical Essays on Theme and Rhetoric*, edited by Rosanne G. Potter (Philadelphia: University of Pennsylvania Press, 1989), xv–xxix.

———. 'Statistical Analysis of Literature: A Retrospective on *Computers and the Humanities*, 1966–1990'. *Computers and the Humanities* 25.6 (1991): 401–429.

Praed, Rosa. *Affinities: A Romance of To-Day*. London: Richard Bentley, 1885.

———. *An Australian Heroine*. London: Chapman and Hall, 1880.

———. *Miss Jacobsen's Chance: A Story of Australian Life*. Serialised by *Leader*, 1886; London: Richard Bentley, 1886.

———. *Moloch: A Story of Sacrifice*. London: Chapman and Hall, 1883.

———. *Nadine: The Study of a Woman*. London: Chapman and Hall, 1882.

———. *Policy and Passion: A Novel of Australian Life*. London: Richard Bentley, 1881.

———. *The Head Station: A Novel of Australian Life*. London: Chapman and Hall, 1885.

———. *Zero: A Story of Monte Carlo*. Serialised by *Temple Bar*, 1884; London: Chapman and Hall, 1884.

Prescott, Andrew. 'Consumers, Creators or Commentators? Problems of Audience and Mission in the Digital Humanities'. *Arts and Humanities in Higher Education* 11 (2012): 61–75.

Probert, Belinda. '"Grateful Slaves" or "Self-Made Women": A Matter of Choice or Policy?' *Australian Feminist Studies* 37 (2002): 7–18.

Radway, Janice A. *Reading the Romance: Women, Patriarchy and Popular Literature*. Chapel Hill: The University of North Carolina Press, 1984.

Randall, Don. 'Charismatic Masculinity in David Malouf's Fiction'. *Australian Literary Studies* 25.1 (2010): 71–81.

Ranken, George. *Windabyne: A Record of By-Gone Times in Australia*. Serialised by *Australian Journal*, 1878–80; London: Remington, 1895.

Readings, Bill. 'The University Without Culture?' *New Literary History* 26.3 (1995): 465–492.

Reskin, Barbara F. 'Culture, Commerce and Gender: The Feminization of Book Editing'. In *Job Queues: Explaining Women's Inroads into Male Occupations*, edited by Barbara F. Reskin and Patricia A. Roos (Philadelphia: Temple University Press, 1990), 93–110.

Richards, James. *Edwin Randolph, or, The Adventures of a Young Australian*. Melbourne: J. Richards and Sons, 188–.

———. *Under a Face*. Melbourne: J. Richards and Sons, 188–.

Romance Writers of America. 'RITA Awards: Past Winners'. Accessed 11 November 2011. http://www.rwa.org/cs/contests_and_awards/rita_awards/past_winners

Rose, Jonathan. 'An Introduction to Book History'. *Book History* 1 (1998): ix–xi.

Rothberg, Michael. 'Quantifying Culture?: A Response to Eric Slauter'. *American Literary History* 22.2 (2010): 341–346.

Rowcroft, Charles. *Confessions of an Etonian*. Serialised by *New Monthly Magazine and Literary Journal*, 1848; London: Henry Colburn, 1852.

———. *Tales of the Colonies, or, the Adventures of an Emigrant*. Serialised by *British Queen and Statesman*, 1842–3, Incomplete; London: Saunders and Otley, 1843.

———. *The Bushranger of Van Diemen's Land*. Serialised by *Hood's Magazine and Comic Miscellany*, 1845; London: Smith Elder, 1846.
Rowe, Richard. *Arthur Owen: An Autobiography*. Serialised by *Month: A Literary and Critical Journal*, 1860; Sydney: J. R. Clarke, 1858.
Ruby L. *Hope Morton*. Serialised by *Australian Woman's Magazine and Domestic Journal*, 1883–4.
Rukavina, Alison. '"This is a Wonderfully Comprehensive Business": The Development of the British-Australian and International Book Trades, 1870–1887'. *Script & Print* 32.2 (2008): 69–94.
Salmon, Catherine. 'Crossing the Abyss: Erotica and the Intersection of Evolutionary Psychology and Literary Studies'. In *The Literary Animal: Evolution and the Nature of Narrative*, edited by Jonathan Gottschall and David Sloan Wilson (Chicago: Northwestern University Press, 2005), 244–258.
Savery, Henry. *Quintus Servinton: A Tale, Founded Upon Incidents of Real Occurrence*. Hobart: Henry Melville, 1830–1.
Schreibman, Susan, Ray Siemens and John Unsworth. 'The Digital Humanities and Humanities Computing: An Introduction'. In *A Companion to the Digital Humanities*, edited by Susan Schreibman, Ray Siemens and John Unsworth (Oxford: Blackwell Publishers, 2004), xxv–xxvii.
Schwartz, Morry. 'Inner-Urban and Outback'. In *Paper Empires: A History of the Book in Australia, 1946–2005*, edited by Craig Munro and Robyn Sheahan-Bright (St Lucia: University of Queensland Press, 2006), 63–66.
Serlen, Rachel. 'The Distant Future? Reading Franco Moretti'. *Literature Compass* 7.3 (2010): 214–225.
Shattock, Joanne, ed. *The Cambridge Bibliography of English Literature, 1800–1900*, vol. 4. Cambridge: Cambridge University Press, 1999.
Shaw, A. G. L. 'English Convicts'. In *The Australian People: An Encyclopedia of the Nation, its People and their Origins*, edited by James Jupp, (Oakleigh: Cambridge University Press, 2001), 279–282.
Sheridan, Susan. *Along the Faultlines: Sex, Race and Nation in Australian Women's Writing*. St Leonards: Allen & Unwin, 1995.
———. 'Generations Lost and Found: Reading Women Writers Together'. *Australian Literary Studies* 24.3–4 (2009): 39–52.
———. *Nine Lives: Postwar Women Writers Making Their Mark*. St Lucia: University of Queensland Press, 2011.
———. 'Women Writers'. *Australian Literary Studies* 13.4 (1988): 319–336.
Sheridan, Susan, with Barbara Baird, Kate Borrett and Lyndall Ryan. *Who Was That Woman?: The Australian Women's Weekly in the Postwar Years*. Sydney: University of New South Wales Press, 2001.
Slater, John. *Butcher of Auschwitz*. Sydney: Horwitz, 1965.
———. *Terror of the Swastika*. Sydney: Horwitz, 1965.
Smith, Eve. *A Woman's Battle With the World. A Story of Hospital Life*. Serialised by *Australian Journal*, 1890–2.
Spence, Catherine Helen. *A Week in the Future*. Serialised by *Centennial Magazine*, 1889; Mount Waverley: Chimaera Publications, 2010.
———. *An Agnostic's Progress, from the Known to the Unknown*. London: Williams and Norgate, 1884.
———. *Clara Morison: A Tale of South Australia during the Gold Fever*. London: John W. Parker, 1854.
———. *Ever Yours: C.H. Spence*, edited by Susan Magarey with Barbara Wall, Mary Lyons and Maryan Beams. Kent Town: Wakefield Press, 2005.
———. *Gathered In: A Novel*. Serialised by *Adelaide Observer* and *Evening Journal*, 1881–2; Sydney: Sydney University Press, 1977.
———. *Mr Hogarth's Will*. Serialised by *Weekly Mail*, 1864; London: Richard Bentley, 1865.
———. *Tender and True: A Colonial Tale*. London: Smith, Elder, 1856.
———. *The Author's Daughter*. Serialised by *Adelaide Observer*, 1867; London: Richard Bentley, 1868.

Spender, Lynne. 'Introduction'. In *Her Selection: Writings by Nineteenth Century Australian Women*, edited by Lynne Spender (Ringwood: Penguin, 1988), 1–3.

——. 'Introduction'. In *Writing a New World: Two Centuries of Australian Women's Writing*, edited by Lynne Spender (Ringwood: Penguin, 1988), xi–xvii.

Spivak, Gayatri. *Death of a Discipline*. New York: Columbia University Press, 2003.

St. Clair, William. *The Reading Nation in the Romantic Period*. Cambridge: Cambridge University Press, 2004.

Stephen, Harold W. H. *Saved By a Ring: An Australian Story*. Sydney: J. J. Moore, 1883.

——. *The Golden Yankee: A Tale of Life and Adventure on the Diggings*. Sydney: J. J. Moore, 1877.

Stewart, Cori. 'We Call Upon the Author to Explain: Theorising Writers' Festivals as Sites of Contemporary Public Culture'. *Journal of the Association for the Study of Australian Literature* Special Issue: Common Readers (2010): 1–14. Accessed 27 June 2011. http://www.nla.gov.au/openpublish/index.php/jasal/article/viewFile/1492/2085

Strauss, Jennifer. 'Are Women's Novels Feminist Novels: An Australian Perspective'. *Cross/Cultures: Readings in the Post/Colonial Literatures in English* 11 (1993): 35–53.

Strehle, Susan and Mary Paniccia Carden. 'Introduction'. In *Double Plots: Romance and History*, edited by Susan Strehle and Mary Paniccia Carden (Jackson: University Press of Mississippi, 2003), xi–xxxiii.

Stuart, Lurline, *Australian Periodicals with Literary Content*. Melbourne: Australian Scholarly Publishing, 2003.

——. 'Colonial Periodicals: Patterns of Failure'. *Bibliographical Society of Australia and New Zealand Bulletin* 13.1 (1989): 1–10.

——, ed. *His Natural Life*, by Marcus Clarke. St Lucia: University of Queensland Press, 2001.

Sussex, Lucy. 'A Woman of Mystery'. *Crime Factory* 2 (2001): 15–16.

Sutherland, John. 'The Ideas Interview'. *Guardian*, 9 January 2006. Accessed 15 April 2011. http://www.guardian.co.uk/books/2006/jan/09/highereducation.academicexperts

——. *Victorian Fiction: Writers, Publishers, Readers*. London: Macmillan, 1995.

Swan, N. Walter. *The Late N. Walter Swan's Famous Australian Story, Luke Mivers' Harvest*. Serialised by *Sydney Mail*, 1879; Kensington: University of New South Wales Press, 1991.

Tally, Robert T. 'Review of *Graphs, Maps, Trees: Abstract Models for Literary History*, by Franco Moretti'. *Modern Language Quarterly* 68.1 (2007): 132–135.

Tegg's New South Wales Pocket Almanac and Remembrancer. Sydney: James Tegg, 1836–44.

Tepper, Steven J. 'Fiction Reading in America: Explaining the Gender Gap'. *Poetics* 27 (2000): 255–275.

Thompson, Frank. 'Sixties Larrikins'. In *Paper Empires: A History of the Book in Australia, 1946–2005*, edited by Craig Munro and Robyn Sheahan-Bright (St Lucia: University of Queensland Press, 2006), 31–34.

Thompson, Nicola Diane. 'Responding to the Woman Questions: Rereading Noncanonical Victorian Women Novelists'. In *Victorian Women Writers and the Woman Question*, edited by Nicola Diane Thompson (Cambridge: Cambridge University Press, 1999), 1–23.

Thomson, Robert and Leigh Dale. 'Books in Selected Australian Newspapers, December 1930'. In *Resourceful Reading: The New Empiricism, eResearch and Australian Literary Culture*, edited by Katherine Bode and Robert Dixon (Sydney: Sydney University Press, 2009), 119–141.

Timperley, W. H. *Bush Luck: An Australian Story*. Serialised by *Boy's Own Paper*, 1889–90; London: Religious Tract Society, 1892.

Tompkins, Jane. *West of Everything: The Inner Life of Westerns*. New York: Oxford University Press, 1992.

Trainor, Luke. 'Australian Writers, British Publishers, 1870–1902: Talking to the Nation?' *Australian Historical Studies* 37.127 (2006): 140–155.

Triffitt, Nigel. *Cheap Thrills*. Fitzroy: Outlaw Press, 1994.

Trollope, Anthony. *John Caldigate: A Novel*. Serialised by *Blackwood's Magazine*, 1878–9; London: Chapman and Hall, 1879.

Trumpener, Katie. 'Critical Response 1. Paratext and Genre System: A Response to Franco Moretti'. *Critical Inquiry* 36.1 (2009): 159–171.
Tuchman, Gaye, with Nina E. Fortin. *Edging Women Out: Victorian Novelists, Publishers and Social Change.* London: Yale Press, 1989.
Turner, Lilian. *Miss Elizabeth.* Serialised by *Australian Town and Country Journal*, 1896.
University of Melbourne Special Collections. 'Douglas Taylor Collection of Pulp and Popular Fiction'. Accessed 7 December 2010. http://www.lib.unimelb.edu.au/collections/special/collections/australiana/taylor.html
Vader, John. *Battle of Sydney.* London: New English Library, 1971.
Vera. *A Life's Sacrifice.* Serialised by *Australian Woman's Magazine and Domestic Journal*, 1883–4.
———. *Adele, A Winter's Sketch.* Serialised by *Australian Woman's Magazine and Domestic Journal*, 1884.
———. *Harold Dane's Legacy.* Serialised by *Australian Woman's Magazine and Domestic Journal*, 1883.
Vida: Women in Literary Arts. 'The Count 2010'. Accessed 19 June 2011. http://vidaweb.org/the-count-2010
———. 'The Count 2011'. Accessed 28 May 2012. http://www.vidaweb.org/the-2011-count
Vidal, Mary Theresa. *Winterton: A Tale.* London: Francis and John Rivington, 1846.
Wailes, Robert. *Me: The History of an Urchin.* Sydney: The Author, 189–.
Ward, Russell Braddock, *The Australian Legend.* Melbourne: Oxford University Press, 1958.
Webby, Elizabeth. 'Australian Literature and the Marketplace'. In *Australian Literature and the Public Sphere*, edited by Alison Bartlett, Robert Dixon and Christopher Lee (Toowoomba: Association for the Study of Australian Literature, 1999), 13–22.
———. 'Before the *Bulletin*: Nineteenth Century Literary Journalism'. In *Cross Currents: Magazines and Newspapers in Australian Literature*, edited by Bruce Bennett (Melbourne: Longman Cheshire, 1981), 3–34.
———. 'Colonial Writers and Readers'. In *The Cambridge Companion to Australian Literature*, edited by Elizabeth Webby (Cambridge: Cambridge University Press, 2000), 50–73.
———. 'Fiction, Readers, and Libraries in Early Colonial New South Wales and Van Diemen's Land'. In *The Culture of the Book: Essays From Two Hemispheres in Honour of Wallace Kirsop*, edited by David Garrioch, Harold Love, Brian McMullin, Ian Morrison and Meredith Sherlock (Melbourne: Bibliographical Society of Australia and New Zealand, 1999), 366–373.
———. 'Introduction'. In *The Cambridge Companion to Australian Literature*, edited by Elizabeth Webby (Cambridge: Cambridge University Press, 2000), 1–18.
———. 'Not Reading the Nation: Australian Readers of the 1890s'. *Australian Literary Studies* 22.3 (2006): 308–318.
Webster, Michael. 'Into the Global Era'. In *Paper Empires: A History of the Book in Australia, 1946–2005*, edited by Craig Munro and Robyn Sheahan-Bright (St Lucia: University of Queensland Press, 2006), 81–85.
Weedon, Alexis, *Victorian Publishing: The Economics of Book Production for a Mass Market, 1836–1916.* Aldershot: Ashgate, 2003.
Whitlock, Gillian. '1901/1933: From Eutopia to Dystopia'. In *The Time To Write: Australian Women Writers 1890–1930*, edited by Kay Ferres (Ringwood: Penguin, 1993), 162–182.
———. 'Eight Voices of the Eighties: Introduction'. In *Eight Voices of the Eighties: Stories, Journalism and Criticism by Australian Women Writers*, edited by Gillian Whitlock (St Lucia: University of Queensland Press, 1989), xi–xxxvi.
———. 'Graftworks: Australian Women's Writing, 1970–90'. In *Gender, Politics and Fiction: Twentieth Century Australian Women's Novels*, 2nd ed., edited by Carole Ferrier (St Lucia: University of Queensland Press, 1992), 236–258.
Whitworth, Robert P. *Mary Summers: A Romance of the Australian Bush.* Serialised by *Australian Journal*, 1865; Canberra: Mulini Press, 1994.
Wilding, Michael. 'Australian Literary and Scholarly Publishing in its International Context'. *Australian Literary Studies* 19.1 (1999): 57–69.

———. 'Michael Wilding on Australian Publishing in a Global Environment'. *Antipodes* 14 (2000): 152–154.

Williams, Christine L. *Still a Man's World: Men Who Do "Women's" Work.* Berkeley: University of California Press, 1995.

———. 'The Glass Escalator: Hidden Advantages for Men in the "Female" Professions'. *Social Problems* 39.3 (1992): 253–267.

Winstanley, Eliza. *For Her Natural Life.* Serialised by *Bow Bells: A Weekly Magazine of General Literature*, 1876; London: John Dicks, 1881.

———. *Margaret Falconer.* Serialised by *Reynold's Miscellany of Romance, General Literature, Science and Art*, 1860; London: John Dicks, circa 1860.

Winter, Thomas Nelson. 'Roberto Busa, S.J. and the Invention of the Machine-Generated Concordance'. *The Classical Bulletin* 75.1 (1999): 3–20.

Wright, Judith. *Kings of the Dingoes.* Melbourne: Oxford University Press, 1958.

———. *Range the Mountains High.* Melbourne: Lansdowne, 1962.

Yarra-Guinea. *Frank Kennedy: The Australian Settler.* Sydney: J. T. Grocott, 1847.

Zifcak, Michael. 'The Retail Book Trade'. In *Paper Empires: A History of the Book in Australia, 1946–2005*, edited by Craig Munro and Robyn Sheahan-Bright (St Lucia: University of Queensland Press, 2006), 202–220.

Zwicker, Jonathan. 'Japan, 1850–1900'. In *The Novel: Volume 1, History, Geography, and Culture*, edited by Franco Moretti (Princeton: Princeton University Press, 2006), 509–520.

———. *Practices of the Sentimental Imagination: Melodrama, the Novel, and the Social Imaginary in Nineteenth-Century Japan.* Cambridge: Harvard University Press, 2006.

———. 'The Long Nineteenth Century of the Japanese Novel'. In *The Novel: Volume 1, History, Geography, and Culture*, edited by Franco Moretti (Princeton: Princeton University Press, 2006), 553–595.

Zyngier, Sonia, Marisa Bortolussi, Anna Chesnokova and Jan Aurache, eds. *Directions in Empirical Literary Studies.* Amsterdam: John Bejamins Publishing Co. 2008.

INDEX

A and A Books 99
A&R: *see* Angus and Robertson
A&U: *see* Allen & Unwin
ABC Books 90
Ace Books 139
Ackland Press 91
Action Comics 64–5, **64**, 67–9, 136, 207n36; *see also* pulp fiction
Active Bladder 93
adventure fiction 33, 69, 118, 119–20, 123, 137 157, 159; *see also* genre fiction
aesthetic value: *see* cultural value
Aether Book Publishing 99, 100
After the Celebration 154–5; *see also* Gelder, Ken; Salzman, Paul
Age 36, 37, 46 Alex McKinley 44
Allen & Unwin 82, **82**, 85, 87, **88**, 90, 91, 156–7
Allen Lane 78
Alpha Books 72
Alyson Books 94
Amazon.com 99
Angus and Robertson 62, 63–4, **64**, 72–3, **74**, 75, 78, 139–40, 145, 148
Annales school 9, 17
Aphelion Publications 92–3
Aquila Books 95
Arac, Jonathan 11–12
ARD Press 99
Argus 35, 36
Artemis Publishing 91, 93
Artlook Books 72
Astley, Thea 141–2, 147, 161
Athenaeum 110
Atlantic 110, 162
AustLit 1, 11, 19–21, 24, 33–4, 37, 40, 63–4, 85–7, 170, 172; biography of 19–21; changes in 20, 24, 201n21; content of 20–21, 98, 136, 194n129, 205n14, 205n14; definition of Australian author 20–21, 33, 182n45; genre categories 20, 85–7, **86**, **87**, **88**, 137, 145–6, 157–60, 206n20; importance of vii–viii; 172; mining of 1, 20, 135, 179n101
Australasian 35–6, **36**, 38, 42, 48, 116
Australasian Book Society 64, 140
Australian 48
Australian in Every Way 91
Australian Journal 35–6, **36**, 38, 48, 115
Australian Monthly Magazine 36, **36**; *see also Colonial Monthly*
Australian National University Press 90
Australian Town and Country Journal 35, **36**, 38, 48
Australian Woman's Magazine and Domestic Journal **36**, 36, 119
Australian Women's Weekly 138
Author, the: *see* self-publishing
AWW: *see Australian Women's Weekly*

Bantam 139
Barnes & Noble 99
Barton, G. B. 114
Baynton, Barbara 107
Bella Books 94
Bentley: *see* Richard Bentley
Bertelsmann 82–3, **82**, 159
Bideena Press 91, 95
Bird, Delys 4, 135, 136, 139, 144–7, 155
Black Dog Books 90–91
Black Lace 94
Black Pepper 98–9
Blackwash Press 95
Blackwell 105–6
Blau DuPlessis, Rachel 106
Blencowe Books 97
Bodley Head 78
Boldrewood, Rolf 40, 42, 114–15, 119–20
book history 3–4, 8–10, 13–16, 17, 19, 21–3, 25, 27, 169, 171, 173; *see also* quantitative analysis, in book history
Book History Reader, The 106
Book Press 99

book volumes: single 32, 46–8, 51, 122; multi 32, 45–8, 51, 122
BookBound Publishing 99
BookPal 99, 100
BookScan: *see* Nielson BookScan
Boolarong 72, 98, 147
Boothby, Guy 48–9
Borgman, Christine 169
Boris Books 91
Boston Review 162
Bowley, William 44
Boyd, Anne 110
Boyd, Martin 140
Braddon, Mary Elizabeth 117
Brake, Laurel 40, 110–11, 119
Brandl and Schlesinger 90, 92, 95
Brolga Publishing 98
Brooks, Geraldine 162
Broome, Mary Anne 44
Brown, Carter 74, 137
Bulletin 125, 126, 128
Burke, Timothy 15
Burn, David 34
Burns, Connie 108
Bystander Press 91

Calvert 64, **64**, 65, 67, 68, 69, 136; *see also* pulp fiction
Cambridge, Ada 40, 41–2, 107, 109, 114, 122
Cambridge Companion to Australian Literature, The 3–4
canon 4, 27, 42, 55, 79, 123, 147–8; critique of 1, 4, 8–9, 105, 123; 176n18
Carden, Mary 151–2
Carey, Peter 160, 161, 162, 165
Carter, David 3, 80, 81, 83, 85, 136, 139, 142
Casanova, Pascale 96–7
Casey, Ellen 110
Cassell 42, 49, 139
Castro, Brian 165
Catchfire Press 91
Cawelti, John 137–8
Centennial Magazine **36**
Century Hutchinson 78
Chapman and Hall 31, 44, **44**, 127
Chatto and Windus 49, **49**, 78, 127
Cheshire 62–3, 140
Clark, Manning 129–30
Clarke, Marcus 42, 44
Cleveland 64–9, **64**, 73–5, **74**, 85, 86, **87**, 89–90, 136–7; *see also* pulp fiction
Companion to the Digital Humanities, A 12, 169–70

Companion to the History of the Book, A 105–6
close reading 8, 11–12, 13–15, 25; criticism of 8, 15; *see also* distant readingCoeur de Lion 92
Colby, Robert 41
Collins 50, **64**, **74**, 76, 139
Collins, Tom: *see* Furphy, Joseph
colonial editions 32, 46, 47, 50, 51, 71, 122, 186 n141
colonial identity 33, 39, 107, 118–20, 128–9; *see also* national identity; regional, identity
Colonial Monthly 36, **36**; *see also Australian Monthly Magazine*
commodity culture 3, 17, 54–5, 89, 101–2, 133, 167; *see also* economic systems
'Conjectures on World Literature' 7, 15; *see also* Moretti, Franco
copayment for publication 32–3, 43, 45–7, 98, 100, 122; *see also* self-publishing; subsidy publishing
Copper Leife 99
Copyright Publishing 99
Corris, Peter 162
Cottage Industry Press 94
Cottrell, Dorothy 141
Coultrap-McQuin, Susan 110
Courtenay, Bryce 63, 162
Coward, Rosalind 144, 152
creative writing courses 101, 163
crime fiction 16, 65, 67, 70, 75, 137–9, 142, 145, 157, 159; *see also* genre fiction
critical attention to Australian authors 105, 107, 133, 134–5, **134**, 136, 155, 160, 162–3, 172, 205n7, 205n8, 208n44; in academic journals 135, 140–41, 146–8, 160–62, 164–5, 208n44; in newspapers 135, 140–41, 146, 147–8, 161–5, 208n44; overall 135, 140–41, 146, 147–8, 161–2, 164, 208n44
Crown Publishing Group 78
cultural diversity and publishing 71–2
cultural materialism 3–4, 55, 128, 170
cultural nationalism 5, 21, 52, 79, 81, 125; *see also* literary nationalism
cultural value 2–3, 6, 10–12, 30, 32–3, 54–5, 60, 70, 80–81, 89, 95–6, 101, 170–71; and British publication 6, 30, 32–3, 41–2, 52, 55, 115, 122–5; and gender 105, 107, 109–11, 114–15, 118, 120, 122–4, 125, 128, 130, 132, 142, 148, 153, 160, 163–7
Currawong 64–5, **64**, 67–9, 136; *see also* pulp fiction

INDEX

Curtain, John 27, 28, 30, 41, 45, 62–3, 66
Cusack, Dymphna 141
Cusack, Mary Francis 50

Dark, Eleanor 140, 141
Darnton, Robert 9, 13–14, 21
Darville, Helen 161–2, 165
data: analysis (*see* quantitative analysis); mining 1, 24, 169–70 (*see also AustLit*, mining of); modelling 1, 8, 23–5, 169–70 (*see also* McCarty, Willard); visualisation 1, 12, 16–17, 22–5, 170, 173 (*see also* objectivity)
Davidson, Cathy 23
Davidson, Harriett Miller 42
Davis, Mark 79, 84–7, 101
Deep End Press 97
Demidenko, Helen: *see* Darville, Helen
deregulation: *see* economic rationalism
detective fiction: *see* crime fiction
Detour Press 93Devanny, Jean 109
Dever, Maryanne 21, 108
Dezsery Publications 72
Diane Andrews 99
Digby, Long and Co. 49
digital humanities 4, 8, 10, 13, 22–5, 169–70, 172–3
Disher, Garry 162
distant reading 3, 9–11, 14–19; criticism of 10–12, 14–19; *see also* close reading; Moretti, Franco
Dixon, Jay 152
Dixon, Robert 117, 120
Dodge, Emerson 74
Dolin, Tim 27, 46–7, 111, 117, 182n51
Dolphin Publications 64
Donaldson, William 38, 53
Dorchester 93, 95
Doubleday 139
Drewe, Robert 165
Duffy and Snellgrove 92
Dykebooks 72, 147
Dymocks 63–4, 140

E. P. Dutton and Company 78
Eagleton, Mary 105
Earls, Nick 162
economic rationalism 7–8, 11, 13, 25, 58, 76, 78–81, 96, 131, 154, 166; *see also* globalisation
economic systems 3–4, 19, 46, 55, 71, 78, 100, 112, 163–5: author earnings 6, 54, 74, 107, 109–11, 114–15, 120, 122–4, 128, 135, 163–4, 170–71; price of fiction 45–7, 51, 65, 69, 75, 99–100, 170, 207n36; tariffs 66–9, 74, 79, 138; *see also* commodity culture; copayment for publication; economic rationalism; self-publishing; subsidy publishing
Eggert, Paul 37, 47, 51, 54
Eidolon Books 92
Eliot, Simon 14, 19, 25
Ellora's Cave 93
Empiricus 98
Eneit Press 92
English, James 11
Ensor, Jason 66, 189n43
Equilibrium Books 90, 98
Esperance Press 91
Evening News 35, 38
Exisle 94
Experimental Art Foundation 72
experimental publishing 72

F. Gleason's Publishing Hall **30**
F. H. Johnston Publishing Co. 64
F. V. White 49, **49**, 127
F. W. Cheshire: *see* Cheshire
Faber and Faber 139
Fabinyi, Andrew 63
fantasy fiction 93, 157, 159; *see also* genre fiction
Farjeon, B. L. 21, 42
Farmer, Beverley 161
Farrar, Straus and Giroux 139
Feather, John 31
feminism 3, 57, 72, 93, 105, 125, 131, 133, 138, 143–4, 146, 148, 151–5, 160–61, 164; *see also* gender trends
feminist literary criticism 6, 105–7, 109–12, 123, 125–8, 131–3, 135, 139, 142–4, 148, 151–5, 161, 162–4, 166–7, 172, 177n27; *see also* gender trends
feminist publishing 72, 93–4, 143–4, 147–8, 152, 157; *see also* gender trends
Finlay Lloyd 92, 95
Finn, Edmund 44
Firestone, Shulamith 151
Five Islands Press 91
Flame Lily Books 99
Flanagan, Graeme 66
Flanagan, Richard 58, 62, 71, 75, 162, 165
Fontaine Press 92
Fortune, Mary 109
Fourth Estate 96

Franc, Maud Jeanne 41–2, 44
Frank Johnson **64**, 65–9, 136; *see also* pulp fiction
Franklin, Miles 109, 140, 141, 142, 161
Franklin, Ruth 162–3
Fremantle Arts Centre Press 72, 147, 148; *see also* Fremantle Press
Fremantle Press 89, 90, 91, 92, 157; *see also* Fremantle Arts Centre Press
French, Jackie 161
Friedman, Michael 17
Frow, John 16, 18–19, 54
Furphy, Joseph 140

Galligan, Anne 70–71, 72, 76, 80, 81, 83, 85
Garner, Helen 161
gay and lesbian publishing 94
Gay Men's Press 94
Gelder, Ken 3, 71, 83, 143, 154–5; *see also After the Celebration*; *The New Diversity*
gender trends 2–6, 18–19, 33, 44, 72, 105–67, **108**, **114**, **116**, **126**, **132**, **133**, **134**, **149**, **150**, 171–2; *see also* feminism; feminist literary criticism; feminist publishing; genre fiction, and gender; literary fiction, and gender; men authors; multinational publishing, and gender; occupational gender segregation; pulp fiction, and gender; reading, and gender; serial fiction, and gender; women authors; women's writing; women's writing and feminism
genre fiction 2, 6, 9, 16, 20, 23–4, 39, 53, 68–70, 74–5, 84–7, **86**, **87**, **88**, 92–5, 102, 170–72; and gender 105, 112, 117, 118, 125, 132–3, 136–40, 142–4, 145–6, 148, 151–3, 154–5, 157–60, 163–4, 166–7; neglect of 2, 54, 60, 69–70, 84, 144, 153; publishers 92–6; *see also* popular fiction; pulp fiction
George Robertson 44–5, **44**, 49–51, **49**, 62, 114, 186n145
George Slater 31
Georgian House 145
Gerstaecker, Friedrich 35
Gilbert, Sandra 151
Giles, Fiona 107
Ginninderra 90, 94–5
Giramondo Publishing 91, 92
glass ceiling: *see* occupational gender segregation
glass escalator: *see* occupational gender segregationGleitzman, Morris 162

globalisation 2, 58, 78–9, 80–81, 83, 88–9, 91–3, 96–7, 99–100, 103, 131, 154, 166; *see also* economic rationalism; multinational publishing; transnational
globalism: *see* globalisation
Goanna Press: *see* Bideena Publishing
Golgatha Graphics 97
Gordon & Gotch 85
Graywolf 163
Greco, Albert 165
Green Candy 94
Greenhouse Publications 72, 78, 147
Greenwood, Kerry 161, 162
Greer, Germaine 151Grenville, Kate 147, 161, 162
Grover, Marshall 74, 137
Goldsworthy, Peter 162
Gottschall, Jonathan 14
Gould, Nat 48–9
government funding: for *AustLit* 20, 170 (*see also AustLit*); for publishing 23, 39, 58, 71–2, 78–9, 86, 103; rejection of 71, 94–5; withdrawal of 79, 163
Graphs, Maps, Trees 7–11, 15–18; *see also* distant reading; Moretti, Franco
Great Bosses 97
Griswold, Wendy 21–2
Guardian 34–5
Gubar, Susan 151

Hachette Livre **82**, 83
Halbooks 99
Hale & Iremonger 72, 73, 89, 91
Halligan, Marion 148, 161, 162
Hamilton, Kirk 74
Hamish Hamilton 78, 139
Hanrahan, Barbara 147, 161
Haraway, Donna 8, 10
Harlequin Mills & Boon: *see* Mills & Boon; Torstar
Harper's Magazine 162
Hart, Jim 70–1
Hartnett, Sonya 161, 162
Hasbro/Wizards 93
Hazzard, Shirley 148
Headline 78, 96
Heartline Presents 95
Heartsong Presents 93
Heinemann 42–3
Henry Melville 31
Hermanson, Scott 12
Hetherington, Keith 137

Hewett, Dorothy 146, 147, 160, 161
historical fiction 157, 159; *see also* genre fiction
Hodder and Stoughton 78
Hodder Headline 76, 78, 82–3, **82**
Hollier, Nathan 80–81
Holtzbrinck **82**, 83, 159
Holyroyd, John 45Hornets Nest 91
horror fiction 92, 159; *see also* genre fiction
Horwitz 64–9, **64**, 73–5, **74**, 85–6, **87**, 89–90, 136–7; *see also* pulp fiction
Hospital, Janette Turner 161, 165
Hudson, Pat 13
Hughes, Linda 53
humanities computing: *see* digital humanities
Hume, Fergus 21
humour fiction 140, 159; *see also* genre fiction
Hunter Publishers 91
Hurst and Blackett 44, **44**, 127
Hutchinson 49, **49**, **64**, 76, 78, 127
Hyland House 72, 89, 91, 145, 147

Ibis Books 91
Illustrated Sydney News **36**, 38
ImaJinn 93
independence 57–8, 70–73, 78–81, 91–3, 95–7, 100, 102–3, 131, 138; *see also* national identity
Independence Jones 92
Indra Publishing 72, 91
Info Publishing 99
Interactive Press 91
Invincible Press 64–5, 67–9, 136; *see also* pulp fiction
Isaacs, Victor 39

J. J. Moore 44
J. R. Clarke 30, **30**, 31, 32, 40
J. Richards and Sons 44
J. T. Grocott 31
J. Walch 47
Jacaranda 63
Jackson, Stevi 151
Jacobyte Books 90
James Hardie 73
James Tegg 31–2
Janus Books 98
Johanson, Graeme 45–7
John Dicks 42, 44, **44**, 127
Johnson-Woods, Toni 34, 39, 46, 53, 54, 64, 66, 69, 74, 81, 117, 118, 137, 138
JoJo Publishing 91
Jolley, Elizabeth 147, 160–61, 162

Jonathan Cape 78
Jones, Gail 165
Joseph Masters 42
Joshi, Priya 7, 14, 19, 21

Kemp and Boyce **44**
Keneally, Thomas 142, 146, 162
Kensington 93
Kent, Larry 74
Kingsley, Henry 42, 44
Kingston, Beverley 116, 117, 118, 119
Kirkpatrick, Rod 39
Krentz, Jayne Ann 152

Lake, Marilyn 125, 138
Lamond, Henry G. 140
Lang, John 30, 33, 34–5, 40–41, 44
Lansdowne 63
Law, Graham 37–8, 53
Leader 35–6, **36**, 38, 48, 116, 130
Leighton, Mary Elizabeth 53
lending libraries: *see* libraries
Lever, Susan 3, 11
Levine, George 8
libraries 31, 44, 45, 47, 51, 52, 111–12, 117, 120, 182n51
Literary Darwinism 10, 14, 175n2, 177n25; *see also* quantitative analysis, in literary studies
literary fiction 72, 79–81, 84–7, 109; critical focus on 78, 84, 101–2, 139, 144, 152–3; definition of 195n148, 205n4; demise of 58, 80–81, 84–7; and gender 109, 132–3, 135–6, 137, 138, 139–42, 144–8, 151–3, 155, 160, 162–7, 172; publishers of 91–2, 94–7, 102–3, 139, 145–8, 156–7
literary nationalism 2, 5, 27, 51–5, 57–8, 60, 62, 70, 97, 102, 105, 109, 125–7, 190 n50; *see also* cultural nationalism
literary value: *see* cultural value
Liu, Alan 173
Local Consumption Publications 72, 94
Locker, Arthur 44
London Review of Books 162
Longman **30**, 31, 78
Longueville 99
Lothian 83, 90, 157
Lovell, Terry 111
Lund, Michael 53, 110
Lyons, Martyn 27, 47, 57, 111

McCabe, Sundowner 74
McCarthy, Justin 44

McCarty, Willard 22–5
McCombie, Thomas 33
McGann, Jerome 23, 170, 173
McNamara, Marygai 108
McPhee Gribble 72, 78, 147
McPhee, Hilary 79
Macdonnell, J. E. 74, 137
Macmillan 31, 42, 44, **44**, 46, 49, **49**, 50–51, **74**, 76, 78, 110, 127
Magabala Books 72
Magarey, Susan 123
Magner, Brigid 71, 72, 75
Malouf, David 160, 161, 162, 165
Marsden, John 162
Martin, Carol 53
Mathers, Helen 50
Matthews, Brian 143
May, Anthony 66, 69, 74, 81, 85
Maygog 99
Mays, Kelly 111, 129–30
Meares, Leonard Frank: *see* Grover, Marshall
Melbourne Books 99, 100
Melbourne Quarterly 36, **36**
Melbourne University Press 62
Melville and Mullens 42
Melville House 163
men authors 105–6, **108**; British 117; colonial 107–16, 118–28, **126**, 130, 171; contemporary 131–2, , **132**, **133**, **134**, 135–7, 139–42, 143–8, 151, 153, 156–62, 164–7; *see also* gender trends
men's reading: *see* reading, and gender; gender trends
men's writing: *see* men authors
Menehira, Hazel 62
Merry, Sally Engle 11
Methuen 46, 49
Miller, Alex 162
Millet, Kate 151
Mills & Boon 73, 95, 139, 151, 152; *see also* Torstar
mining: *see* data, mining
MirrorDanse Books 92, 95
modeling: *see* data, modelling
Modjeska, Drusilla 107
Modleski, Tania 152
Mofussilite 34
MonkeyBrain 93
Month 40
Montpeier Press 91
Moorhouse, Frank 162

Moretti, Franco 7–12, 14–19, 21, 23, 176n5, 177 n25, 184 n81
Morrison, Elizabeth 32, 36, 37, 38–9, 45–6, 48, 53, 112, 114, 117, 120, 122
Mudrooroo 160
multinational conglomerates: *see* multinational publishing
multinational publishing 2, 58, **59**, 60, **60**, 73, **73**, **74**, 75–6, **76**, **77**, 78–90, **82**, **88**, 96, 102–3; commentary on 80–81, 83–4, 96–7; definition of 76, 78, 194n126; and gender 131, 144–5, 148, **149**, **150**, 151, 154–6, 158–60, 163, 166–7; opposition or resistance to 80–81, 83–5, 94–7, 100, 159
Mundania Press 93
Munro, Craig 27, 28, 30, 41, 45, 62, 63, 66
MUP: *see* Melbourne University Press
Murray, Les 160, 161
Murray, Simone 81
Myers, David 80–81, 101
mystery fiction 157, 159; *see also* genre fiction

Naiad Press 94
national identity 33, 39, 62–5, 68–72, 75, 79, 81, 89, 91–7, 100, 102–3, 107, 118, 128–9, 138, 190n59; *see also* colonial identity; regional, identity
national sentiment: *see* national identity
neoliberalism: *see* economic rationalism
New American Library 78
New Diversity, The 3–4, 154–5; *see also* Gelder, Ken; Salzman, Paul
New Republic 162
New York Review of Books 162
New York Times 169
New York Times Book Review 162
News Corporation 73, **74**, 76, 78, 82–3, **82**, 96, 159
News Limited: *see* News Corporation
Nielson BookScan 84–6, 172
Nile, Richard 52, 66
Nimrod 72

objectivity 10–12, 15–19, 21–5
occupational gender segregation 110–11, 114–15, 136–7, 153, 155, 163–6; *see also* gender trends
Ocean Publishing 99, 100
Olsen, Mark 172
Openbook Publishers 90
Oracle Press 99

Otford Press 91
Otmar Miller Consultancy 99
Outback Press 72, 145
Outlaw Press 94
Oxford, Johnnie 67

Page, Michael 63
Pan 78
Panmacmillan 76, 78, 82–3, **82**, 159
Paper Empires 58, 62–6, 68–9, 70–71, 189n39
Papyrus Press 91
Paris Review 162
Parker Pattinson 99
Pascoe Publishing 72, 147
Paterson, Banjo 162
Peacock Publications 72, 99
Pearson **74**, 76, 78, 82–3, **82**, 158–9
Pearson, Jacqueline 111
PenFolk Publishing 99
Penguin 78, 162–3
Pennon Publishing 99
periodical publishers 3, 5, 20, 28, 31–2, 34–50, 52–4, 106, 110–20, 121, 124–5, 128, 130, 135, 138, 162, 171; *see also* serial fiction
Pierre, DBC 162
Poolbeg Press 94
popular fiction 27, 41, 50–51, 111–12, 117–19, 127, 129–30; *see also* genre fiction
Post Press 92
Praed, Rosa 44, 107
Prichard, Katharine Susannah 109, 140, 141, 142, 147
PrimeBooks 93
pseudonyms 109, 119, 136–8, 145, 206 n23
Puffin 78
Pulp Fiction Press 92, 95
pulp fiction 2, 64–70, **65**, 73–6, **76**, 78, 81, 84–5, 89, 102–3, 171; and gender 132, 136–9, 142, 143–5, 151, 153, 166–7; neglect of 2, 60, 69–70, 79, 82, 142, 171
Puncher & Wattmann 91

quantitative analysis 1–4, 7–25, 169–71, 172–3; in book history 8, 9–10, 13–15, 19, 21–3, 25; criticism of 2, 4, 7–8, 10–12, 14, 25; in literary studies 7, 10, 14, 175 n2; as representation 4, 12–14, 21–5; *see also* distant reading; Moretti, Franco; objectivity
quantitative methods: *see* quantitative analysis
Queenslander 48

R. Mackay 44
Radway, Janice 152
Random House 76, 78, 82–3, **82**, 159, 163
reading 1, 2, 5, 27–8, 31, 33, 34, 36–7, 41, 43, 46–7, 50–56, 62–3, 65, 68–70, 74–5, 91, 94, 102–3, 170–72; Anglocentric model 5, 27, 111–13, 119 (*see also* Lyons, Martyn); and class 129–30; criticism 3–5, 9, 17–19, 27–8, 34, 36, 45, 46–7, 50–55, 58, 71, 101–2, 111–12; and gender 111–12, 117, 119–22, 123–4, 127–30, 132, 137–8, 142, 145, 151–3, 159, 163–5, 166–7, 207n36; self- and subsidy publishing 45, 86–7, 97, 99–100; *see also* close reading; distant reading
Red Hill Books 91
Reed Elsevier 82–3, **82**, 159
regional: identity 39, 96, 130; publishing 38–9, 72, 91–2, 96, 103; *see also* colonial identity; national identity
Religious Tract Society 42
Remington & Co. 42, **44**, 49, **49**, 114, 127
Richard Bentley **30**, 42, 44, **44**, 114, 122, 127
Richard Willoughby 42
Richards, James 44
Richardson, Henry Handel 109, 140, 141, 142, 146, 148, 161
Rigby 63, 64, 72–3, 75, 78, 140
Rigmarole Books 72
Riley, Matthew 162
Riverhead 162
Rivington 31
Robbery Under Arms 114, 119–20
Robert Hale **64**, **74**
Rodríguez, Clara 165
romance fiction 20, 65, 67, 69, 75, 83, 93, 105, 112, 118, 119, 125, 1323, 137–9, 144–5, 148, 151–3, 158–9, 166–7; *see also* genre fiction
Ross, William 33
Rothberg, Michael 10, 22
Routledge 30, **30**, 31, 44, 49, **49**, 106, 127
Rowcroft, Charles 34, 40, 41, 42
Rukavina, Alison 50–51

S. W. Silver 114
Salzman, Paul 3, 71, 83, 143–4, 154–5, 161, 210n102; *see also After the Celebration*; *The New Diversity*
Sampson Low 42, 44, **44**, **49**, 127
Saunders and Otley **30**, 31

Scholastic 83
science fiction 92, 93, 139, 157, 159; *see also* genre fiction
Scott, Kim 165
Scott, Walter 117–18
Scribe 90, 91
Sea Cruise Books 72
Seaview Press 90, 98–100
self-publishing 5, 20, **30**, 32, **44**, 45, **49**, 58, **59**, **61**, **73**, **74**, **76**, 82, **82**, 86, 89, 97–8, 101, 103, 163, 171; and gender 156; neglect of 101–2; *see also* copayment for publication; subsidy publishing
sensation novels 117; *see also* genre fiction
serial fiction 2, 5–6, 20, 28–30, **29**, 33–43, **38**, 45–56, 70, 138, 171; and gender 106–7, 109–11, 113–24, **114**, **116**, 127–30, 171; neglect of 2, 34, 47, 52–6, 109, 171; *see also* periodical publishers
serialisation *see* serial fiction
Serlen, Rachel 15–18
Serpent's Tail 95
Sheridan, Susan 107, 109, 112, 118–19, 125–6, 135–9, 141–2, 167
Sid Harta Publishers 90, 98–101
Simmonds and Ward **30**
Simon & Schuster 83
Sisters Publishing 72, 147
Sleepers Publishing 91
Smith, Elder **30**, 31
South Briton, or, Tasmania Literary Journal 34
Spectrum Publications 99, 100
Spence, Catherine Helen 33, 44, 107, 118, 123
Sphere 78
Spinifex Press 91, 93, 157
Spivak, Gayatri 10–12, 15–17
Stead, Christina 142, 146, 147, 161
Stephen, Harold W. H. 44
Stothard, Peter 163
Stow, Randolph 142
Strauss, Jennifer 144, 152Strehle, Susan 151–2
subscription libraries: *see* libraries
subsidy publishing 5, 45, 86, 89, 97–103, 156, 163–6, 171; definition of 98, 198n222; and gender 156, 163–5; neglect of 101–2; *see also* copayment for publication; self-publishing
Sun Books 63
Surridge, Lisa 53
Sutherland, John 110
Swan Sonnenschein 49

Sybylla Press 72, 147
Sydney Mail 35, **36**, 38, 48, 116, 120, 130
Sydney Morning Herald 35, 38

T. C. Newby **44**, 127
T. Fisher Unwin 49, **49**, 127
Tally, Robert 10
technology and publishing 31, 37, 52, 93, 97, 99–100, 103, 183n67, 198n217
Tennant, Kylie 141, 142
Text Publishing 90, 91, 92
Thompson, Frank 63, 66, 85
Thompson, Nicola 110
Thomson Organisation **74**, 78
three decker books: *see* book volumes, multi
three volume books: *see* book volumes, multi
thriller fiction 159; *see also* genre fiction
Tillotson's Fiction Bureau 117
Times Literary Supplement 162
Times Mirror Company **74**, 207n37Timperley, W. H. 41–2
Tinsley 42, 44, **44**, 127
Tomato Press 72
Tompkins, Joanne 138
Torquere Press 94
Torstar 73, **74**, 76, 78, 82–3, **82**, **149**, **150**, 151, 158–9, 194n128, 194n129Trafford Publishing 99
Trainor, Luke 50
transnational: approach 2, 27, 52–3, 96–7, 106, 170–71; corporations *see* multinational publishing; identifications in publishing 91–7, 117, 120, 125, 127–8, 135–6; trends 2, 6, 83, 106–7, 110, 112, 115–20, 123, 125–8, 135–6
Triple D Books 91
Trojan Press 97
Trumpener, Katie 10, 14–15, 54
Tsiolkas, Christos 165
Tuchman, Gaye 110–11, 113, 118, 123, 127, 141, 153
Turkey Tracks Press 97
Turner, Ethel 141

University of Queensland Press 72, **74**, 75, 82, **82**, 89, 90, 145, 147, 148, 157
UQP: *see* University of Queensland Press
Ure Smith 63, 64, 140

Vanark Press 91, 92
Verso 163
Vida 162–3, 167

Viking and Kestrel 78
Virago 78
visualisation: *see* data, visualisation
The Vulgar Press 196n180

Wakefield Press 90, 91, 95
Walker, David 52
war novels 65, 67, 75, 137–8, 145, 167; *see also* genre fiction
Ward, Lock 30, **30**, 40, 44, **44**, 49, **49**, 50, 127
Ward, Russel 138 *Waverley*: *see* Scott, Walter
Webby, Elizabeth 3, 27, 35, 39, 47, 57–8, 112, 119, 121, 129, 131–3, 135, 143, 154–5, 165–6
Webster, Michael 65, 97
Webster Publications 67–9, 136; *see also* pulp fiction
Weedon, Alexis 27, 32
Wennerberg **74**, 192n87
West, Morris 162
westerns 20, 65, 67, 70, 75, 137–8, 139, 145, 167; *see also* genre fiction
Wharton, Robert 165
White, Patrick 101, 142, 146, 160, 161, 162
Whitlock, Gillian 143, 165
Wild and Woolley 72, 98
Wilding, Michael 58, 80–81, 84
Williams, Christine 165
Williamson, David 161
Winstanley, Eliza 42
Winton, Tim 162, 165

women authors 105–6, **108**; American 110, 115, 117, 119, 171; British 110–11, 113–19, 171; colonial 106–28, **126**, 171; contemporary 131–5, **132**, **133**, **134**, 137, 139–40, 141–2, 143–8, 151–3, 155–67; early twentieth century 107–10; neglect of 106, 109–10, 112, 123, 128; success of 106–8, 120, 123, 128, 171; *see also* gender trends
Women's Press, The 94
women's reading: *see* reading, and gender; gender trendsWomen's Redress Press 72, 147
women's writing: as a category 105–6, 144, 152–4, 164; growth in 6, 131, 133–4, 139, 143–5, 147–8, 151–60, 162, 163–7, 172; *see also* gender trends
women's writing and feminism: association of 131–5, 143–4, 152–3, 154–5, 161, 166–7, 171; critique of association of 105–6, 144, 154–5; disassociation of 144, 154–5; *see also* gender trends
Wren Books 72, 145
Wright, Judith 140, 141, 146, 147, 161

Xlibris 100

young adult fiction 140, 151, 157, 159, 162; *see also* genre fiction

Zeus Publishing 82, **82**, 90, 98–100
Zwicker, Jonathan 14

www.ingramcontent.com/pod-product-compliance
Lightning Source LLC
Chambersburg PA
CBHW021823300426
44114CB00009BA/304